# IN DESPAIR:

*A Socio-Economic View
of Today's India*

# IN DESPAIR:
## *A Socio-Economic View of Today's India*

### DR. RAYASAM PRASAD

eShore

Pittsburgh, PA

ISBN 1-58501-0693

Trade Paperback
©Copyright 2001 Rayasam Prasad
All rights reserved
First Printing—2001
Library of Congress #00-107579

Request for information should be addressed to:

CeShore Publishing Company
The Sterling Building
440 Friday Road
Pittsburgh, PA 15209
www.ceshore.com

Cover design: Jeffrey S. Butler—SterlingHouse Publisher
Page Design: Bernadette Kazmarski
CeShore is an imprint of SterlingHouse Publisher, Inc.
Cover photos supplied by author

## This book is dedicated to

# ANJANI

Printed in Canada

# *Foreword*

AS THIS BOOK goes to print, India is struggling to reverse more than forty years of socialism whose devastating effects on the economy the various newspapers and magazines have tried to describe. By any standard, recording these changes in this vast and complex country is a tall order. To this, add the attempts to observe and record the non-economic effects of socialism—such as those on the individual, culture, and the society as a whole. The exercise goes beyond being brave; it becomes overwhelming, if not downright foolish. Nevertheless, this book is written in the belief that what has happened in India over the past half century has to be chronicled. It has to be done to continue the civilized tradition of recording history. It has to be done for posterity.

Despite all the outside aid (private and public), the country still has 320 million people below the poverty line: those that do not have purchasing power to meet their own specified minimum caloric requirement of food. This number does not include those that subsist, but do not have adequate health care, education, and other necessities that are taken for granted in most advanced countries. This number does include millions of babies who go to bed hungry every night. What the hundreds of millions of such poor people in developing countries need is not more aid, but a legal-economic structure which lets them produce all the goods and services they need. Benefits of such a structure go beyond ensuring a better quality of life; they go beyond helping them to lead a life with dignity and self-respect. Such a structure induces quite a few phenomenal changes in the individual and the national psyche. Based on my experience as an immigrant, I have tried to document them in detail in this book. For this, I used many sources. They are listed in the bibliography. At the end of each paragraph (just as I have done for this paragraph), the reference number(s) for the source(s) of information in that paragraph is listed. Also, please note that the exchange rate between rupee and dollar has varied from eight to one (during the seventies and early eighties) to forty-four to one. (498)

But for the help of many caring professionals, this project would have remained incomplete. I sincerely thank the staff at the Lee Shore Agency, especially Ms. Megan Davidson, the editor. Ms. Davidson's valuable suggestions transformed a bunch of incoherent essays into this book. Thanks are due to the wonderful people at SterlingHouse Publisher for their help in getting this book ready for publication. I particularly thank Ms. Cynthia Sterling, my Publisher, and Annick Rouzier, the Acquisitions Editor.

From the bottom of my heart, I want to thank my lovely wife, Anjani, and our children, Ravi and Renu, for their encouragement and never ending support.

# CHAPTER 1
## *Fly Now, Pay Later*

I SURVEYED THE scenery at JFK Airport in New York. From lounge chairs and luggage carts to airline counters, everything at JFK seemed so out of this world, so despicably dust-free. So many people, yet so much room.

It was a far cry from the crowded and not so clean Bombay airport, which I had left a couple of days earlier. Suddenly, the years of filling applications, preparing for and taking examinations, and what felt like endless waiting to come to get the visa, seemed worthwhile. I was eager to start my new life. I couldn't wait to go to work as a resident physician in Lincoln Hospital in Bronx (New York). Please note, I was yet to visit Bronx.

The novelty of my first intercontinental flight was also yet to wear off. Just one day after getting our *green cards* at the US Consulate in Madras (India), my wife and I boarded the Swiss Air flight to New York. Why Swiss Air? It was the only airline which would let us taste a slice of our life in America in advance. We bought our tickets on credit. The airline called the plan "*Fly now and pay later.*"

That we certainly did, especially the pay later part. At an astronomical interest rate of eighteen percent (about which my travel agent *forgot* to inform me), I borrowed the money to buy the tickets. After little more than a glance, I signed the loan papers. It was several years before I would hear the famous warning: "Buyer beware."

With eight dollars—the amount of foreign exchange generously allowed by the government of India—and a telegraph from my friend promising to meet us at the New York airport, my wife and I got off the plane and walked toward the terminal. Hardly the giant steps that mankind was used to, but nevertheless, our first steps through any airport conduit.

My friends did show up. They relieved my poor, wretched, and hungry self of what turned out to be an unnecessary fear that I might be left wandering in the large jungle of a New York airport.

"His first name is Rayasam. *R* as in *Robert. A* as in *Apple. Y* as in...," my friend was confirming my appointment to meet a member of the administrative staff at Lincoln Hospital. I thought it was a strange way to spell. Did my friend say the letter o for zero?

He was speaking softly into the phone. For the first time I realized that one could whisper into a public telephone and still be heard. I was impressed by the quality of telephones in the U.S. To be audible during a long distance call in India, it was necessary to shout to the point of weakening the structural foundation of the building.

Spelling my name into a telephone was one of the several things that my friends taught me and my wife to help us survive the next several years in America. After we had returned from Macy's with fifteen dollar pillows and expensive bed spreads, for example, they introduced us to the concept of discount stores. We also learned to buy only items on *sale*. In no time our shopping vocabulary grew to include such gems as *exchanges, returns, refunds,* and *replacements.* If I bought a tableware set that happened to have a broken dish, no problem. I would write to the company for a replacement.

Despite all the fun and excitement, in a few days I came down with the ailment very few immigrants could escape. I felt homesick. By the time I arrived, my friends had already caught it. We missed everyone and everything from India. To cope with our loneliness, we clung to each other, listened to movie songs from back home (or the eighties' version: watching video tapes), and ate carefully-packed Indian pickles. We told each other that we would eventually go back. Actually, most of us laid down a definite timetable. Modeling after the government of India, we called ours a five-year plan. We planned go back in five years with lots of money.

At the end of the first five years, however, few of us could meet our *plan targets.* We owed more than we owned. We would have to start from scratch in India, a dreadful prospect that had made us skip the country in the first place. We did what any sane two-legged being would do; make up a second five-year plan.

While zipping through the next five years, we came up with a lot of excuses as to why we couldn't go back. For example, "the children were too *Americanized* and would have problems coping with a culture totally alien to them," or the wife had "become too *independent*" to survive the oppressive atmosphere of a combined family in India. After all, she would have been heavily criticized if she would leave her children with a babysitter to go to parties.

In reality, it was not just the children and wives that had become *Americanized.* We all had changed profoundly and done so for good.

More than any other time, just after returning from each of my trips to India, I become acutely conscious of the changes that have taken place in me. It is a time filled with mixed emotions. The terrible depression of leaving behind the loved ones is mixed with a sense of relief. For a few more blessed years, I can forget about the long flights, messed up airlines' schedules, snobby customs officials, heavy luggage, stomach upsets,

children's prostration from diarrhea, and those hot sticky afternoons, which, thanks to those god-awful blackouts (from the
serious power shortage in India), seem to get hotter and stickier
with each passing year. At 110 degrees (Fahrenheit), a running
fan is man's best friend.

Relief is just one of the feelings I experience immediately
after returning to America. I also sense that a part of me is
slowly disappearing. I realize that besides the obvious decrease
in my body's tolerance to such elements as hot weather and
infections, my thoughts, emotions, logic, perspective, and reasoning have undergone a slow mutation. This perception leaves
me feeling uneasy. But the struggle goes on. I keep saying to
myself, "Money isn't everything. Why should I give up the land
of my birth? I am not from Europe. This Western country can't
become my home. I don't belong here."

I also notice that most of my friends are in the same boat;
they, too, are struggling with the same emotions. A few get
tired of the conflict and put this reasoning to test. They try to
move back to India. I especially watch one or two couples. I
believe them to be braver and smarter than me. They are certainly more patient and committed than I can ever be. If any-
body can make such a move work, surely they can.

And it happens. They hurry back in a year or two. Each one
recites the same story. Typically, within a month or two, the
modern adventurer to India gets used to the hot afternoons
and blackouts. Even his stomach settles down, and he no longer
feels like a bubble boy. The children easily acclimatize to their
"new way of life." He and his wife also find out that the "oppressive atmosphere of a combined family" is the least of their
problems. Very few families stay combined anymore.

Nevertheless, one particular problem refuses to go away. To
our Indian emigrant, "back home" no longer feels like home.
He no longer fits in the place he has grown up. The people he
has grown up with are on a slightly different wavelength. To
be sure, the country and its people might have changed some,
but it's hardly as if they have undergone a collective brain sur-
gery. On the contrary, it is the transplants to America that have

changed profoundly. Thanks to their mutation, they feel like aliens in their native land.

Following this major discovery, these modern explorers return to America. For the benefit of all the future Vasco da Gamas[1], they give the following pointers.

When you go "back home," **Never**:

Go to work or start a meeting on time if you work for the government. Otherwise, you will end up talking to yourself and risk being labeled as *strange*. If during a general strike, called by any group, you go to work, the same fate will greet you, that too, if you are lucky enough to escape from the hands of the agitators. That you hate them, their message, and their methods is hardly a license to act dumb.

Use the telephone to request a document (which should have been on your desk in the first place) from another department. Instead dictate a memo and let your secretary type it. Once you correct the memo and your secretary retypes it, ask the attendant to take it to the department (which is usually next door). If your colleague from the other department (who sees you in the officers' dining room every day) asks for a written clarification of your memo, don't be surprised. As a matter of fact, be prepared to get your document only after reclarifying the first clarification of your initial memo.

Use a telephone to call your subordinates into your spacious office. Otherwise, the attendant, who lives to tell these guys "*Sahib* wants you in his office" and watch them sweat, will feel useless. He may even refuse to do your personal chores.

Try to have a technical conference with your subordinates. Even if the battleship you are building for the country has as much a chance to crank up as a car with a dead battery, they will agree with everything you say and wait for you to ultimately make a fool of yourself.

Tell your superiors that the ship they are building is as good as your son's paper boat in strength and design.

They will pull rank on you and transfer you to places you never knew even existed. Just sit back and relax. And when their ship sinks, be prepared to look grim.

Be surprised when you overhear one of your colleagues inquiring of another whether you are, in his words, "our guy." He simply wants to know whether you belong to his caste or religion.

Work outside your own state. Otherwise be prepared to endure a lot of rude treatment, often dished out in an alien language.

Write your memos in plain English. You have to perfect the *officialese.* Nobody wants to run the risk of being intelligible to an average high school graduate. The same goes for clarifications and reclarifications.

Ever discuss politics. The fact that you can't even write a decent memo will invariably come up in the discussion.

**Never** do any chores at home. That is, **Never**:

Help your wife cook, clean dishes, or serve coffee to your friends. Or else, you risk a thorough evaluation of your manhood.

Ever fetch yourself a glass of water, even if you feel like you are paralyzed from the waist down from sitting too much at work and home.

**And Never**

Be shocked when you see a politician, in his Gandhian attire, walk around with bodyguards who sport ruffled clothes, hairy chins, and machine guns.

Try to raise money for a *worthy cause,* unless it involves buying machine guns for your favorite member of the parliament. Otherwise, very few will donate.

Vote and risk getting caught in a crossfire between the opposing factions. Also stay away from any place where a (voting) booth capturing is in progress.

At great personal cost, your friends accumulate all this wisdom and pass it on to you.

While living in India, you knew all this stuff. You seldom allowed yourself to be bothered by it. After living in the U.S. for a few years, and particularly soon after returning from a visit to India, you vaguely feel that quite a few changes have taken place in you. For sure, they run deeper than the deforestation of your scalp.

Slowly you let go of the idea of "back home." You take full responsibility for deciding to settle in America.

You validate the words of the Viennese librettist who has said: "Home is where you are happy." (1)

*Morley Safer (of 60 Minutes, the CBS news magazine): What is it about this country that you like the best, that impressed you the most? (2)*

*Ms. Zarharchenko (a Soviet Attorney): People! people!*

*Mr. Padolsky (another Soviet Attorney): It's nice to see Americans, well, smiling, just even if they don't know you, just smiling on the streets, kind of saying hello or whatever.*

*Mr. Bluger (a third attorney): I just love the way people work here, how hard they work. How right they work. How friendly they are to each other. You have only positive emotions here.*

What these Soviet attorneys are saying, in so many words, people from the various countries and cultures express through their feet. Voluntarily and happily, these immigrants settle in America. They do so because they, too, feel the *positive emotions*.

If you are one these immigrants, eventually, some of the *positive emotions* get inside and initiate the changes that take place in you. First and foremost of these changes is the belief that you control what happens to you. You realize a simple fact. Regardless of your lineage, caste, religion, and ethnic group, and the language you speak at home, and whether or not you enjoy connections with people in high places, you can have a shot at a decent life. Having reasonable goals, and being committed to achieve them, mostly decide whether you get ahead or not. Your actions, well thought out or otherwise, determine the outcome.

More than likely, you refuse to whine about not being handed a job. You seek one out. Or you try to be on your own by starting a productive venture. In either case, to the extent you or your employer have to compete with the other producers, you have to be efficient. You go to work not to kill time but to make the best use of it. You promptly show up at the office, keep appointments, and start conferences and meetings. In all likelihood, you have little time for leisurely lunches and useless or unintelligible (to your average consumer) memos and clarifications. If, however, you squander time on any such worthless pursuit, you are the one who pays the price.

If the proverbial battleship your outfit is building goes under, more than likely you and your colleagues do too. They tell you what they really think of its chances. No matter what your position in the organization is, you have got to spare them of the niceties. That's your job, your key to survival.

From wherever possible and by whatever means, you try to gather the resources you need to accomplish the task at hand. Whatever the color of your skin is or the nation of your origin, whether or not you attend his church, as long as you are efficient and productive, your employer would be foolish to lose you to another company, especially to his competition. As long as you deliver, you seldom need to boost his ego by visiting his private office four times a day.

Much more so than in most other countries, your attributes as an individual dictate your status in life. Whether you belong to a certain predetermined group matters very little. Your vision, instincts, education, patience, persistence, and ability to communicate all set the pace of your upward mobility. When you employ even a few of these inherent assets and produce tangible results, you feel good about yourself. You feel worthy of the rewards that befall you. You feel confident and *positive*. You can make a difference. First you attempt to improve your lot. Soon, you will be searching for ways to improve that of the others you care about. Whether by giving money to charities, taking up volunteer work, or simply serving your consumers well, you benefit the others. You leave your mark on their life.

You like to help, primarily because you identify with the beneficiaries of your actions as individuals with inherent worth. You slowly learn to value other people not due to such extraneous factors as sex, race, or religion, but to the simple fact that you can relate to each one of them as an individual who possesses internal assets similar to your own and who shares your goals, desires, aspirations, and even values. It gets harder and harder to discriminate against someone "who is just like you." Your ego is boosted more when you stick to these standards than when your subordinates suck up to you. Naturally, you can never view your spouse as a person whose only mission in life is to fetch you glasses and glasses of water, beer, or mineral water.

Another reason why you grab your own Perrier from the refrigerator might be that you like whatever exercise you can get out of the day-to-day activities. Feeling in charge, you take more responsibility for your physical well-being. You work out, partake in some physical sport on a regular, or at least periodic, basis, think about exercise, or, at a minimum, have a stationary bike rusting in your basement. And you refuse to model yourself after your friends and relatives from "back home" who behave as if life is a drag after the ripe age of thirty-five.

To state that every immigrant undergoes this magical transformation overnight is a clear exaggeration. There is little about these changes that is easy, quick, absolute, or invariable. Relative to how they have felt before coming to America and when compared to their friends and relatives from "back home," more likely than not, the immigrants exhibit these changes in their psyche. Most immigrants first struggle to reconcile their previously held beliefs with the new ones. Many transform at a snail's pace. A few flatly refuse to change. Even the latter, however, can hardly avoid the *positive emotions* that surround them. More than likely, their friends, spouses, or children suffer from the *new values*. An occasional Indian might struggle to make his daughter understand how important it is to befriend people from their own caste or socialize within their sub-caste. He had better be prepared to fail. For starters, the poor girl might have a tough time pronouncing such words as *Brahmin* (not to mention *Kshatriya*). In all probability, she will refuse to choose her friends on the arbitrary basis of caste or region. The dad will end up as a cheap imitation of Archie Bunker.

Considering that these immigrants have spent their formative years in another culture, the fact that most of them change at all is very revealing. It shows that such traits as despondency, apathy, laziness, tardiness, and religious and caste bigotry are hardly ingrained in their psyche. Also, people from different countries exhibit varying levels of these traits. They vary in the level of confidence a typical individual (from each country) feels about his ability to control what happens to his body, mind, and his environment. They also vary in the strength of the belief that he is responsible for what happens to him, those he cares about, and even those who live in Somalia or Bosnia. All these variations, however, have little do with the racial, religious, or cultural factors unique to each country. By working as a sort of controlled experiment, the immigrant experience proves as much. Despite their vastly different backgrounds, cultures, and geographic locations, these people come to America, undergo similar transformation, and do so in a relatively short span of a few years. There is only one explanation for this phenomenon: their shared experiences in this country.

These experiences, in turn, are made possible by the legal system in America that guarantees relatively more economic freedoms than the laws in most other countries. It's because of this system that an individual can start a business by overcoming relatively fewer hurdles and run it with fewer regulatory millstones around his neck. These laws also let him enjoy more of the fruits of his labor. The ease with which one can engage in, and benefit from, productive ventures leads to higher levels of economic activity. This naturally translates into higher levels of employment. Either by running his own show or by getting a job, an average American—native born or immigrant—has a better shot (than his counterparts from most other countries) at making a living by his own efforts. Whether or not he succeeds is largely dependent on his instincts in spotting a good opportunity and his ability to take risks and work hard to exploit it. Naturally, he feels both responsible and confident.

The unique experience of the immigrant goes beyond establishing the benefits of a freer economy. By allowing for a comparison between him and those like him who happen to stay back and live with fewer economic freedoms, it contrasts different legal-economic systems, especially the way each one affects the human mind.

When compared to a capitalist country (such as the US), in a socialist country (such as India) government confiscates and distributes a higher share of the wealth. Owing to their pervasive control over the economy, officials in a socialist country are more likely to decide such things as who thrives in productive ventures, who gets jobs, and who starves. How well an individual lives has little to do with his ability to produce and perform. His opportunities mostly depend upon his connections. Those who are able to influence the officials get ahead. The rest suffer from shortages and joblessness. They enjoy little control over their lives. Naturally, they feel helpless and despondent. Many of them give up responsibility for their welfare and that of the others. Those who refuse to give up feel frustrated and angry. They vent their impotent rage through strikes, public demonstrations, burnings of property, and other forms of violence.

Such an accumulation of powers in the hands of the authorities sets the stage for rampant corruption. People who view government service as a means of amassing great wealth fill both the bureaucracy and the political networks. Regardless of their party affiliations, the politicians behave as if they have only one mission: By hook or crook, acquire the office and use it to stay in power as long as possible and make as much money as possible. To this end, they employ all the powers of the state, especially those that involve the redistribution of wealth. Officials bestow such goodies as jobs, bank loans, and exclusive licenses and permits on their supporters with political muscle.

Eventually, the voter choices are limited to one set of the criminal politicians or the other. Despite the periodic elections, the people have few means of cleaning up the system. Government and its organs lose their credibility. Under the veneer of a semi-orderly life, a state of anarchy prevails. Many people try to pressure the government by forming vote banks. They dangle votes in front of the politicians and vie for special rights (such as job quotas) for their groups, formed along the lines of existing divisions based on caste, sub-caste, religion, region, or language. This fight for group rights goes beyond voting in blocks. It separates people into sects and makes their divisions more entrenched. It pits one against one's neighbor. It leads to endless factional fighting and ultimately threatens to pull the country apart. All this decay has little to do with any historic, religious or cultural factor unique to a country. It's the inevitable result of the socialist laws.

In short, a closer look at countries such as India and a review of the immigrant (to the U.S.) experience reveals the following: By affecting the individual experience (and thus behavior and thinking), one way or the other, the legal-economic framework in each country exerts a major influence on the collective consciousness of the populace, the predominant social values, and what kind a society these values produce. The more the laws allow for political and economic freedoms, the better is the chance to build a civil, peaceful, prosperous, and generous society. Unfortunately, the converse also happens to be true.

Implications of advancing this theory are far reaching. If it's not some vague and predetermined factor such as religion, culture, or history that shapes a society but the legal-economic system, then there is hope. Unlike these other factors, the legal system is changeable. Countries that are ripe with shortages, despair, and endless civil strife can slowly but surely take steps to remedy the situation. The benefits also extend beyond rescuing the third world countries. Those areas of the advanced countries, such as the inner cities, which have followed the third world policies to reproduce the third world results, can also hope for a better tomorrow.

If the ultimate benefits of pursuing economic freedoms go beyond producing a few jobs to ensuring the creation of peaceful, prosperous, and caring societies, all of us who hope to build such a world will embrace these freedoms whole heartedly. We will no longer view free market policies as desperate measures only to be used sparingly and temporarily to rescue us out of stagflation and the other economic woes. Without giving up on the leftist goals of equality and fairness, we can resist the leftist policies which still hold an enormous appeal to the hearts of many caring people. Especially when these people find out that the redistributive policies harm not only economic growth, by discouraging the individual initiative, but also the individual's self-confidence, his ability to care and live peacefully with others and, thus, the very survival of a nation, they will run away from these policies.

With this realization, we, the people, can put in place a legal-economic system that can prevent America from becoming another France, France another Sweden, Sweden another Argentina, Argentina another India, and India another Burma, Rumania, or even Somalia.

In the absence of such a system, our individual freedoms will wither away in no time.

*Morley Safer: Do you think that Americans are spoiled by all this stuff that we have? (2)*

*Mr. Bluger (a soviet Attorney): It seems to me that sometimes people don't realize how happy they are... how lucky they are to have all this, to go to the grocery store just once a week to get it all and to, you know, just to avoid the problems—they probably have no idea how people in the other parts of the world might live.*

It's very tempting to jump on the locals who have taken life in America for granted. To forget to count our blessings, however, is rather easy. In my case, for example, in addition to hot pickles, sizzling credit card receipts, and a prayer that everything is all right at my house and work, I always return from India with a warm feeling towards the good life in America.

Within a few days, however, I too suffer from a severe memory lapse. As to be expected, life intrudes. Daily concerns grab my attention. I get busy. Just like millions of other Americans, I will be soon forgetting that people from very few other countries can claim as their birthright the ability to pick up groceries or take a hot shower (not at the same time, of course) at two in the morning.

The ultimate reason why immigrants from all over the world make America their home, however, goes well beyond such amenities. Quite a few of these immigrants are (actually or potentially) rich. Their ranks include businessmen and professionals who know that in their own countries their expertise is highly valued and easily marketable[2]. All these professionals and businessmen, when, and if, they go back to their native countries, have a real chance to avoid the *rat race.* They face minimal or no competition and limited expectations. They usually end up in the higher echelons of the society. Whatever one might say about their performance, the elites in their own countries are one relaxed group, *siestas* and all. To return to such a privileged life, a person can easily give up such amenities as 24-hour grocery stores. What about the hot showers at 2 A.M.? Hired help (if he doesn't mind such an arrangement) can get his water hot and running at any time. And who needs the fast American highways, as long as he can afford an inexpensive chauffeur "back home?"

When they come to America, the immigrants leave their loved ones back. They arrive into an alien culture. Language seems to be beyond rules and grammar. Few locals seem to care about the newcomers. Despite all the pain and the hurdles, however, time and again, immigrants from the far corners of the earth settle in this country, mostly, because they are aware of one simple fact: When they go back, these men and women can make up for all of their losses, but for one; the ability to enjoy basic freedoms, civil and/or economic.

*Morley Safer: Do you think that we have too much freedom? (2)*

*Mr. Zukmataius (Soviet attorney): No, no. I don't think so. It is impossible to have freedom too much.*

If I get up every morning screaming, "Freedom!" my spouse will surely commit me to an asylum and free me of my freedoms. But to feel free is addictive. One hardly misses it until one experiences less of it. It's also relative. There is no such thing as absolute freedom.

Because it means different things to different people, freedom is tough to define. For an unemployed person, it comes in the form of a job. For men and women, who have broken free of a combined family, it means acting out of self-interest (for example, earning money and spending it on your children rather than on your cousin's) without being labeled as "selfish." For a teenager, or a grown-up who feels like one, it means not having to explain every move and admit every mistake to his parents. After coming back from India, where one has to depend upon one's family and its connections to thrive and thus feels obligated and answerable to one's relatives, I see little need to explain to others my every action, attitude, or behavior, rational and otherwise.

Ludwig von Mises, an Austrian economist, hits the mark with his definition: "Freedom and liberty always refer to inter-human relations. A man is free as far as he can live and get on without being at the mercy of arbitrary decisions on the part of other people." (4)

In other words, free societies are founded upon the cement and steel of voluntary cooperation and mutual benefit. We depend on each other, but serve none.

Passage to America has become a one-way street to the majority of its millions of immigrants, rich or poor, overtly persecuted in their native countries or not. For living here, each of them has his own reason(s). Each time they contemplate a trip to "back home," however, to these immigrants, the idea of freedom ceases to be abstract.

As to where all these freedoms lead, says Henry Grunwald (of *Time* magazine): "Freedom is the ultimate value, whether aesthetic or political. Sooner or later most immigrants learn that freedom is not about what one wants but about what one can do and, ultimately, must do. Freedom won't let one be. It pursues one relentlessly, like a secular hound of heaven, challenging, provoking driving." (1)

---

[1]Vasco da Gama, a famous Portuguese navigator whose voyages to India during the fifteenth century opened up new sea-routes from Western Europe to the East.

[2]According to the United States (1980) census, seventy eight percent of the men and fifty two percent of women from India have college degrees (versus twenty percent of all Americans). (3)

# CHAPTER 2
## *A Journey Back Home*

AFTER BEING SUFFICIENTLY provoked, challenged, and hounded (by his sense of freedom) to help his native country, an occasional immigrant to the U.S. might wish to go back to India. In such an event, more likely than not "back home" will feel less and less like a home. It will feel more like a ship consumed by the flames of frustration.

All he has to do is to keep his eyes open, be sensitive, and apply his ears to the ground. He can see, feel, and hear the helpless rage that fills India.

The anger is intense. Its heat is felt in such mega-events as the frequent burning of public property, secession demands, violent demonstrations, and widespread terrorism that has already consumed thousands of ordinary citizens and two prime ministers. The mass frustration frequently shows up in private conversations. It spills into news magazines. Forget the tough problems such as the recent Punjab upheaval, laments an editor:

> "We can't even control the traffic in our cities. Why are we such a stupid people? We don't run our trains and buses efficiently. Our postal and telegraph services are a shame.

*Communication in Africa with drums is more efficient than in India with its advanced electronics. Don't remind me that we make aircraft and nuclear reactors. We make bad pins, bad exercise books, bad textbooks, bad houses, bad bridges, bad dams, bad medicines, bad cassettes and bad almost everything. The first priorities for India should be water, sanitation, literacy and public health. A people, who have not realized this, have no right to be called civilized or intelligent."* (5)

The frustration permeates all the way to the top. After his electoral defeat, said Rajiv Gandhi: "I have been worrying for the last five years. Now it is Viswanath's (then the new prime minister) turn to worry." (6)

For Rajiv Gandhi, this was quite a turnabout.

In 1985, he said: "India today is not the same India that it was in the early '50s. We have management capability, we have production capability, we have technological growth capability that we didn't have then." He added: "Our investment is almost 90% our own." (7)

In listing India's capabilities, he is hardly alone. U.S. Defense and Foreign Affairs (1989) rates the country higher than France in many areas related to defense. India has launched *Prithvi* (Sanskrit for earth), its first surface-to surface missile, and followed it with *Agni* (fire), an intermediate range ballistic missile. Thus, it has joined the exclusive club of the five with missiles: the US, USSR, France, China, and Israel. (8,9)

On paper, India's economic progress looks promising. Production of food grains has doubled between 1960 and 1980. During the five years preceding 1989, it has gone up by another thirteen percent; investment has increased by thirty nine percent; organized industry has grown by fifty percent; and India's real GDP has risen at an annual rate of 5.1 percent. Seventy million of the one hundred million or so Indians belonging to the middle class earn, on average, more than the mean European income. The Indian constitution has adopted some of the best features of the Western democracies. It's also highly idealistic and guarantees food for all. (10)

Notwithstanding such promises and promising statistics, up until the mid eighties, the number of people below the (official) poverty line kept on raising. Close to fifty percent of all Indians continue to be poor. On an average day, fifty-five million children toil away for sixteen hours or more. Twenty percent of Indians eat less than two meals a day. UNICEF estimates that every night seventy five million Indian children go to bed hungry. Owing to malnutrition and lack of proper health care, each year 200,000 of them—mostly under the age of five—go blind. (11)

A recent story on rural poverty in the *Illustrated Weekly of India* paints a even more vivid picture of the suffering. During his trip to a remote village, the reporter offers a banana to an emaciated child. The boy promptly pockets it. The boy's mother explains: "He had something to eat yesterday. I have trained my children to feel hungry only once in two days." (11)

All this happened despite the promises of equality by Indian socialists. These promises meant only one thing: extensive planning, also known as unending regulations which survive political parties and chief ministers. Until recently, these laws severely handcuffed enterprise. For example, they limited what an industry could produce in any existing line, prevented the companies from expanding into a new line and prohibited them from changing the product mix without the explicit consent of the authorities. Observed J.R.D. Tata, a famous industrialist, "It makes no sense." As a manufacturer, he was required to obtain separate licenses to produce soap and its ingredient, a fatty acid. (12)

Owing to such laws, without jumping through government's sky-high hoops, few could start and sustain a productive venture in the country. Rich or poor, a person could earn a living only with the official blessing.

Naturally, Tata spent his energies not in making a better soap but in devising new ways of greasing the officials. But why should he complain? He faced only token competition.

The same rules that made life hard for him made it impossible for the lesser human beings to engage in enterprise and compete with him. He and the other monopolists like him could sell whatever they made, at whatever price they came up with. All they had to do was to pay off the various officials and, maybe, even slightly bow before the bureaucrats. These businessmen could squeeze the consumer to their heart's content and at the same time get rich.

Besides the exclusive licenses and permits, those with influence can obtain everything the officials can still dole out: jobs, bank loans, and protection from tax raids, to name a few. Naturally, the well-connected have gained big. The top ten percent of the rural households in India own 49.5 percent of the assets, while those in the bottom ten per cent own a mere 0.4 percent. With corresponding figures of 58.1 percent and 0.1 percent respectively, the inequality in towns and cities is even worse. (13)

The poor remain poor because they live with few economic rights. Without connections or paying bribes, they can't start, or survive, simple ventures such as street vending. They are the true apartheid of India. Any street vendor will tell those who care to ask how the authorities harass him on a regular basis.

"I want to pay tax, but they are demanding bribes," complained a fruit seller from Bangalore (in the state of Karnataka). For refusing to pay *the usual* to a local politician, muscle-men razed his stand to the ground. The fruit vendor felt desperate. When, along with his wife and children, he tried to commit suicide, a few officials took pity on him. They helped him to rebuild the stall. What the king giveth, however, he can taketh away too. Soon other officials came along and declared his brand new stand "illegal." That prompted a reporter from the *Illustrated Weekly of India* to say: "Now the poor vendor does not dare refuse to pay the necessary bribe. Truly honesty is a luxury virtually nobody can afford these days." (14)

Selling fruits from a stand is one of those thousands of productive actions that the all-encompassing legal system in India has made close to impossible to engage in. In the name of planned growth, year after year, this machine spews out so many laws, regulations, clarifications, and reclarifications that finally almost every activity—with the possible exception of the very basic functions of the body—have become illegal, unless of course carried out with the official blessing. Those, who have no way of winning the nod and yet want to do more than just attending calls of nature, do business outside the purview of law. They would rather pay the price and make a living. Officials are more than happy to oblige. Over the years, they have learned to regard underground production as a source of income and the illegals a fair game. In return for a promise of being left alone, these businessmen pay off the officials.

To extort, an official need not risk a visit to some dark alley in his city. All he has to do is to just take a stroll in any busy street.

"Have you ever walked down the streets of Bombay without being addressed or harassed by hawkers?" ask S. Bana and S. Rajhans of *India Tribune*. They answer: "Unlikely. Because the streets and pavements of Bombay are littered with stalls, carts, boxes, baskets, stands of hawkers, selling anything from fish to fruit, from hankies to hair clips, from belts to bags, from trousers to towels." (15)

Naturally, according to the thousands of laws on the books, if not more, such hawking is illegal. One can certainly justify a few of these laws by saying that Bombayites have the right to walk without being addressed by the hawkers. These *rights*, however, clash with those of the consumer who buys the goods and, more importantly, of the hawker who tries to engage in productive work and make a living.

In any event, these laws have little to do with rights. As in the case of our fruit seller (from Bangalore), who lost everything even though he was willing to obey the law and pay taxes but not bribes, they serve only one purpose—making the officials rich and powerful. While at it, the restrictions that have made hawking, and every other productive activity illegal, cramp enterprise and reduce the number of productive, legal jobs. The poor have to either hawk or die. Being run-of-the-mill, non-suicidal human beings that they are, many just choose to peddle on the streets. Day after day, they try to dodge the elements and corrupt officials.

To this end, the hawker often changes his location. In the process, he might lose his loyal customers. He certainly suffers through the physical ordeal of carrying his merchandise with him. Using simple common sense, one can conclude that he would like to settle in a small shop somewhere, deal within the legal system, and lead a less adventurous life. Even if somehow the hawker obtains a license to do business, however, there are not enough shops to rent. The various building and zoning codes and high property taxes allow for very limited construction of commercial space. More importantly, rent control and urban ceiling laws (the latter restrict how much land a person can own) muddy up property rights. In the absence of security of ownership, let alone a good return on the investment, very few dare to build new space. Owing to a limited supply of shops, the hawker just lives with a pipe dream of having a place of his own. Meanwhile, he just shares the streets with pedestrians.

On a lucky day, he does survive in his *illegal* trade. On others, he watches helplessly while the municipality checkup van takes away his possessions. The police who eat off his palms have their own problems too. Each of these lawmen must meet his "quota." To fill the coffers of BMC (Bombay Municipal Corporation), he has to collect certain amounts of penalties from the hawkers. The officials love to round up the hawkers, and, depending upon the nature of the business, levy fines of five to twenty rupees on each one. They love it so much that they have stopped issuing licenses. The authorities keep hawking illegal, suck these poor guys dry, and each day collect fees of about 200,000 rupees. (15)

In return, these businessmen get nothing: no water, electricity, or police protection. Someone else with more muscle power can encroach upon their space, rob them, or simply topple their stands. To protect his business, the hawker also pays money to goons. Naturally, small-time ring leaders, gangs, and even underworld dons have proliferated in this city. (16)

Actually, the whole operation brims with efficiency. These mafia types join hands with the police and form a criminal-police nexus. It's one of those win-win-shoot situations. Police use these criminals as middlemen to collect bribes from the various establishments and individuals who operate on the wrong side of law. The lawmen find using goons this way to be a cleaner, safer, easier, and more dignified approach. Gang members keep a portion of what they collect as a "service charge," estimated to be 100,000 to 150,000 rupees a day for one such gang. The rest they give to the police. (16)

For a while the gangs divided the territory, and each operated in its own domain. Soon, however, some of the gang members grew a bit more bold. They entered into turf wars. In a matter of a couple of weeks (in 1990), twenty-two of them died fighting each other. Reports of these killings moved Sharad Parwar, then chief minister of the state (of Maharashtra), to act. He ordered the police brass to prepare a list of the corrupt officers. He got it in no time and transferred many of these officers to out of town, to not *so lucrative* outposts. (16)

Showing how pervasive the mafia influence was in the ruling party, Parwar canceled his transfer orders within a few weeks. He had to. Without the support of the politicians friendly to the gangs, he couldn't survive a day as the chief minister. (16)

Most of these hawkers are villagers who have tried to escape their hopeless poverty. In search of work, they have migrated to cities. The government, however, is under constant pressure from the elites to clear the sprawling urban slums and *beautify* the cities. Consequently, the authorities try to relocate the poor using force. Especially, during the so-called *emergency period* of the seventies they destroyed huts, packed many slum dwellers into transport buses, and shipped them to remote areas. As soon as the buses left, however, these slum dwellers would return to the city and rebuild their huts.

For several decades, half a billion poor people in India have suffered through such abuses of their fundamental rights and degrading poverty. They entertain little hope for a decent future. They feel very powerless, except, perhaps, once in five years, when they vote between the Tweedledees and Tweedledums. Small wonder that the poor feel enraged.

✦     ✦     ✦

A typical scooter owner in India has this funny habit of waiting until he is down to a few ounces of gasoline in the tank—not gallons or even liters, but ounces. To reach the petrol bunk (gas station), he tilts, shakes, drags, and pushes his poor machine.

To these men and women, petrol is, indeed, black gold. At thirteen rupees a liter (approximately two dollars a gallon in the late eighties), one could go bankrupt trying to maintain a car. This explains why many Indians risk their lives by riding tiny scooters with wheels the size of a dinner plate. A lot of factors have contributed to these horrendous prices. Price controls and other regulations discourage production and distribution of fuel. Efforts by successive governments to "protect" India from experienced oil drilling companies from outside the country have also curtailed the supply of gasoline and pushed up prices. Thanks to a weaker rupee (owing to a poor economy), it costs a lot to import oil. Add to this high petrol taxes and you have prices which can make even Donald Trump shake his scooter.

Scooter owners in India, however, rarely complain about the high cost of petrol. They are happy to ride their two wheelers. As recently as the mid-eighties, many waited as long as six years to get their hands on one. Also common were long waiting lists for cars, telephones, cooking gas, and construction materials.

Even today, many daily necessities command high prices and, on many occasions, are available only through the black market. Middle class workers spend as much as forty to fifty percent of their take home pay to feed their families. The usually high income taxes take a big bite out of their salary. As if this is not bad enough, these workers pay a lot more money— four times that of direct taxes—through indirect taxes. A variety of excise taxes and import duties bleed the consumer white. Despite the heavy taxation and a high cost of living, there are those who skimp on necessities and manage to set aside a small savings. In due course, however, constant double-digit inflation decimates the buying power of these savings.

Nevertheless these Indian workers are the lucky ones. They are the minority who happen to have jobs. They can afford to worry about such things as taxes, inflation, waiting lists, not having enough money for savings, and how to get their hands on the hardcover edition of a particular book with its lock on the meaning of life. Using religion and philosophy, they can, at least, try to escape the harsh realities of day-to-day life. Their problems, and especially their jobs, their unemployed brethren would kill to have.

Those who have jobs but live in relative poverty and the others who live in absolute poverty feel helpless. They seethe with anger. They blame their plight on everything and everyone except the real culprit: socialist planning.

In the spirit of this time-honored philosophy, politicians of every stripe resorted to the rhetoric of class warfare. They turned the public against the wealthy and discouraged creation of wealth. In other words, they discouraged the production of goods and services that were needed to be produced in unbelievable quantities to assure even a minimum standard of living for the hundreds of millions of Indians. The end result was a tragic paradox: To stay afloat, consumers needed enormous amounts of soap, cloth, cement, two wheelers, and everything in between. The enormous numbers of unemployed were willing to work, produce all these materials, and eliminate the shortages. In the name of preventing the rich from getting richer, however, officials blocked the entrepreneurial activities which, otherwise, would have productively employed the unemployed and paved the way for the creation of wealth.

As might be expected, stunted enterprise results in anemic revenues for the government. Despite this, the government insists on providing most services, including banking, railroads, power supply, telecommunications, air transportation, and television and radio programs. Populist measures such as subsidies and cheap loans to farmers and businessmen take their share of the pie, leaving very little capital for such basics as sanitation and water supply and building infrastructure. In the absence of adequate power supply and transportation, enterprise suffers some more. Naturally, all this government spending coupled with low revenues has led to horrendous deficits. When successive governments finance these deficits by printing more money, the result is a devastating inflation. Weakened currency further harms the already moribund economy.

In short, pursuing their cherished goal of equality, these socialists have planned the whole country into a state of shared deprivation and into one giant sustained depression. A former US ambassador to India summarizes the country's economic problems: "Over there, they follow the London School of Economics. They behave as if it's wrong to make money."

Notwithstanding such opinions and the images Westerners see in filmed documentaries, quite a few Indians do make money.

Their ranks include those who operate largely outside of the system and the monopolists who enjoy exclusive licenses and/or permits. Even these privileged men and women, however, lead a sort of double life. To the extent possible, they hide their incomes and shield their operations from the authorities. To this end, most businesses employ two sets of books. With the bureaucracy they play a constant cat and mouse game, which ends up, happily, in bribes paid to the officials.

Actually, from all the regulations and government-owned enterprises, the authorities gain a lot more than bribes. They gain a strangle hold over the life of each and every one of their countrymen. To whomever they want to, these officials hand out such things as jobs, business subsides, the golden goose called exclusive license, and other protections from competition, as well as ownership of a telephone before its time. A network of thousands of politicians and millions of bureaucrats controls this distribution process. How well an individual lives or dies depends upon such factors as where he is situated in this lattice and how well he can influence its bright spots—the officials. Regardless of their qualifications, those with connections live very well. Naturally, many savvy young men prefer having a minister for a father-in-law rather than a fat dowry.

The middle class youths who are not that lucky try to stay in colleges as long as possible. "Education is not connected to the future anymore," says the head of a department in the University of Calcutta: "It's their [the Indian students'] pastime. 'We cannot get jobs any more,' the boys say, 'so let's go to school.'" (17)

Government has spent a lot of money to educate these young men and women, but by restricting the enterprise and job growth it hampers their ability to produce in every way it can[3]. In the end, it has managed to waste their talents in unemployment lines. The socialist planners did, however, create eighteen million largely unproductive jobs in the public sector. Lured by the job security and powers enjoyed by the bureaucrats, and unable to get the few jobs in private industries or engage in production by themselves, smart students in India prefer joining the government service. Many actually dream about it.

Majority of these youngsters can only dream. Each and every politician has his own formula for the distribution of government jobs. For example, most state governments have passed laws reserving jobs for people from within the state or, sometimes, within a region in the state. Such laws render many young men and women ineligible for jobs outside their own states or even regions. Even if your family has lived in a state for a couple of generations, if you speak a different language (than the state's official language) at home, you are out of luck. One such student assumed his mother's family name to gain admission to a medical school. That's okay except for one thing: In his own country, his father has suddenly become an alien whose children are treated as second class citizens.

Thanks to job quotas for the minorities, you are also damned if you are born into one of those so-called upper castes in India. Regardless of your qualifications, you become ineligible for a big chunk of government jobs and seats in professional schools. These positions are reserved for people from *Scheduled Tribes and Scheduled Castes*, formerly known as untouchables. Under this system, Siddalingaiah, a poet belonging a Scheduled Caste, was tipped for a professor's post—a reserved one—in the Kannada (language) department of Bangalore University. He said about one of the candidates who was bypassed in the process: "Not only is he my teacher, he is also more deserving." (18)

Siddalingaiah goes on to explain, "[But] there is no escape from reservation [the quotas] as long as we continue to be a prejudiced inhuman society." He is both honest and correct. These former untouchables, especially those who live in villages, endure abject poverty and unending humiliation. Owing to the economic stagnation, most can't find reasonably productive jobs. They scrape here and there. The whole family toils for mere subsistence. Quota system or not, a poor man needs his children helping him at home providing food, not *wasting* their time at school. (18)

Many leaders who had fought the British hoped that the caste system would wither away, but the quotas ensured exactly the opposite. These quotas linked one's survival to one's caste, made the divisions entrenched, legitimized the age-old caste boundaries, and (in the words of Rajiv Gandhi) splintered the country much more effectively than the British could ever do. They also led to mindless violence. During the summer of 1990, for example, close to one hundred students died in clashes over the extension of the reservation program.

Time and time again, one also hears about atrocities against poor Scheduled Caste members by politically powerful local bosses and their thugs in the rural areas. When the perpetrators rape, beat, or burn their victims, however, the general public takes these incidents in stride. It does so for many reasons. For one thing, it's desensitized by the pervasive violence. A lot of people also feel too powerless to stand up to the political bosses. A few keep quiet mainly because they project their resentment of the job quotas on all members of the Scheduled Castes. This resentment against poor Scheduled Caste members is not only inhuman, but also highly misplaced. The reservation program largely benefits those that are relatively better off. Mostly children of middle class families and even top officials belonging to the Scheduled Castes benefit from the quotas.

In short, an inherent feature of any re-distributive system kicks in with vengeance: Such group rights as quotas mostly benefit the well connected and the relatively better off members of the group. On the subject of job quotas for the so called

*Other backward Castes* (other than the former untouchables), reports Javeed Anand in *India Tribune*:

> *"Politically powerful and economically better off sections within the backward castes have managed to manipulate state policy to consolidate their economic status not only vis-à-vis the more vulnerable groups within the OBCs (other backward castes) but also in comparison to upper castes."* (19)

In other words, even the all-powerful officials have too few jobs, college seats, and other vehicles of opportunity to accommodate the hundreds of millions in the country. They can only help a few groups, and that too, only a tiny minority in each group. They can ill-afford to waste these plums on the weak and the dispossessed risking the wrath of the powerful and the influential. Most successful politicians thrive only because they patronize those who deliver a lot of votes and money. For these leaders, job quotas are just another bait to build and maintain their following.

About such notoriously corrupt Indian politicians, says Madhu Jain of *India Today* , "Once upon an unevil time, one looked for villains on the [movie] screen. Today, they crowd the newspapers and the neighborhood—Gandhi-capped politicians, underworld dons, terrorists and God-men." (20)

In commercial societies, people with drive and ambition become entrepreneurs. Some of these daredevils get rich. In the process, they create jobs, make loans, and build such things as airlines, automobiles, cable televisions and cordless phones. For them, a political career is just a waste of time.

In socialist countries, the ambitious mostly work for the government, or, even better, they enter politics. They immediately proceed to convert their enormous powers over economic decisions into money. Corruption thus starts at the head and rots the society all the way down. In India, if you ask a policeman why he accepts bribes, he invariably points his fingers to the top.

A few Indian politicians have reduced the whole process to a science. They become chief ministers for a month or two and amass great wealth. Of course, most live with a more long-term philosophy: By whatever means it takes, "get elected and stay elected."

N.D. Tewari knows what it takes. Before the 1989 elections, the then chief minister of (the state of) Uttar Pradesh spent money, meant for upgrading schools, to buy necessities such as jeeps and revolvers. (21)

No. He was not into mobile schools that teach revolver shooting. He just needed all this ammunition for his electioneering, so alleged his own colleagues from the Congress(I) party. They did so because Tewari showered his largess on an anti-Congress(I) leader, Mulayam Singh Yadav. Tewari hoped that Yadav would defeat one of Tewari's rivals from his own Congress(I) party. Such tactics and the misappropriation of funds are pretty routine in Indian politics. Another politician, interviewed for this news story, says that only a small portion of the funds (earmarked for building schools) actually go into the buildings and the grants to educational institutions have been a source of rampant corruption. (21)

Naturally, over the past few decades, day-to-day corruption has become a fact of life for most Indians. Those who won't, and can't, bribe stay behind. Among the rest, in each group of friends or family, there is at least one person who can "get things done." He can fetch seats in trains, or obtain large quantities of otherwise rationed cement, or cash checks at a nationalized bank in no time. He knows how to bribe.

Such corruption extends beyond back alleys and smoke-filled rooms. The press openly calls some ministries, such as the Public Works, "lucrative." Small wonder that politicians do almost anything do keep their lucrative jobs. To aid their reelection efforts, they extort money, vehicles, and even gasoline for the vehicles from businessmen. They go after much more than just rich businessmen. The politicians blackmail, cajole, and pressure anyone who depends upon them. Most law enforcement officials have proved to be no exception. To survive, they too cater to the politicians and cover up the latter's crimes.

Many law enforcement agencies work as personal detective services for the ruling politicians who find such help indispensable.

Devi Lal, an anti-Congress(I) leader, alleged that the CBI (Criminal Bureau of Investigation)—the top investigative agency in the country—had become the "Congress(I) Bureau of Information." To back up his accusation, he cited the cover-up in the Bofors case (a now-famous, arms purchase scandal involving Rajiv Gandhi and his Congress-I party) and other politically motivated cases inspired by the CBI against members of the opposition parties (see chapter 9). Devi Lal, however, is hardly a saint. He illustrates how even those who oppose and criticize the politically dominant Congress (I) and are supposed to serve as an alternative to it, themselves, have a few hidden skeletons of their own. His skeletons involve both his public and private lives. Devi Lal, for example, made his famous comment when (in 1989) a few members of the Congress(I) party smelled blood and demanded a CBI inquiry into his family affairs. The list of these affairs was very colorful. Jagdish, Devi Lal's younger son, was accused of rape. Doubts were also raised about the *accidental* death of Supriya, daughter-in-law of Om Prakash Chautala, Devi Lal's eldest son. In the end, however, few such allegations get investigated. Owing to the political control of the law enforcement apparatus and the horse trading that goes on between politicians of various parties, few officials can afford to snoop around. (22)

Naturally, many criminals found politics a safe haven. They joined one political party or the other, acquired money and influence, and used them to cover up their crimes and that of their followers. Eventually such criminal-politicians just about filled the political networks. So much so, no one was surprised when, recently, the state government of Gujarat released ten hardcore criminals from prisons to enable them to run for office in the municipal elections of Porbandar, incidentally the birthplace of Mahatma Gandhi. (23)

Seventy of the 108 candidates in this election had criminal backgrounds. Of course, people could have voted against them. But how? Not only were most of the ordinary citizens too scared to vote (much less campaign) against these hooligans, quite a few of these criminal-politicians ran unopposed. (23)

Voters also have too many other pressing concerns on their minds to worry about how their legislator has made his first million or how many heads he has cracked to rise to power. Such things as job quotas, rising prices, and arms purchase scandals mostly command their attention. Besides, the voters' choices are very limited. Every political party has its share of criminals.

So does every department of the bureaucracy.

What Nikloy Shmelyov (an economist at the Institute for U.S. and Canada in Moscow) says about the eighteen million or so Soviet officials aptly describes the mindset of the Indian bureaucrat: "Who will break our managers, especially the high-level ones, of their feudal ideology, caste-like haughtiness, confidence in their own invulnerability and 'God given right' to command? Why should they think that they are above the law and immune to all criticism?" (24)

Indian bureaucrats—who too number about eighteen million—also command the huge public sector, which includes such entities as steel plants and five-star hotels. They certainly feel invulnerable and above the law. Most are very arrogant. They virtually pass and implement the thousands of regulations whose original purpose was to ensure government's planning of the economic activity.

Few elected officials can keep up with the majority of these rules. Most people in the country are too busy surviving these regulations to notice what these bureaucrats do. To pay my college tuition fee, I remember going to three different institutions: the revenue office, the State Bank of India, and the university office. Such nonsense could frustrate even Mother Theresa or Mahatma Gandhi.

To survive the regulations, businessmen routinely pay extortion money to officials. For their children's college seats, parents bribe education bureaucrats. To obtain loans, farmers pay off bank officials. Passengers pay bribes for their train seats. A few contractors in the state of Tamil Nadu paid to get around the land development laws and built taller buildings than allowed. G.V. Ramakrishna, a special adviser to the governor, spotted the infractions. In this land of shortages, he asked the engineers "to find ways of demolishing unauthorized upper-story structures [of course] without damaging the lower ones." (25)

To get their work done, people usually pay *fast money.* To prevent their files from reaching Ramakrishna's desk, builders in this case paid *slow money.* Said the reporter from *India Today*, "You can't beat the bureaucracy in ingenuity when it comes to corruption." (25)

Ingenious or not, most officials get rich quickly. By choosing one set of corrupt politicians over the other, the average person can vent his feelings, albeit temporarily, in the voting booth. But he can do precious little about corrupt bureaucrats. Once appointed and confirmed (usually in a year or two), government officials can't be easily fired. Their jobs are permanent. They get promoted strictly by seniority. These *public servants* fully realize their staying power. They sleep well at night and lead long and happy lives. And they enjoy generous pension benefits and paid holidays.

In their world, performance simply means getting along with their superiors. It has little to do with doing their jobs effectively or treating their consumers right. Naturally, these modern maharajas rule the public with an iron hand. They control everyone from businessmen and judges to politicians, and even sometimes the reporters. Their tenacious grip over various parts of the society allows these officials to live above the laws they themselves have created. Even Rajiv Gandhi found out that, as a group, they became formidable over the years. While the bureaucrats chewed on the foundations of his economic liberalization program (see chapter 12), he watched helplessly. They had little use for his talk of accountability. Instead, they liked to talk about annual rises and special allowances, which, regardless of the state of the economy and at a great cost to the taxpayer, they had gained for themselves. During the five years prior to 1987, for example, the economy grew at an annual rate of five percent. Per-employee expenditures of the Indian Railways, however, doubled to 21,000 rupees. With a corresponding figure of 30,900 rupees, the usually inept and notoriously lazy bank employees did even better. (26)

All most all officials behave as if they are entitled to benefit from the whole state apparatus. Few of them hesitate to use their subordinates for personal chores. These officials also believe in the age old system of bartering. With great efficiency, they network and exchange favors. Education officials and revenue officials help each other out. Sales tax collectors and the police work hand in hand to extort small businessmen. Doctors take good care of the income tax officials. For that matter, most everyone takes good care of the income tax officials.

Whatever amenity they can't exchange, such officials sell. They operate a giant, but invisible, supermarket. In it, a person who can afford to pay them off can buy jobs, loans, permits, licenses, college seats, or just plain protection from the officials.

Those, who can't afford to pay, have to kiss good-bye not only to their economic rights, but also the other basic human rights.

My first exposure to police brutality occurred when I was in the middle school (during the early sixties). The cries of agony from the nearby police station used to scare me quite a bit. I felt sorry for the victims of the police beatings. I also vividly remember a policeman dragging a nicely-dressed woman by her hair. Few on the street seemed to object to this act of a policeman, who, all at once, was playing the roles of an arresting officer, judge, jury, and the enforcer. Someone explained to me: "She is a prostitute."

As recently as 1992, Amnesty International has cited India for widespread police brutality. Even the local press considers the stories of police excesses a staple. According to one such news story in the summer of 1988, after serving a warrant in a village in (the state of) Madhya Pradesh, a head constable failed to return to his job in time. (27)

His colleagues from the police department suspected foul-play. Within the four days the constable had been missing, they rounded up scores of villagers and brought them to the police station for questioning. The police detained about fifty villagers, including five women and eleven children. The police methods also included hitting with a baton, pricking with pins, and holding back food and water. Showing his injured hands, Naresh, a ten-year-old boy said, "They removed one of my fingernails with tongs." The police unleashed so much terror that two of the villagers confessed to *the murder*. Soon, however, there appeared a small hole in the case. As a living, breathing self, the alleged murder victim showed up. He was unharmed. (27)

Apparently, on the day he had visited the village, this constable got into fights with a few village youths. He became worried that they might complain against him. On his own, he took some time off hoping that the affair would be forgotten by the time he returned to his job. Ramesh Saxena of Peoples's Union for Civil Liberties (PUCL) said: "Dube (the head constable) was drunk. It is suspected that he did not return to the police station apprehending a report against him by the villagers." (27)

For his *murderers*, however, Dube's reappearance hardly spelled the end of their troubles. The police refused to let go. Although the murder charges were withdrawn, the accused were denied bail. They were charged with beating up and detaining the head constable. The police knew all about an ounce of prevention and a pound of cure. For challenging their authority and complaining to the press, they wanted to teach these villagers *another lesson*. The police continued to harass the villagers and detained another member of the family of the accused. Only this time, however, news reports, efforts by PUCL, and an opposition censure motion in the state assembly stood in the way. Owing to the adverse publicity, and almost a month after the original incident, the authorities announced a high level official probe. They also ordered medical examination of the victims and transferred seven police officers to another location. (27)

These kinds of checks and balances are more an exception than the rule. Anuradha Dutt, a reporter for the *Illustrated Weekly of India*, narrated the story of one Chander Parkash Bhasin of Delhi. In 1978, police charged Bhasin with possession of arms. Even though an internal inquiry by the assistant commissioner of police had exonerated the poor man, he had to wait for ten years before being cleared of the charges. Meanwhile, he was harassed by the police and lived like a "convict on the run." Such abuses were so widespread that Dutt accused the police of behaving like a security force in a banana republic by "denying citizen's rights enshrined under the constitution." (28)

The police can afford to do so. Rarely, if ever, are they charged, much less tried for abusing citizens' rights. When in trouble, they bribe their superiors and the politicians and get these higher authorities to intervene on their behalf. Come election time, the police pay back their friendly politician by protecting his hooligan friends and turning a blind eye to, or even assisting in, the booth capturing. Small wonder that they can easily get away with denying the citizen his basic rights that are enshrined on a piece of paper.

The victims have few places to turn to, certainly not to the government which has gotten involved in so many activities and spread itself so thin that it no longer is capable of carrying out one of its unquestioned responsibilities—maintenance of the law and order.

Do all these stories of top to bottom corruption, criminalization of politics, erosion of law and order, and abuse of human rights, reflect sensational reporting? Quite a few in the country don't think so. "In India truth is sensational," says Sudip Mazumdar of *India Tribune*, "The nexus between the politician, criminals, and the police is complete and India is their fiefdom to be sucked dry. And they do form bureaucracy to judiciary." (29)

This atmosphere has caused a lot of inequities. Most pernicious of them, however, is the sense of insecurity and the loss of dignity victims must live with. Many nurse their wounds and seethe with rage and desperation. They lend their ears to those who preach revolt.

By doing such things as preaching revolts in his movies, Amitabh Bachchan became a mega-hero of the Indian screen. His 1988 movie *Shahenshah* was expected to be a blockbuster.

Amitabh also happened to be a close friend of the, then, prime minister, Rajiv Gandhi. They were so close that both vacationed together. Following a rumor that the film would be pirated on videocassettes on a massive scale, Bachchan's comrades at high places decided to protect his interests. They turned loose the police force. Fifty police officers descended upon Delhi airport and searched peoples' baggage for the cassettes. Even though they found nothing, they made a simple point: vacationing with the prime minister has its own rewards that involve a whole lot more than enjoying the sand and surf. (30)

*Shahenshah* bombed out at the box office. The movie-goers defied the wishes of an almighty prime minister. Market forces gave the consumer the power to do so; in a small yet significant way, they gave back to him the control over his life.

Small wonder that the officials hate the market forces. They know a simple fact: The more the consumer gains such sovereignty, the more they will turn into number crunchers, or even worse, into public servants, in true sense of the word. They will possess fewer means to collect bribes, hand out money and perks to their followers, and retain their positions of privilege. To this plague of economic democracy, officials have discovered a potent antidote—the culture of statism that is the hallmark of socialism. In this culture, being friends with them goes a long way. As discovered by Mr. Bachchan (in the case of *Shahenshah*), it enables one to rent the awesome government machine to do one's dirty work.

What tops being friends with a powerful politician, however, is being related to one. Rajiv, a reluctant entrant to politics, soon joined the innermost circle of advisers to his mother, who herself (being Nehru's daughter) became prime minister by virtue of her lineage. In this world's largest democracy, soon after his mother's demise, Rajiv inherited her post. He was, after all, her sole living heir.

Very few political princes are that lucky. Most have siblings to compete with. After the 1989 elections, Devi Lal, the, then, chief minister of (the state of) Haryana got a promotion. He became the deputy prime minister of India. Within hours, both his sons and their followers lined up for a succession battle in his state. To settle this sibling rivalry, Devi Lal simply followed the example of ancient Hindu kings. He convinced his younger son, Ranjit Singh, to withdraw in favor of the older son, Om Prakash Chautala. (31)

The next best thing to being related to a politician is to help him win elections: deliver money, an audience for his meetings, or supporters for his agitations (designed to topple his opponents from power), and, most of all, deliver votes.

Labor union leaders, for example, can promise all three. With the help of very favorable labor laws and using intimidation, they collect dues from union members and pass some of it on to needy politicians. The bosses dispatch workers to political meetings, strikes, or whatever. These Jimmy Hoffa types even throw in some muscle power, just in case. In return, politicians pass some more labor laws that enhance the power of union bosses. Also, by shielding the latter from law enforcement agencies, the politicians help to turn a few of the unions into criminal enterprises (see chapter 7). Consequently, union members enjoy little control over their unions and the bosses.

Thanks to its hold on the all-encompassing government apparatus, organized labor, in the private and public sector, receives a huge slice of the country's production. Until the economic liberalization of the mid-eighties (see chapter 12), its members actually formed the bulk of the middle class in India.

That these labor laws are stacked heavily against the owners is hardly a surprise. Despite the outward appearance, however, they also hurt the workers, especially the unemployed ones. As seen in a couple of states, Kerala and West Bengal, if strictly enforced these laws drive out the capital and, along with it, jobs. These regulations also help to push enterprise underground and strip the workers of the protection of the other laws, such as those covering minimum wages, occupational hazards, and pension benefits. In the end, militant unions help their members some, but they work against the rest of the workers, especially the very poor. Union leaders and politicians do benefit from these outfits. Not surprisingly, quite a few wear both hats.

On occasion, government itself imitates the unions. It organizes strikes. In (the state of) West Bengal, for example, the ruling Marxist communist party routinely commits such an incest and paralyzes the state. (32)

Mostly due to such antics, many industrialists abandoned the state. A lot of people in this state lost their jobs. The chief minister, Jyoti Basu, did "not want to make the state into a desert" and started to tone down his anti-investment policies. He tried to attract the capital, and thus, jobs back. His opposition—another communist party and the Congress(I) party— jumped at the chance to attack him. They served Basu a dose of his own Marxist concoction and accused him of abandoning labor "by discouraging strikes, without taking action against the management who declare *illegal* [my italics] lockouts." (32)

Such an accusation could rattle even Karl Marx. Basu, a dedicated Marxist, soon regained his rational thinking. He washed off his sins with a compromise: a joint strike by the left-wing parties against the jute industry. Jyoti Basu obviously made the correct political move. He was one of the very few politicians who survived the recent (1989) anti-establishment vote in the country. Promoting economic growth and helping the poor to get jobs hardly guarantees votes for a politician. Courting unions and their bosses works better. (32)

Organized labor, its successful strikes, and the politicians who back them teach the rest in the country one simple lesson: in a statist economy, numbers mean safety and strength.

Any leader with a sizable number of committed followers has a good chance of getting the government to pass laws favoring the group. To many in his group, he, his promises, and the power of the group represent the only hope for survival, however slight it might be. Recently, for example, prostitutes in Delhi marched demanding licenses to practice, a pension scheme, proper health care, adoption of their children, and nomination of their representatives to the upper chamber of the parliament. (33)

When properly instigated and organized, many in the country naturally form groups. They unite on the basis of caste, sub-caste, religion, region, language, occupation, or, if necessary, the way they wear their loincloth. The individuals identify themselves more as members of their group than citizens of the country. To gain its share of the government handouts, each of the groups votes as a block. To win more group rights, it protests every chance it gets. Some groups protest not having high enough job quotas. Others protest that there are too many.

Many students have quickly caught onto this idea of big numbers producing tangible results. Routinely, they go on strikes. They demand everything from postponement of examinations to "reasonable prices" in local restaurants. By and large, students win their demands. Owing to the fear of reprisals from the usually well-connected parents, law enforcement authorities look the other way, when, during these strikes, students mob and harass the university officials. On occasion, students even prevent the university officials from going to the bathroom for a long time. Under such duress, most officials cave in. They grant whatever is asked of them.

This might look unruly, but students know that mob rule works well in their country. Without any show of collective strength, they and their demands will be ignored: Their vice-chancellors (VCs)—CEOs of the universities—are political appointees and as such are answerable only to the ruling politicians. The politicians kick around the VCs just as the striking students do. Naturally, in this power game the VCs feel more and more like hockey pucks than educators.

In (the state of) Bihar, in early 1989, the chief minister, Bhagwat Jha Azad, sacked all of the VCs in his state. He merely wanted to assert his control over the universities and bring them into his fold. Azad, however, faced a hurdle. It arose in the form of the governor of the state, Govind Narayan Singh. Both Azad and Singh belonged to the same political party, Congress(I), but they despised each other. Singh, for some time, had wanted to settle a score with Azad. He complained that, during a river festival, he received "a third-rate motor launch [state owned], while the chief minister reserved for himself one [motor boat] of superior quality." (34)

Shortly after the VCs were fired, citing further deterioration on the campus, Singh invoked his powers as the constitutional head of the state. Without even consulting the chief minister—the duly elected head of the government—Singh appointed new VCs. (34)

Most colleges and universities are rife with this kind of cynical politics. Such things as whims of politicians and ability to put pressure on the government rather than the desire to educate determine job security. Feeling demoralized, teachers have little interest to teach. They also enjoy union protected jobs. As such they have little need to teach. They just show up and collect their salaries. Rich kids pay them for private tuitions, and, sometimes, even for grades. The other students go on frequent strikes. If that fails, they burn property, both public and private.

Students are hardly alone in using strikes and other forceful means to achieve their ends. By pushing everyone to conform to its plans and by catering to only those who exert pressure on the officials, government makes the use of force an integral part of the culture. Anyone who refuses to convert to this new religion ends up as a loser. Quite a few villagers in (the state of) Uttar Pradesh found this out the hard way. Their troubles started when the government bought their agricultural lands "to build houses for an ever-increasing urban population." (35)

Due to land ceiling, zoning, and other laws, these villagers had to sell to the government only. Naturally, its housing agencies behaved like typical monopolies. They offered to pay less than two rupees per square foot, a small fraction of the market value. After spending, on average, five to seven rupees to develop, these agencies planned to sell the lots for twenty five to forty rupees per square foot. (35)

Notwithstanding these contracts, however, the agencies refused to pay even these paltry sums. The reason was simple.
Government was a little short of cash. In this state, the bank
balances of all the relevant agencies put together amounted
to 600 million rupees. To the 1,300,000 or so farmers, however, the government owed 5,500 million rupees. Its housing
agencies in cities (such as, Kanpur, Meerut, and Lucknow) across
the state were in default. (35)

The ruling politicians refused to allow such a silly problem to
hinder their construction of housing "for the poor." What they
had lacked in funds, the authorities easily made up for in legisla-
tion: They passed a new Emergency Land Acquisition Act. (35)

Owing to its provisions, the officials could confiscate a parcel of land just fifteen days after they had issued an acquisition
notice. They argued that because the housing shortages were
very acute, the authorities desperately needed these emergency
powers. Governed by a philosophy that had preached little
respect for private property, they readily embraced the idea of
robbing many villagers of their land. (35)

The officials were committed to this plan for a very important reason. On paper, their housing agencies were supposed
to help the weaker sections of the society, but in reality the list
of the beneficiaries mostly included the officials themselves,
their family members, a few of their friends, and anyone else
who had the right connections. For example, Lucknow (a city
in Uttar Pradesh) Development Authority, promised to allot
forty percent of the newly built houses to the poor. The real
figure, however, was closer to ten percent. The rest were
gobbled up by the ruling elites. (35)

These attempts at the land-grab angered many landowners. They hated to stand by and watch the politicians steal
their property and redistribute it to the developers and
homeowners friendly to the high priests of power. The villagers banded together. They refused to yield control of their lands
to the government agencies until the latter paid them the
agreed-upon purchase price. When the authorities ignored their
demands and proceeded to build on the disputed land, the
villagers resorted to violence. On February 11, 1988, a group

of 200 attacked gang contractors and workers who were digging foundations for a housing colony. (35)

Someone in the gang fired, injuring six villagers. Soon, about 5,000 villagers showed up. They blocked a major highway. Their sheer numbers and show of strength impressed the local politicians who started to backpedal. They assured the villagers that the construction would restart only after the compensation issue was settled. (35)

"We can store wheat and grow vegetables. So we can't go hungry. But the government won't get our wheat without paying a fair price," says a victim of the government's food procurement policy. Using its powers, the government tries to procure wheat and rice from farmers at low prices. That makes many farmers very angry. On many occasions, they refuse to sell. To keep their election promises of cheap food, however, the authorities need all the food they can lay their hands on. They have little problem in using the force of law. Using threats of fines and jail sentences, the authorities loot the villagers of their food stuffs. (36)

Farmers in (the state of) Utter Pradesh decided to meet force with force. Galvanized by the calls for direct action from *Bharatiya Kisan* (Indian Farmer's) *Union (BKU)*, they demanded an increase in procurement prices. To their wish list, *BKU*'s leader Mahendra Singh Tikait added a few items of his own: writing off the government loans, rents, and the previous year's electricity dues; concessions in electricity rates; pensions for farmers; better payment for lands acquired by government; and representation for farmers in the Agricultural Price Commission and in other local development bodies. (36,37)

Per the instructions of their leaders, many villagers held back payments on electricity bills, house taxes, and land revenues. The farmers even refused to let the government employees enter the villages. Said one agitator, "If Tikait [leader of BKU] says burn your crops, uproot railway tracks, stop traffic, we will do it. It's more honorable to be shot by the police than to seek alms from the Government." (36)

Faced with such a show of solidarity and a staggering loss of revenues (up to twenty five percent), the authorities finally backed down. They offered to withdraw court cases and waive the electricity dues for six months. (38)

There was one small problem. Asked an official, "what of farmers who have stood by the government and paid the dues?"

The answer is simple. Until they can form a group, burn properties, bury the public under endless agitations, threaten bureaucrats with bodily harm, and put pressure on politicians, the decent and honest will have to grin and bear it.

---

[3] The organized private sector was so stunted that by the mid-eighties, it had created only eight million jobs. (17)

# CHAPTER 3
## *"We Indians"*

MOST INDIANS ARE quick to explain what has gone wrong with their country: something about their countrymen, and of course women, that makes them lazy, unruly, and quarrelsome.

This explanation finds its currency in books, magazines, newspapers and informal discussions. Says an editor in the *Illustrated Weekly of India*:

> *"In my present despair I am inclined to think that ours is an accursed land, that we are like some of the unfortunate characters in a Dostoyevskian novel, that we are like a whole nation possessed.... Could an entire nation be bitten by a hitherto unclassified bug, bitten into behaving in the most grotesque manner?"* (39)

Kushwant Singh, a distinguished author, knows what possesses India. In his book, *We Indians,* he says: "Racial, linguistic and religious divisions are older than and therefore deeply embedded in the Indian mind than the sense of Indianness which is less than 150 years old." He particularly holds the Indian religions (such as Hinduism and Sikhism) responsible for, among other things, envy, pettiness, insensitivity, having two sets of books, and dealing in black money. He connects the intro-spective nature of the religions and their emphasis on pursuit of inner peace to apathy, arrogance, self-importance, and lack of team spirit. Singh also rails at entrepreneurs, industrialists, suppliers, and middlemen. It's as if the scum of the earth has settled in India. Or, just as in a third-rate ghost movie, have these ugly traits snatched the collective consciousness of the public? Who do we call? *Greed Busters?* (40)

Every religion, however, encourages its followers to look in-side and pursue inner peace. Countries such as Japan and Ko-rea are influenced by Buddhism, an Indian religion. Still these people have prospered. Their religion poses little hindrance. It seems that they rather count their yen and dollars than en-gage in mind dulling introspection.

Also, few Western writers can get away with such a bigoted theory. They would be sternly reminded that for centuries Eu-ropeans, too, fought on the basis of geography, religion, and language. After all, even during these enlightened times, both the world wars and communism spread from Europe. By vir-tue of the color of their skin, however, Indian pundits such as Kushwant Singh can get away with their race-based explana-tions for the plight of India.

In all fairness, Singh just says it loud. During my frequent trips to India, I hear many people echo similar sentiments and engage in rabid self-depreciation. When asked about the state of affairs in the county, these Indians typically begin, "Our people...."

The theory that something is unalterably wrong with Indi-ans has as much of a logical foundation as the one that blames the plight of the country on the position of stars at the time of its independence. Both theories are utterly convenient, yet won-derfully vague. Particularly the former fails to explain why the same individuals are prospering and disgustingly behaving themselves in other countries. Of course, one could subscribe to another equally ridiculous theory that while all the smart ones skipped the country, the dumb jacks stayed back and screwed up India.

A more plausible explanation might be that when exposed to similar forces, that have discouraged hard work, risk taking, and self-reliance in other places (such as Africa, Sweden, South America, and eastern Europe), Indians, too, have developed most of the traits.

But the experts are less into plausible explanations. They are more into vague race-based theories and celestial prescriptions. For all the maladies. Kushwant Singh comes up with his own remedy: By some mysterious means, re-elevate the truth in all its dimensions "to the status of God." He yearns for the good-old-days of a leader who could tell the people that hard work is real worship. Then everyone would follow this messiah and turn into saints. (40)

India, however, started out with such leaders. They not only preached everyone to sleep but also tried to legislate their values and force-feed morality to their countrymen. Among all such pious laws, my very favorite is the *Guest Control Order.* This law prohibits entertaining a hundred or more guests at successive feasts. (40)

Singh also drags Freud through all this. He says that a "God-less West" liberated itself of sexual inhibitions and learned to be more truthful. (40)

In his magnificent book, *The Other Path,* Hernando De Soto, gave his best shot at being truthful. Because the theme (of *The Other Path*) rests on the idea that the legal-economic system— rather than some mysterious force or a few dead-end cultural explanations—determines a country's plight, the book's inferences just might apply to nations such as India. (41)

*The Other Path* was based on a study of the black market in another third world country, Peru. ILD (*Instituto Libertad y Democracia*), De Soto's organization, conducted the study. (41)

As a part of their efforts to examine what an individual had to go through to start an industry—if he would refuse to pay bribes, except as a last resort, or use influence—ILD researchers actually set up a dummy cloth factory. To register this *factory,* it took 289 days, the full-time labor of the group, and $1,231 (equivalent to thirty two minimum monthly wages in Peru). The researchers also calculated that to obtain a legal license for a vending cart one had to toil for a total of forty three days and spend 590 dollars. To procure a vacant lot and development and building permits for a house, going through the ministries and bureaucracies alone consumed seven years and $2,156 (fifty six monthly minimum wages). (41)

Whether from India or Peru, most people have these legitimate desires. Each likes to have a job and a roof over his head. When the legal system erects such obstacles as those documented in the study, creates a (in De Soto's words) "legal and economic apartheid," and frustrates these desires, people have only two options: to starve and die, or use their energies to survive by any means, such as paying bribes and running illegal ventures.

The choice is obvious to and must be welcome by anyone with an IQ higher than his height in feet. Small wonder that Peru has a burgeoning underground economy. It enables many Peruvians to make a living. The "informals" operate sixty percent of the Peruvian economy. In the city of Lima alone, the black market employs about 439,000 workers. A few of them run mini-busses and cars without a license and formal recognition. These informals shuttle around ninety five percent of the city's commuters, who otherwise would be left stranded. Of the 331 markets in the country, the illegals have developed 274 (83%). While the state has spent $173 million in low-cost housing, these law breakers have built houses worth forty seven times as much—for a total of $8,314 million. (41)

Peru is hardly an oddball of a country. The International Labor Organization reports that in all the developing world the informal sector employs about sixty percent of the urban labor force, more than twice that employed by the modern industries. In India, during the twenty years prior to 1985, underground markets created twice as many jobs as the "law abiding" ones. In all these countries, but for the underground economy, millions more would have been unemployed, deprived, miserable, and angry. (42)

De Soto hardly glorifies the black market. He actually lists the many drawbacks to the society. Illegals evade taxes and deprive government of revenues. They unfairly compete with legal manufacturers who pay taxes and try to abide by the rules. Most of all, the informals function without the advantages and protections of a legal system. In spite of their initiative, imagination, and hard work, they run clandestine operations which are inefficient. To avoid detection, for example, these illegals keep a low profile. They shy away from such instruments as advertisements. They reach their potential consumers by word of mouth. Without large-scale advertising and brand name loyalty, quality of their products is, at best, variable. (41)

To obtain capital for a new business or expand the existing one, the owner has to raise funds through illegal channels. He has to either pay high, black market interest rates or wait for his rich uncle to die. Starved of funds, these operations tend to be small and inefficient.

Also, even if any of these businesses has written agreements with its suppliers or customers, in case of a default, it has little recourse. Obviously these illegals can't go to court and obtain justice. They thus operate without legal contracts. Contrary to appearance, enforceable contracts do much more than pay orthodontist bills for attorneys' kids. These binding agreements build trust among total strangers. Owing to legal contracts, workers, investors, managers, and suppliers from diverse backgrounds and faraway places know that they will be paid for their efforts, interact with each other with confidence, and efficiently produce everything from pencils to 747s and laser devices. Without the benefit of legal contracts, an informal in Peru does business only with those he knows and trusts, such as people from his village, who form a network of *cousins* and *uncles*[4]. (41)

In short, deprived of easy credit and enforceable contracts and to avoid detection, most of these illegal enterprises tend to stay very small. Also, why take risks and kill oneself to build a large business if one is unable to safely transfer it to one's heirs or to a buyer for profit? Small wonder that in many predominantly socialist countries, economies of large scale are mostly confined to university textbooks and air-conditioned classrooms.

Being small and inefficient, underground businesses produce fewer jobs than when allowed to function in the open. For the consumer, they produce smaller quantities of cloth, cement, two-wheelers, candies, washing powder, and everything else. Their workers and consumers are beyond the protection of many laws, including those that apply to children in the workplace.

Thanks to a legal structure riddled with hurdles to the enterprise, however, only those who have connections engage in formal businesses. Only they can obtain the exclusive permits and licenses, necessary clearances and protection from the complex laws. By whatever means necessary, these monopolists protect their exclusivity. They and their official patrons relegate the rest of the producers to underground markets. Pretty soon, most people find out that it's more profitable to spend their efforts to influence the authorities than to invest and innovate and produce with efficiency. Those who enjoy a lock on the market by virtue of their official patronage make shoddy goods and get away. They manufacture bad pins, bad textbooks, bad dams, and bad every thing. In a cramped economy, the consumer has little choice. He has to buy this junk. To work around these restrictive laws and to obtain exclusive licenses, quite a few people bribe the officials. The reputations of the public servants gets so bad that most decent individuals stay clear of the public service. They yield to criminal politicians who, in due course, snuff out the political freedoms, notwithstanding the elections held every so often.

Regardless of religious or cultural background, few can escape these dynamics.

The conditions that have weakened countries such as Peru seem to have existed in early seventeenth and eighteenth century Europe.

Based on writings of Coleman, Devries, Clapham and Heckscher, De Soto paints the picture of a typical European city from that time:

*"Since the urban wages were relatively high, the more ambitious peasants migrated to cities... When they arrived in the cities, migrants from the countryside found that there were not enough jobs for them... Some entered domestic service or worked only on a casual basis... Since it was the only feasible alternative, however, informal activity spread quickly... Legions of peddlers invaded the streets, smuggled and illegally produced goods invaded the markets, and illegal suburbs flourished on the cities' outskirts."* (41)

This description fits most cities from the present third world. For example, the following excerpt from a 1989 article in the *Illustrated Weekly of India* also talks about the conditions that promote migration to Indian cities:

*"Isn't it ironic that in an agricultural economy, the average villager cannot even earn the Rs.10 [forty cents] a day that he can just by rag-picking in Bombay?...the villager will migrate to the urban centers in search of work."* (43)

De Soto finds the similarities between the early Europe and the present third world more than coincidental. In both the situations, a huge web of regulations and restrictive laws pushed most production underground. They made shortages and corruption inevitable. According to an English ordinance (1692) quoted by Heckscher, British inspectors went to factories only to collect their dues and did not examine the goods at all. In 1601, a speaker in the House of Commons defined the justice of the peace as, "a living creature that for a half dozen chickens will dispense with a whole dozen of penal statutes." (41)

Owing to such widespread corruption, very few Europeans respected or trusted the authorities. In more ways than one, their officials behaved as if they were the spitting images of officials from the present third world. Both offered handouts and froze prices. Unaware of the root cause of the corruption, they appealed for a return to morality and prescribed harsher punishments for law breakers. Both tried to bribe the public to conform to their planning. To push the poor and the retired away from the cities, for example, authorities in early Europe offered assistance only to those who would return to their parishes of origin (for example, Poor Law adopted in Britain in 1834 and a number of laws passed during years 1662, 1685 and 1693). These band-aides simply failed. More unrest, crimes and violence ensued. Law and order became hostage to politics with the consequent loss of relevance of the state. All this eventually spelled the end of the mercantilist status quo. (41)

For an Indian, Peruvian, or an Egyptian, if this sounds all too familiar, De Soto can be forgiven for the egghead thinking that says regardless of race, religion, or culture, human beings have a lot in common, especially the way we all respond to economic oppression.

To those who agree with this simple premise, hope to learn from history, and chart the future course of their countries, what happened in eighteenth and nineteenth century Europe should be of great interest. In England, the illegal activities became too widespread to be ignored. Its politicians finally realized that these informal markets sustained production and employed many people who would otherwise remain unemployed. Using massive deregulation, they proceeded to incorporate the underground economy into the legal structure. They passed laws that guaranteed property rights and access to business activity to the entire population. Because most everyone could engage in enterprise, organized businesses faced stiff competition. To sell, they had to produce quality goods at low prices. In their quest for efficiency, they economized on the use of resources, planned long-term, and came up with new technology. Levels of production and employment shot up. Small wonder that in just a few decades, the average standard of living in England rose by more than 100 percent. This so-called Victorian boom led to a time filled with peace, order, and respect for the state. (41)

France and Spain—the other major colonial powers and beneficiaries of the industrial revolution—refused to adapt. They repressed the informals. Disparities between those who have connections and have-nots accelerated. After the massive upheaval during the French Revolution, most of the European countries learned their lesson. They reformed their legal systems. (41)

Russia failed to reform until it was too late. Its economy failed to grow. Its people were stuck with a low standard of living. Largely owing to the inevitable and widespread discontent, Russia ascended the garbage heap of Leninism. It dragged with it many other countries, some close by and others as far as Cuba. (41)

There are several ways by which an all powerful and unscrupulous researcher can examine how modern societies evolve.

This supreme being, for example, can conduct a sort of controlled study with a few crossover provisions. He can choose a reasonably homogeneous society and split it into two countries. One country embraces political and economic freedoms more than the other country which imposes communism on its people. To carry His research further, He can experiment with varying degrees of democratic socialism and democratic capitalism in the first country. What happens to these countries and their people can teach a thing or two about human behavior.

Does this sound far-fetched and ludicrous? Maybe to everyone except, perhaps, Germans. Over the past few decades, something close to the above scenario took place in their country. Of course, not as an experiment, it just happened that way.

West Germany after the Second World War was prostrate. Its cities were reduced to rubble. Thirteen million refugees were pouring from the east. A pound of meat and half a pound of butter was all each family allowed to have per month. Black market was rampant. Rather than working for worthless currency, many preferred to stay home hungry. Physically, emotionally, and spiritually, the country lay in ruins. In such a situation, bare physical needs override any ideology. There is little room for intellectual pretenses and fancy economic notions about government enforced equality. (44)

Immediately after the war, an administrative board of five members—constantly under the watchful eyes of the occupation authorities—ruled West Germany. The board reformed the currency. Prodded by Ludwig Erhard, one of its members, the board put in place a market-oriented economic plan that, among other things, repealed rationing ordinances and price controls. (44)

Erhard's plan was a big hit. Germans behaved as if they woke up from a bad dream. Freed for the second time, they produced what they needed, and some more. They flooded the market with goods. Prices became stable. Just like in a Hollywood movie, over the next eight years unemployment faded into the background. (44)

In their pursuit for a better life, the newly-confident workers beat back the demons of poverty and unrest, which in the past had led to totalitarianism in their country. This so-called German miracle made its neighbors jealous. Enno von Lowenstern, editor of the German daily *Die Welt,* said, "As the West German economy boomed in the 1950s, the envious British and French used to joke that it was a shame they hadn't lost the war, for then the Americans would have made them as rich as West Germany." Britain and France had also received the Marshall Plan funds. They could have become as rich as West Germany, if they followed Erhard's course. Explained von Lowenstern: "But Britain had voted Labor after the war, which meant rationing, price controls and redistribution…and France opted for re-creating prewar political chaos and economic protectionism." (44)

Initially, Britain's Laborites detested Erhard. They balked at his plan. He, however, stood firm and closed the West German doors to the export of their deadly ideology. Soon, they relented. German socialists, however, refused to budge. In their eyes, Erhard committed the deadliest sin of all—being correct. These Social Democrats managed to turn Erhard into a caricature. They trivialized his policies. (44)

They also played the right kind of politics. They embraced the rhetoric of class warfare, championed union causes, appealed to the good intentions of the majority, and came to power. Owing to their policies, during the seventies the West German economy stagnated. Just like Jimmy Carter, who blamed the American stagnation on a *national malaise,* the pundits decided that somehow West Germany attained *the middle age.* It had become flabby and sclerotic. How does any country reach middle age? What are the signs to look for? Probably, everyone wears thick eye glasses and walks around wearing ties with soup stains. But then how does a nation develop malaise? (44)

During the eighties, under the relatively more market-oriented policies of Christian Democrats, Germans picked up where they had left off. They kept on moving. By 1989, with a GNP of close to 0.9 trillion (U.S.) dollars, their country had the fourth largest economy in the world. It exported one-third of its output and registered a trade surplus of $75 billion. Its per capita income rose to $11,000. What happened to the pundits? They quietly shelved their theories. (45)

East Germany—the other half of this controlled experiment— put in place structural Stalinism, complete with a central committee, politburo, and a general secretary.

They enforced their collectivist polices and put the famous *German work ethic* to a severe test: the individual was supposed to receive according to his needs (as decided by the officials) but work according to his ability. The overwhelming majority of the East Germans, however, proved to be just like the rest of us. In the absence of guarantees to enjoy the fruits of their labor, they refused to work and produce. They suffered severe shortages.

After the fall of the Berlin wall, most East Germans found out that, all along, they were worse off than West Germany's lowest one-third. Roger Thurow (of *The Wall Street Journal)* recited the story of residents of a East German town who literally went bananas after visiting a border town in West Germany. They went on a buying spree that left the West German town banana-free. Explained Thurow: "East Germans, some of whom have never seen a banana, yellow or green, have bought 10 tons of the precious fruit." Under communism, East Germany's industries stagnated, became inefficient, and poisoned their country's air, water and land. Yes. The savings rate was high—close 150 billion East German marks. In the absence of property rights, however, where does one invest all these savings? (46,47)

Communist party officials used their control over the economy, armed forces, and secret police to establish their own dictatorship. A few even took extra precautions. They developed private armies with their mafia-like arms' networks, funneled weapons to the third world countries, and made millions. In 1989, Heinrich Toeplitz, head of the commission investigating the abuse of power by the communist officials, said that Eric Honecker (East Germany's chief executive) and the other ousted leaders squirreled away $54 billion in Swiss bank accounts and spent huge sums on hunting lodges, luxury vacation homes, and other indulgences. As an example of life imitating art, Honecker behaved like an evil king in a fairy tale. While his countrymen were starving, he had corn stored to feed deer during the winter season. (48)

Nevertheless, in country after communist country, many western reporters—who otherwise profess a healthy dose of skepticism, disbelieve their authorities, and insist on checking out the facts for themselves—turned in their investigative lenses and masks at the borders. They faithfully swallowed the official line. Declared Ferdinand Protzman of the New York Times: "East Germany is the communist world's vaunted economic success story, held as proof that hard work, discipline and thrift can translate Karl Marx's theories into reality." (49)

Apparently, such reporters never wondered why people were risking their lives to run away from this utopia. Soon, however, during the remarkable events of 1989-90, the physical and informational barriers that had helped the likes of Mr. Protzman to get away with their shoddy journalism collapsed. A free flow of information revealed the truth. Not withstanding the government propaganda, Karl Marx's theories fostered widespread apathy, laziness, despondency, and a mental state of dependency. East Germans ran out of options. They started to look up to their filthy capitalist cousins from the West to come to their rescue. The former demanded a market based economy and its *trickle down prosperity*.

Of course, free market system offers a lot of opportunities and very few guarantees. The East German social welfare network did provide jobs, albeit of the make—believe variety, which produced very few goods and services. Naturally the workers dreaded the prospect of losing their jobs when and if their inefficient industries would fold. They also feared losing many social benefits. For example, East Germany provided free education for all, of course with a heavy emphasis on the now-useless *scientific Marxism*.

News anchors and editors from the West warned against this rush toward a market economy. They hoped that the economy would improve without giving up on socialist guarantees. They wondered whether the majority would support such a radical idea as private property. To the surprise of these pundits, the former East Germans showed that they, too, loved to make a buck. In less than two years after the fall of the Berlin Wall, a million of these Germans applied to start new businesses. (50)

The theory, which, at best, revealed a static if not racist thinking—that some how Germans were inherently aggressive—surfaced again. Its proponents worried about the emergence of a united and strong Germany which might threaten its neighbors. These theorists, however, ignored history. They forgot that the all-promising-but-unable-to-deliver social democratic policies of the Weimar Republic (during the decade after the First World War) made its leaders look weak. Naturally, Germans yearned for a statist system that "could get things done." Hitler, with his promise of national socialism, did fit the bill. Mr. Schoenhuber, a fascist *Republicaner*, hopes to repeat the history. He hopes to come to power by following Hitler's formula. He asserts, "we have to redistribute." He thus illustrates the marriage between fascism and socialism. (51)

Socialist theorists who share his zeal for redistribution might be better off listening to an East German plumber who, before the fall of the Berlin Wall, partook in anti-communist demonstrations. He said, "The 40-year experiment in socialism here has failed and there's nothing left." (52)

✦    ✦    ✦

Lech Walesa agrees: "We have nothing. I don't have a good ballpoint pen. I don't have a typewriter or tables...People here are discouraged in a different way. Life is doing a crossword puzzle. But one crossword is about food..." (53)

The Leninist-Stalinist structure, which left Poland, East Germany, and many other nations in shambles ravaged its birthplace. The Soviet experience revealed how ineffective and wasteful central planning was. According to Leonid Abalkin— a leading Soviet economist and director of the All Union Economic Institute in the Soviet Union—by 1988 a staggering $700 billion worth of unusable products filled the Soviet warehouses. (54)

Before the 1917 revolution, Russia used to be a major grain exporter. After the communist takeover, despite the huge imports, almost all the former Soviet republics rationed food. To boost agriculture, Soviet planners spent a lot of funds: on fertilizer which was incorrectly used, on grandiose irrigation projects that failed to increase the yields and harmed the environment, and on a distribution system that had worked halfway, before Gorbachev, and collapsed as soon as he stopped using brutal force. (55)

Government failed to allow for production of sufficient food for its countrymen, but it did create a lot of oddities. To house cows, for example, officials built concrete livestock sheds. For sure, these cows lived better than many Soviet citizens. Each of their bungalows cost more than a small apartment. After such high living, however, these poor cows (as well as pigs) lined up for days outside the government owned slaughterhouses. The reason was simple: a shortage of cold storage space. At the other end, for their meat, consumers lined up for hours in stores. (55)

Witnesses to such devastating failures of central planning started to sing the praises of free market. Some of these sayings could put both Adam Smith and Milton Friedman to shame. "I consider the open-market economy to be an ultimate achievement of mankind for which no alternative has yet been found," says Ante Markovic (the Premier-designate of, then, Yugoslavia). He called for an "urgent introduction of shares and bonds, private initiative and entrepreneurship in the Yugoslav economy and an end to government interference in the running of businesses." (56)

Most social democrats in the West (Germany, Sweden and France, for example) distance themselves from communism. They disagree with its undemocratic means and use of brute force, but marvel at its beautiful vision of equality. More importantly, in their own ways, they go along with its gospel of confiscation and redistribution of private property. They lure voters with their promises of forced equality. With the despotic backing of the majority, these leaders trample on the rights of those who disagree with them. For example, they nationalize industries and send the former owners packing. These social democrats also force sellers to sell at controlled prices, and owners to rent at controlled rates. With their protectionist policies, the leftists make consumers pay more for imports.

Early communist leaders such as Lenin—upon whom fell the burden of applying socialist theories—found this approach slow, cumbersome, and only marginally effective. These comrades spotted an inherent conflict between the ideas of forced distribution and that of fundamental freedoms such as the right to own property, to free speech (victims of forced redistribution might point out the inequities), to vote (horrified by the use of force, the majority might vote against the socialists), and to due process (an independent judiciary might slow down the agenda of forced equality). These communists found a surer and faster way to expropriate property. They established leftist dictatorships and simply dispensed with these *bourgeois* freedoms.

Just like their social democratic friends, these communist officials used the powers they had accumulated to confer a higher standard of living on the privileged few: eighteen million or so Soviet bureaucrats and a few thousand party officials. Also included in the ranks of the super-rich are those who have the official backing—high-ranking scientists, athletes, artists, and diplomats.

While blessing the rich with more riches, the communist rulers shrunk the opportunities for the poor and made the

inequality even worse. Alexander Zaichenko, an expert on Soviet living standards, made this point when he presented his
case in *Argumenty Fakty*, a Soviet weekly with a circulation of
twenty million. Because of the restrictions on ownership of private property, he used ownership of consumer goods as a proxy
for wealth. (57,58)

According to Zaichenko, 11.2 percent of the Soviet population belonged to the middle class by Western standards, in
that they had owned separate apartments or houses, furni-
ture, appliances, or maybe a summer home. In most advanced
countries, this figure was close to fifty to seventy percent. Of
the Soviet people, 2.3 percent were wealthy; the other eighty
six percent or so were poor. In the US (which might rival the
Soviet Union in terms of natural resources) the corresponding
figures for upper, middle and lower classes were roughly twenty,
sixty, and twenty percent. Most in the bottom group had a
better standard of living than the so-called middle class of the
socialist countries. (57,58)

Also, the well-to-do in a free market economy get ahead
because they have anticipated the consumer needs and met
them better than the competition. In the Soviet Union, the
rich got richer owing to their connections. In their universe, all
rubles were not created equal, either. Because of their access
to specialty shops, the Soviet elite could buy more for their
money. They also bought quality items the lower classes could
only dream of. Whatever they left back, the store mangers
would sell in the black market at high prices. (57,58)

Even from Gorbachev's reforms, some 400,000 top brass—
the newly-rich managers of the cooperatives—have benefited
more than the others. Whither the revolution; using their grip
over the system, quite a few of these former officials are emerging as millionaires. (57,58)

In the name of equality, the communist leaders trampled on
fundamental freedoms. Their revolutions left tens of million of
people dead, tore families apart, and installed a reign of terror.
The end-result, however, was an extreme inequality. Commenting on the system of *Nomenklatura* (a heirachical network of
politicians and bureaucrats in the former Soviet Union), a widow

of a famous poet who was killed in the Stalinist purges said: "They have divided everybody into categories, and we all starve, or eat, according to rank." (59)

Inequality happens to be the least of problems for Japan. In a survey, more than ninety percent of Japanese say that they belong to the same category, which has little to do with their perverse liking to raw fish. They belong to *the middle class.* (60)

Japan comes closer to being a classless society than the so called socialist countries. Its equality is one of shared wealth rather than shared deprivation. As a result, it's relatively peaceful. News of strikes or mass civil disturbances rarely fill its front pages. Its lead in science and technology runs everybody scared. In this country, education is mandatory and universal. Progress is merit dependent. (60)

Japan, however, started out as anything but a level playing field. As late as the 1860s, the society was hierarchal and had a well-defined caste system. A Japanese could enter only the profession prescribed by birth. He was prohibited from taking up any other. Confucius and Buddha, whose ideas are very close to Hindu thought, influence Japanese religious traditions. (60)

Compared to many third world countries such as India, Japan commands fewer per capita natural resource. Despite this, the Japanese produce and export enough wealth to make up for whatever they lack: virtually all of their iron ore, cotton, wool, and rubber, and half of the lumber and wood pulp, wheat, feed grains, cooking oil, and soybeans and most of the meat. Foreign imports meet fifty percent of Japan's caloric needs and eighty percent of the energy needs. They export all this stuff to Japan with pleasure. They love to earn the strong yen, not because it's backed by Japan's Central Bank, but by the country's production—cars, stereos, cameras and that most basic commodity of all, the Nintendo game system. (60)

One of my friends, a representative from the Indian Chamber of Commerce, found out the secret of Japan's success: "It's a warrior race."

Buffalo wash! Just like all the other racially biased theories of human behavior, this one, too, is rooted in fiction. Before 1868, Japan undertook only one major foreign expedition: Hideyoshi—one of the three leaders responsible for unifying this hopelessly divided country—executed a brief (1592–1598) military operation in Korea. During the following 250 years (*Tokugawa* period), the Japanese led a very peaceful and sheltered life. Even the warrior Samurai class turned into bureaucrats and petty functionaries. They wore swords for the same reason that a banker would wear his tie. (60)

Owing to this isolation, however, Japan got behind technologically. So much so that a modest American fleet under Commodore Perry forced them into submission (1853–54). Japan opened its ports to the West. It signed unequal treaties and gave away trade concessions. After this humiliating experience, the early *Meiji* government (*Meiji* period: 1868–1912) vowed to modernize Japan. In a rush, it started new industries and sent students abroad. (60)

To finance all these ventures, the government needed money. These were pre-World Bank years. Due to high interest rates, private loans were prohibitively expensive. Out of necessity, Japanese started to sober up. Matasukta Masayoshi, the then finance minister, initiated a few crucial reforms. He disposed off many state-owned enterprises, such as small industries and pilot plants, to private owners. With this new money, the government balanced its budget and stabilized the currency. (60)

These were just side benefits. Soon, private owners turned these industries around, with cotton spinning leading the pack. Owing to reduced costs, effective management, and improved quality, these industries showed profits. Japan's share of the world markets started to rise. This set off a chain reaction of increased employment, higher personal earnings, higher consumer spending, rapid economic growth, and further increases of employment. With the additional revenues, the government built railways, roads, and power plants, employing still more people and pushing the economy into even higher gear. Historians called all this the "Meiji Miracle," and loved the alliteration. (60)

The Second World War, however, rained on this parade. As if swallowed by a giant snake, the country ended up well behind square one. Two million Japanese died. The war destroyed forty percent of the aggregate area of the cities and reduced the urban population (and, consequently, skilled industrial labor) by fifty percent. Agriculture, short of equipment and fertilizer, was in shambles. Six million Japanese, living abroad, returned. They strained the resources further. (60)

Over the next few years, America handed Japan a half billion dollars as a sort of seed money, but the funds came with a price tag. The occupation government forced-fed an otherwise good constitution that was a bit left-leaning. For example, instead of leaving it to market forces of competition, government sought to splinter the big industrial houses and break up their monopolies. The constitution also paved the way for labor strikes. All this threatened the economic growth. Over the next few years, Japanese leaders, such as Yoshida Shiguru, under the guidance of the Dodge Commission (ironically named after a Detroit banker), dropped many of the "reforms." The government scaled down its efforts to break up big industries. It also banned strikes by civil servants who were threatening to become very uncivil. (60)

After 1950, year after year, Japan's economy grew by ten percent. Because of compounding effect, Japan's output doubled every seven years. By 1980, its per capita income exceeded $10,000. Many experts started to talk about the *workaholic Japanese.* Peter Jennings of ABC News said, "The average American spends 18 to 20 hours [a week] in leisure activities; the average Japanese, 10 to 13 hours." (60)

This widely-held notion that Japanese are inherently workaholics, however, clashes with views held by many Western travelers to *Meiji* Japan. Milton Friedman, a noted economist, quotes an early (1867) foreign resident in Japan: "Wealthy we do not think it [Japan] will ever become. The advantages conferred by Nature, with exception of the climate, and the love of indolence and pleasure of the people themselves forbid it. The Japanese are a happy race, and being content with little are not likely to achieve much." (61)

Maybe only recently have the Japanese have embraced workaholism. They have probably done so after being guaranteed the opportunities to earn and keep wealth regardless of the status of a person at his or her birth. More than likely, their culture or genes have very little to do with their work habits. Before the "*Meiji* miracle," they were chained by the hierarchal setup. They had refused to work hard because, just like under a socialist system, their progress depended less on their efforts than on other extraneous factors.

By imitating and successfully reproducing the "Japanese model," the other so-called newly industrialized nations (NINs)—Taiwan, South Korea, Hong Kong, and Singapore—have made tremendous strides in development. By doing so, they relegate most of our race-based explanations for economic success to the ranks of hearsay. For example, Koreans are as much of a warier race as Michael Jackson is a heavyweight boxer. Time and time again, China and Japan have mangled this country. In the past two decades, however, South Korea has increased its annual per capita income by 25-fold to about $2,400. (62)

How free are these "free enterprise" systems? After all, countries such as Japan have giant business houses. Their governments *coordinate* commercial activities.

Just like the frictionless model in physics, however, an absolute form of free enterprise is strictly a theoretical concept.

During most of the nineteenth and early twentieth centuries, the US, Britain, and Sweden came closer to this model, in that government left individuals mostly free to enter in contracts with each other as long as they stayed clear of other peoples' basic rights. Consequently, these countries enjoyed unprecedented prosperity and egalitarianism[5]. With their central planning, high tax rates, business subsidies, rent controls and price freezes, most third world governments, on the other hand, heavily interfered with the enterprise. In the name of national-ization, which Michael Harrington—a devout and self pro-claimed socialist—called "a flawed memory at best," some even engaged in large scale confiscation of private property. These governments tried to manufacture everything from rubber bands to rockets. What they produced in larger quantities, how-ever, were waste, fraud, and inefficiency. (63)

Prior to 1950, the Asian *Tigers,* such as South Korea, belonged to the category of the third world. In terms of resources, edu-cation, and per capita income, they were no better than India. Economies of these Asian Tigers, however, grew rapidly over the past few decades because their governments moved closer to the free enterprise model by taking one important step. They showed a moderate respect for individual property rights. They, thus, encouraged creation of wealth. Seeking *windfall* profits, and disciplined by competition, producers in these countries showered consumers—at home and abroad—with quality products, just in the right quantities and at right prices. In these countries, market forces coordinated and planned the produc-tion and distribution of wealth much better than any planning commission living, dead, or suspended in between. Owing to the economic growth, without any help from Marx or his brand of *worker advocates*, workers in the Newly Developed Asian Countries (NDACs) started to live better.

To the extent any country deviates from the absolute model of free enterprise, however, it pays the price. In Japan, for ex-ample, government *coordinates and streamlines* a lot of pro-ductive activities. To this end, the authorities have passed a lot of regulations and grabbed a lot of discretionary powers over the enterprise. Many people, such as farmers and ship build-ers, have organized as groups and seek to influence the offi-cials. Each group tries to get the officials to *coordinate* its way and bilk the average Japanese. For example, the farmers' lobby uses its influence on politicians to keep up protectionism. As a result, the consumer pays high prices. He suffers, relatively, a lower standard of living than otherwise. A Japanese worker, who makes eighteen dollars per hour and spends three to six dollars per apple (due to restrictions on imports of apples), is going to be poorer than his American counterpart who makes as much but can buy an apple for thirty cents. Even a planning commission member ought to know this much.

The recent Recruit scandal (see chapter 7) shocked many, but not as much as the realization that the corrupt practices are widespread in Japan. But there is no surprise here. In every country, such corruption is in direct proportion to the discretionary powers the officials enjoy over the economy.

In the NDACs, corruption and cheating might be more common than most of us realize, but it's hardly the natural order. Most of the economic planning is still carried out by private individuals. As a result, the citizens are spared the often mind boggling, omnipresent and colorful corruption of the socialist countries. They are also spared the unrest, divisiveness, and disenchantment that has become universal in most socialist countries. Assured of property rights, these individuals rather direct their energies towards achieving prosperity instead of fighting each other for government handouts. They enjoy a greater control over their lives. As such they are much more hopeful and confident.

On both these counts, the Swedish seem to be slipping. Over the past few years, their self-confidence and hope in the future seem to be on decline. A report (Nov. 22, 1990) by Knight-Ridder newspapers quotes Madeleine Olsson, mother of three children: "I work evenings with old people. My husband works days on construction.... Everything is so expensive, especially the food. The only time we eat meat is when my husband hunts down a moose." (64)

Early on, Swedes did benefit greatly from their economic freedoms. They prospered and built a very civil, happy and egalitarian society. When they abandoned the free market in favor of a welfare state, however, they, too, paid the price.

Social Democrats ruled Sweden for fifty one of the last fifty eight years. Their regulations and high taxes (with a marginal rate of seventy two percent) ensured that roughly sixty percent of the country's production went to government for redistribution. To assure cradle to grave welfare benefits, government spent these revenues on an enormous system of subsidies. Rather than equality of opportunity, all these measures promised an equality of outcome regardless of effort. They destroyed incentives and encouraged rampant absenteeism. To make up for lost productivity, the government continuously depreciated kroner and fueled inflation, which, during the eighties ran double the European average. By embracing socialism, the once-prosperous Swedes suffered a nose dive in their standard of living. (64,65,67)

Social Democrats ran out of choices. They started to beat a retreat. "The Social Democratic government [in Sweden] on Friday began dismantling the welfare state it built, proposing sharp cuts in benefits and state jobs to stop the country's economic decline," said an Associated Press report (Oct. 26, 1990). Early that year, Ingvar Carlsson, the prime minister, announced a two year freeze of wages, prices, rents, dividends, and local government income taxes. "To guarantee continued full employment, the basis of a fair society," he called for a ban on strikes. A ban on strikes? Was he saying that strikes might hurt the poor by reducing the number of jobs available to them? (65, 66)

All along, socialists, such as Carlsson, have credited unions for workers' gains, but most evidence fails to support this viewpoint. In the US, for example, over the past seven decades, non-union workers increased their wages faster than the union workers. During the eighties, despite the anti-union polices of the Republican administrations and the fact that a low seventeen percent of the American workers belong to unions, the personal income of American workers has shot up. When compared to workers in countries with massive union power such as India and the Philippines, workers in Japan and South Korea enjoy a very high standard of living. Organized labor temporarily augments salaries and benefits of a few privileged workers,

but certainly prevents expansion of business activity and hurts
those who are unemployed and underemployed. In the long
run, such matters as how many are employed and how well
they are employed are decided by the rate of economic growth
which rests upon worker productivity. Carlsson agrees with such
*capitalist propaganda.* He notes that in Sweden, over three years
prior to 1990, production has grown by two percent, while
salaries have increased by twenty eight percent. That, he says,
is throwing the economy off balance. (65)

Compared to most other European countries, West Germany,
especially under Christian Democrats, followed more
pro-growth policies. To the extent it had interfered with the
enterprise, however, even this country did pay the price. The
recent scandal involving Kohl and his party has revealed the
degree of corruption that has corroded this country.

Even within the same country, regions which are statist suffer from higher levels of corruption, unrest, violence, and
politicization. For example, in Italy, for whatever reason, the
south lagged behind economically. To help the region, the Italian government allocated funds for quite a few public works
projects. As to what happened to the money, David Lawday
and Alexander Stille (of *US News and World Report*) recounted:
"Rome recognizes that many of the fattest contracts for
public-works projects in the South have ended up in Mafia
hands. But the last thing the feudal minded Mafia wants is
modernization, and these projects frequently have been left
half-finished once the billions from Rome have been soaked
up. As a result, Sicily is cursed with unusable highways and
dams." (68)

Why couldn't government abolish these wasteful subsidies?
The reporters explained: "Southerners dominate the central
government and the bureaucracy. Northerners enter business
and finance." Largely entrepreneurial northerners stayed out
of civil service and created their own opportunities. Their cousins from the south, however, found a better way. Their leaders
hung on to the government. They held the purse-strings and
used their grip to confiscate someone else's production. Their
efforts to distribute the loot naturally politicized the region.

Lawday and Stille said: "Southerners traditionally opt for politics, the South's main and most lucrative industry." (68)

From the founding of the Republic until 1929, the US government mostly resisted the lure of socialism.

It limited its role to basics such as national defense and printing the currency. According to Milton Friedman, federal spending typically amounted to three percent or less of the national income. Most of the rest its people were free to spend, save and invest. Fired by a limitless profit motive, they made the best use of the country's resources. Free and ambitious, they pushed the edges of knowledge and handed the humanity the technology to produce all the things we take for granted: cars, movies, telephones, airplanes, electricity, and, of course, chewing gum. By guaranteeing economic freedoms, the legal framework let loose an unprecedented boom. It helped to build a superpower out of this ragtag country made mostly of refugees. (69)

Within the last few decades, however, even this fortress of capitalism fell victim to the tide that had swept the rest of the world. Americans, too, found the lure of forced equality and a life without risks irresistible—politicians started to build a safety net, albeit a limited version that consisted of such entities as social security, farm subsidies, health care for elderly and poor, loans to small businesses, protection against bank failures, and housing for residents of inner-cities.

The media which routinely devalues individual initiative and pushes government intervention to correct all ills—real and perceived—prods the majority to trade freedom for security. More and more news stories close with prescriptions of increased intervention by the state. Such a consciousness permeates beyond the evening news, editorials, and cartoons. Invariably, when most journalists ask a politician what he is going to do about a certain problem, such as the deteriorating standards of education, they mostly mean one thing: "How much of the taxpayer's money is he willing to spend on this so-called unmet need?"

Unfortunately, American politicians love to answer such questions with actions. They love to spend the taxpayer's money. So much so that they can't get enough of it. As the government gradually enlarges its scope to areas hitherto left alone, it confiscates a much higher percentage of the country's production—up to twenty four percent in the mid 1980s, and twenty one percent by 1990[6]. As a result, even during the *mean* decade of the eighties, federal government just about doubled its spending to more than $1.2 trillion. (70)

In order to survive, most politicians follow the consensus and cater to the various interest groups. This includes even the so-called conservatives. Says Mickey Edwards (a member of the US House of Representatives): "If you were to try to find a conservative who always disregards the interests of his constituents, you would have to look real hard." (71)

Beneficiaries of these various federal programs—such as the elderly and the men and women who build every thing from $1,000 toilet seats to housing projects—have developed a sweet tooth for the taxpayer's money. They have formed political action committees. The more they get, the more they want. They fill up election chests. Politicians naturally distribute money in favor of any group that will help them win votes and political contributions; known as bribes in other countries but made legal by the American politicians. Members of the U.S. Congress have followed this simple and effective formula. Small wonder that they have mostly maintained a very high reelection rate of ninety percent.

It's true that voters resist their attempts to raise taxes. Compared to the vested interests (beneficiaries of the government programs and the politicians), however, the taxpayers are too ill-organized to stop individual programs. For example, a handout of $100 million to 1,000 people will cost each taxpayer a dollar or two—too little to arouse his concerns. The 1,000 beneficiaries, on the other hand, have every incentive to keep the program alive and thriving. Few will hesitate to give a measly $10,000 as a political contribution and make $100,000 each from the government. The next thing the beneficiaries will be clamoring for is a further enlargement of the program.

Naturally, many of the federal programs, which start out very small, soon invoke the images of the marshmallow monster. As late as 1960, for example, government spent a mere 5 billion dollars for civilian health purposes (omitting the veterans). By 1977, the figure has swollen to $68 billion and by the late eighties to $100 billion. Despite this, lobbies of senior citizens and *advocates of the poor* howl at cuts even in future increases. To extract more money, each day health care providers come up with new and ingenious ways of billing. As long as Uncle Sam pays, who's counting? Also, his spending habits proved to be very catchy. They set the trends for private insurers who had to match his payments based on procedure coding. As a result, between 1960 and 1990, total U.S. health expenditures (private and public) zoomed from $27 billion to $666 billion. (72,73)

More importantly, someone else—usually the employer— ends up picking up most of the tab. Naturally, the consumer harbors little interest in controlling the costs. The employer can attempt to reduce his premiums, but he has only a limited say in controlling the expenditures. He can't veto this test or that operation. By attempting to limit the providers' choices too narrowly, he will surely invite the wrath of the employees and their unions. It's as if the boss buys his employees' groceries. He has little flexibility. He can seldom get away with buying the store brands. Minimum benefit packages decreed by various state governments also limit the employer's options. In any event, why should he lose sleep over the high premiums? His expenses are tax deductible. Interestingly, employee-paid health care, which transfers the responsibility for and the control over the provision of health care from workers to the employer and perversely affects the market incentives, is a relic of another socialist measure, wage controls that were imposed during the forties. To circumvent the controls, employers sweetened their offers with such benefits as *free* health care. In the end, consumer thrift—the only element that could have controlled the costs and kept insurance premiums down just as it has done in the case of auto insurance—plays little role in the affairs of health care. Naturally, the costs have escalated. Very few average Americans can afford to get sick anymore.

For similar reasons, very few can afford a college education by themselves. Parents (and an occasional student) insist on a quality education from colleges but not economical one. As voters, all they have to do is to elect *education presidents* and congressmen "who want to invest in the future of America." These elected officials will make sure that the taxpayer will pick up the tab. Between 1981 and 1988, for example, they have increased federal aid to higher education from $9.7 billion to $14.4 billion, a forty eight percent jump. During the same period the consumer price index has risen only by twenty-five percent. (74)

If a taxpayer thinks that he is forking out all this money to educate and civilize the current crop of party lovers, he is in for a surprise. Just like in any other area of bureaucratic intervention, administrative costs soak up most of these funds. Not only do some of the monies pay for expensive yachts and make-believe research programs in the universities, forty-four percent of the funds just cover the defaulted loans.

One of the reasons why the average taxpayer rarely objects to all this spending is because he feels for those whom he perceives as less fortunate than he is. He hopes that his money will throw a life raft for the needy, such as the struggling farmers. He fears that without his handouts their way of life might disappear. He forgets that for centuries, without any help from the government, farming has burgeoned. In America, by the turn of the twentieth century, farmers have built the most efficient, productive, and awesome machine in the world. So much so, each farmer has fed close to twenty mouths. This he has done without using any subsidies. (75)

Ever since, politicians have discovered a way to win elections in the farm states; by handing out subsidies to the once independent and proud farmer and make him the ward of the state. They do so by proclaiming that these funds primarily help the needy. In reality, however, few politicians can afford to waste money like that. James Bovard (of the Cato Institute), author of *Farm Fiasco,* identifies the major beneficiaries of the farm subsidies: in 1988 alone, 323,000 of these farmers (up from 271,000 in 1980) have had sales over $100,000. Median net worth of these full-time farmers is more than one million dollars. During the eighties, consumers and taxpayers shelled out $260 billion to feed these starving millionaires. The farm lobby destroys any politician who questions such a transfer of wealth. It has defeated the many attempts to reform, including the one that limits the aid to those earning less than $100,000 a year. Even those reforms that are passed are eventually diluted. (76)

Despite all this, Hollywood still makes movies about farm foreclosures. News anchors pile up ratings on farm-related stories. We learn to love *the farmer.* We pay him from both the pockets: as taxpayers and consumers. As a direct aid to peanut farmers, for example, the taxpayer shells out a measly $4 million. More importantly, the US government limits the number of farmers who can sell peanuts. It all but forbids peanut imports. Naturally, prices stay high. Each year, all those peanut butter and jelly sandwiches stick the consumer with an additional bill of $369 million. Officials decide who gets this dough: farm by farm, county by county, state by state. This peanut quota is a sure ticket to riches. More than a third of the nation's 44,000 quota owners rent their quotas to other farmers. They enjoy profits without ever being involved in the production. Some even live in distant cities. (77)

Peanut quotas are just one example of how by using promises of risk free lives, an *all caring and all providing* government hurts the little guy. Not only do politicians tax him and shower their favorite constituencies with money, they also pass regulations which restrict competition for the producers and make sure that the consumer pays more in the form of higher prices. Actually, most politicians find protectionism to be a very handy tool in helping their benefactors. While, at least, voters might resist some tax increases, they know very little about, much less protest, the damage caused by laws that restrict competition.

Such laws shield producers from competition, both from outside and within the country. Owing to textile protectionism, for example, the US consumers pay an additional $25 billion a year for their clothes. This amounts to an extra $238 a year per family. Such restrictions also reduce the credibility of the US trade representatives, who demand free trade from the third world countries. (78)

These tariffs and trade quotas only help the producers who are infinitely smaller in numbers, but are richer and much more influential than the consumers whom they bilk. Even among the producers, the usually more powerful management benefits much more from the protectionism than the individual worker. Not only does the general level of employment become higher in an open country, these workers are consumers too. A textile union might lobby against imports. If politicians follow this prescription and restrict most imports, they will hurt the consumers, some of whom are textile workers themselves. By paying more for low quality cars, video recorders, and television sets made by protected companies, the workers get much less for their dollar. Their standard of living declines. What if a few of them refuse to buy from foreigners and insist on buying from domestic companies such as the Ford? These consumers still come out ahead in an open market. Due to a stiff competition and poor sales, for example, recently it seems that the Ford has decided to make "quality as job one."

Also, either in the case of school boards of New York or that of grain boards of Africa, the more numerous and complex the regulations are, the higher are chances for official corruption. In short, to the extent a government regulates the economy and appropriates and redistributes the national wealth, it nurtures all the elements of the statist system: loss of consumer choices, destruction of individual initiative, official sponsored privileges, widespread corruption, loss of respect for law and order, unrest, over politicization and an ever enlarging state that slowly and ultimately threatens most individual rights.

Regardless of the race or religion of its people, or its geographical location, no country can escape these dynamics. America, the cradle of the Bill of Rights, is hardly an exception.

To find out what an all powerful, all interfering, and redistributive government can do to the standard of living of those that are at the bottom, all one has to do is to take a peak at an American inner-city.

To be poor and living in an inner city is beyond rough. It's dangerous. A recent study, published in the *New England Journal of Medicine*, concludes that adult males in Bangladesh live longer than those in Harlem (New York). (79)

Notwithstanding improvements in child mortality rates, between 1960 and 1980, death rates for males between the ages of 25 and 65 living in Harlem went up. These men mostly died from homicides, cirrhosis, accidents, drug dependency, and cardiovascular diseases. McCord and Freeman, authors of the study, looked for causes behind these causes; among other things, these researchers came up with poverty, malnutrition, substance abuse, psychological stress, and inadequate access to housing and health care. The good doctors prescribed an intensive educational program to improve nutrition and reduce the use of drugs, alcohol, and tobacco. They called for a heavy dose of "political commitment," also known as more funds. They believed that the new programs would provide the poor residents of Harlem access to adequate income, useful employment, and decent housing. (79)

Prescribing more funds from government sounds reasonable, but there's a problem. Such a program consisting of clinic and drug treatment centers has already been in place for decades. Also, more than ever before, Harlemites live on public assistance. Despite all this "political commitment," poverty, unemployment, substance abuse and violence have kept increasing. (79)

McCord and Freeman looked at the facts. These researchers wondered for an instant, but refused to be confused by their own data. They saw few alternatives to more government spending. They were entrenched in their belief that government was the only agent of progress.

So were the intellectuals and planners of the third world. Instead of promoting a legal framework that would let the individual create his opportunities and earn what he needs, they,

too, embarked on the path of "more political commitment."
With their pie-in-the-sky promises of government engineered
prosperity and equality, they seduced the poor into inaction.
By erecting hurdles to those who liked to engage in production, they would further discourage individual initiative. The
poor were led to believe that the only way to prosper was to
receive alms from Big Brother. He failed to come through, and
they paid a heavy price.

Both Bangladesh and Harlem—a poor third world country
and an American city—followed similar policies. They stripped
the individual of control over his life. Both released him of responsibility for his future. In either case, without an active participation from the individual in his care, no amount of infusion of money and services would make a difference. In both
places, a combination of good intentions and bad policies invariably led to more poverty, desperation and inequality.

These policies did so because they ignored or, much worse,
tried to repeal certain immutable natural laws. One such basic
law relates to property rights and creation of wealth. Without
guaranteed property rights, few will toil to create wealth. With
the help of rent controls, restrictive building codes, and other
regulations, for example, the planners in New York city abridged
the property rights. The city naturally ended with very little
wealth—in this case fewer rental units. Successive governments
in New York robbed the landlords and paid off the tenants. For
many units, the laws allowed rents that would fail to cover
even the maintenance costs. As recently as 1984, the government passed a law which stipulated that just because the owner
wanted to occupy his property, he couldn't evict a tenant who
had lived in the apartment for more than twenty years. The
owner first would have to go to court, bear the legal costs, and
prove undue hardship, defined as an annual return of less than
8.5 percent. One might support such laws by arguing that
"These guys are rich. Surely, they can afford the lawyers and
the court fees." An Arthur D. Little study (1985), however,
showed that most landlords owned one building and had income between 10 to 40,000 dollars per year. Many were immigrants. Asked Gordan Crovitz of The Wall Street Journal: "Who

else would be naive enough to invest in residential apartments in New York?" (80)

The poor renters whom the government was trying to protect were, in fact, very upscale. Their ranks included many influential politicians and judges. They would beat back the many attempts at even modest reforms, such as the one limiting rent controls to poor and middle income families. Just like any other socialist policy, rent controls, too, helped those with clout. They would add to the perception of widespread official corruption. (80)

To win votes among the poor, politicians did promise *enhanced commitment*—more public housing. By doing so, not only did they emerge as the champions of the poor, these officials could, then, turn around and use the funds to help their friends: builders and contractors. Even during the *housing cuts* of the eighties, the American politicians spent more for subsidized housing: Federal spending rose from $8.3 billion in 1980 to $16.1 billion in 1988; the number of HUD-subsidized rental units actually increased by almost fifty percent—from 2.9 million units to 4.1 million; the number of families living in these units went up by one-third. (81)

All these plans to "house the poor" provided dwellings. They, however, stripped the occupants of the only incentive to maintain these houses, ownership. As to be expected, bureaucratic landlords managed these buildings like they managed everything else. To everyone's surprise, the houses failed to self maintain. Where were the *homeless advocates* that had demanded for all this *political commitment*? They were too busy agitating for more of the same. They refused to be held accountable. That their policies wasted a lot of taxpayer's money only to fill the urban landscapes with dilapidated houses meant little to them. (81)

This scenario repeated itself in as many cities as there were *homeless advocates.* In the US, for every house the government built since the sixties, it condemned and/or destroyed four. As recently as during 1988, even though not a single residential building permit was issued in many (Oakland, Woodlawn, and East Garfield Park) neighborhoods in Chicago, the city officials granted permits to demolish thirty one buildings from these areas. Such demolition would cost money too. (81)

Besides housing, in many other areas American cities have tried their best to create a socialist utopia. In New York, the public school system employs more educational bureaucrats than all of western Europe. Despite this, the standards of education keep sinking. Parents can do little about the problem. They enjoy little control over the big education machine. On occasion, to prevent the officials from totally behaving like autocrats, the parents have ended up organizing protests. (82)

Just as they did to many third world countries, within a matter of a few decades, such policies tore down the fabric of this once lovable city. Now, it has 830,000 people on welfare. Around 500,000 in this city are drug users. Each year 10,000 babies are born toxic. (82)

While blaming the "Reagan cutbacks," Mitch Snyder—an advocate for the homeless—however unwittingly, demonstrated the similarity between a third world socialist country and an American inner-city. He said: "Nothing came from Mars or Venus to make New York city look like Calcutta." (83)

---

[4]Similarly, mega-industries in India are run like *mom-and-pop* stores. To survive, these entities have to break so many otherwise impossible rules that they run semi-legal operations. Their owners, too, can't trust a stranger, who might get them in trouble with the authorities.

[5]The obvious exception is the treatment of African-Americans who were denied citizenship and individual rights.

[6]Because of the economic expansion, the dollar figures, adjusted for inflation, kept increasing up until 1992 when higher taxes dampened the economy and reduced the government revenues.

# CHAPTER 4
## *Excuses, Excuses and More Fig Leaves*

THOSE WHO DO whatever it takes to survive—such as the people who make their living in the underground markets of Calcutta— also know that they can ill afford to blame their plight on some mysterious forces from Venus or Mars. Otherwise, these Indians risk inaction, starve, and die.

Politicians, on the other hand, love to blame the poverty and deprivation on the heavens. They love to divert the public's attention from the fact that their socialist policies have planned the whole country into a deep morass. Few of them can afford to come clean, utter this whole truth, and implicate themselves and their ideological forefathers.

Recently, a commentary about eastern Europe analyzed the predicament of such leaders. It's hard enough for an individual to accept his mistakes, mend his ways, and build a life from ruins. How can leaders of an entire nation do it? Owning up to their blunders takes a lot of courage. It amounts to taking responsibility, taking charge. It starts with saying, "We had the power to screw up. We can fix it too."

Thanks to Glasnost, all of a sudden the situation in Eastern Europe got out of hand. Marxists could no longer hide behind their iron curtains. The ensuing flow of information exposed the phenomenal failure of their ideology. These leaders found themselves standing naked in the public's view without a fig leaf of an excuse. Successes of their Western counterparts left these communists with few alibis. For example, the East German leaders were at a loss to explain why their country lagged so much behind West Germany.

The Indian leaders, however, are a luckier bunch. Their country has no such direct *counterparts,* not even among the giant nations of Asia. When they bother to, these politicians simply explain away the successes of the other countries: "The Japanese are a warier race," "Koreans work hard," "America has a lot of land," or "Singapore has a lot of people."

These opinion-makers stress the unique characteristics of India. They stroke national pride, even the perverse kind. They say, "We can't compare ourselves to others. We are so much different. What has worked elsewhere won't work here" They turn the differences—some real and some assumed—between India and other countries into explanations for India's poverty and unrest. Using their total control over the broadcast media, the officials peddle these "excuses" and evade accountability. It's a ruling politician's heaven.

With constant repetition, these excuses start to sound believable to the public. From high school textbooks to doctorate theses in economics, most analyses buy into this conventional wisdom. In a sort of unintentional conspiracy, newspapers, magazines, and other private media join in the chorus and pass these excuses for the truth.

Anyone who points out that the king is wearing his birthday suit is dismissed as irrelevant, or worse, anti-national.

What are these famous excuses which pass for the conventional wisdom?

The first, foremost, and universally agreed-upon curse plaguing India is its people: *There are just too many of them.*

Whether this surfeit population is the cause of whatever has gone wrong in the country or its effect is debatable. There is, however, little doubt that visitors to this country can feel, witness, and even smell the Malthusian specter. More than likely, they need a few days to get used to the sea of humanity.

It works the other way too. Most first-time visitors from India to the West miss the closeness that one feels with the other human beings in an overcrowded country. My father likened my suburban home in the U.S. to an *ashram* (hermitage). That he hardly saw anyone on the streets, amazed him. In my case, while strolling through streets of Zurich, the first European city I ever visited, I said to myself, "Switzerland is such an empty place."

The census takers confirm that India is an overcrowded country. During the past half century, just about half a billion people have joined the rolls. The population grows at a rate of fifty per minute—an annual growth of 2.13 percent or sixteen million. As a result, by 1990 close to a sixth of all humanity, more than 800 million people, have called themselves Indians. (85)

In the ever-crowded city buses, commuters just about kill for standing room. The unemployed are equally desperate for jobs. Consumers struggle to obtain basics such as kerosene. Between 1950 and 1985, the national income has grown at an annual rate of 3.5 percent, but the per capita income at a measly rate of 1.5 percent. To provide just basic education for all the new babies, close to 150 primary schools will have to built every single day. (85,86)

Experts trace the growth in population to an increasing life expectancy. From twenty years in 1911, it has gone up to fifty years in 1980. A drastic fall in death rates (from 31 per 1,000 people in 1941 to 15 in 1981) has conspired with a slower fall in birth rates (49.2 per 1,000 people in 1911 to 37.2 in 1981) to explode the population charts. In other words, *too many Indians live too long.* (87)

They do so because, compared to the past, more people eat better and receive semi-decent medical care. Advances in public health (a cleaner water supply, better immunization rates, and so on) also make a quite a bit of difference. India's neighbor, Sri Lanka, illustrates this point more dramatically. In just one year, its death rate plummeted by a whopping thirty-four percent. DDT, a cheap insecticide now banned in the West, greatly reduced the incidence of malaria and conferred longer lives on Sri Lankans. (87,88)

At one time or another, every industrialized country went through a similar phase. During the *Meiji* period (1868–1912), Japanese doubled in numbers. Within twenty-five years, after attaining their independence from the British, so did the Americans. During the late nineteenth century, there were frequent references to "overcrowding" in Europe. Prophets were screaming, "Standing room only." (89)

If for any mysterious reason, the population problem has failed to materialize in India, its politicians would have invented one. They love to talk it up. They use it as a neat diversion from their failed ideas and policies. Instead of allowing for people to employ their resources, create their own opportunities, and enlarge the economic pie, these politicians shift the debate to how to reduce the numbers.

To address this national obsession, officials hire experts and form committees, and commission studies. By and large, these experts pin the blame on the victims—the poor, who usually have large families. The pundits, especially, find fault with the widespread illiteracy and *ignorance*. They blame the religious beliefs. In doing so, however, they themselves ignore that for centuries, in the West, Christianity has opposed artificial birth control. They also complain about such things as early marriages and fathers being fanatical about having sons. These academics encourage politicians to pass some more laws that further intrude into the private lives of their countrymen, such as the one requiring marriages at a late age, another of the many largely ignored laws of the land.

Successive governments have also tried to spend their way out of this explosion. Between 1977 and 1987 alone, they have allocated 30,000 million rupees ($2 billion)—three times the total amount of money spent during the previous three decades.

However, it seems that one can't simply throw money at such problems or expect the usually uninterested bureaucrats to deliver. The officials simply collect their salaries, but have few results to show for. (85)

Even if they tried, they would have failed. They are working against the basic human nature, especially the instinct to survive. In the absence of economic growth, and, thus, decent jobs, those at the bottom need their children to eke out a living. The poor villagers naturally resist any and all attempts to curtail the family size. Shireen Jejeebhoy, director of research, Family Planning Association of India in Bombay, says, "People are not breeding like rabbits." They breed for valid reasons. Says one villager, "I need five children, one to look after my goats, one to look after my cows, another to tend to my sheep, one to help me on the field, and one to help my wife at home." (85)

Owing to the lack of savings or pensions, children also represent the only financial security such parents will ever have during their old age. As reflected by the high mortality rates, however, quite a few of the children fail to make it to adulthood. Besides poor obstetrical care, preventable diseases, such as diphtheria, whooping cough, tetanus, and diarrhea, kill one out of ten babies before the first birthday. The lucky survivors add greatly to the population numbers. The mortality rates, however, are just high enough to make the parents fearful of being left childless. Naturally, most poor villagers produce more than two, just in case. (85,90)

Add to this the need to have children as helping hands to survive, and lack of any hope of providing a decent future for their children, and it's easy to understand why most Indians produce a lot of babies. They listen to health workers, nod their heads, and simply forget about family planning. Despite the offers of financial rewards, most poor people shun the sterilization procedures. Condoms and other devices handed out by the government simply collect dust in attics. Regrets a health worker, "You can't be hiding in their bedrooms and finding out whether the condom is being used." (85)

As much as they love to peep, these health workers are otherwise busy. They have quotas to meet. Out of fear of losing out on promotions and raises, they do the only thing they do well—cook up the figures. They make matters worse by neglecting the other issues of health care. One worker says, "Our worry is how to complete the target in the register." (85)

One way or the other, health workers try to "complete the target." Many times, they perform vasectomies on eighty-year-old men. To earn an additional 180 rupees ($5), some people go through the operation a second time! If all else fails, the officials fill their registers with imaginary persons. On occasion, health workers borrow a few famous names for their fake subjects. Uttar Pradesh Basic Health Workers' Association released a photocopy of a certificate—bearing the medical officer's stamp—which states that *Rajiv Gandhi, son of the late Feroze Gandhi*, underwent sterilization on April 4, 1987 in a primary health center. Armed with their phony numbers, politicians insist that their programs are working. Year after year, they report a record number of vasectomies. As if babies are a disease, the officials talk about the increased percentages of "protected couples." (85,91)

To get a more realistic picture, one can look at the spectacle of rising birthrates as if it's a tale of three countries—India, China, and South Korea. Between 1960 and 1965, on average each Indian woman had 5.8 babies. Women from China and South Korea registered fertility rates of 5.9 and 5.4 respectively. During the next twenty-five years, to a varying degree, all these women had fewer babies. For India, the fertility rate declined to 4.3 (1985–90). If you believe the official statistics, at a rate of 2.4, Chinese women did better, but not as well as the South Koreans whose rate plummeted to 2.0. (92)

South Korea hardly begs for funds for some centralized family planning program, if, indeed, it has one. By themselves, its men and women plan their families small. Without any help from the "Peeping Toms" of their government, on a voluntary basis and out of self-interest, they have fewer children.

But so do many middle and upper class Indians. Just like the South Koreans, these Indians know that their children have as much chance to survive into adulthood as those from the developed countries. They are less likely to produce a lot of kids saying "*just in case.*" These parents make enough money. They are also less likely to view their little brats as helping hands to survive.[7] Compared to poor people, they enjoy a greater control over their lives. These middle and upper class moms and dads feel empowered and responsible. To build a better future for their children, they do whatever they can, including having fewer babies. In the process they thrash the many culture-based explanations peddled by population experts. Also, the so-called "selfishness" actually works to slow the population growth. These couples realize that with fewer children they can spend their incomes on items other than food and other basics. Says one Mr. Sunil Lahari in his letter to *India Today*, "Development is the best contraceptive. This is evident from the increasing number of young couples in the cities who are delaying the first child and spacing the second." (93)

India and South Korea, however, differ from each other in one respect. Thanks to economic growth, a lot more South Koreans have incomes comparable to middle and upper class Indians and as such they have one or two children. In India, on the other hand, those who do well economically and limit the size of their families are outnumbered by the very poor that are very fertile.

With regards to drops in fertility rates (between 1960–65 and 1985–90), only a few African countries, such as Kenya (from 8.1 to 6.7), have done worse than India. Corresponding to their economic growth, Egypt (7.1 to 4.8), Mexico (6.8 to 3.6), and Brazil (6.1 to 3.5) fall between these extremes. With a fertility rate of 1.57, when it comes to making babies, the Japanese seem to be hardly that hard-working. (92)

The Chinese do disrupt this direct relationship between prosperity and population growth. By using the kind of force that is unthinkable in any democratic country, government has forced the people to limit their families drastically.

Such findings leave the Indian planners in a fix. Because it runs contrary to their economic ideology, they like to stay clear of the South Korean prescription. The Chinese method, however, makes them uncomfortable. In any democracy, such use of force is invariably met with voter resistance. The Indian politicians instinctively realize that socialism and human rights are incompatible. Some of them, however, like to shove the Chinese medicine down the throats of their *ignorant* and rather *thankless* countrymen. To these leftists, democracy is just another nuisance. One such economist complains that India can't do as well as China because, "Politicians who go to polls every five years can't be relied upon to find the will to implement hard decisions." This, however, is hardly due to lack of effort. Under pressure from late Sanjay Gandhi—heir apparent to, then, the prime minister, Indira Gandhi—during the *emergency period* of the seventies, officials did force sterilizations on many villagers. Largely owing to a popular backlash against such barbarism, Indira Gandhi lost in the ensuing elections. (85)

As fashionable as it is to criticize such efforts, the younger and more impatient Gandhi has only attempted what a lot of Indians believe must be done. They typically complain about too many people rather than too few jobs or too little food. These well-to-do and the well meaning feel overwhelmed by the problem. They want the poor to be forced or bribed to follow birth control. They see few other alternatives. Their socialist background tells them that a human being is another mouth to feed rather a than a pair of hands, capable of accomplishing practically anything that one can dream of. By chaining these hands in every which way and preventing them from creating anything of value, the socialist framework promotes the idea that every human being is a burden on the society. In the process, life, itself, loses it value. It becomes rather cheap. Small wonder that few in the country show sympathy for victims of various disasters; even fewer help the needy with donations or voluntary service.

Hitler—the undisputed master of devaluation of life-hoped to take care of his "crowded" country by doing two things: Reduce the numbers and provide more *lebensraum*, or living space.

Of course, he would do so by using force. His way differed from that of the Chinese. He had no qualms about pruning the numbers of other races, even if it involved using a few not so conventional means. At the same time, Hitler could never have enough Germans. To help them live better, he came up with his own prescription: "Why not get them more living space and increase their natural resources?" To him and the various socialist politicians, the shortage of natural resources and over-population make two sides of the same coin.

Stalin, too, liked the idea of "more natural resources." To access the resources of central Europe, he made a few deals with Hitler himself. The Molotov-Ribbentrop agreement of 1939, for example, gave Stalin control over oil fields of Ruma-nia. These dictators found the foreign adventures to their lik-ing. When successful, these aggressions increased the land area. At the very minimum, they killed quite a few people. More importantly, the citizens became too distracted to complain about their own poverty.

Unfortunately for most Indian politicians, such an avenue is virtually nonexistent. They are unable to increase the *living space* for Indians. The leaders, however, love to talk about the "lack of natural resources." They use this as yet another excuse for the country's semi-permanent seat in the abyss. They argue that these resources are fixed, little can be done about it, and, as a result, India remains poor. Many Indians, including some very educated people, have bought into this argument. They give the politicians a free ride.

Actually, these leaders have done even better. They have convinced most everyone that the resources are so scarce that these materials will have to be *managed* carefully. The authori-ties, thus, justify their regulatory approach which helps them to acquire power and prosperity.

To decide how scarce the resources really are, in the ab-sence of an infallible yardstick, one can look at the density of population—the number of people per square kilometer. As of the late seventies, on average, 221 Indians have lived per square kilometer, pretty crowded, but not as bad as in the Nether-lands which has had 329 people per sq. km. England (with a density of 229) and Japan (221) come very close to India in population density. Prosperity of these countries makes mockery of the claim that India is too dense to be rich. It's true that the US, with its density of 22, is much better off. But it's richer than not so dense Australia (2), Argentina, and poverty-ridden Brazil (12). (94)

What happens to the standard of living as a country becomes more crowded? It goes down. Or, does it? In India in 1931, only ninety people have lived per sq. km. (vs. 221 in the seventies). Indians also have had more cultivable land (1.1 acres per person) in 1911 than in 1978 (0.26 acres). Despite this, currently they live longer and better. In 1987, Indians have successfully weathered the worst drought of the century (see chapter 12). (95)

Besides, if the resources are so scarce, it makes more sense to do away with the wasteful planning and the voracious public sector. When compared to market economies, for example, to produce each unit of GNP, the ever-planning communists (in the former Soviet Union and eastern Europe) have spent one and one-half times the energy. The oil and the other energy sources that Stalin managed to grab, he and his followers managed to squander.

Japan, Hong Kong, and Singapore have very few natural resources, except, of course, for their hard working, resourceful, and ambitious people. They efficiently produce a lot of goods needed by the foreign consumer and exchange these materials for whatever they want. To them and the others, who live in a resource-poor country, such a fluent international trade represents the best hope. It's their key to oil, food, machinery, and other commodities from foreign lands. These people perish under protectionism.

Of course, to be able to compete in open markets, a people should squeeze the most out of their own resources and export quality goods at low prices. To anyone who wants to measure such efficiency, Nikloy Shmelyov, an economist at the Institute for the U.S. and Canada in Moscow, offers his own yardstick: "Over the centuries, humankind has found no more effective measure of work than profit. Only profit can measure the quantity and quality of economic activity and permit us to relate production costs to results effectively and unambigu-ously." As to how to punish those who squander resources, he says, "And the producer must be faced with the real possibility of loss and even total bankruptcy if the goods he produces cannot be sold." (96)

Such business failures represent a self-corrective mechanism inherent to market economies. Any government that banishes such failures is akin to a Pope who rejects the notion of hell. In both cases, sinners get off easy, keep sinning, and take down everyone with them. By letting the failing businesses to go under, on the other hand, bankruptcies shift resources to those who produce efficiently. It doesn't take a genius to separate winners from losers. The former make profits. They supply what the consumer wants at the best price. They do so with as little waste as possible and make money.

Many a businessman might help the needy with his chari-table donations. By pursuing profits, however, he economizes the use of scarce resources. He, thus, helps to build the infra-structure for creating jobs, products, (and consequently) pros-perity and social order. By engaging in his business, he thus renders a much more valuable service. Even Helmut Schmidt, a social democrat, defended profits. When harassed by his more leftwing colleagues, he has called today's profits tomorrow's investments and jobs. (97)

Anil K. Malhotra, a senior member of the Oil and Natural Gas Commission of India, did his bit to bring in a brighter tomor-row for India. During the early eighties, he helped to dramati-cally reduce India's oil imports. He beat Al Gore by six or seven years when he prescribed a cure for India's problems, "The challenge is to bring about institutional reforms so that we institute modern management practices in all our public en-terprises." (98)

The key word here is *management*. A lot of otherwise smart people attribute the failure of the planned economy to poor management. In spite of its legendary non-performance, to them, government, with its huge public sector, embodies the sole hope for the country. As far as they are concerned, the only thing that needs to be fixed is its management.

Of course, public enterprises in India are riddled with mis-management. This is hardly because the managers are dumb. All of them have college degrees. The top officials could get into government service only because they have scored high in a, relatively, honest (civil service) testing system. They are the cream of the crop, but why should these managers care? What do they gain from quality and extra output? Promotions? They advance strictly on seniority. Job security? They enjoy permanent jobs. When people entrust their government with a lot of functions and erect a huge public sector, and turn around complain about the "poor management," they forget that they have based their results on a plan which works against the basic human nature. An overwhelming majority of us, on an overwhelming majority of occasions, work to promote our individual well-being. We, however, expect the officials to be different. We expect them to be superhumans. When the managers prove to be just like the rest of us and fail to perform because they have little interest in the outcome, we groan and moan. We fault them rather than our plan.

Besides, not only do the managers have little to gain from well run operations and lose nothing when the output is meager, they enjoy little control in running these enterprises. These managers answer to politicians, whose reelection chances rarely depend upon the performance of the public sector. The politicians benefit a lot more by catering to powerful groups such as unions. Obviously, few managers can afford to fire the lazy workers and risk the wrath of politically powerful unions. Also, to maintain their grip over the public sector and demonstrate who is in charge, Indian politicians very often shunt these managers from job to job. As such the latter have little time to get to know the operation, much less improve it. The managers just fill papers, cook up figures, and find excuses. Even the very best turn into lousy pencil pushers.

"A Japanese considers his office an extension of his home and not a separate thing. There's a sense of values, a commitment to the organization, which is now lacking in India," says V. Krishnamurthy, chairman of a joint (public and private) venture, Maruti Udyog. Such analysts disregard the fact that these Japanese work for private owners who love commitment as long as it helps their company's bottom line. The owners thus hire and elevate only those who display lots of commitment. (99)

A few Indian officials did try to imitate the *Japanese* methods to fix the "managerial problem." They hoped to encourage worker involvement and boost productivity by promoting and providing such things as: a common canteen and uniform for workers and managerial staff, offices without partitions or cabins, daily shop floor meetings between supervisors and workers, emphasis on workers cleaning their work places at the end of the day, low inventories and quality circles—periodically bringing groups of workers together for problem solving sessions. How much of an improvement had come out of all these changes was unclear. Clearly, little of whatever had come out was spontaneous. In the absence of true incentives, people just went through motions. After one such required presentation at a quality circle, an executive commented: "The first time you see it, you wonder whether the workers have been tutored." (99)

The joint canteen idea bombed too. Officers sat together, but separate from workers. The former enjoyed nice sounding titles. Regardless of their performance, they earned decent paychecks. They, however, had few powers over the workers. The only way the managers knew how to feel better about themselves was to maintain a *healthy* distance from the *riffraff.* Workers, for their part, owed little to their superiors. Thanks to their unions and their politician friends, all these workers had to do was to just show up. They had little use for new ideas or initiatives. The Japanese, too, found them to be very unresponsive. One manager said, "It's very difficult to get the worker's cooperation and understanding. Here workers are only doing what they're told [by the superiors]." (99)

Workers from a few companies did respond better than others. For example, at Maruti Corporation, a car manufacturer, workers who had turned out more than 25 vehicles a year earned two and half month's wages as a bonus. They did perform better. Every worker, no matter where he comes from, can easily feel motivated by this value. He understands the language of incentives. It presents few cultural barriers. (99)

To fix permanently the "management problems" plaguing India, Rajiv Gandhi, the then (the late eighties) prime minister, recruited his friend Sam Pitroda, a telecommunications expert, and a few other repatriates from the US. They gladly accepted the assignment. Just like many Western intellectuals and politicians (such as Gary Hart, Jerry Brown, Al Gore and, of course, Bill Clinton), Pitroda and his colleagues believed that somehow modern technology could solve India's managerial problems. They promised to advance the country into the twenty-first century. To boot, they came armed with a catchy slogan: "*chakra*[8] (wheel), community and, of course, the chip." (100)

To upgrade the standard of living of villagers, these supermanagers targeted five problem areas: low immunization levels, illiteracy, shortage of drinking water and oil seeds, and the notoriously bug-ridden telecommunications system. Later on, they added to this list flood control, housing, and wasteland development. They worked on these projects for a few years. In the end, however, they got as far as Gary Hart had gotten with his presidential ambitions. (100)

They started their journey from America in which government had allowed *greedy* individuals to create a huge economy and a solid infrastructure. From there, Pitroda and company landed in India in which, owing to the socialist policies, economic growth was anemic and the infrastructure was primitive. Largely unmet were even the basic needs, such as water supply, sanitation and that essential element for any modern economy, energy supply. During the power failures, more than food would get spoiled. For example, due to interruptions in refrigeration, effectiveness of polio vaccine was reduced to one third of what it should be.

Besides ruining valuable medical supplies, the stunted economy in India handicapped disease prevention by several other means. For example, it kept the standard of living so low that severe malnutrition became a fact of life for many poor people. It also hurt the literacy rates. When a person was so poor that he needed his youngster to work at home, how could he send the child to school? The oil seed policy did work, but only because the government dropped its senseless import restrictions.

In their privately owned American businesses, Pitroda and his friends had the powers to manage their way into success. They could fire the lazy, the timid, and the stupid. In place of such control, during their stint with the government of India, all they had were a few high-sounding titles. As to be expected, when the usual bureaucratic inertia and turf fighting haunted their efforts, they could do little more than sit and watch. In the 1989 elections, the opposition politicians defeated Rajiv Gandhi. They had known Pitroda as Rajiv's boy and viewed him with suspicion. Using his American greetings, "Hi! Haven't we met before?", Pitroda tried to get chummy with them, but to no avail. Later on, they forced him to resign. (101)

At the same time, it was entirely possible that the culture of officialdom had finally caught up with Sam Pitroda. After the elections, he faced many allegations: financial irregularities, such as using the state owned Center for the Development of Telematics (C-Dot) to enhance business interests of his own companies in the US, arbitrary recruitment of favorites to crucial posts, and giving false progress reports. (102)

Upon the outcome of British colonialism in India, commented O.S. Shrivastava, an Indian economist, "The per capita real and net incomes would have been much higher without the intervention and occupation of the British..." (103)

At one time or another, we all tend to blame our problems on others. Entire nations can also indulge in such a futile exercise.

It's futile because not only does it shift the blame but also the responsibility to make amends to others. It makes us feel helpless. We are too powerless to prevent someone else from breaking our nation. Naturally, we can't fix it either. Only the *someone else* can fix it for us. We are neither capable nor responsible to solve our problems.

Shrivastava claimed that British colonialism had destroyed the self-sufficiency of villages and semiurban areas in India. Yes, there was self-sufficiency, but just like in any other pre-industrial society, only at a subsistence level. With high mortality rates, short life expectancy, and hand-to-mouth existence, the majority went through their lives as if it was a chore. A few privileged Indians did live well, but they did so before, during, and after the British, especially after. If anything, despite all the oppression, the British did bring in certain decent legal, social, and political ideas. (103)

A few go to the other extreme: "It used to be better under the British." For several years after independence, I heard many Indians longing for the good-old-days of the British Raj. That the country either needed or owed its modernization to colonialism was as ridiculous as saying that the British had permanently impaired India. China, Japan, and a host of countries in the Middle East progressed without someone like Robert Clive[9] ever setting foot on their shores.

Just like any other occupying power, in questions of trade, the British were anything but benevolent. They levied high taxes on Indian exports such as textiles. Hundreds of thousands of rural families who were dependent on this age-old industry bore the brunt of such protectionism. By losing free access to these goods, however, so did the British consumers. At their expense and that of the Indian workers, British industrialists profited from the remnants of such mercantilist laws.

Besides these protectionist laws, there was another reason why Indian workers failed to compete with their British counterparts. To be sure, it had little to do with their Indianness. Owing to their primitive production methods, these Indian workers had no prayer against the more efficient British mills.

In this respect, they were hardly alone. Early on, many European artisans, too, suffered the same fate. Highly productive modern industries effected tremendous increases in the supply of goods and, thus, unprecedented prosperity, a higher standard of living, and longer life expectancy. In the process, however, they wasted their competition that clung to primitive and, thus, relatively inefficient and wasteful methods of production.

Early European artisans bitterly fought this modernization. Using the state apparatus, they managed to severely restrict the competition from modern industries. The French government, for example, yielded to pressure from its workers' guilds and passed detailed laws on textile production (1666–1759), which covered such things as what types of threads and needles should be used by the manufacturers in Lyons, Paris or Semur. To ensure consumption of the goods produced by the artisans, in 1571, British government required all citizens to wear English woolen caps on Sundays. Such laws simply delayed the progress. They wasted resources and promoted inefficiency. Levels of production sagged, depressing the standard of living, especially for those at the bottom. (104)

When mill cloth threatened the Indian artisans, they, too, fought back. They recruited the great Mahatma for their cause. He made a religion out of this issue and took to spinning. He prescribed handspun cloth for all patriotic Indians. Soon, no one could call himself a "Gandhian" without wearing this uniform, complete with a Gandhi cap.

What British colonialists could not accomplish, however, in due course the Indian politicians did with flair. They stripped this icon of its dignity. By using it as their uniform, they tainted it with their sins. Quite a few who revel in the good-old-days feel that Mahatma Gandhi should have retired the dress code when he could.

"In fact it can be said without the fear of contradiction that the Industrial Revolution of Great Britain was fed by the ruthless exploitation of its colonies in countries where brown and black people lived," says Shrivastava. The likes of Shrivastava are at a loss to explain why the other colonial powers failed to live as well as Britain. If anything, the French and the Spanish exploited their colonies with more vigor. Britain, however, did something the others failed to do. It let its citizens produce. (105)

Despite the evidence to the contrary, the idea, that somehow one can follow protectionist policies, rob another country of its resources, permanently damage it, and, with the spoils, build one's own nation, is still a fashionable theory peddled by many left-leaning intellectuals. Using similar logic, they also claim that the post-war (WWII) boom in the advanced countries was founded on the exploitation of the third world. Michael Harrington, a firm believer in socialism, disagrees. He observes that the poor nations partake in only a minuscule portion of the world trade. At the most, they marginally affect the advanced economies. For example, by the late eighties, India's share of the world markets dropped to 0.5 percent (from 1.56 in 1957), too small to have any significant impact on the advanced economies. (106)

Nevertheless, many third world politicians insist, "we are poor because you are rich." Most of them know that it's a lie, but make such an argument for a few good reasons. It offers them a scapegoat for their failures. It allows them to explain away prosperity of the advanced countries without acknowledging the phenomenal successes of free market ideas, which they loathe, and it injects a dose of guilt into the Western thinking. These socialists gladly offer the advanced country a chance to atone for its sins, past and present. All it has to do is to give the poor nations a few pounds, dollars, or maybe yen.

This scheme worked well. To "improve" the third world, its first world cousins sent in unprecedented amounts of loans and aid. Despite this, the poor countries stayed poor. It seems that no amount of money transfers can rescue a socialist economy. Whatever happened to the money? In the case of India, its officials turned out to be pretty non-discriminatory. They didn't care whether the money came from the Indian taxpayer or the Western one. They squandered it with equal vigor. They spent the foreign currency on their junkets. They used it to import gizmos that they forbade for the ordinary citizens. Using it, the politicians also imported essentials such as food, but mostly before elections. It couldn't be otherwise. Why should they be frugal?

For a while, IMF and the other agencies did go along with this *developmental model,* which mostly developed the estates of the political elites, but yielded little else, not certainly the economic growth needed to pay back the loans. The real lenders, taxpayers from the developed countries, balked at the idea of writing off these loans. Under such pressure, the lending agencies demanded repayments of the loans. Instead of pushing pro-growth policies, however, these lending agencies emphasized a few austerity measures such as tightening the money supply. These measures hurt the poor people some more. One could only imagine what would have happened if, instead of handing out money to the bureaucracy, the rich countries had let their efficient, profit-seeking and result-oriented private companies invest the funds in the poor countries.

Phenomenal progress by countries such as South Korea and Taiwan has laid to waste the argument that somehow past exploitation by colonial powers can explain the plight of the third world. Also—faced with a progressive deterioration of the conditions in India after its independence—of late, very few young Indians jump to blame their country's past rulers, the British. They are proud to say that the current mess is totally indigenous in its origins.

"How many more villagers could benefit if only they could mobilize the labor power of the village and construct a link road for themselves, or dig wells…?" laments O.S. Shrivastava. What does he think poor villagers should do? Build a road all day and go home hungry? Will any such economist work for free while his family is starving? Delinking behavior from (dis)incentives certainly makes his a dismal science. (107)

Shrivastava happens to be author of an economic text—book (*Economic Development and Planning in India,* New Delhi: Allied Publishers Private Limited, 1988), which I have picked up at random from a college bookstore in Hyderabad (South India). He is typical of many economic scientists in India. They use a lot of data, right words, and complicated equations, and come up with excuses, explanations, and solutions which form the intellectual backbone for the socialist legal framework. On many occasions, however, they defy their own logic.

Shrivastava analyzes how poor savings set in motion the vicious cycle of low investment, poor capital formation, dismal productivity, meager wages and profits, and even lower savings. At the same time, he and his fellow economists view with suspicion most investments (unless they come from government) which could set in motion a virtuous cycle of high productivity, high wages and profits, and more savings. These economists especially hate investments from outside the country. The restrictions on multinationals that they support scare off most outside investors. These leftists also back policies that make sure that very little of investment comes from inside India. They know that the poor and the middle class, in general, save little. These intellectuals realize that, in most countries, it is primarily the rich who save enough to invest. At the same time, however, these leftists support policies that tax these monies away from the rich. (107)

They also blame the rich for investing in jewelry and lands. For sure, many well-to-do flaunt a boundless avarice for acres of dirt and tons of yellow metal. If, however, a rich man could realize a better return from a productive venture (than from investing in land or gold), he is expected to have the financial savvy to do so and treat gold or land just like any other commodity—to buy only when he needs it. But starting any productive venture and running it only guarantees headaches with the officials. (107)

The rich primarily employ their black money to buy lands and gold. In order to conceal the amount of money used to buy lands and to avoid high stamp duties (needed to register the sales), they routinely under-report the sales' prices. It's close to impossible to do such juggling with huge productive investments that involve high employment, complex operations, and large credit requirements. What happens to the money that changes hands in these land deals? Thanks to the crushing burden of regulations, it finally gets invested in the unaccounted for and inefficient underground economy.

These elites routinely come up with a lot of excuses for India's plight. They use these explanations to prescribe such cures as protectionism, heavy taxation, and even more regulations. These leftists, however, do their worst damage when, with their excuses, they dissociate results from specific actions and lead most people to believe that poverty somehow happens, something beyond human control has gone wrong and precious little can be done about this deprivation of staggering proportions.

Hidden among Shrivastava's revelations is this cutest excuse for India's failure: "It is also a fact that the people in less developed countries do not have the same civic sense to put money in the hands of the governments so that they can discharge their essential development functions." (107)

Is he saying that people from developed countries pay taxes more out of "civic sense" than of fear of punishment for tax evasion? He probably thinks that these people are delighted to pay their taxes. If so, what a great idea for another Hallmark card:

*"Happy tax giving!"*

---

[7]This is hardly unique. In all the forty-one countries that the Harvard School of Public Health has chosen to study, low infant mortality rates are associated with low fertility rates. (90)

[8]Icon from the period of Ashoka, a famous Indian emperor.

[9]By winning a very crucial battle in south India, Clive, a British officer, helped the East India Company to ultimately subjugate India.

# CHAPTER 5
## *Welcome to Real Voodoo Economics*

IN ALL FAIRNESS, the men and women whose blueprint turned India into an economic basket case were great individuals and dedicated patriots.

After independence, they were fired up with hope and confidence. They knew that they would be able to lead their people out of poverty. Did they not prevail over the mighty British? They envisioned a self-contained and self-sufficient country devoid of *the usual* problems of the West such as inequality. Filled with social justice, their India would be nothing short of an utopia.

To get there, these leaders laid out a charter whose basic ingredients they imported from the same place that many other countries had done theirs, Britain. "Foreign countries may take their cuisine from Paris," said Margaret Thatcher, "but they take their economics from London." (108)

Japan, in the late nineteenth century, sent its students to Britain and copied the prevailing economic system, democratic capitalism. When leaders such as Nehru—who, later on, shaped

India's public opinion, its policies, and ultimately its destiny—studied in Britain (the early 1900s), they were caught up in the intellectual rage of the time, democratic socialism. At that time, the old Liberal Party was fading. In its place, the Labour Party was holding the torch for the poor. Fabian socialism was its religion. It was a historic accident that these opinion makers from India were looking towards the West at a time when the latter was slowly embracing the socialist dogma.

Once in power, Nehru and his followers turned their beliefs into government policies.

For example, these erstwhile revolutionaries embraced one of their instruments of protest against the British, hand-spun cloth. To them, it somehow embodied the soul of India, and a cure-all for the problems. Despite the large-scale establishment of cloth mills, owned and staffed by Indians, these leaders used the government machine to push the hand-spun cloth very hard.

To this end, they urged the consumers to resist the *Western influences.* Their message sounded good to a country which, after its independence from the British, felt just like a teenager. It was searching for recognition and identity. It wanted to prove to the world—and, more importantly, to itself—that this nation-building could be done by Indians themselves and with their own ideas. India wanted to be unique and refused to "ape" the West.

Whether it was from the West or western Sahara, however, the consumer could spot a value. Regardless of their social class or educational background, most Indians went for the cheaper and more durable mill cloth. Only the rich politicians, hanging on to the loincloth of the Mahatma for votes, could afford the more expensive hand-spun. Despite the democratically-expressed preference for the mill cloth in the market-place, these charlatans were determined to impose their values. To this end, they would use the taxpayer's money. They gave away subsidies and set up specialized stores to sell the hand-spun cloth.

After years of spending money, which could have provided badly needed capital for modernization of India, all these planners can show is an indigenously produced poverty. On average, 3.1 million weavers each work 194 days a year and earn about 8,600 rupees (approximately, $470). Some one million of them fare even worse. As of 1988, they have earned a per capita annual income of 1,200 rupees ($72), abysmal by any standard. These weavers mostly produce meager amounts of cloth. For example, 0.58 million households weave between one to three meters, 0.7 million between three to ten meters and 1.5 million just one meter (39 inches) per day. (109)

Naturally, by charging five to ten rupees per meter (the average wholesale price of mill cloth), only very few can make enough money to buy all the necessities of life such as food, housing, education, and most important of all, movie tickets. It is a question of simple arithmetic. Even to enjoy a basic standard of living, most have to sell their cloth for tens of rupees per meter, if not more. Because very few consumers can afford, or want, to buy the cloth at such ridiculous amounts, the price of hand-spun settles at a much lower level, but higher than that of mill cloth. In the end, despite all the subsidies, the weavers stay poor. They produce very little. And very few consumers use their product.

Before it could prosper, without exception, every country had to abandon such primitive and inefficient means of production. Leaders in India, however, clung to an old way of life. Besides hand-spun cloth, they subsidized various other small cottage industries whose outputs would be anemic. By choosing the "self-sufficiency" over the highly productive, market-coordinated, industrial production, they attempted to repeal the basic economic law that linked efficient production with a higher average standard of living. Naturally, they failed.

It was hardly as if government gave subsidies to the age old industries and wished them well. It also tried to shield them from competition. It *reserved* many areas for small scale producers. It banished large companies from these industries. The planners argued that India, with its hoards of workers, could ill-afford the labor-saving machinery of the big industries. With the hope of artificially protecting the jobs, government tied the hands of large companies that otherwise could have produced the same goods and services with far more efficiency and in much larger quantities and eventually employed many more people. In the process, the planners ignored a basic reality. A job was a wonderful means to even a greater end, production of goods and services. The sole social purpose of one's job was to produce something that one could exchange for whatever one wanted. If, collectively, everyone made very little of what everyone else wanted, mostly everyone would stay poor.

The Indian planners thus created a few make-believe jobs in a make-believe economy that had produced too little cloth, too little food, too few houses and, despite the original purpose of avoiding "technological unemployment," very few decent jobs. In short, these leaders ended up hurting the very people they were so desperately trying to help.

Nikloy Shmelyov, an economist at the Institute for U.S. and Canada in Moscow, suggested a better alternative to such planning. He said, "In place of fruitless efforts at central planning of our entire industrial production (some 24 million items), we should introduce contracts between supplier and consumer." (110)

Adam Smith called it the *invisible hand*. He credited the guiding force of self interest, tempered by free competition, for efficient production of wealth. The founding fathers of modern India, however, neither believed in the guiding force of self-interest, nor did they have a taste for free competition. They hoped to retire such instruments of free market as demand and supply. They dismissed as hearsay the idea that freely contracting suppliers and consumers would automatically and efficiently set prices and direct the patterns of production.

Rather than working with the basic human behavior that drove these markets, these leaders hoped to improve upon it. It mattered little to them if, in the process, they worked against it. To run the economy, they would rather use the visible hands of uninterested bureaucrats than those of consumers and producers with an enormous stake in the outcome of the transactions. The officials would decide what would be produced, how it would be produced, and in what quantities. They would decide at what price most goods would be sold. All this they would decide using heavy regulations and their famous five-year plans. Through these plans, they would channel the country's resources towards achieving a few predetermined goals.

For the first five year plan (1951–56), the government set a goal that was nothing short of putting India on a road to self-sufficiency in food production. To this end, the officials made agriculture their top priority. They allocated close to thirty-seven percent of the investable resources to agriculture and irrigation. (111)

Under "priority sector lending," they forced banks to lend farmers money to invest in agriculture. To prevent price gouging by the producers, government would control the distribution of fertilizers needed for this *Green Revolution.* During the first plan, and for decades afterwards, officials put a lot of taxpayer's money where their mouth was. In the year of 1988-89 alone, for example, they gave away a whopping 43,000 million rupees as fertilizer subsidies. Government also spent hundreds of millions of rupees to establish rural extension offices. Through them, it hoped to teach the villagers about the newer methods of production. (112)

That these farmers could have used better materials and methods was beyond any question. In market economies, producers of agricultural wares educated their consumers on how to use the new technologies. Only when all the components would fall in place and improve the farm yields, did both the producers and farmers realize profits. Out of an ingrained distaste for such grubbiness, Indian planners let government undertake all these functions. The farmer soon found himself at the mercy of the bureaucrats. Despite all the monies spent, many bottlenecks hampered the distribution. A lack of timely availability of fertilizers and other supplies plagued the agriculture. If it treated its customers with such disdain, any private company facing competition would have gone out of business. Its workers would have lost their jobs. Few agricultural bureaucrats, however, needed to satisfy their consumers, or lose sleep over the farm yields. Whatever had happened on the land, they reaped their promotions and moved on to bigger and better positions.

The program was hardly a total washout. Government concentrated its resources in a few states such as Punjab and Haryana with encouraging results. Later on, however, it couldn't repeat this trick in other places. Owing to a depressed economy, it would never have even a fraction of the unbelievable amounts of funds needed to cover this vast nation.

Besides robbing the whole country to benefit a few areas and creating a lot of animosities among the various states, officials also started to micro-manage the agriculture in other ways. For example, they gave priority to cereals. They directed all assistance, including R&D, to cereal producers. More importantly, government allowed for imports of better seeds. In thirty seven years (1951–88), per capita availability of the cereals did show a modest increase—from 334 grams to 429 grams. Nevertheless, on many occasions, cereals had to be imported. (113)

The supply of other foods fared much worse. As if it were a sin to produce anything with a profit motive, the officials called non-cereals the "cash crops." They simply ignored the production of oil seeds and pulses (legumes, such as peas and beans), the latter being a better source of protein than the usual rice and wheat[10]. Between 1951 and 1988, production of pulses remained static at eleven million tons and per capita availability dropped from sixty to thirty six grams. (113)

In a market economy, such a shortage would have led to increased prices, higher profits, more producers, and, without any boost from the officials, higher production. In advanced countries this chain of events had led to a remarkable abundance to the point that most would think malnutrition meant obesity. Few policy makers in India would sit and watch such a travesty. As a part of their agricultural program, and a good election strategy, they maintained strict price controls. By following a certain immutable natural law—which links price controls and the resulting lack of profits to anemic production—the farmers produced less.

When, mostly due to such meddling, prices go up, government addresses the problem with more planning. For example, it sets import-export quotas. A host of smart officials engage in a bunch of complicated calculations and decide such things as what should be imported, by whom, from where, when and at what price. This sounds great. The only problem is that even these wise guys cannot possibly predict all the fluctuations affecting one commodity, much less hundreds of items needed by the consumer. After disabling the self-corrective mechanisms inherent to free market with their controls, they routinely overshoot or undershoot in their calculations. In the process, they end up shooting their own countrymen and women in the feet.

For example, in January of 1989, the government projected that about ten million tons of sugar would be produced. It called for exports. Within a few months, however, it slashed its projection to 8.7 million tons and attempted to import sugar. While the various administrative agencies were haggling over such matters as which ministry should handle the program (Commerce, or Food and Civil Supplies) and to whom it should award the purchase orders (to registered dealers or non-registered ones), world sugar prices went up by sixty percent, costing the taxpayer millions of rupees. Meanwhile, in just one month, the consumer paid thirty-three percent more for his sugar. (114)

Politicians know where to assign the blame. They rap hoarders, speculators, and smugglers (how?). They go beyond the price controls and planned imports of food. To keep their election promises of cheap food, they get directly involved with its procurement and distribution. About half a million government employees earn their daily bread doing just that. They buy twenty percent of India's total wheat; cultivators keep thirty percent; the rest flows through private channels. In this business, officials simply follow the rule my stockbroker has used to invest my money. Buy high and sell low. Using taxpayer's money, the officials try to please both farmers and consumers. (114,115)

Despite, Indian farmers have ended up as one of the most unhappy and politicized groups in the world. It's hard to blame these farmers. Many feel cheated. In due course, they have discovered a simple fact: The emphasis on distribution of wealth sounds great to them as a group. In real life, however, it leaves the individual at the mercy of the officials. To farmers without any influence, the high procurement prices seldom translate into big profits. Explains one farmer, "In the old days, we could fight with *arhthis* [grain merchants], but after the food grain takeover, we can't stop these government *babus* [masters] from cheating us. They under-grade or short-weigh our crops." In the olden days, private grain dealers used to advance loans to farmers. "But," says one farmer, "today we are totally dependent on banks and the government where nobody bothers about the common man." (115)

Consumers, who are supposed to benefit from all this food procurement, are hardly pleased either. Despite the many pre-election promises, they end up with either high black market prices or the usual headaches of ration shopping: long lines, shortages of essential commodities, and substandard or adulterated goods.

Naturally, very few of the consumers feel in control. A lot of forces—not the least of which are the whims and interests of the authorities—impact the day-to-day life of the Indian consumer. For example, in the city of Bombay, in one year (1988–89), the officials allowed for a large number of ration shops to close. Owners of these shops got "sick" all at once. Each cited genuine health reasons, but the reporters got suspicious about this epidemic of varied illnesses. They soon traced the underlying problem to an anemic disease—low profits. (116)

Saying that they make a measly six percent profit rather than the required minimum of ten percent, explains one owner: "Ration shops are not as profitable as we want them to be, so we are closing down and opening other business on the same premises." When asked about the consumers, he says, "It is for the government to worry about that." (116)

How could these owners get away with their mass closures? Before they folded, each one had sought and obtained the official permission. In the first place, they had probably paid bribes for the licenses to open their businesses. But then, they paid again to close their shops. (116)

Over the years, food supply has naturally became a hot button issue for politicians. Most of them fight like dogs over the distribution. In 1989, a minister from the, then, opposition-ruled state of West Bengal accused the Central government of "supplying rice not fit for human consumption." The Central minister shot back by saying that it had been cleared by the state officials. He alleged a breakdown in the state's distribution and procurement system and said that the state government had "surrendered to the rice mill lobby." Politicians know the power of such accusations. Just before the 1989 election, said Ajit Singh, then an opposition politician, "Each time you mention the issue of inflation the crowds respond wonderfully." (117,118)

After the elections, Singh's party came to power. Prices kept increasing "wonderfully," at least for many members of Congress(I) now sitting in the opposition benches. They promptly put up posters comparing these prices with those from five months before, when Congress(I) had been in power. These guys know this game too well. Prices do make politics. (119)

The main reason behind the inflation, of course, is the gradual debasing of the currency brought on by huge increases in money supply not sufficiently matched by the meager increases in supply of goods and services from an economy stunted by hyper-regulation and heavy taxation. Between 1984 and 1988, for example, the money supply went up by close to 100 percent (from 489,500 million rupees to 968,670 million rupees). At the same time, the real income (production) grew at an average rate of five percent per year. A lot of dough chased a little flour, sugar, petrol, and everything else. Prices had nowhere to go but up. Even after 1988, they continued to do so, because politicians stayed their course[11]. During the next two years, prices of pulses doubled. That of meat, fish, and poultry went up by twenty-five percent in one year. One commentator complained that the inflation had led to domestic fights and, in some cases, even to the breaking up of families. (118)

The effects of such inflation are very skewed. Government officials make sure that their salaries keep up with the price increases. Because their incomes and profits rise, the top fifteen percent of the population gain from inflation. The bottom fifteen percent buy very little. In any event, they can't get worse off. For another ten percent, who belong to the upper rungs of the middle class, the effects are neutral. (118)

The high prices hit the rest hard, those who toil day after day to survive. Within three months in 1990, for example, rickshaw pullers and other laborers watched the price of a cup of tea jump from sixty paise to one rupee (100 paise). The price of a plate of food, sold on the roadside, rose to three rupees from two. (118)

Hundreds of millions of Indians—some of whom are not even as lucky as these laborers and rickshaw pullers—watch helplessly the price increases, while their children starve and eventually fall prey to severe malnutrition. They wonder about the promises of self-sufficiency. What angers them is that, while more than a third of them have to do with just one meal or less per day, their government declares its *Green Revolution* "a success."

What demoralizes these poor Indians further is to hear their leaders tell them that there is no better way out of the poverty than socialism. To cure the country of its shortages, the leftists prescribe more of the same and push such ideas as land reforms. Says S.K. Ray, a noted economist, "More than a decade prior to independence, the Indian National Congress underlined the importance of land reform in agronomic development." (120)

"Land belongs to the tiller," was more than a revolutionary slogan. It was yet another means of wholesale destruction of property rights. As to be expected, it would hamper creation of wealth, in this case food production, and aggravate the shortages.

Shortly after independence, government passed laws to dispossess those who had owned more than a few acres of land. The tracts government had managed to confiscate, it gave away to the landless, some of whom had little experience in cultivation. Just like the tenants of rent-controlled houses, even these beneficiaries enjoyed few secure and complete rights. According to the various laws, the new owners wouldn't be able to sell the land. Unable to benefit from the increased value of land, and due to other uncertainties, most would hesitate to invest their labor, money, and time to improve the land. Very few engaged in long-term planning such as crop rotation or worried about soil erosion. As long as they had a parcel of land, the new owners hoped to extract the maximum out of it. It made little sense to buy expensive farm machinery. Also, unlike the brutal collectivization programs of communist countries, which produced huge tracts of land, these reforms, where implemented, created tiny pieces in which one had little use for such machinery. Small wonder that, despite better seeds and other advances, farm yields in India failed to keep up with population increases.

Many local economists complain about the low productivity. What upsets them is that one American farmer can feed twenty people, while eighty percent of Indians (who are engaged in agriculture, one way or the other) have failed to make their country truly self-sufficient. To fix the problem of low productivity, these intellectuals prescribe "a better implementation of land reforms." In other words, these planners go beyond claiming that land reforms are equitable; they explain at length why these reforms will improve the harvests. It's as if they say "destroy land ownership rights. By itself, food will jump right out of the farms." (111)

Most politicians go along with the reforms, not because they are sure about the abundant harvests of rice, but the improved harvests of a more important commodity—votes. This social democratic approach has rarely succeeded in producing anything else. In country after country, it has only served to deprive the land of its most important social and humane function—food production.

Actually, the situation could have been worse. But for the usual corruption and bureaucratic inertia that has sabotaged this program, these laws could have easily reformed India into a giant Ethiopia. Many landowners simply pay the bribes. With creative bookkeeping and distribution of the assets to even unborn and dead family members, they keep their lands and limit the damage. A report on the seventh five-year plan (1985–90) says: "Only 46 percent of the land declared surplus under revised ceiling laws has been distributed." This still sounds impressive except that mostly useless dirt has been divided upon. Concludes the report: "What is distributed is only one percent of the net area sown." (111)

On the land they have managed to keep out of the clutches of the government, a few Indian farmers do work hard. Pursuing profit, they try to produce to the best of their ability. On occasion, they might even end up with a bumper crop. For example, in 1987–88, farmers from (the state of) Uttar Pradesh harvested seven million tons of potatoes (compared to 5.5 the previous year). Going by the hundreds of Indian movies about villagers, one would expect these peasants to be singing, dancing, and throwing bright colors at each other in the streets. (121)

Our potato heroes, however, were hardly smiling. They faced a major problem. With the state's 770 cold storage facilities overflowing, their potatoes started to rot in piles. Said agricultural secretary, R.M. Sethi: "We can store only about 32 percent of the crop as against the requirement of 60 percent." In other words, the planners expected a whopping forty percent to remain unprotected even under the best of the circumstances. (121)

This situation is hardly unique. Owing to a shortage of storage and transportation, a lot of food spoils in this country, teaming with hungry masses. Few market economies are that wasteful. In these countries, the other *greedy* people smell profits in storing and transporting food. They build the necessary infrastructure, and some more, just in case. Farmers, who hate to lose their produce, gladly pay for these services. At every chance it gets, the media decries such "greed." People from advanced countries nod their collective heads in assent. While at the same time, they go to stores and buy sacks and sacks of potatoes and other foods as if all this stuff grows in the asphalt parking lot of the supermarket.

Time and again, the government of Uttar Pradesh curbed such greed. As recently as 1988, it fixed the rents on the storage to 24 rupees per quintal (100 kg.). Politicians refused to allow even meager increases of 2 rupees. Such assaults on property rights invariably kill creation of wealth. In Uttar Pradesh, for example, only eighty-one storage facilities were built during the next five years (compared to 233 built between 1979 and 1982). The 2.5 million farmers, who probably saved a few rupees each in storage rents, saw the tons of potatoes they toiled to produce go to waste. A few farmers even faced bankruptcy. They are hardly the first ones to go down the highway to hell paved by the supposed great intentions of the socialists. Whether in Paris, or New York, such rent controls work like a charm to create shortages. (121)

Indian cities proved to be no exception. The politicians at least allowed for some meager increases in rents for the potato warehouses. In the case of accommodations for the other bumper crop of the country, people, government passed even stricter laws and pegged rents well below the market rates. For decades, it froze rents on houses and shops. It also passed laws that would shield tenants from eviction even after the lease had expired. In short, the legal structure reduced the right to own rental property to a zero. The usually-backlogged court system conspired with these laws to effectively yield control of the properties to renters.

Early on, some fools have parted with their money in new construction. Soon, their numbers have dwindled. So have the number of jobs in the construction industry and available rental units. Of course, these rent controls do help the *needy*—such as the rich businessmen in Connaught Place in Delhi, one of the most popular shopping places in India. These lucky tenants rent shops for 285 to 500 rupees. The real market value of each unit is actually 100,000 rupees or more! These controls also help a few other poor people, such as myself. While visiting India, I have bought dresses and leather goods in this premier shopping area at lower prices than in my small town. (122)

What about the other poor, the real kind? By living in huts and unauthorized colonies, many of them live beyond the realm of the rent control laws. Don't these laws aid the middle-class families that can afford the controlled rents? Not exactly. For a simple reason, even they live beyond the realm of the rent controls. Few of them can afford the *pugree* (deposit or key money), which roughly equals the purchase price of the unit in the black market and amounts to tens of millions of rupees. The landlord knows that renting amounts to quasi-selling. By the power vested in them by the rent control laws, renters virtually enjoy the ownership of the property. Without the usual headaches such as property taxes and maintenance costs, they can live in these units as long as they want. In many cases, they can pass on these benefits to their children. Only by collecting astronomical sums of money as a deposit can the landlords recoup their investment. Due to a shortage of housing units, they demand and get a very high *pugree*—usually in the form of tax-free black money, the kind only the filthy rich can come up with. (122)

Even after paying these outrageous deposits, however, the renters own, virtually, but not totally. They can't sell the unit, for example. Also, with the help of a few musclemen, an occasional landlord can forcibly evict his tenant. Naturally, most renters refuse to spend their money on maintenance and the necessary repairs; so do the landlords who have already made their money and enjoy very few guarantees of ever regaining control of their property. Between them, the landlords and the tenants have reduced many areas in cities such as Delhi, Bombay and Calcutta to slums. Quite a few have even stopped paying property taxes. Because the taxes are fixed according to the rental value, even those who pay, deposit only meager amounts. According to one estimate, in Bombay, alone, government loses revenues worth 500 million rupees per year. (122)

To address the inevitable shortages, government passes some more rent control laws. Recently (1988), for example, it has passed another new and improved Rent Control Act in Delhi. With annual inflation rates constantly running in double digits, it generously allows for a ten percent increase in rents every three years. It exempts from these increases tenants, who pay less than 3,500 rupees as rent. The idea is to give a few middle-class Indians a break. In reality, however, the law protects from rent increases the privileged people who have been renting at rock bottom rates for decades. (122)

The officials have taken care of themselves by slipping into the new law a heartwarming feature: civil servants, police and army personnel who own a single house can evict a tenant within a year before or two years after retiring. Any other owner, who tries to evict a family on the "false pretext" that he needs the premises for his own use, however, risks fines and imprisonment. (122)

The authorities have implicitly recognized the power of rent controls to freeze new construction, when they have decreed that for ten years (1988–98) new buildings will be exempt from the rent controls. That should lead to more construction, except that the property owners still enjoy what amounts to short-lived property rights. Also, judging by the past record and the prevailing support for rent controls in the public, they won't be surprised if, with a stroke of a pen, the government reimposes rent controls on the units that are currently enjoying the exemption. To recoup the value in ten years, the owners charge astronomical rents. (122)

Besides rent controls, the owners face many other hurdles to new construction. They will have to overcome the various building codes and ordinances that are close to impossible to comply with.

They are close to impossible to comply with, unless of course, the owner is well connected. In 1988, Congress(I), then the ruling party, planned to build for itself an All India Congress

Committee office. It failed to produce various documents required by the many laws: a copy of the registration certificate of the architect, a few ownership documents, an affidavit needed to satisfy the Urban Land Ceiling Regulation Act (1976) and a structural stability certificate. City officials recommended to reject the permit. The Building Planning Committee of the New Delhi Municipal Corporation, however, had no stomach to stand up to the all powerful Congress(I) politicians. It gave its blessings for the construction. (123)

Such impossible regulations and hard to satisfy requirements, go beyond frustrating the entrepreneur. They kill his spirit. Well before he launches his venture, he is doomed. On occasion, even the officials themselves say as much. While announcing their new (1988) electronic policy, for example, they acknowledged that it would take almost one and one half years to clear a project in the industry (electronics) whose products become obsolete in less than a year. (124)

Government restricts every aspect of the enterprise, including expansion of existing businesses, construction of multi-storied buildings, relocation to cheap areas, or installation of modern machines. It issues exclusive licenses to a few companies. Even for them, it sets production quotas. Recently (1989), Reliance Industries and Tamil Nadu Petroproducts, Ltd. (TPL), holders of such exclusive licenses to make LAB (Linear Alkyl Benzene, a raw material used in the manufacture of synthetic detergents), shut down their plants for one month due to a perceived glut in the market. Revealing the power of government engineered oligopoly, both hiked their prices by ten percent. Lured by these guaranteed profits, several other companies also wanted to make LAB. It was not as if by meeting certain predetermined criteria they could do so. The officials were too smart to permit such anarchy. Only they would decide who the lucky recipients of the licenses would be. (125)

In their infinite wisdom, these Solomons concluded that there was room only for three companies. Out of the applicants, seven companies made it to the *final list,* which the officials had altered several times. Citing market or technical reasons, they would drop a company which, early on, they had deemed suitable. "To prevent another glut," they staggered the issuing of new licenses. Paranjoy Guha Thakurta (of *India Today),* however, suspected that they had delayed the licenses to newcomers for a political reason: lobbying by then the very influential Reliance corporation, which hoped to idle its competitors and enjoy a few more years of oligopoly. (125)

These businessmen can rob consumers and workers and keep both poor only because they own not just businesses but monopolies and oligopolies. Under a regulatory economic framework, the distinction between these entities is one of ability. The more influential a businessman is, the more he can use the government and its regulations to tighten the screws on his competition. Those who are already rich, have famous last names, and play the right kind of politics, naturally build mega-industries. They establish their own clans. Comments O.S. Shrivastava, an economist, "Industrialists and entrepreneurs in less developed countries do not normally come from all classes but from limited caste-class groups." (111)

Actually, few monopolies can survive without the active help from government in restricting the competition. On many occasions, they might not have to even lobby for the exclusivity. In a planned economy, they enjoy a natural advantage. Owing to the regulations, very few can start a venture and give the existing businesses a run for their money. As a matter of fact, the ease with which one can start a business is the single most important indicator of the level of competitiveness in a country. Many politicians, who impose all kinds of work-place regulations and license, and other, fees, contend that every business has to live with these limitations and, as such, the effect on competitiveness is neutral. In reality, larger and more influential companies can absorb these costs and cope with the rules much more easily. They come out ahead because the regulations disproportionately hurt their small competitors, who have little room to maneuver. In the case of a startup business, such laws can kill it, before it has a chance to take its first breath.

In India, for example, just because a person comes up with a marketable idea and, maybe startup funds, he can't go and set up a joint, unless, of course, he has the necessary connections. In such a society, someone like Steve Jobs (who used a mere fifteen thousand dollars to buy the necessary equipment and start the Apple Computer company) or Bill Gates (of Microsoft) might have to spend most (if not all) of his seed money just to grease palms. Actually, even after all this bribing, he might fail to get the necessary licenses and credit, unless he has connections with powerful politicians. More than likely, such a person will end up as a hopeless dreamer or master black marketeer.

Naturally, authentic rags-to-riches stories are hardly commonplace in India. Very few think of such things as marketable ideas or startup funds. Very few are surrounded and inspired by those who have succeeded in starting and running profitable businesses. It's uncommon for an average Indian to come across a relative, friend, or acquaintance, who has built up a business from practically nothing. One can't look at one's boss and say, "If this bozo can pull it off, I can do so too." One knows that "the bozo" has something one doesn't—connections. One hesitates to take the plunge.

These rules—which frustrate production, destroy growth and kill the entrepreneurial spirit itself—duplicate, accentuate, attenuate, negate, and dismember each other. Some of them even frustrate tax collection. Says a tax consultant, once a collector of customs in Bombay, "If the government is interested in collecting more excise duty, it should simplify the rules. They are changed so frequently that even excise officials, leave alone companies, cannot keep track of them." (126)

How this process has become so chaotic is easy to explain. On each day of the work week (praise your God for weekends and holidays), the eighteen-million-strong bureaucracy generates these rules at the thousands of offices scattered over this vast land. Even the most sophisticated communications network in the world (much less the bug-ridden system in India) will be unable to coordinate these diverse, widely dispersed, uninterested bureaucrats and their dictates. Besides, the career civil servants can only claim, at best, very roundabout legitimacy for their rule-making powers. An overwhelming majority of their rules fly over the heads of the elected officials. Few can remember, or care, about the original purpose of many of these regulations. Even fewer can keep up with this avalanche.

Certainly, most businessmen, who undertake their ventures to make a profit, not to gain proficiency in understanding the official *Gazette,* feel lost. Just to survive, they break most rules. It's as unavoidable as walking in water naked without getting wet. Many textile mills, for example, fail to cope with the various rules that cover the excise taxes. A complicated system of price slabs, directed by such things as weight and blending proportion, decide the amount of taxes each company has to pay. This complex disease of over-regulation lends itself to a simple cure—good, old-fashioned cheating. The mill owners routinely undervalue the cloth and understate the width. They pass off synthetic cloth as cotton because duty on synthetics is four times higher. The sheer amounts of the materials preclude any close supervision. According to the official estimates, over the many years, these businesses have managed to evade as much as 1,500 million rupees in taxes. (127)

To bring them in line, on June 27, 1989, the tax department moved in with the agility of Her Majesty's Secret Service. Based on reports from undercover informers, 450 of its James Bonds swooped down on six processing mills and forty-seven cloth merchants and charged them with evasion of excise duty. (127)

Most businessmen live with a constant fear of such attacks. They naturally prefer more civilized behavior. They want to be left alone. To this end, they just pay up. Why can't they hire hordes of accountants and lawyers, follow the rules, pay the taxes and run clean operations? It's not that simple, either. Even if they pay all the taxes and seek official blessing to as much as taking a leak, they are hardly home free. Officials not only disbelieve these numbers and routinely assess higher taxes than reported, they also saddle these businessmen with various other impossible obligations. A few of these businesses, for example, have to earn foreign exchange. To each of these companies, officials allot "export quotas." They demand that the company does its bit to satisfy their insatiable thirst for foreign currency. Recently (1989), Dinesh Singh, the commerce minister, required many big industries to report to him in three months regarding how they would deliver on this sacred mission. According to him, "It's an obligation, a duty, to earn money for the country and for themselves..." Or, is it an example of government-mandated *greed*? (128)

Even if a company performs well and meets its export "obligations," it can't expect to live happily ever after. The officials always need more dollars, pounds, and deutschemarks. Naturally, they take the next logical step. As found out by many diamond traders, government increases the export obligations of successful businesses. (129)

By any standard, these traders perform very well. In 1988 alone, they earned a net foreign exchange worth 12,000 million rupees. They worked diligently to build a thriving industry and a loyal overseas clientele and developed the export market. Owing to their efforts, two out of every three diamonds processed in the world are worked on in India, making it the largest diamond-cutting center. Every second, Indian workers cut and polish eleven diamonds that come from mines in the former Soviet Union, Australia, Botswana and South Africa. Without any subsidies or other handouts, the traders export all these rocks. (129)

For earning all this foreign exchange, however, they hardly receive medals or one of those coveted titles that government bestows on its favorite subjects. It has little time to pat these businessmen on their shoulders. It's busy harassing them, raising their export obligations, and warning them of fines if these quotas are not met. If the businessmen complain about the rude treatment, officials retort with rightful indignation. Complains an official from the Central Board of Direct Taxes, "Diamond traders think that, because they bring in so much foreign exchange, they should be immune from investigations." (129)

Commerce officials and taxmen are always willing and ready to inspect these businesses. Unless of course the necessary bribes are paid, they love to report any breaking of rules. On a given day, any trader could enter his office only to run into the waiting clutches of a taxman. For their part, officials claim that every time they search they come up with "unaccounted stocks of diamonds or cash." A foreign dealer, on the other hand, paints a different picture of the same tax-evading diamond traders: "They are not saints. But they are honest with their customers." Why the discrepancy? The diamond merchants have black money for the same reason that every other merchant has black money, to avoid high tax rates. Thanks to these rates, if a stupid, but honest, businessman reports all his income, he ends up with little for the troubles and risks he takes. In addition, he faces the wrath of the bureaucrats who expect and thrive on the bribe money. To survive, most businessmen doctor their records. They underprice their stocks. In their warehouses, they hoard unreported stocks of diamonds or other merchandise. They give the bureaucracy more excuses for its extortion. It harasses them some more. By April of 1989, over 50,000 diamond traders had had enough of it. They marched protesting "'an intolerable level of harassment' by way of raids and rude treatment by tax officials." (129)

Quite a few the traders didn't bother. They simply moved to Antwerp, New York, Hong Kong, Bangkok, and Japan. In these foreign lands, they enjoyed more freedoms. (129)

They also enjoyed a very high credit rating. Apparently, private banks gladly lent them the capital needed to build huge businesses. In Antwerp alone, these Indian traders owned forty percent ($9 billion worth) of the diamond business. These refugees took jobs and even export earnings with them. Said one of them, "We have regrets for India, but not for leaving it." (129)

All this confiscation and redistribution, the leaders call mixed economy, "You make it, we spend it."

Kamal Nath, a Congress(I) MP (member of parliament) from (the state of) Madhya Pradesh, came up with his own formula to spend. During 1988, he embarked on "a long march towards development," by arranging for 220 million rupees to be given as loans to his constituents. The plan covered 2,000 villages. Its beneficiaries included every third tribal and Harijan (formerly untouchable caste) family in the district. The vast official machinery went into high gear to distribute the money. (130)

Nath is just one of the thousands of politicians who, just before the elections, invariably come down with a bad case of philanthropy. These politicians give their handouts very clever names. "The losses under *priority sector lending* [author's italics] are always high," said the chairman of the Central Bank of India, while supporting this project. Nath's priority sector embraced, among other things, goat breeding. Some of the beneficiaries, however, never before bred goats. When asked about repayment of the loans, one perplexed breeder queried, "Will they want the money back?" (130)

More than likely not. Recouping the loan money is quite messy, if not downright futile, more or less like making hay out of horse manure. Politicians quickly learn how to use other people's money to advance their careers. They are even quicker to learn that asking for the money back throws the process into a reverse. It makes them lose elections. In any event, why bother? Their whole operation is so professional that the real lender, the taxpayer, is oblivious to the fact that every day his money is squandered on new and improved vote-getting schemes.

While he slumbers, his leaders promise more and more. For example, before the 1989 elections, the ruling Congress(I) party came out with a huge anti-poverty program with a price tag of 40,000 million rupees. The opposition front did one better. At an estimated cost of 100,000 million rupees, its members baked a few more pies in the sky. They proposed to, "deploy more than 50 percent of the investable resources for rural economic development." They promised farmers crop insurance, strict land reforms, guaranteed remunerative prices, a county-wide network of warehouses, improved access to water resources, and a waiver of previous loans coupled with even more and cheaper loans to cover future needs. (131,132)

This handout business got intensely competitive. In (the state of) Tamil Nadu, during 1989, four rival parties tried to top each other with promises covering just one subject, rice. Shortly before the elections, between them, these parties promised: provision of free rice during important festivals (cost to the treasury, about 250 million rupees), rice at one rupee a Kg. (1,000 million rupees), an increase in rations of rice (600 million rupees), and better-quality rice (300 million rupees). (133)

As to be expected, in trying to keep some of their promises Indian politicians have created huge budget deficits.[12] To finance the programs, they borrow at home and abroad. A recent (1989), confidential report by the Washington-based Institute of International Finance calculated that India's total debt was 963,200 million rupees, which exceeded the official figure by a whopping 413,200 million rupees. Besides robbing the private sector of productive capital, all this borrowing landed India in a serious debt trap. Just to pay the interest, the government had to borrow some more. (131,134)

The original mind-set that has made such ideas as "goats for votes" an integral part of the political system and led to these deficits, rests on a simple belief: Whether dealing with rice or radio sets, it is more important to decide how to distribute the wealth than to create more of it. Because government produces little of value, it has to get the wealth from someone who is smart enough to produce it, but weak enough to part with it. Among other things, such a plan involves astronomical tax rates of up to ninety-seven percent and robbing homeowners and farmers of their profits. For that matter, it involves robbing every producer blind.

Founding fathers of modern India have failed to realize that such confiscation hurts the creation of wealth and causes shortages and unemployment. From their socialist mentors in the West, they have learned the opposite: No matter how much a government destroys the incentives, people still produce. All the authorities have to do is to lecture to their countrymen about "work ethic."

These Indian leaders have ignored that, in the West, a very established and countervailing force of conservatism prevents the leftists from completely destroying economic freedoms. Guaranteed of property rights, people from the advanced countries produce wealth, a portion of which their politicians distribute. Without a thriving economy and the huge revenues, they can forget about such handouts as Medicare, social security, and unemployment benefits. In other words, the pro-market politicians have saved the leftists from themselves.

In India, on the other hand, thanks to the consciousness nurtured by leaders such as Nehru, most of the public and the political parties have embraced socialism in one form or other. There are probably more five-legged donkeys in the country than there are free market politicians. In the absence of any challenge from *the right*, its socialists keep on destroying the incentives to produce. They end up with much less to distribute.

What little they collect, they would rather spend on such sexy vote-getting schemes as goat breeding than on desperately-needed basics such as sanitation, health care, and water supply. And they have every reason to do so. Consumers of these basic services are too diverse, too poor, too naive, and too demoralized to exert any kind of political pressure on their rulers.

Naturally, the money finds its way toward the pockets of vested interests. To obtain subsidies, for example, many businessmen routinely bribe the politicians. The former also know that their profits will be taxed away in no time. To prevent the government from snatching with its left hand what it has given with its right hand, they transfer the subsidy money into their underground operations.

To begin with, they showcase their blueprints and plans, and obtain grants of loans and land from the government for ventures which, according to O.S. Shrivastava, "are to remain non-starters." In other words, they just build a facade. They display products from their other companies as if they are produced by the venture in question. After the subsidy is released by the government, and after bleeding the fake unit white of cash, they declare insolvency. (111)

This kind of waste and abuse prompted Rajiv Gandhi to say, "India cannot afford socialism…instead of generating resources, the public sector has been eating up the wealth of the nation." (135)

This was true in every country. Officials in the former Soviet Union adopted wastefulness as their religion. In 1990, the United States Senate Budget Committee reported that at least thirty billion defense dollars were spent on unnecessary spare parts, uniforms and other equipment. Stories of one thousand dollar toilet seats and wrenches shocked the American taxpayer. Regardless of culture or political system, in every country, bureaucrats routinely come up with ingenious ways of eating up the wealth of the nation. Neither periodic elections nor a well functioning secret service agency can cure them of their prodigal ways. (136)

Much more than the US, however, India has enlarged the scope of its public sector far beyond essential areas such as defense. In the four decades since independence, they have thrown more than 3,000,000 million rupees into this black hole. Despite a glut in the market, for example, they built steel mills. Now society—a.k.a politicians and bureaucrats—owns 214 such mega enterprises. They manage these industries just as they manage everything else. Between 1975 and 1980, for example, return on these investments has dropped from a measly three percent to an abominable -1%. During the same period, private companies have seen their average returns nearly double, from eight to fourteen percent. Forget about the return. Under government ownership, the principal has no prayer. By the early nineties, losses in the power sector alone amounted to 130,000 million rupees. (137)

While the industries they have started are going down the tubes, the planners confiscate many private concerns such as banks and coal mines and push them down the same path. K.S.R. Chari, a former coal secretary, said that production and financial performance of many coal mines deteriorated since they had gone into public (state) ownership. By 1988, for example, the state owned Coal India LTD. (CIL) lost 20,000 million rupees. (138)

Politicians appoint and sack managers of the public sector companies faster than one can say *inefficiency*. Whims of ministers, rather than performance, determine these moves. Says one such manager, "We have to please everyone in the ministry from the section officer to the secretary. The ability to manage the secretariat (which houses the executive offices of ministers) is more important than the ability to manage the company." Just to hang on to their positions, these managers hang around the corridors of the secretariat. They cater to the egos of ministers and their staffs. (139)

Despite this, these managers get shunted around with a dizzying pace. In the twenty years before 1989, for example, the State Trading Corporation, with its annual turnover of 26,000 million rupees, saw fifteen chief executives come and go. Barely a half a dozen of them worked on a *regular* tenure. One CEO lasted for twenty-seven days. (139)

Such juggling further compromises what little efficiency these managers bring to their jobs. Out of frustration, quite a few good managers leave the public sector for private companies. Politicians and top bureaucrats, however, couldn't care less about retaining the best. They hate the idea of anyone making more than they do. At best, only mediocre yes-men languish in these positions.

With the help of their unions, despite poor productivity, these employees get regular raises. To this end, they make use of the lopsided labor laws and organize frequent strikes. On occasion, they do so just to maintain the pressure. In the spring of 1988, 2.2 million of the workers struck for three days. Their demands included not only pension schemes and wage hikes, but also jobs for dependents of retired employees and halting the sales of sick (unprofitable) units. Besides the inconveniences that the public had to endure due to interruption of services in such areas as transportation, this strike cost the economy more than 7,500 million rupees. (140)

Even when they are not on strike, these workers are notorious for their laziness, incompetence, and total cynicism. They waste unbelievable amounts of resources. Knowingly or otherwise, they make sure that the country stays poor, jobless, backward, and even lethargic. Nevertheless, each of them behaves just like you or I do in a similar situation. It's as if your boss has told you, "Show up whenever you can. You will get your steadily escalating paycheck. Do as little as you possible can. Unless you stir up the nest, you will get your promotions." How many of us would shun secure jobs, guaranteed raises and freedom not to work?

By disregarding human nature, especially the way it responds to negative and positive reinforcements, the dreamers in post-independent India have put in place a structure which ensures such a non-performance. Their huge public sector has been doomed to fail. Managers and workers benefit little from the company's profitability. Their survival has little to do with their performance, or the lack of it. Their progress largely depends upon the ability to influence the politicians.

What they lack in the department of motivation (lest the reader searches for one, there is no such agency in Delhi. At least, not yet.), however, the leaders hope to make up by endlessly preaching how the public sector should perform. Of course, they name their sermons "goals and targets," which they declare through an agency, *The Planning Commission*. Actually, this commission does a whole lot more than setting goals and targets. Except in a few areas such as defense, subsidies, and interest payments, this Commission recommends how the government should spend its money. The prime minister serves as its chairman. That didn't prevent Rajiv Gandhi from calling his commission members "a bunch of jokers." (141)

These funny gentlemen are highly innovative. To cover up the politics behind their spending, they and their political bosses utilize all kinds of instruments (such as setting high targets to justify their massive fund allocations) and the most fancy equations. Endlessly, they establish boards and commissions, including my own favorite—the Central Molasses Board. On occasion, such performance confounds even a few of the commission's members. L.C. Jain, one of them, said, "It is time the Planning Commission delivered goods instead of statistics." (142)

One of the statistical numbers that government officials do deliver is the so called targets of production. These unicorns have little to do with the real world and its compulsions. Bureaucrats pull these numbers out of their hats. In 1988–89, for example, the country harvested 170 million tons of food grains. The agricultural ministry set a target of 175 million for the next year. By doing so, however, it terribly disappointed the prime minister's office. The ruling party was facing a crucial election. It liked to look good, if not by performance, at least by predicting higher numbers on paper. The prime minister's office raised the target to 185 million tons. It was hardly as if these officials would stare at ceilings at night and worry about such things as how to get there. They let the ministry sweat out such petty details. Concluded the report, "So the agriculture department suffers another high-yield headache." (143)

The planners forget that by just channeling more of the taxpayer's money to pay salaries and perks to agricultural bureaucrats, one can't prod one's farmers to produce more. After all, with their land reforms, low procurement prices and wishy-washy fertilizer policies, and by discouraging building of such necessities as storage spaces, the officials have stung many previously hard-working farmers.

When the results fall short of the targets, as they invariably do, the dreamers get mad. On everyone and everything connected with the already failed process, they come down hard. They even claim that India has given a bad name to the ideals of socialism. Laments S.S. Gill, a former high-ranking official and an ardent supporter of socialism: "The planning process [in India] itself has gradually become an exercise in wishful thinking. The plan projects are seldom backed up by adequate resources, the plan targets have little relevance to actual achievements and the plan projections are mere expressions of populist aspirations." (144)

In 1988, the National Airports Authority of India recommended importing certain electronically controlled air traffic equipment to be installed at the various airports. (145)

A few of the machines were manufactured locally. To ensure the safety of the flying public, however, engineers and technicians of the agency decided to import the gadgets which they felt were better-made abroad. The department of electronics, however, had a more sacred mission, promoting "self-sufficiency." Saying that indigenous products must be given priority, the department put its foot down. (145)

Such a talk invokes the images of a country subjected to frequent and total blockades. As if they are getting their countrymen ready for a final showdown, the politicians push the so-called self-sufficiency. In the name of protecting local industries, which they otherwise oppress with regulations and high taxes, these officials throw all kinds of hurdles against imports.

Consequently, the consumer pays more for everything from electronics to daily wear. He naturally does so for imported goods with tariff-inflated price tags. When the duties on capital equipment are passed on to him, he pays more for locally finished products. Because such protectionism restricts competition, he also forks out a lot of money for the shabby goods that are built from scratch by the local monopolists. Under the protectionism, the rupee of an average worker buys less than otherwise. His standard of living suffers.

Forget about luxury items and arcane air traffic equipment. The officials also keep out life saving medicines that aren't even produced locally. Despite this, the majority in the country just go along. To them, these are a few more rules to tread around. They routinely buy smuggled goods. Owing to an overwhelming xenophobia and leftover anti-colonial sentiments, however, few demand a change in the policy. To an average Indian, foreign manufacturers awaken the memories of the East India Company, which, with the help of the British government, played a crucial role in subjugating India. Of course, Indian politicians are more than happy to stroke these phobias. They exhort the consumer, "Be Indian; buy Indian."

At every chance they get, they beat up on foreign investors. Says K.N. Singh, a top Congress(I) leader, "They come through cola as a window dressing: the real purpose is to serve the designs of imperialist forces. Do we need Pepsi at the cost of the country's security?" What Singh is talking about is not some attack aircraft, but Pepsi Cola, just hyped-up sugar water. Even China and the USSR have been more receptive to cola companies than India. (146)

With their high tax rates and other anti-business policies, Indian planners prevent the accumulation of capital inside the country. When a multinational tries to come in with capital and technology, provide jobs for the unemployed and cater to the scarcity-plagued consumer, the likes of Singh whip up nativism. They erect all kinds of hurdles for the investor, unless of course he is willing to bow before them. Pepsi bowed exceptionally well. It agreed to a variety of conditions, which included not using its brand name and exporting fifty percent of its product. The company had to promise that the soft drinks would represent only a quarter of the business. The rest involved fruit juices, potato chips and other kinds of processed foods. A few in the country supported Pepsi's bid because they expected the deal to improve food production by transferring agricultural technology. After all, by using its patents, the company had doubled per-acre yields of potatoes in Mexico in just three years. (146)

Potatoes or chips were the least of the considerations of the domestic soft drink manufacturers, whose list included a few big power houses. These businesses cried for government protection. These producers wrapped themselves and their intentions in the flag only to avoid something they hated passionately—competition, foreign or domestic. In this, they behaved like any other monopoly—the East India Company, for example. They tried to use the many organs of the state to earn more than just profits. They hoped to gain a wise grip over the consumer and the worker. (146)

It's not just the local producers who want to keep the multinationals, and, thus, technological advances, out of the country. Politicians and their researcher friends also love to squander the country's precious resources to reinvent the wheel. Even the Gandhian kind, if funded enough, they will make from scratch.

If enough bribes are paid by a foreign investor, however, all these hurdles melt away just like that. By playing this game by its implied rules, however, the company gives the opposing politicians an opportunity to howl about "those corrupt multinationals." Coke, too, tried to come in. The All India Soft Drink Manufacture Association howled, "Here is another case of 'things are brought in big jars and put in small jars.' " Pepsi, just being a Roman in Rome, joined this protectionist frenzy. To plead its case, it sent a nineteen-member team to Delhi. It seemed that in no time Pepsi had learned about doing business in a statist society: It was not how well your cola fizzed, but how well you and your friends were fizzing with power. (147)

The founding fathers, who preferred self-sufficiency over the mutually beneficial free trade and laid foundations for such protectionism, were unable grow above their anti-British, anti-colonial rhetoric of pre-independence days. They filled the atmosphere with a fear of things foreign. They refused to let the capital and technology from more advanced countries help them build a more wealthy nation. Thanks to their blueprint, the officials enjoyed a veto power over most decisions concerning foreign investment. While most countries were benefiting from free trade and Europe was planning to break down its internal barriers, Indian politicians stood in the door and sang patriotic songs.

The results proved to be devastating. Foreign investment in India stayed as low as $200 million in 1988, compared to 980 million in relatively tiny Sri Lanka and $8 billion in not-so-big Thailand. China's trade figure was $3.5 billion, proving that even communist nations were ahead of India in realizing potential for economic growth from "capitalist exploitation." (148)

But then, why earn if you can beg?

After rejecting the infusion of foreign capital from multi-nationals, Indian politicians use *friendly persuasion* to get donor countries to make *spontaneous* offers of aid. In 1988, alone, using this technique they hoped to rise $1.15 billion. (149)

In following this map to deprivation, even among the different Indian states, some fare worse than the others. For a student of political economy, a probe into their affairs is akin to undertaking a controlled study; it's more or less like a time travel for an anthropologist. (150)

In (the states of) Kerala and West Bengal, for example, democratically elected communist leaders followed their religion. Their policies produced scanty economic growth rates. Even by Indian standards, they were abysmal, for example, 0.3% to 0.5% in 1988 (versus the highest rate of 12.6% in the state of Utter Pradesh, 7% in Andhra Pradesh and 3.3% in Karnataka). Kerala became so backward that it ended up with only 210 large and medium-scale industries. As a result, in this workers' paradise very few could find jobs. Of course, communists in Kerala were ready with an explanation, the old faithful. They blamed the poor growth on the "lack of natural resources such as iron, copper, and aluminum." (150)

This ridiculous explanation appealed to only those who believed that Kerala lived under some kind of internal embargo and couldn't get its materials from the rest of India. Also, "the lack of minerals" failed to explain why agro-based industries had slumped too. Just as in the rest of the Third World, Kerala's economic depression had nothing to do with natural resources; it had everything to do with the abilities of Marxist governments to destroy property rights and drive away investors. For example, ninety percent of the country's rubber came from Kerala, but almost all the rubber-based industries were located outside this state. (150)

With the help of communist politicians, unions in these states turned very militant and very unreasonable. In one industry, for example, the unions prevented the use of forklifts to handle cargo weighing up to 850 kg., even though such loads were too heavy to be lifted manually. Following hurried consultations, the union leaders relented, but only after the owners agreed to pay 1,000 rupees to them for every truck that would be unloaded by a forklift. (150)

Small wonder that Chandan Basu—son of Jyothi Basu, chief minister of one of these states, West Bengal—said that if he wanted to start a industry, he would do so outside his state. Owners that were not as well connected as Chandan had no prayer. Many of them either closed down their shops or, more commonly, moved out and took their jobs with them. As a result, in jute industry alone, forty percent of workers lost their jobs. In the real world, the newly unemployed were reduced to menial chores, or worse, begging or suicide. They had no safety net to fall into. Thanks to its depressive policies, government had little money for welfare programs such as unemployment insurance, a major feature of productive economies. (151)

As to be expected, Marxist politicians turned to using force. They tried to prohibit the owners from moving out or closing down the industries. The leftist governments passed strict lockout laws which prescribed fines, and even jail time to punish the violators. Such laws would clutter the books and scare the potential investors some more. Otherwise, they were largely useless. Even the communists realized as much. Said D.K. Ghosh, the labor secretary of West Bengal, "We can prosecute the management. But the entire legal process takes years." (151)

Now-a-days, government only brings unions and owners together for negotiations. It refuses to arm-twist the producers and make a bad situation worse. If the owner closes down, or so much as delays reopening of his plant, more workers will suffer. By limiting investment opportunities and, thus, the level of employment for years, the communists have created an ever-increasing demand for such jobs. They ironically strengthened the hands of the *filthy capitalists*. At present, owners hold all the cards. Workers and their erstwhile firebrand unions have few choices. During most disputes, they just give in. According to a 1989 report in *The Illustrated Weekly of India,* the management of Bata shoe factory in Batanagar locked out close to 10,000 workers. Only when the union agreed to the management's charter of demands, which the former had rejected early on, did the factory come back to life. (151)

Owners' control extends beyond such negotiations. There are serious allegations that they squander employee pension funds—close to 1,320 million rupees in the jute industry alone. In this depressed economy, officials can't prosecute the management and risk a factory shutdown. Workers simply won't go for it. Says Kamaljeet Rattan (of *India Today),* "After all, asked to choose between his salary and his provident [retirement] fund, the worker would unhesitatingly choose his pay." (151,152)

Also, by sending the rogue owner to jail, officials gain little for themselves, certainly not as much as if they let him pay them off and cope with their laws and, of course, their supervision. A lawyer representing the workers alleges that most government officials "are in collusion with the owners." What about the union leaders? Why don't they protect the rank and file? But then, why should they? They too partake in this feast. Says Piyal Singh of the *Illustrated Weekly of India,* "The semi-literate worker is duped by this manipulative species [union leader] who fills his [the leader's] personal coffers and promises a large vote bank to the local politician." (151)

Among other things, this invasion of corruption and politics into union affairs hurts another socialist experiment, worker self-management. Such questions as, how to conduct union elections to pick the worker representatives, confound the officials. Despite its pro-worker rhetoric, for example, the Congress(I) party runs as fast as possible from the idea of intra-union democracy. Its politicians even claim that secret balloting has "always encouraged irresponsibility." Apparently they can ill-afford to anger the typical union boss who thrives on coercing the workers to vote for him. (153)

The "pro-labor" politicians in these states, and for that matter in the rest of India, have passed so many regulations that they push most jobs into the underground economy. Even the legal businesses employ quite a few on a casual basis and under short-term contracts only; some of these men and women might even work on the premises. Naturally, most of these illegal and semi-legal workers live beyond the purview of the many laws that cover, among other things, pension plans, health care, and safety in the work place. (154)

Describing the conditions of more than 40,000 workers in tobacco processing units in (the state of) Gujarat, says Uday Mahurkar (of *India Today*): "The working conditions are inhuman, the hours long. Diseases due to tobacco dust are common. The pay is a fraction of that prescribed by the Minimum Wages Act. As for medical allowances, gratuity and bonus, most workers haven't heard of them." (154)

---

[10]At present, the majority of Indians derive their protein mostly from rice and wheat.

[11]During 1989, for example, the money supply went up by nineteen percent as opposed to a 4.5 percent growth in real Gross Domestic Product. (119)

[12]For example, 61,000 million rupees in 1988 and an estimated 75,000 million in 1989. (131)

# CHAPTER 6
## *Cut Trees—Give Votes*

TO CRISSCROSS INDIA by its trains is to touch its soul.

The scenery can be hypnotic. Just as in any other country, one feels cradled by the oscillations; the rhythmic sounds of wheels can be very soothing. In India, however, an another dimension is thrown in. Frequently, the train becomes a nice social setting, a sumptuous buffet to sample the public opinion.

One can partake of this feast without moving one's finger. There is little need to be nosy or ask personal questions. As a matter of fact, the best way to enjoy the serving is to keep one's mouth shut and just listen. Travelers speak with emotion. From personal matters and social issues to politics, they cover diverse topics.

The rhythm, music, feel, and engaging conversation can be fascinating, but they are nothing compared to the risk and the adventure that are part of the experience. For starters, you have to get seats for the journey. To reserve your tickets in this government-owned and operated Indian Railways—the only train system in the country—you can't just call or send in the money by mail. You, or someone you know, should take the time to go to the station of departure ten days or so before the trip. Or, you can purchase the seats after the train arrives on the platform. That's easy, if you know how to bribe a total stranger in front of tens of other total strangers. And you must do so very fast.

If he turns down your offer, you hop into one of the unreserved compartments, push and shove others, step on a few feet, and create a place to stand. As to the colorful cursing you might hear about your ancestors, pay no attention. If the coach is bursting with people, learn to enjoy an outdoor ride with one leg on the step, one hand clutching the railing, and your brain praying that the foot will be steady and the palm will stay dry.

As incredible as it sounds, the adventure can get even better. All you have to do is, before you leave home, read a report by N.K. Singh (of *India Today*): "Safety: The First Casualty." He says, "In this world's second-largest railway system, the problems are daunting: primitive maintenance methods, aging tracks and machinery. And as traffic burgeons, the odds are mounting." (155)

Singh lists the gory details: "One fifth of the total length of railway track in the system—13,000 km out of 62,000 km—needs to be replaced. But this has not been done. Continuing use of old and weakened track leads to metal fatigue and fractures—a major cause of accidents. The number of rail fractures has increased from 4,517 in 1980–81 to 6,272 in 1987–88." Singh is also concerned about the condition of the bridges, aged engines, and passenger coaches. In the ten years prior to 1989, due to fewer but more serious accidents, the death toll went up from 172 to 244. (155)

A special working group of the Planning Commission looked into the problem. The panel recommended that to launch Indian Railways into the twenty-first century, compared to the 105,000 million rupees it spent during the last five year plan (1985–90), government should allocate another 416,000 million in the next plan. Sounds great, but where's the money? (155,156)

What should keep all the passengers lying on their gyrating berths wide awake with anger is that only a small portion of the meager funds available goes toward fixing the structural problems. The ever increasing payroll eats up a big chunk. Besides, the officials love to spend on speed and style. They allocate close to eight million rupees a year to provide, of all the things, plastic cups to passengers—an idea picked up by the railway minister, Madhavrao Scindia, during one of his foreign trips. (155)

To the likes of Scindia, such ideas make a lot of sense. Politicians get credit for running trains on time and for making them look good. What if the lack of attention to safety details leads to a disaster? Well. It's all preordained. When people consider human life as disposable as a plastic cup, there is hardly any clamoring for safety.

Families of the accident victims have no place to turn to, not certainly to the courts. They find it impossible to sue and win against the state-owned railways. If a private corporation every so often killed so many people by such negligence, not only would it have been pushed into bankruptcy, its board of directors would be in jail by now.

During my actual train ride, however, I see or hear very little that makes me nervous. It lets me mentally settle back. Especially when I return to India after a hiatus, the journey lets me catch up with the latest trends. If it happens to be a night train, I even sleep off my jet lag. Once or twice, I have almost missed my station.

While cruising on Indian roads, however, I refuse to even blink. No. I don't suffer from some kind of highway phobia, road insomnia, or whatever. Only that I find a car ride in India to be by far the most bloodcurdling experience of my trip. So do many of my friends who used to operate vehicles before they emigrated from India. Now they refuse to so much as touch the steering wheel. They leave the driving to locals and simply ride with the facial expression of someone who has planted his bare bottom right in the middle of an ant farm. From gossiping pedestrians, over-stuffed busses, and two and three-wheelers and cars that every few minutes or so miss his by only a few inches, to cows that leisurely answer nature's calls in the middle of the road, a whole cast of characters send butterflies to explore the confines of the visitor's stomach.

It's bad on the beast too, I mean the mechanical one. Cars bump up and down on the roads which, in comparison, make the moon's surface look like a skating rink. The automobiles keep on ticking only because owners spend an estimated 20,000 million rupees on vehicle maintenance alone. A recent World Bank report calls both road network and road building technology in India obsolete. The traffic has clearly out grown this network. Even on major highways, many bridges allow traffic just one way each time. Before attempting to cross one of them, the driver has to make sure that there are no oncoming vehicles. (157)

Owing to a minor mishap on one such narrow bridge during my trip, the traffic got backed up for two hours. Soon, we were coughing from dust and vehicle exhausts. Scooters and rickshaws were trying to pass each other on footpaths and between heavy trucks. The trick was to somehow avoid being crushed by the monsters. This would take a lot of skill on the part of the driver; the trucks themselves were constantly backing out from the gaps in the traffic they had crawled into early on. To make matters worse, a few amused pedestrians and adventurous bikers brought back confusing traffic bulletins and misled the drivers some more.

I started to inquire about the road conditions in general. That proved to be a big mistake. From the annoyed taxi driver and my tired relatives, I got an explanation that would leave a worse taste in my mouth than the combination of dust and diesel fumes. Government did allot money for the roadways, but only a small portion went into improvements. Private contractors in collusion with corrupt officials digested at least one half, if not more. Even now, it's tough to get a job in the public works department, which the media often calls "lucrative." To be posted as an engineer, one has to pay close to 100,000 rupees as a bribe. For those who can pay, however, this is a wise investment. In no time, they recoup their principal and a whole lot more. On their trail to this financial nirvana, however, they leave behind bad roads, weak bridges, vehicles that wear down fast, and countless injuries and deaths. Compared to an accident rate of 1.8 (per 10,000 vehicles) in

Japan and 3.6 in the U.K., the rate in India hovers around 45. (157)

Also, trucks overload. Truck operators bribe the officials and pass through the government check points. This has become such a routine that even when they carry the loads within regulation, the truck operators just pay up; income tax officials even treat the payments as legitimate business expenses. While waiting at the check points, trucks burn fuel worth more than 10,000 million rupees every year. (157)

It's hardly as if the country has fuel to burn. Recently, an oil coordination committee has taken into account oil demand, indigenous supply, and refining capabilities and submitted its report to the petroleum ministry. According to these estimates, to fill gaps in the energy sector, by 1995, India will have to import close to thirty-six million tons of crude oil. Even if the country somehow comes up with the cash to buy the oil, it has a slight problem. It lacks the necessary wherewithal to handle such a flow. With their licensing controls and price freezes, and by barring big industries from this area, the planners have effectively hampered the growth of necessary infrastructure. (158)

Thanks to such policies, the power situation in India has gotten so bleak that fewer than half of the 576,000 villages, where the majority live, have electricity. In the luckier half, seeking the farm vote, politicians sell electricity to farmers at subsidized rates. Largely owing to such *generosity* and mismanagement, by 1988, state electricity boards have lost a total of 70,000 million rupees. They can only supply limited quantities of power. Naturally, the country suffers from frequent blackouts and brownouts. These shortages cripple industries, reduce output, and retard job growth. They, however, more than make up for the damage; they interrupt movies and shut down the television. (159,160)

Few movie theaters, small industries, and other businesses can afford to lie idle. Most carry on their work using power generators. So do quite a few rich households. These contraptions are highly inefficient. They burn a lot of oil and add to the pollution.

Just to keep up with the demand for energy, between 1990 and 1995, the country would have to produce an additional 38,000 mega-watts—more than half of the total power generated in forty-one years of India's independence. Even if by some miracle it reaches this goal, it still has to maintain the current average power cut of twenty percent during the peak periods of demand. During a fit of sanity (in 1989), officials floated a proposal to allow large private sector companies into power generation. Soon, they sobered up, got busy, and engineered a few roadblocks. The investor would have to come up with sixty percent of the money. He would not be allowed to borrow from the public sector financial institutions, the only large ones that were allowed to thrive. For the equipment, he would have to place orders only with the indigenous units. It was as if the officials dared the producer who would try to spread his wings and lift the country out of this mess: "You move, we clip." (160)

Not counting such mindless obstructionism, whether involving trains, planes, automobiles, or power plants, the reason why the infrastructure is moribund is threefold. Thanks to the economic depression—borne out of the socialist polices which have failed everywhere—government earns fewer revenues than needed to acquire, repair, and maintain all this equipment; the bureaucrats have little interest to build it right in the first place, maintain it well, or fix it properly when it's broken; they have absolutely no reason to treat the consumer right. Thanks to their monopoly over these services, he has few alternatives, private or public, to turn to.

So do the entrepreneurs, who might venture into the ice-cold waters of the Indian investment world. They, too, have to contend with the limited infrastructure which stands out as a monument for the failure of public policy in post-independent India. Owing to various bottlenecks in transportation, for example, these businessmen face problems shipping their cargo. Their industries live with energy supplies that are, at best, scanty. Forget about three-way conference calls or zipping documents via fax machines; most are happy to settle for a semi-decent long distance phone connection. Private investors who hurry to fill these gaps are told to wait for years before the monopolistic phone company bestows on them such privileges as a fax line, of course, at the bargain basement price of several thousand rupees a year. By restricting the growth of infrastructure, government limits the enterprise some more. It stunts the economy and ends up with fewer revenues than needed to satisfactorily fix the broken rail tracts, supply power, pick up garbage, or provide cargo planes.

Small wonder that it leaves many basic human needs unmet and lays the foundation for many an acute human tragedy. In the absence of minimal sanitation and safe drinking water, epidemics, such as diarrhea and hepatitis, which have been banished from most other countries frequently rear their ugly heads in India. For a while, Malaria did come under control: While in medical school, I remember to seeing few cases. In just a few years, by the time I was doing my residency, the disease had become rampant. Now the parasite is largely resistant to such common drugs as chloroquin.

In Bombay alone, sixty percent of the children fail to receive their basic immunizations. Such a breakdown of preventive measures, combined with inadequate health care and widespread malnutrition, has resulted in an infant mortality rate of 129 per 1,000. According to a World Bank report, eighty percent of India's villages and fifty percent of its urban population have to do without safe water supplies. As to be expected, for all the money it has thrown at these shortages, government has very few results to show for. Bunker Roy (of *India Today*) even accuses the bureaucrats in Delhi and state capitals of using the wrong technology: such as deep-well (India Mark 11) hand pumps in the shallow water-table regions. Despite their past failures, the officials insist on a real hands-on approach. They know that the villagers are "incapable" of making complicated decisions, such as where to locate water taps. So the officials make that decision, often to the chagrin of the villagers, especially the house wives who must sometimes carry water for long distances. Government also spends 1,000 rupees to maintain each hand pump, which the locals can take care of for a mere 300. In spite of such high-class maintenance, if a pump happens to break down—as many do—scores of families must survive without tap water for days, or even weeks, while the high priests of the bureaucracy take time to approve the repairs. (159,161)

Such bureaucratic indifference also haunts another area, garbage disposal. Overflowing and filthy garbage containers are an ubiquitous sight in almost all cities and towns in India. According to a recent (1988) news story, in the capital city of Delhi, one committed citizen wanted to deposit her garbage in a proper dump. Only after a ten km. bike ride, did she find one. In any case, this lady must have dropped from wherever the ET had. To dispose of their garbage, very few in the country even take ten yard walks, much less ten-kilometer bike rides. Most dump their trash wherever they can. As far as they are concerned, the closest street is their eternal landfill. It's very tempting to criticize this "lack of civic sense." But what does one do? Leave garbage in neat bags that will stay in the street for eternity before being ripped apart by all God's living creatures? (162)

In 1988, an outbreak of cholera killed many slum dwellers in Delhi. Rajiv Gandhi, the prime minister, lashed out at the officials. He demanded an inquiry and a report on the level of pollutants in the water supply. He did so in public and scored a few points with viewers of the government-owned television network. It displayed his fury at length and repeatedly. After a while, he did get the report, but quietly shelved it. It was embarrassing. Some of the contaminants were 100 or even 200 times higher than the safe levels. He simply assumed that few voters would remember the incident or bother about the report. (163)

He has assumed right. The majority of the voters don't know how to read a newspaper, much less the report written in the newest member of the Indo-European language family—officialese. Very few people have the opportunities to learn even the basic skills. Even those who attend public schools get precious little in the form of creature comforts. In a survey conducted in (the state of) Bihar, forty-four percent of the schools don't even have semi-permanent buildings. Quite a few function without blackboards and only with one teacher. (164)

The state of Goa is famous for its pristine coastline. A while back (1989), its chief minister wanted a few industrialists to take advantage of his beautiful state and set up a "bureaucratic hassle-free electronic township." (165)

After listening to the sales pitch, the businessmen responded with an advice of their own. They asked the minister to first talk to the officials in the civil aviation department and get the schedules of the Indian Airline's flights to Goa (from Delhi) changed. One can't blame these poor souls. Who wants to limit his flying to the ungodly hour of 5:15 A.M? (165)

When Nehru nationalized India's seven airlines in the early fifties, little did he realize what was in store for the consumer, whom he left at the mercy of an unresponsive, irresponsible, and highly bureaucratic air travel system. As recently as 1988, this system confounded Rajan Jetly—then the managing director of Air India. All Jetly wanted to do was to run this international airline just like a private carrier. To cut costs. Among other things, he proposed limiting free first-class travel only to a few high level employees—deputy directors and above. His investigations showed that just two out of every sixteen first class seats were paid for. Employees earning 2,500 rupees and above and their dependents took up the rest. Complained one traveler, "What annoyed me was that due to comradeship, Air-India staff was offered more personalized services than full-fare paying passengers like me." Few public sector officials in India tolerate such an attack (as the one by Jetly) on their birthrights. True to the tradition, Air India employees promptly struck, costing the airline 40 million rupees. (166)

Besides such strikes and a lack of personalized service, the consumer puts up with delayed flights, stiff schedules, shortage of seats and cargo piling up at various airports waiting to be piked up by the planes. Also, airports have obsolete landing aids. As of 1989, barely twenty percent of the Indian airspace is under radar surveillance and the control towers are heavily understaffed. To make matters worse, pilots and engineers receive inadequate training and medical supervision. To all this add poor licensing procedures and incomplete airworthiness checks, and you have air travel that is truly a life-risking adventure. After a disastrous Indian Airlines' crash at Bangalore (in 1990) which had killed ninety people, said Prakash Narain, chairman of the National Transportation Safety Board , "The level of safety is still highly unsatisfactory." (167,168)

Besides all those things that move, the government builds, owns, and maintains many other structures whose level of safety also remains highly unsatisfactory. At an alarming rate, bridges crack or even cave in. So do many buildings. For example, during the spring of 1988, Children Hospital of Jammu Medical College collapsed killing ten children and injuring twenty-five. During the previous year, in just two districts about twenty new (16 months or less) school buildings also bit the dust. (169)

Under centrally financed "rural development schemes," contractors close to the ruling politicians built all these schools. Such contractors routinely maintain the bureaucracy on their payroll. Naturally, they can rob the taxpayer to their heart's content, do a shoddy job, and easily get away with the murder and mayhem. (169)

The ability of the indifferent and corrupt officials to transform buildings and other innocent objects into instruments of death—worthy of 007's arsenal—also threatens another area with far-reaching consequences. To address the energy shortages that it has skillfully engineered, the government has gotten into nuclear power plants. About one such plant says Guha Prasad (no relation to the author) of *India Today*: "It was designed as the show piece of India's nuclear power technology. Kalpakkam today resembles a mute monument to failure—" a monument which has cost the taxpayer 2,450 million rupees, twice the original estimate. (170)

There are fears that this monument might not stay mute for very long. After a few *incidents* at Kalpakkam, the auditor general and comptroller expressed serious concerns about quality control in the construction of two units. Prasad dated the first major incident to June 25, 1986: About fifteen tons of heavy water coolant leaked out of the core of one of the units. Ever since, this unit was regularly plagued by leaks. In a what the officials termed a "unique accident," for example, fuel rods were dislodged while the spent fuel was being removed. He quoted an obviously exasperated official, "How do we cope with such substandard equipment?" Prasad ominously concluded, "As it is, the problems at Kalpakkam are indicative of serious problems in the entire atomic energy program." (170)

While riding a cab on *Rajpath*—a scenic road in Delhi—I became aware of another serious problem. At first I was very impressed by Rajpath. It looked as colonial as a road could be. It ran between a memorial gate and the presidential palace. It was flanked by several majestic buildings that housed the various federal ministries. In short, it ran through the most dense accumulation of all political and economic power in India.

Not withstanding, one of these buildings, Vigyan Bhavan— the site of many national and international meetings, including the summit of the Non-Aligned Nations (1983)—caught fire during 1990. The fire surprised many who expected the building to have enough safeguards. After all, Vigyan Bhavan did undergo expensive renovations in 1979. Despite prior complaints from the chief fire officer of Delhi about the lack of fire prevention facilities, however, officials did little in the way of fire safety. Instead, they spent the monies on cosmetic changes and improvements to the audio system. (171)

Such amenities as fire services are standard fixtures in most towns and villages in the advanced countries. The fire at Vigyan Bhavan illustrates how woefully inadequate such basic services are even in the nation's capital. (171)

Nevertheless, I doubt whether the millions who live in Delhi— or for that matter in any other Indian city—lose sleep over a lack of decent fire control service. I doubt they even care. They are too busy surviving the urban jungle.

To say that every city in India is exploding at its seams is hardly an exaggeration. In 1951, 1.4 million lived in Delhi. By

1991, close to nine million tried to do so. During the same period, Bombay registered a population explosion from three to eleven million. (172)

For the privilege of living in these cities, each resident pays a heavy price. To a degree not matched by most people in the West, rich and poor alike in Indian cities breath polluted air and sit through traffic jams. The wage earner spends an awful lot of time commuting. Most try to cope with frequent interruptions of essentials such as the water and power supply. A fourth of the urban population have to do without tap water or sewage facilities. Owing to a shortage of electricity, a third live in darkness on a regular basis. (172)

The droplets that mostly make up this sea of humanity, the very poor, are drowning in it. Says Raj Chengappa (of *India Today*): "In East Delhi's Nand Nagri and Seema Puri, man and animal live alike. Human excreta float around in clogged open drains, rats and rag pickers scurry around in reeking garbage piles, pigs roll in the slush, queues around public water taps stretch for a mile, and at night, people lie littered around in corners with torn tarpaulins as roofs and newspapers as blankets to beat the cold." (172)

Government estimates that more than thirty million live in such squalor. Shocked by these conditions, most Western TV reporters just shoot their footage in the city and leave. They rarely ever venture into the countryside. Incensed by the images rather than the plight of those who are in the images, Indian politicians promise *proper planning* to deal with the urban overcrowding. (172)

They come up with cures that are far worse than the disease. A case in point was the Urban Land Ceiling Act of 1976. Using it, officials planned to confiscate *excess* land, give it to the needy and curb speculation and profiteering in these shortage-plagued urban centers. In reality, however, property owners simply paid bribes and evaded the law's provisions. So much so that the government ended up with too little—only thirty four acres in Calcutta and two acres in Delhi—"to house the poor." To avoid the confiscation, owners also sold their *excess* land to the squatters. Just to have "a place of their own," the latter bought these pieces. Said B.D. Shukla, a planning officer of the Gujarat Slum Clearance Board, "The Act is a major headache for us. With the landowners trying to make as much as possible from their excess land, the number of slum areas is shooting up." (172)

The sellers and buyers use the slumlord to protect their properties from any encroachment. They have little choice in the matter. They have nowhere to turn. The legal apparatus, which is supposed to protect their property rights, has resorted to confiscation. Small wonder that it has pushed land-dealing underground and caused gangs and crime to proliferate.

The slumlords routinely keep many politicians and law enforcement officials on a retainer. The criminal gangs thus operate without fear and enforce their rule. With their backing, a few powerful owners tightly control the markets. Also, because of the shortages these owners can sell on their terms. They display little interest in providing roads or sewage. To make matters worse, the bureaucracy destroys what little it creates. A road paved by one agency is dug up by another such as the telephone department. (172)

Many movies and novels glorify villages in India. To an outsider, compared to the cities, living conditions in the villages seem much more tolerable. Most slum dwellers, however, disagree. They refuse go back to their villages for the same reason that they have come to the city in the first place: in search of work. By following this one-way migration, they prove that the urban slum may be a living hell, but rural poverty, though not as graphic, is far worse.

Naturally, these city dwellers doom all attempts by government to resettle them. In (the state of) Gujarat, for example, government gave each of more than 5,000 slum dwellers a house in the outskirts. In no time, many of the beneficiaries sold their houses. They quietly moved back to the city. A house may be a castle, but the lord needs his job. (172)

To understand the fundamental forces behind the overcrowding of cities, it is important to realize that those who desert their scenic villages are hardly a bunch of mirage-chasing fools. Cities do have most of the decent jobs. In India, the majority of important government offices, businesses, and commercial centers are concentrated in the hearts of cities. In Calcutta, for example, this amounts to only two sq. km. A third of motor vehicle tires produced in India come from Calcutta's factories. So do the bulk of the country's wagons, jute, and rolled steel. Bombay now has one out of five joint stock companies in the country and ten percent of the total factory work force. (172)

That the majority of government offices are situated in main cities should surprise few. Where else would the all-powerful officials like to locate? In a faraway god-forsaken village? Not if any of them can help it. Even now, when posted to a small town or a village, many officials frantically try to reverse the transfer orders.

What very few realize, however, is that the centralized economic power—a hallmark of socialist planning—also mandates concentration of private investment in cities. In a heavily regulated economy, whether they like it or not, managers of private industries have to deal with government on a day-to-day basis. To ensure the very survival of their company, they have to develop personal contacts with the officials who enforce the various regulations. Also, the managers have to stay very close to the top tax officials. Naturally, few managers can afford to sit in a faraway village and hope to cultivate friends in state and central cabinets and thousands of government offices. The private investors simply concentrate around the seat of the power. They bring capital and, thus, jobs to cities.

Each of these private and government workers, in turn, creates jobs for a few others. She sets in motion the so called multiplier effect. In other words, a few find jobs in selling her groceries or appliances. Many others survive doing such things as teaching her children, laundering her clothes, or showing her movies. Each of these employees in turn creates a few more jobs around him, in this case, in the already congested cities.

Another kind of multiplier effect also promotes the migration to cities. It's based on hope. Each person who has any kind of job serves as a role model to several other unemployed men and women from his village. He inspires them to come to his city and look for work. All this leads to a spiraling of population growth in cities.

Managers and investors in market oriented countries also have to deal with the government, but to a lesser degree. They can live far off and still thrive. A company near New York City, for example, can afford to stay 200 miles from Albany, capital of the state, and still survive. In other cities, too, the suburbs house a lot of industries. For the time being, relatively, a lot more economic power still rests in the hands of the individual. For this reason, the cities are less dense.

To the extent a country allows its people to move freely, overcrowding in its cities is directly proportional to the degree of concentration of economic powers in the hands of government. This is true even in the developed countries: Those with a high bureaucrat-businessman interaction are subject to similar demographic pressures. Despite Japan's healthy agricultural economy, for example, the cities are very overcrowded. To ensure protectionism, and to obtain export licensing, loans from the highly-regulated banks, and a host of other benefits Japanese investors do depend upon their government. They bring their industries, jobs, and people with them and choke cities such as Tokyo and Osaka.

Many argue that industries concentrate in and around cities because the latter happen to have the necessary infrastructure. Usually, however, the development of infrastructure goes hand in hand with industrialization and consequent population increases in cities. Also, electricity is generally produced far from cities. It's brought to cities only because the officials decree that it should be brought there.

Adding to all the misery is the heavy pollution in India's cities. Levels of air contamination in Delhi are higher than the limits of human endurance, as specified by the W.H.O (World Health Organization). In this capital city, the incidence of respiratory diseases is twelve times higher than the national average. Just as in most other cities in the world, motor vehicles are the major culprits. The Delhi Transport Corporation happens to own a few of them. A mere eighteen percent of these state-owned buses conform to the prescribed standards of emission. The rest merrily add on to the pollution. (173)

It seems that the leaders in Delhi, who try to control every facet of human activity in their country, are unable to even control the quality of air they, themselves, breathe.

Nor can they control the quality of food they and their countrymen eat.

In 1984, a multi-center study sponsored by the U.N. Food and Agriculture Organization (FAO), analyzed 1,500 samples of cereals, pulses, milk, oil, and meat from different parts of the country. It found that almost all the samples were contaminated with DDT (dichloro diphenyl trichloroethane) and BHC (benzene hexa chloride). In as many as twenty-five percent of the samples, residue levels crossed the W.H.O.'s safety limits. According to the Industrial Toxicology Research Center (ITRC) in Lucknow, one third of the sweets tested contained dyes banned by the government. (174)

Farmers use DDT and BHC to protect their crops. These chemicals are cheaper, easy to handle, and attack a wide range of pests. Nevertheless, owing to safety concerns, governments in many other countries have altogether banned these chemicals. For Indian politicians, however, to show high yields and, thus, how successful their *green revolution* is a much higher priority. Owing to their efforts, in the past three decades (1960–90), consumption of pesticides such as DDT and BHC has risen ten-fold. K.N. Mehrotra, president of the Society of Pesticide Science, points out, "The government is the largest peddler of this dope." Hindustan Insecticides, a public sector company, manufactures all the DDT that's being used in the country. This firm along with another public sector company, Hindustan Organics, also accounts for a sixth of the BHC production. (174)

There are alternatives to these chemicals. Switching to relatively safer malathion, however, costs six times as much. Not only is the government strapped for funds, but what little it has it spends on art exhibits and goat breeding schemes. And thanks to its price ceilings and land reforms, Indian farmers—unlike their Western counterparts—make too little to spend that kind of money on safer pesticides. (174)

Use of these pesticides has far-reaching effects. Milk taken from fifty lactating women has shown DDT and BHC residues four times higher than in other participating countries. Only milk taken from Chinese women has had higher residues. Mehrotra says, "We are not only slowly poisoning ourselves, but jeopardizing our future generations too." (174)

"Cut trees and give votes."

With this message, Amarsinh Chaudhary, then a forest minister, hoped to win in the assembly elections in 1985. Thus emboldened, tribal members and timber contractors plundered the forests. Soon the forestry officials ran into stolen wood worth 170 million rupees. Only then the story became public. Officials estimated that this loot represented only a third of the total wood harvested. A few of them complained that Chaudhary had pressured them to look the other way. Chaudhary denied the allegations. He contended that the trees had been chopped down after the elections. Subsequent investigations, however, revealed otherwise. And most tree felling had taken place in his constituency. (175)

The government owns huge pieces of land in this vast nation. This includes many precious forests. As a result, politicians and bureaucrats get to decide who can use these forests and how they can use them. Just as they have done with other public properties, many officials barter these natural resources for votes and money. All-around corruption and the decimation of law and order have turned out to be disastrous for the environment too.

Nevertheless, it is not tree felling or even poisons in food, but government's plans to build two giant dams over the river Narmada that has launched a credible environmental

movement in India. The protesters are fired up for a good reason. When completed, the project will make Narmada valley
extinct. One of the dams will create the largest man-made lake
in the world. It will submerge 100,000 acres of prime teak
forests and 110,000 acres of cultivable land. The second dam
will submerge another 100,000 acres of land. Environmental
damage from the project is estimated to be around 390,000
million rupees. More importantly, the project will displace
200,000 Indians from 500 (some of which are 1,000-year-old)
villages. Said a villager, "No government has any right to make
us homeless." (176,177)

The architect of this despotic irrigation policy was none other
than Jawaharlal Nehru. In his speeches, Nehru hailed the irrigation dams as modern temples of India. Just like the ancient
kings who had built the real temples, he and his successors
lavishly spent taxpayer's funds on their dreams. In the four decades before 1990, they threw 337,710 million rupees at these
projects. (178)

These projects had the potential to irrigate and increase food
production in about 200 million acres. Unfortunately, however, officials brought their usual vigor and commitment to
these projects and made sure that this centrally planned strategy would fall far short of its targets. Compared to the expected 2,024 kg., due to waterlogging and siltation, each acre
would yield, on average, only 688 kg. of food grains. Also,
many farmers were left hanging in the mid-air. C.G. Desai, an
adviser to the Planning Commission, said that because of bureaucratic bungling, "We are not able to tell a farmer whether
his land would come under irrigation or not once the project is
complete." (178)

These irrigation dams, however, yielded definite results in
one area. They played havoc on the environment. They had
invariably created huge lakes that would submerge forests and
even cultivable lands and displace many from their villages.
The damage might have been worse except that, by 1989,
182 projects remained incomplete. The villagers and the environmentalists should probably tell the officials, "Thanks for all
the incompetence." (178)

Despite its record, the government remains steadfast in its commitment. By 2010, it plans to spend an additional 1,000,000 million rupees on the projects, and irrigate 279 million acres. Whither the villagers and the environmentalists, the government has a sacred mission: "to feed the hungry." (178)

Few can disagree with this goal. Experts such as I.P. Abrol, deputy director general of the Indian Council of Agricultural Research, however, claims that there are better ways to raise farm yields. They point out that tube wells and other traditional irrigation systems are both environmentally safe and economical. According to one estimate, it costs about 3,200 rupees to irrigate an acre through the traditional systems. To do the same with a large project, it takes about 16,200 rupees. This figure does not even include the cost of draining water-logged land—estimated (by the Central Soil Salinity Research Institute) to be 10,120 rupees per acre. (178)

A few environmentalists from the West attribute the ecological disasters of the communist countries to the absence of feedback from the public. India, however, is a fairly open society. Its planners certainly hear from their detractors. Victims of their strategies have the right to protest. The officials, however, mostly ignore all the complaints. They can afford to. Each project displaces only a few thousand people whose clout is no match for the official machinery. Using their control over the broadcast media (see chapter 9), the officials promise "to feed the hungry" and rally the rest of the country behind their plans. All this shows how, in any country, a simple majority rule can easily perpetuate tyranny, unless of course there is a heavy emphasis on individual rights,

Few Indian politicians care about individual rights. They love to switch on irrigation dams. It is much more sexy than to open a tube well, or even two. The huge dams are their Pyramids. As for the irreversible ecological damage and trampling on human rights, did pharaohs worry about such minor details?

The politicians also found it to their advantage to hop on the bandwagon of the environmental movement that had swept the West. "To protect the environment," they could pass a few more restrictions on the industry. They elevated the department of environment to a full-fledged ministry. To provide a single focus for environmental issues and to plug loopholes in the existing laws, in 1986, the government passed an Environmental Act. (179)

Nevertheless, *friends of the Earth* have few reasons to jump with joy. The environmental ministry functions just like any other governmental organ. Sunder Lal Bahuguna, a leading environmentalist, claims that instead of doing any useful work, the department uses much of its funds to meet its wage bills. He even feels that it should be closed down. (180)

Notwithstanding, on occasion these environmental officials truly earn their salaries. They come up with fantastic ideas. Under the exhilarating influence of one of those creative flashes, forestry officials in (the state of) Andhra Pradesh, decided to ban, of all the things, rearing goats. They simply wanted to keep goats away from the seedlings that they had sown to grow forests. What about those who eat meat? No problem. They should grow rabbits and eat bunny meat instead. (181)

At this point, I must confess that I have met few rabbit eating Indians. Besides, this plan might not protect the tender seedlings yearning to become trees. You see, rabbits, too, like to eat these seeds. And they breed faster than goats. (181)

If all the bureaucrats do is to come up with such slapstick schemes and pay themselves to do nothing, that is great. Unfortunately for the country, however, the new environmental laws vastly enhance their control over many projects. In keeping with their time-honored tradition, officials use their powers to the hilt. By 1988, the ministry held up as many as 115 big and small power, mining, chemical, and steel projects. It bombards managers of the various industries with endless queries. It buries them under layers and layers of regulations. It delays these projects and increases the costs. (179)

Ironically, these environmental cops try to strangle many public sector companies also. This leads to a few turf battles between the various departments. Officials from the environmental ministry, who can always ignore the private investors, have to defer to their colleagues from the public sector industries and powerful politicians. In other words, politics, rather than environmental concerns, drives the government to act. That troubles Anil Agarwal, an environmentalist. He is worried that, with their political influence and promises of later actions, managers from the public sector might speed up the clearances and open industries which might greatly add to the pollution. What if the managers fail to undertake the remedial measures which they have promised early on to obtain the environmental clearances? As much as they love to, the environmental officials will be unable to close down a factory that is already operational. The workers will kill them. (179)

The corollary is that any project can be delayed indefinitely before it's operational. And the poor men and women, who would have been employed but for these delays, will never know how the environmental ministry keeps them unemployed, poor, and miserable.

For Maneka Gandhi, the, then (1990), new federal minister for environment, politics and turf battles were hardly new. As widow of Sanjay Gandhi, Indira Gandhi's son, Maneka had a running feud with her mother-in-law and brother-in-law, Rajiv Gandhi. She worked for the anti-Congress(I) national front which ascended to power in the 1989 elections. She joined its Central cabinet as a minister for environment. True to her reputation as the first *green politician* of India, Maneka, announced that the government would set up special "environmental courts," designed for "speedy disposal of environmental cases." (182,183)

She also mixed her militant environmentalism with the enormous powers of the government of India. Maneka armed the Environment Protection Act with harsh penalties for offenders. The law was so heavy-handed that she herself called it the "Hail Hitler" act. She also followed some of the great Fuhrer's tactics. She demanded that the chief minister of (the state of) Rajastan should either provide funds for her pet project, a bird sanctuary, or forget about a fertilizer project in his state. She came down even harder on private industries. Combining the roles of prosecutor, judge, and enforcer, she threatened to cut off electricity to tanneries near the city of Kanpur, unless "they stop polluting the river Ganga." (183)

Many admired her efforts, especially those to educate the politicians. God knows how tough that is. Maneka, however, gained a reputation for abrasiveness. By erecting obstacles to such projects as building hospitals, she angered the public. She also hindered the political objectives of her colleagues. In the process, she lost their support. Her clout diminished to the point that she was unable to stop such environmental disasters as the Narmada Valley Project and Tehari dam (in the state of Uttar Pradesh). Biju Patnaik, the chief minister of (the state of) Orissa, ignored her instructions to cancel the lease granting seventy acres of land—previously reserved for a wildlife sanctuary—to Oberois' East India Hotels Ltd. Tens of millions of rupees allegedly changed hands in this deal. As far as Patnaik was concerned, Maneka Gandhi had no business being in his way. (183,184)

The innate desires of the politicians to do whatever it takes to get reelected and of the bureaucrats to do whatever it takes to get rich render many laws, including the environmental ones, impotent. As a matter of fact, the officials turn the environmental movement to their benefit. They simply use it to grab a little more power and, of course, more money.

Naturally, the high officials have little problem brushing aside those who try to chip away their power. To tame Maneka Gandhi, her party leaders appointed Nilamani Routry as an environment minister with a higher cabinet rank. (183)

Greens from the West have inspired the likes of Maneka Gandhi. Few, however, can ignore the levels of pollution that haunt the cities in the developed countries. Naturally many otherwise market-oriented thinkers believe that the industry is unable to police itself. Environmental activists know a thing or two about such concerns. They transform these feelings into phobias, rally the public behind their causes, and by and large, attempt to increase the power of the state. As far as these Greens are concerned, the private sector is the source of all pollution and the state is the white knight that will save the ailing Mother Earth.

*Glasnost*, however, rained on their parade. It revealed what an all-powerful state could do to the environment. Communist planners largely ignored the environmental impact of their policies. At best, they were preoccupied with the increased production goals; after killing incentives and, thus, engineering shortages, they had to do something to increase production. At worst, they couldn't care less about the environmental concerns of their people. As holders of the truth, these former *peasant guerrillas* answered to no one.

More importantly, in the absence of free competition, state-owned industries in the communist world became highly inefficient and, thus, highly polluting. To produce each unit of the GNP, these socialist countries used fifty percent more energy than their free market counterparts. Even the most rabid Green has to agree that the generation of extra energy adds to pollution. To beat their competition, on the other hand, companies from free market economies have to be efficient. They have to conserve. After the oil shock of 1973, for example, to keep their costs down, many companies such as 3M (and all the individuals who pay their own energy bills) have taken a lot of measures to save energy. As a result, between 1973 and 1989, even though the U.S. economy has grown by fifty-four percent, in real terms it has increased its energy consumption only by nine percent. (185)

Besides polluting the Soviet Union, the inefficient production methods have turned eastern Europe into an environmental basket case. Emission levels per square mile are almost seven times as high as in the U.S. The air has become so dirty that it accounts for one out of every seventeen deaths in eastern Europe. In Czechoslovakia, seventy percent of rivers are heavily polluted. Forty percent of all sewage is untreated. In Poland, the government declared five regions as ecological disaster areas. Sixty percent of food from the Krakow region was unfit for human consumption. So was ninety-five percent of water in Poland's rivers; fifty percent of this water was unfit even for industrial use. People living in Bulgaria, Hungary, and East

Germany have their own stories to tell. After the reunification, West Germany hopes to give a nice bath to its cousin from the East. To clean up the east German environment, West Germany plans to cough up $600 million. (186,187)

Many environmentalists agree with such plans. They want the Western taxpayer to foot the bill to cure environmental problems all over the world. The Greens demand that their governments not only use force to vanquish the *environmental villains* in the West, but also shove similar statist solutions down the throat of the third world. The activists contend that the third world governments should acquire more powers and further destroy individual rights, especially the property rights.

This presents a problem or two. Most third world governments have more powers than they should have in the first place. These environmental regulations only help to further strengthen the hands of the ruling politicians. The last thing *Mother Earth* needs is for her precious resources to be placed in the hands of the uninterested and unaccountable bureaucrats and politicians. To enhance their status, they will gladly sell her to the highest bidder. The regulatory approach can also derail any liberalization program which, otherwise, can increase production, create jobs, and increase revenues for the government. The private and public institutions in the developing world desperately need the additional funds for, among other things, cleaning of air, water, and food.

Says Tatiana Zarharchenko, a Soviet attorney: "We can't resolve our environmental issues while we don't resolve our economic issues. Because real environmental protection needs a lot of money." (188)

# CHAPTER 7
## *Corruption,*
## *an Indian Dharma?*

"WE ARE ALL fish swimming in this ocean (of corruption)," concludes a character in a story.

This story is about an official who comes to a town (somewhere in south India) to investigate corruption by the principal of a local college. The official finishes his job and gets ready to leave for another town for a similar engagement. Finding himself without a seat in the train, however, this bribe-buster bribes the conductor.

Most every Indian can identify with the investigator. It's hard to miss comments such as, "we are ruled by scoundrels." Says an editorial in *India Today*, "Institutionalized malfeasance and misfeasance, graft and bribery are as familiar to Indians as a mother's bosom to her suckling infant." Kushwant Singh, author of *We Indians*, agrees: "In every profession—law, medicine, architecture, soldiering, engineering, teaching, arts, sports—dishonest outnumber honest." If an Indian claims that he has never given a bribe, you better think twice before you buy his used car. (189,190)

The minute you walk out of the airplane to visit the country, corruption stares into your eyes. The customs official, while tabulating the duties, surveys your luggage for a scotch bottle, (or, if he is a *god-fearing* teetotaler) cassettes, or watches. Corruption in India carries a language of its own that's full of rich words such as *the usual*, and *the weight*. A few use novel means to bribe. Recently, a voter attached to his ballot a twenty rupee bill and a note requesting that the money be distributed between the president, prime minister, election commissioner and the state's chief minister. Hardly a big fan of these guys, he pleaded in his note, "Please get my work done now." (191)

Ask Indians why their countrymen and women have become so corrupt so fast, most fall back on the old faithful: "It's their nature." Kushwant Singh declare, "We flatter our gods with prayers, bribe them with offerings…, and pay the priests to carry our expensive rituals on our behalf." He also chastises the old habit of offering gifts to kings. Singh, however, is too smart to ignore that kings everywhere have thrived on gifts, and rituals are as ancient as man. Like everyone else, Singh is plain frustrated and resorts to such self-denigration. (190)

Others try total denial: "The Congress party is just like the (river) Ganga. It is pure and can never be dirtied." Either this guy is smoking something illegal, or he is one of those totally dishonest Congress(I) politicians. Any bets? (192)

Quiet a few take the whole mess in stride. Says a film hero, famous for his patriotic movies: "Corruption has become India's Dharma [natural order]." (193)

Rajiv Gandhi performed a great service to India. He defrocked the myth that a smart, honest, and committed leader could clean up the system and make it work.

All along, this is one superstition most Indians have lived by. In editorials, letters to newspapers and private conversations, many sound wishful, "If only we have had a good leader…" They mostly wish for someone who could make socialism work.

For the country's problems, they naturally suggest a simple cure: A leader who can make the whole thing work "the way it's supposed to."

Most pundits agreed that Rajiv Gandhi was the one. Why? He didn't even covet the position. When his ambitious younger brother died in a plane crash, his grieving mother begged Rajiv to move into politics. Being a good son, he reluctantly obliged her. After the sudden demise of Indira Gandhi, his party men viewed him as their meal ticket. He became their natural choice. For a while, he even made them nervous. He lifted the country's spirits by declaring, "We [the Congress-I party] obey no discipline, no rule, follow no principle of public morality, display no sense of social awareness, show no concern for public well-being. Corruption is not only tolerated but even regarded as a hallmark of leadership." (194)

Only a Gandhi could say such things about the very people that had elected him as prime minister and get away with it. As far as Rajiv was concerned, he walked in with a clean slate. He owed few political debts. He made no back room deals. As the sole heir of the Nehru/Gandhi dynasty, he didn't have to. Media fell in love with this rebel with a great cause. It discovered in him a prime minister who was tough, smart, and open-minded. It enlarged the legend and sang his praises. He won big in elections and earned the mandate to turn things around.

Four years later, just before the 1989 elections, Rajiv reminisced, "I found when I tried to change the system, to push the system to deliver, I came up against blocks, vested interests which just wouldn't let go." (195) By then, this feeling that he had failed on most counts (see chapter 12) became almost universal. An obviously disheartened print media dumped on him. It talked of, "a return of wheeler-dealers and muscle-men to the ruling party, and the beginning of the end of the reformist process Rajiv had initiated in the winter of 1984." (196)

Rajiv himself manifested a new avatar. In the face of dwindling public support for his policies, to keep his position, he sought help from his party members—the same people that he had castigated before. He renominated eighty percent of the sitting MPs. He even claimed that Congress(I) was the only party that fought for the down-trodden, and it was the only party of principle. (194,196)

In short, the system had chewed, swallowed, and spat back a caricature of this former *Mr. Clean.*

Rajiv was hardly alone. To many before him, the system had done the same. As leaders go, few countries have kicked off with a better bunch. If good, decent, and selfless leaders could make socialism work anywhere, it had its best chance in India. After the British had left, Nehru, Patel, Rajaji, Kripalani, and thousands of other freedom fighters threw themselves at building a model nation. They were determined. They were honest. Naturally, the public rallied firmly behind them.

In due course, how such patriots have been replaced by the current crop of criminals is a story to tell.

This is a tale of human beings, a few extraordinary and many normal ones. It is about how they have failed to resist the lure of tremendous powers that have been handed to them in the name of planning and how, in spite of all the checks and balances, most have turned into tyrants, sycophants, and despots. It's about dispelling the notion that corrupt leaders just happen. It's the story of socialism everywhere. Certainly, it's the story of post-independent India.

It starts with Jawaharlal Nehru. With every one of his subatomic particles, this first prime minister of India loved his country. Even his worst critics didn't accuse him of corruption, graft, or laziness. As the legend went, he put in years of eighteen-hour workdays and pushed his agenda for the country. He delivered what he had promised—democratic socialism.

This meant that government had to make millions of economic decisions. An oxymoron, a saint-politician, would be in charge. He would erect a massive public sector and the second largest bureaucracy in the world; he would control the appointments for both; he would tax away most of the country's production and decide where and how all these funds would be spent; and he would decide who would have the rights to produce and who would enjoy the fruits of all this labor. At the same time, he would have to remain so detached that he would not abuse all these powers for personal gain. More importantly, without using force and by some mysterious means, this leader should make the rest in the government overcome their instincts to improve their lot and put other's interests ahead of their own.

In real life, politicians and bureaucrats brought to light the built-in contradiction in this policy. As far as they were concerned, industrial licenses or bus routes assured the investor business minus competition. Such goodies guaranteed prosperity. The officials saw nothing wrong in sharing the profits. After all, they were "only taking away from the rich."

One by one, they started to cash in on their abilities to bestow such privileges. For example, permits to export and import were issued on a selective basis, a fact not missed on K.D. Malaviya, a central minister. In 1963, he allegedly asked for a bribe of 10,000 rupees from a private company. In return, he would forward to the ministry of commerce and industry an application to import twenty million rupees worth of equipment from Czechoslovakia on a private barter deal against the firm's manganese ore. (197)

When this became public, however, Malaviya had to resign. That was because, during the early days, the abuse of power was neither as rampant nor as respectable as today. Some of it was even amateurish. For letting a government doctor accompany him during an election campaign, Pratap Singh Kairon, an ailing chief minister, took a lot of flack. Of course, his sons did engage in a few shady deals, but the money involved was peanuts, at least when compared to even the village-level politics of today. (197)

The corruption and nepotism which, early on, only infested a few *lucrative* economic departments such as commerce and public works, soon started to spread. The hitherto revered Congress Party saw its membership deteriorate in quality. In 1963, its president concluded, "Congressmen who were paupers in 1947 are millionaires and multi-millionaires." (190,197)

Many attempts were made to curb these tendencies. Mahatma Gandhi, himself, reprimanded T. Prakasam for accepting a donation of 50,000 rupees. Prakasam, an otherwise illustrious leader and a famous attorney, did so only when, due to his involvement in the independence movement, he was reduced to abject poverty. On a more formal note, government established a permanent Public Service Commission that was supposed to make appointments strictly on the basis of merit. To investigate the corruption, government also appointed a number of commissions. Kushwant Singh lists them: "The railway corruption inquiry committee [1953], the Vivian Bose commission [1962], the Santhanam's committee on prevention of corruption [1964], and Wanchoo committee report on black money [1971]." (190,197)

In due course, most of these commissions and the promises of investigations would be forgotten, thanks to new scandals. Their recommendations would collect dust in paper cemeteries. So would a number of *service conduct rules* and anti-corruption laws. During the regime of Indira Gandhi, for example, section 293-A of the Company Act banned all donations by private companies. With regard to enforcement, however, the 55 mile per hour speed limit on American highways had much better luck. In 1985, Indian government realized as much and lifted the ban on donations. (198)

These laws, committees, and, supposedly, the best-written constitution in the world failed against the combined power of the self-interest of the officials and unlimited opportunities they had to indulge it. It turned out that a system which largely depended upon the saintly behavior of its officers would only work for monasteries. Of course, there were those who ignored their self-interest and revolted against the corruption, but their numbers were small. Such officials were mostly ignored. Some even faced banishment to remote places. Out of fear, many more kept quiet. Their corrupt counterparts retired rich and content.

In due course, everyone learned his lesson. There was no point to be honest and end up poor. If you sealed your mouth, someone else would eat. Trends toward widespread nepotism and corruption accelerated. To get, and keep, positions of power and to enrich oneself, blessings from the top were indispensable. Sycophancy became another official *dharma*.

One of the Congress(I) chief ministers raised sycophancy to an art form. He coined the slogan: "India is Indira." (194)

"I don't want to know reasons. I want results," said M.S. Yadav, then the chief minister of (the state of) Uttar Pradesh. He demanded that villagers in his state be provided electricity for fourteen hours a day. (199)

The officials had a problem. They had limited power supplies. As such they couldn't meat this demand, but they were smart. So smart that they could teach a thing or two to King Solomon. They divided the villages into two zones. Each zone would get power for fourteen hours, but only every other day. Each, also, lay in darkness every other day. (199)

Politicians such as Yadav promise only because their words deliver—of course not the stuff they have promised, but votes for them. Besides electricity, they promise such goodies as jobs, cheap rice, and rents at controlled prices. Once in power, such politicians realize that there is not enough money to deliver even a few of the promises. They are unable to please even a sizable segment of the voting public. They realize that at any moment the angry electorate could abandon them in favor of those that promise more. Owing to this electoral insecurity, most politicians gobble up as much money as they can and do so as fast as they can.

Also, even if they want to, ministers who enter and exit at regular intervals have little time to gain expertise in their departments. They depend upon, and have no way of curbing, the ingrained corruption of the eighteen-million—strong bureaucracy. More commonly, for politicians the temptation has proven to be too great to resist. Whoever comes to power simply profit from the built-in channels of corruption that spread the money from the bottom to the top.

Eventually, in city after city, state after state, regardless of party or ideology, such plunderers have taken up almost all the space on the ballots. Instead of choosing from "Robin Hoods," voters mostly end up having to choose among these hoodlums. Lack of decent voter choices further emboldens the politicians. Each points his finger at the next one and robs at an accelerated pace and each day adds to the number of stories of corruption that fill most magazines, newspapers, and private discussions.

In (the state of) Assam, for example, to help two hundred thousand farmers hurt by floods, the government established a potato seed project. It seemed that the officials were just like the rest of us. As long as someone else was paying, they didn't mind buying the seeds at double the market price. The media and voters, however, failed to appreciate this generosity. After many complaints, when a legislative committee investigated the affair, it found out that money had been doled out to many fake suppliers. Barely a half dozen of the twenty *suppliers* were in existence and none had prior experience in dealing with potato seeds. They were so well connected that most even refused to divulge their fathers' names. (200)

These suppliers were hardly the first ones to benefit from influential fathers or fathers-in-law. On any given day, one can just walk into any public institution, pick any number of employees at random, and bet all the money one has that close to one hundred percent of them have had connections to the elites. On such a pick, it's hard to lose. Only those who have found a way to return favors to top officials fill the thousands upon thousands of government jobs that open up each year. The giant public sector with its banks, telephone services, steel companies, and car manufacturers is there for their picking. Besides the jobs, as a group, the well connected Indians obtain lucrative contracts to do business with these public sector industries.

Even if a businessman is crazy enough to value his freedom and forego all the profits that such contracts might bring him, he still needs help from the above to run his private business. Otherwise, he will go under. Says a cloth dealer, "Today no one can do any business without keeping these *dada* [criminal type; my emphasis] politicians in good humor. If this comes through paying some money, we don't mind." (201)

Soon, most say, "Why not?" To them, in terms of immorality, to break the law and get away once or do so a million times is the same thing. Besides handing out bribes, many a businessman might keep a car or two ready for the officials, and let them use his private guest house. Instead of striving to compete in the marketplace and please the consumer, these businessmen spend more time in the corridors of power and gain exclusive licenses, cheaper (government-owned) land purchases, import credits, and special tax concessions. The more they reap handsome rewards from this behavior, like the most of us, the more they repeat it.

To some, the possibilities to enrich themselves seem endless. These aggressive businessmen go beyond all the petty bribery. They maintain a host of bureaucrats and politicians and even a political party or two on a retainer. They go for all the insurance they can get their hands on. Said a partner in one of these (peanut) oil companies, "We do provide funds to all political parties out of compulsion. We don't know who will come to power tomorrow." For this company it was money well spent. Manoharsinhji Jadeja, a civil supplies minister, tried to implement a few stiff measures against it. That proved to be a mistake. He was denied his party's ticket to contest in the next election (in 1985). (202)

With friends in high places, such businessmen, for the most part, benefit from every law, rule, and policy, including those that cover the piecemeal *liberalization* (see chapter 12). In one of its budgets, for example, the government slashed excise duties on polyester staple fiber and polyester filament yarn. Reliance corporation made out big on these concessions. This was, however, hardly the first time that this influential company profited from the government and its benevolence. Recently, cumulative savings from all such special concessions far exceeded the company's annual profits. (203)

Later on, Reliance faced an investigation for evasion of taxes close to 1,200 million rupees. It had allegedly undervalued the

yarn to avoid these whopping duties, but there was no problem. The collector of customs, K. Viswanathan, cleared it of
any wrongdoing. He had to. At that time Congress(I) was in
power, and its politicians liked the owners of Reliance very much.
Naturally the anti-Congress parties felt little love for the company. After the 1989 elections, their new government transferred Viswanathan. All of a sudden, his colleagues found the
courage to question his judgment. (204)

Besides Reliance, this administration also went after many
other friends of Congress(I), such as the Hindujas—billionaire
Indians living in Britain. Politicians know that, with all the rules
on the books, each and every company will have at least a few
skeletons in its closet. They first raid the target, usually an unfriendly company. Only later do they look for violations. They
very selectively apply justice and remind those with money
who's in charge. In the end, such officials not only gain bribes
but also votes for "being tough on rich businesses." (204)

Naturally, "being tough" on outside investors sells even better to the voters. As a result, foreign businessmen face even
closer scrutiny. To start their businesses and conduct them prof-
itably, just like local businessmen, these foreigners find out that
they have to end up on the right side of the ballot box. They,
too, get embroiled in the country's politics and, eventually, its
scandals. Reporters for *The Statesman* recently dug up information detrimental to the Sumitomo Corporation of Japan. To
obtain an order of steel pipes worth 1,000 million rupees from
the Oil and Natural Gas Commission, a public sector concern,
the company allegedly paid commissions worth 66 million rupees. Sumitomo handed this money to a corporation owned
by wife and mother-in-law of Lalit Suri, a noted businessman.
Sumitomo hoped that, through his friend and ex-tenant, Satish
Sharma, Suri would do its bidding. (205)

Satish Sharma, a pilot, had other friends besides Suri. One of
them was a famous ex-pilot, Rajiv Gandhi. When questioned
about a marble-tiled swimming pool in the house of this friend
and adviser, Sharma, Rajiv gave a statement that soon made
him the butt of many jokes: He declared that it was normal for
pilots to possess such pools. Unfortunately for him, most Indians

knew that few pilots had big enough salaries to afford such luxuries as marble-tiled pools. (205)

After the 1989 elections, V.P. Singh's government started to look into the Sumitomo affair. It opened up the Coke and Pepsi deals. The government also started to investigate the now famous Bofors deal and the purchase of HDW submarines from a West German company. The new rulers promised that the "guilty" companies would be barred from India. (206)

Managers of private companies, however, are in business to earn profits, not prison terms. Quite a few know where they are welcome and drift there. The others, who invest in the country, serve their masters. They pay *the usual* to the bureaucrats and ruling politicians. If a new party comes to power, in due course, they buy off its members too. As a result, even though one hears the initial rumblings of investigations, seldom do the final quakes ever happen.

If there was ever a sure-fire formula to build a corrupt society, this was it. Thanks to its dynamics, what had happened in post-independence India was all but inevitable. It was as predetermined as the occurrence of an eclipse. Besides corrupting all those *Mr. Cleans* who came to power, these dynamics replaced the honest ones with the current crop of crooks who, rather than waiting for the offers of bribes, would even approach the multinationals for *the usual*. Said an executive of one foreign company, "In an election year, particularly, we are deluged with requests and demands for funds." (207)

When I was young, children of the prohibition officials had all the neat stuff. Even a low-level inspector in that department made more money than a high court judge. When such massive corruption and bootlegging caused a great deal of stink, governments in many states dropped the prohibition.

The politicians went on to regulate alcohol consumption and discovered another gold mine—the liquor industry. In (the state of) Karnataka, for example, such control meant taxing liquor at each of the several stages of its journey—breweries to distributors, to wholesalers, to retailers and to consumers. To evade all these taxes, the owners followed a simple shortcut; they smuggled liquor out of their breweries to the retailer. The profits involved in the operation were mind-boggling. The manufacturing cost of a case of liquor was close to 100 rupees. After all the levies had been slapped on it, the case was sold to the consumer for 700 rupees. A case of smuggled liquor also fetched 700 rupees. It, thus, yielded a net profit of about 600 rupees, or 600 percent. (208)

To carry out their illegal activities, these owners paid an estimated one million rupees a day as bribes. In response to many complaints, in 1989 the government announced a new policy: It would purchase the liquor from the companies, sell it to the consumer, and put the middlemen out of business. By doing so, it hoped to earn 500 million rupees a year. There was, however, one slight problem. Besides getting into the grimy business of selling a product which it had banned until recently, the government would have to depend upon its corrupt machinery to implement the new law. (208)

Of course, politicians seldom come out and say, "give me powers so that I can enrich my family and friends." Instead, they cite their great goals. They appeal to the values and morals most people hold close to their breast. They say, "We all hate alcohol and what it does to our poor people. I will control its usage and help build a moral society." They go on, "Just like you, I love equality. I will use the government and its laws to take from those who have and pass it on to have-nots. Don't worry about orphaned children. I will take care them." And, "On your behalf, I will decide who are the right people to run all these orphanages and liquor companies."

In (the state of) Tamil Nadu, the government handed out licenses for manufacturing and distributing liquor. Then the chief minister, M.G. Ramachandran (M.G.R.)—an extremely popular movie star turned more popular politician—awarded the retail outlets to his favorites, each for a paltry sum of 20,000 rupees. If, instead, had it auctioned the privileges, the treasury would have made 250 million rupees. From such an open auction, however, the authorities would have gained only a sore throat. (209)

Why did the opposition parties in this state condone all this nepotism and corruption? The rumor on the street was that everyone who had paid bribes to the ruling party members was advised to pay to the opposition legislators also; too bizarre even for the country's standards.

Few thought that it was bizarre when, recently, a college sold 30,000 application forms for just 500 seats. (210)

Just as in other countries, students in India know the financial benefits higher education brings them. Moreover, to most Indians a seat in any engineering or medical college represents the only shot at decent income. To get in, they compete intensely. Each batch of students works harder than the previous one. Standards and scores keep rising.

For the majority, however, these high scores lead to nowhere. There are never enough colleges to accommodate all these millions of bright young men and women. This mismatch, combined with a lack of jobs for high school graduates—rather than an unbridled thirst for knowledge—has engineered a phenomenal demand for college seats. (210)

To help their children get ahead, many parents are ready and willing to do much more than assist with the homework and pay for private tuitions. For these seats, they will gladly pay thousands of rupees. Students know what's going on. Well before they leave high school, they receive a hands-on training on how to survive their adulthood. On occasion, the help they receive gets creative. In a school from Raipur district, for example, parents of some one hundred students entered into a *contract* with the headmaster: At a cost of 1,000 rupees per brain, the children would be allowed to cheat in the exams. Unfortunately, however, the inspectors showed up uninvited and doomed the plan. To get back their deposit of 500 rupees (per student) from an unwilling headmaster, the parents approached police. (211)

That they could go to police to get back the bribe money shows the extent to which corruption has become a norm for the country. Naturally, very little of this surprises most Indians. They have come to accept corrupt officials as a fact of life. One might even hear compliments such as, "He might take *the usual*, but at least he does the job." Such an attitude further lowers the standards by which the public gauges its officials. It broadens and deepens the corruption some more. It leads to a sort of downward spiral of expectations, to the point that most officials regard each law, regulation, or official clarification as a way of earning money to get their daughters married off, send their sons to good colleges, build houses, or fund retirement plans. Even matchmakers ask how much the prospective groom makes "over and above."

If he was alive today, Shakespeare would love the irony when, sometimes, the bureaucrats, themselves, become the victims of the power-money game. On many occasions, they find themselves at the receiving end of the so-called *transfer business*. What happened recently (1988) in Madhya Pradesh illustrated how this business would operate and bring untold rewards to top politicians and bureaucrats. In less than four weeks, some 30,000 of the state's 600,000 government employees received transfer orders. In a matter of a few days, one of them was transferred to three locations. Unable to pack bags and move at such rapid rates, most flocked to the capital city. They scrambled to find the middlemen, pay *the usual* to the top officials, and stall the orders. This maneuvering could get very expensive. According to one estimate, the market rates for arranging transfers or canceling them ranged from 5,000 rupees for a sub-engineer to 100,000 for a superintending engineer. Besides rank, the place of choice would also affect these rates. (212)

A few side industries also proliferated. Newspapers published these transfer lists. On occasion, for fifty rupees or so, peons at newspaper offices smuggled out copies of the list before the normal distribution schedule. Because of haste and conflicting interests, a few foul-ups did take place. For example, two people would show up for the same position. To prevent any confusion, the officials issued a clarification: The later the order, the more authentic it was. (212)

Was all this done out of ulterior motives? Not according to Arjun Singh, then the chief minister. While admitting to the active involvement of his party legislators in this transfer business, he came up with an excuse. Frequent transfers would prevent the bureaucracy from becoming "arrogant and insensitive to public needs." (212)

Two professors, who simultaneously got the orders posting each as the chairman of the department in which I later served as a resident, hardly fit this description. All they did was to *try* and get this job. After all the troubles he took, and possibly spending wads of money, each was determined to keep the post. Each occupied the chair (used literally) on a first-come basis. For their subordinates, they caused quite a few headaches and occasional comic relief.

"When one looks at the democratic systems of the US and the UK and compares it with ours, the greatest difference noticed is the precedence of national interests above party politics," laments an obviously exasperated Indian in his letter to the editor. (213)

Such misconceptions notwithstanding, in almost every country, the level of corruption is strictly proportional to the degree of involvement of the state in the economy. India's problem is that, at higher levels of government meddling, corruption increases by geometric proportions.

One after another, American cities that rival the third world countries in their social welfare policies have landed themselves in a similar predicament. In a (CBS's) *60 Minutes* interview, Coleman Genn describes how bad the situation has gotten in New York. He ought to know; besides being a school superintendent, Genn has worked as an undercover agent to investigate corruption in the city's school boards. According to his estimates, each year salaries of employees engaged in make-work jobs cost the taxpayer about one million dollars. Many of these workers have gotten their jobs primarily due to political patronage. It seems that close to half of the school board members are corrupt. Genn also claims that discrimination against Jews and Blacks is rampant. (214)

The scandal that has implicated many top officials in the department of Housing and Urban Development (HUD) also lays open the anatomy of political corruption. Citing great goals, such as providing houses for the poor, politicians unzip the taxpayer's wallet and scoop out his money. They hand it out to those with influence, such as building contractors. For a while, politicians who controlled the HUD funds did function within a few guidelines. Soon, they found a better way. They created a slush fund, albeit the legal kind. The committee members who controlled this fund enjoyed a lot of discretionary powers. They spent it on their pet projects which had little to do with housing the poor; a performance arts center in Newark, N.J. and a job retention program for sugar mills in Hawaii, for example. Showing how such programs are easy to launch but next to impossible to terminate, recently, despite all the scandals, the legislators have increased this fund by $28.4 million. (215)

Just like their colleagues from the third world, American politicians know the power that such politics of distribution can bestow upon them. Naturally they crave more and get the government deeper and deeper into the economy. In the case of government's guarantees for the savings and loan industry, for example, they have robbed both the present and future taxpayers. Quite a few, such as Charles Keating, Jr.—the chairman of American Continental, parent company of Lincoln Savings & Loan which failed, costing the taxpayer a lot of money—discover how beneficial it is to have a few legislators on their side. Between them, such favor seekers and their powerful benefactors make corruption inevitable. Regardless of their background and original intentions, very few can escape the lure. (216)

Says David Gergen of the *U.S. News And World Report*: *The pity is that the quality of people in office [U.S. Congress] today is higher than in the past—most are well educated, sensible, and honest—but they feel trapped by forces beyond their individual control. To stay in office, a lawmaker must answer to an army of lobbyists, fund-raisers, political consultants and party leaders, all far removed from people back home. (217)*

To pacify the public, the Congress has imposed a few limits on campaign finances. Quite a few American politicians, however, routinely find their way around these restrictions. For example, they derive support from many tax exempt and charitable foundations, despite the official non-partisan status of these organizations. The list of such groups include Cranston's voter registration groups, Bradley's Fair Tax Foundation, Rostenkowski's Charity Foundation, and The Dole Foundation. Such foundations and groups collect unlimited, unreported contributions from corporations and individuals. They use these monies to help their friends in the U.S. Congress get re-elected. As demonstrated in country after country, no such campaign finance laws, but an across-the-board limiting of the role of government, can prevent a typical politician from realizing his innate and supreme desire—staying in power forever. (218)

Notwithstanding Japan's economic success, its politicians, too, fit this mold. In the name of coordinating industrial production, they put in place a lot of regulations. They, thus, gained a lot of powers. They were free to bestow such favors as special licenses, tax breaks, and protection from the restrictive laws. The situation in the country was ripe for corruption. Small wonder that the Recruit scandal shook the foundations of the ruling party (LDP). (219)

Recruit was a relatively obscure company before it diversified into real estate and telecommunications, both heavily regulated fields. When the company ventured into these areas, at minimum it faced 150 regulations and special taxes. In matters such as zoning and building heights, the officials had Recruit at their feet. After taking considerable risks to expand, owners and managers of this upstart corporation faced two options: either win the obstructionist officials on to their side or fail. These businessmen spelled their relief in the form of bribes. They paid handsomely, sometimes in the company's stock. When Recruit went public in 1986, the stock prices went up by thirty percent, benefiting the original shareholders, including many officials. When the scope and the nature of these transactions became public, they effectively ended the careers of many politicians. (219)

The Recruit affair, however, is hardly an exception. It seems that in Japan most ministries and their bureaucracies serve only their benefactors—industries and special interest groups, not the consumer. Says Kenichi Ohme, managing director of McKinsey & Co:

*The ministry of Agriculture and Fishery actually is a ministry for farmers and fishermen instead of a ministry of provisions. The Ministry of Health and Welfare is a ministry of doctors and pharmaceutical companies rather than an organization dedicated to protecting the health of the people. The ministry of education is nothing but a cartel for licensed teachers, and certainly does not act on behalf of students. (220)*

In 1688, England must have been a great place for lawyers. They comprised three percent of its population. (221)

Most of them thrived because of a simple reason. There were too many laws. They were so many that Oliver Goldsmith, the famous playwright, said (in 1762), "There is scarcely an Englishman who does not almost every day of his life offend with impunity some express law..., and none but the venal and the mercenary attempt to enforce them." (221)

That for a few bucks every venal and mercenary politician will gladly sell refuge from the laws and cause corruption is easy to fathom. These all-encompassing laws also promote corruption by another way. They make almost everything illegal. By attempting to regulate every activity, economic and otherwise, they make an offender out of everyone who is trying to just muddle through life, much less to better his lot. Few have a choice in the matter but to break one law or the other. As a result, the distinction between those who offend the un-natural and unnecessary laws (which have little to do with the protection of the basic rights of citizens) and the criminals who thrash the natural and just ones (that are supposed to prohibit them from infringing on the basic rights, such as to life, liberty, and private property of other citizens) gets blurred.

In other words, whether one operates an otherwise safe busi-ness without a license or robs one's neighbor's house, it's the same. It matters little whether you sell alcohol to a willing con-sumer or beat up another person. The courts will punish you the same. Few differentiate between the actions of a private citizen who hides his property from the land reformists and that of the official who, for a few bucks, lets him do so. In general, everyone feels that everyone else is cheating and uses it as an excuse to do whatever he or she can get away with. The avalanche of laws overwhelms the public. Consequently, most people learn to accommodate to lawlessness and live with a culture of corruption.

Most Indians can relate to this scenario. They find it hard to tiptoe through life without offending some rule or regulation. For example, consumers instinctively know that they have a natural right to spend their hard-earned money on goods of their free choice, even if this stuff is produced in foreign lands. Due to protectionism, however, these goods are expensive in the open market, if they are even available. As a result, just about every Indian used to buy (before the recent reforms) smuggled goods such as VCRs, watches and that dire need, razor blades. Thanks to the price ceilings and rationing—an-other hallmark of the socialist economy—almost everyone also used to shop in the black market. I know how one feels when one does such clandestine stuff. One feels guilty or even dirty. Moreover, one feels like a hypocrite. One loses the moral cour-age to criticize others who break laws, even the just laws. When their officials extort businesses and take bribes or their police commit robberies, most in the country just look the other way.

When millions, who seldom infringe on others' basic rights (and by the standards of any civilized society qualify to be normal and decent) participate in these activities, they embolden the real criminals who trample on others' basic rights. If questioned about their crimes, the later simply shoot back, "Who's perfect?" As an example, they point to the millions who routinely bribe the train conductors or those who cheat the voracious taxman. Such illogic ignores the fact that every person who bribes the conductor loves to buy his seat by paying the regular price but can't do so, thanks to the government-engineered shortages and the powers the officials enjoy to cash in on the demand. As for high taxes, they themselves put a serious dent in a few important natural laws: If complied with, these taxes will confiscate most of what an individual produces or owns. Only a fool or saint will pay them. Kushwant Singh (of *We Indians*) points out that it's more profitable to evade taxes on 30 rupees than to honestly earn 100 rupees and that, when the marginal tax rate is 97.75 percent, net profit from concealment can be as much as 4,300 percent of the after-tax income. (222)

No less a person than Mahatma Gandhi arranged for government land to be given to his biographer, D.G. Tendulkar. (223)

On this piece of land—located in a great location in Bombay—Tendulkar built a bungalow. He made Mahatma look good by donating this real estate to Bal Kalyani, a voluntary organization devoted to the education and welfare of poor children. (223)

Notwithstanding the worthwhile end, the means by which he has gotten the land is based on the idea (a.k.a planned development) of ownership of huge tracts of land—many in prime locations—by government. Government itself, however, is owned by politicians and bureaucrats. After spending a lot of energies, and of course money, to get their positions, these officials view the power to release these lots for building everything from apartments to five star hotels as their just reward.

They have even given this process a nice sounding name—dereservation. (223)

And they love to *dereserve*. They make a lot of money and a lot more friends. In any case, to hang on to and gain from their positions, most officials are ready to dereserve their mothers. If necessary, a few will throw in their firstborn as a tip. In their world, even the gift from the *father of the nation* enjoyed little safety. With blessings from Sharad Parwar, then the chief minister of (the state of) Maharashtra, officials managed to subdivide the piece of land formerly donated to Bal Kalyani. They leased one portion to Angarki Cooperative Housing Colony Society to build homes for influential tenants. Why lease? It had a better ring than *sell*. The well connected beneficiaries hit the jackpot when they got the apartments at a fraction (one hundredth or less) of the market value. (223)

Trustees of Bal Kalyani went to court. The judge, who ruled in their favor, listed a few statements by the officials. Some of them even sounded like a "Bureaucratic Bill of Rights." They challenged the citizen's right to question such matters as government's allotment of land to its officials. As far as the officials were concerned, it was an "internal arrangement of the administration." (223)

For a very good reason, they called it an *internal arrangement*. All along they had used it to take care of their own. In Bombay, for example, government dereserved one of the most coveted pieces of real estate in the world. It allowed for building of four multi-story housing cooperatives to accommodate a few top bureaucrats (IAS and IPS officers) and politicians. Only a court order stopped the construction of another building meant for the present and retired politicians. Otherwise, the developers would have destroyed a hospital, police barracks, and a welfare center. (223)

Such land dereservation scandals are commonplace in every state of the country. The situation could have gotten far worse except that, occasionally, the courts do step in and prevent the officials from overdoing the dereservation.

But judges have needs too.

In 1985, Shekhar Gupta, a noted journalist, interviewed Chandrachud—a retired chief justice of the supreme court. Gupta inquired about the allegations that His Honor got a car out of turn[13]. Ignoring that there was a waiting list for these cars (which was why he was accused of bypassing the other potential buyers in the first place), Chandrachud explained, "Probably the company decided to allot cars on priority basis in order to boost their sales." (224)

He also talked about his other needs. He recommended that, to control corruption, each retiring judge should be allotted a house through the housing board. He reminded Gupta of his own housing application. (224)

Soon, justice Chandrachud realized his dream. The government provided houses for him and twenty-seven other sitting and retired judges of the Bombay High Court and the supreme court. First, it dereserved a few pieces of land in Bombay. On these plots, it built houses that the judges could lease by paying as little as 0.4 percent of the market value. A few such as M. Rahman—a reporter for *India Today*—called for moving the cases that challenged the dereservation to a high court in another state. If justices from the country's supreme court were involved, however, where could the plaintiffs go for appeals? To the Privy Council in London, perhaps, out of the pre-independence habit? (223)

For a while after independence, a majority of the judges tried to stay honest, but they, too, slowly got trapped in the culture of high officialdom. First, a few used police and the other officials to gain minor favors; to obtain rationed supplies, to get a private bus or two to make a special stop at their houses, or to attend movies without paying money.

Later on, the more malignant corruption plaguing the rest of the society started to eat away at the roots of the judiciary. Nepotism, casteism, and politics also heavily infested its institutions. E.S. Venakataramaih, a former chief justice of the supreme court, observed that in most (state's) high courts several judges had sons and other relatives practicing. A government report alleged that Ramaswamy, the chief justice of the high court in (the states of) Punjab and Haryana, had misused funds. Despite, he went on to become a supreme court justice. Said Soli Sorabji, the, then, attorney general of India, "The standard of judicial integrity seems to have fallen down alarmingly." Kushwant Singh (of *We Indians*) talked of high court justices who, to prolong their periods of service or to get promotions, would simply forge their birth certificates. During one of my trips, I learned that a bribe of 200,000 rupees could get one appointed as a county magistrate. (190,225)

Politicians compromised the judiciary in other ways. They appointed their favorites to various commissions and overseas jobs. Said a report in the *Illustrated Weekly of India*, "The nomination of Chief Justice R.S. Pathak to the International Court of Justice… has set the staid court rooms abuzz. Attorney General K Parsaran, former Chief Justice P.N. Bhagwati, and former Law Minister Ashok Sen, have come out strongly against the selection of a sitting judge for such a plum job." (226)

All this further compromised the checks and balances of the democratic process. Small wonder that the once-in-five-year elections turned out to be too inadequate to stem the tide of the natural tendencies that led to the massive corruption.

In no time, this led to the next stage: criminalization of politics. "There are several ways in which politics is criminalized," a report in *India Tribune* quoted a senior police officer from Bhopal, "But it begins from interference with routine police work by politicians. It may be related to delay in the arrest of an accused or the release of the accused on bail." (227)

The political machine shields the accused from the law enforcement apparatus and helps them to carry out their lucrative businesses, such as selling protection to those who cannot and will not approach the law enforcement officials. For example, the hooligans protect underground businesses and help to sustain the black market. Also, in many cities where the land prices keep increasing but the tenants keep hiding behind the rent control laws and refusing to either increase rents or vacate, landlords hire muscle-men to carry out evictions. Obviously that's illegal. The criminals can engage in this enterprise only when they have blessings from the top. Sometimes, for the would-be evictors, the politicians themselves provide what amounts to one-stop shopping. Says the report, "The local MLA [state legislator] is approached and he arranges for his goons to get the premises vacated for a reasonable fee." (227)

By failing to protect property rights and, thus, promoting underground economy, the legal structure has corrupted the various public institutions, including the law enforcement apparatus. Naturally many in the country believe that only crime pays. And they are correct. Following the ultimate destruction of property rights—nationalization of private holdings—for example, crime has especially paid handsome dividends to politicians and the mafia-type unions, they have controlled.

After a few coal mines in (the state of) Bihar were nationalized in 1971, for example, political involvement in the unions naturally deepened. For a long time, Bhindeshwari Dubey, a local politician, controlled the dominant coal union. Eventually his rivals, with blessings from the top politicians, split it into factions. They did so with naked force and shared in the control of this major public sector industry, Bharat Coking Coal, Ltd. (BCC). Dubey fought back. As the state's chief minister, in 1988, he launched a *mafia elimination drive*. He obviously targeted his enemies. Suddenly dons, some of whom had literally ruled the area for all these years, faced court cases and long jail sentences. And the media started to take note. (228,229)

Many of these criminals were once just fourteen-rupees-a-week laborers. By joining hands with politicians, in a few years, they turned into multi-millionaires. They had done so in a variety of colorful ways. They forced the workers to pay five to ten percent of their salaries to the trade unions. By terrorizing businessmen at gunpoint, these hooligans collected tolls. The latter cornered all the coal mine contracts and, in collusion with the officials, ran a job racket within the company. Allegedly, several hundred fake employees drew salaries from this state-owned company. Some of these impostors forcibly replaced the genuine workers and got paid under the latter's names. Also, just like their patrons in high places, these union leaders knew how to exploit the various laws. They distorted one company law which had allowed workers above the age of forty-five, especially women, to voluntarily pass their jobs on to their dependents. Suddenly, an estimated 10,000 women were replaced by their sons-in-law. There was, however, one minor snag. Very little of this massive replacement was voluntary. Many of these women had no idea that they were about to lose their jobs. Some didn't even have sons-in-law. (228,229)

When questioned about the fake employees, Suryadeo Singh, one of the union leaders, didn't bother to even deny the allegations. He claimed that his rivals had appointed more impostors than he had. (228)

For politically-well-connected criminals, looting the poor and the weak was only the first step in their climb up the social ladder. Soon, many became smart. They sought to make a living by methods that were a little less illegal. To this end, in return for renting their muscle power to politicians, these criminals won such goodies as government grants and transport permits. Using these privileges, they ran legal businesses and moved closer to the mainstream. Some did even better. They used their connections to infiltrate the government cooperatives and other profitable entities. Besides sharing in their profits, politicians used these musclemen for various electoral chores: to protect or steal polling booths or to intimidate opponents.

In (the state of) Madhya Pradesh, for example, successive chief ministers appointed members to a commission that administered a major developmental program and controlled seventy percent of the state's budget. Each chief minister sacked his opponents and appointed his supporters to the vacant positions. At one time, the newly appointed commission members included many criminals, including one, who had gone to jail and had thirty-two criminal cases registered against him. He apparently had been involved in rapes, murders, plunder, and disposal of corpses using captive crocodiles! (230)

The list of charges against the other commission members included gambling, murders, armed robbery, sodomy, and rapes (once in a state legislator's rest house). Very appropriately, the commission also graced itself with a convicted murderer. When this illustrious group met, their behavior was so unruly and insulting that the officers' association threatened to boycott. (230)

Finally, many such criminals took the next logical step. They eliminated the middlemen. Despite their police records, they entered politics. In 1989, for example, people with criminal records of hooliganism, murder, and kidnapping won berths in the State Congress Committee of Uttar Pradesh. Even prior to this appointment, few people were willing to testify against these mafiaesque members. These goons were so well connected politically that the law enforcement apparatus was impotent against them. They were widely feared. (231)

Brij Lal, a local police superintendent, tried to buck the trend. He arrested one such politician, Shrivastava, who was involved in forty criminal cases, including four murders. For his audacity, Lal faced an immediate transfer. An obviously dejected colleague of Lal said, "If Congress(I) has decided to give party posts to criminals then at least the law and order is beyond the DMs [District Magistrates] and SPs [Superintendents of Police]." The appointment of hooligans to top posts in their party also dismayed a few Congressmen. Said Raja Mohammed Amir Mohammed Khan, a local legislator, "If the party has opened its doors for such people, it is time for the saner elements to bow out." (231)

Balram Singh Yadav, a leader of the Congress (I) party in the state, explained why he let the criminals in, "If such persons are given responsibilities of a public nature, they will mend themselves." Notwithstanding Yadav's criminal rehabilitation program, the only mending such criminals liked to do was to rearrange the body parts of anyone who dared to stand in their way. From their positions they derive too much money and too much power to behave otherwise. (231)

It has gotten to the point that only very few of those who have no criminal backgrounds even think of contesting in elections and risk their lives and that of their loved ones. Says a reporter, "It can be said that there is hardly any Lok Sabha [parliament] member from [the state of] Bihar who has 'honestly' won elections in 1984." (232)

*The India Tribune* quotes a Lincolnite teacher: "We now talk of a government of the criminals, for the criminals, by the criminals. (232)

For the Amethi region, the eighties must have been a godsend.

Amethi happened to be Rajiv Gandhi's parliamentary seat. For returning him to this supreme legislative body, voters in this area fared quite well. Between 1980 and 1989, for example, the number of primary health centers went from twelve to thirty-six; that of villages with drinking water rose from twenty-eight to 1146; the number with electricity increased from 330 to 1254. Said a villager, "We get power 24 hours, the whole year." Today, fifteen big and 1,231 medium and small-scale industries grace this area. All trains, including the super-fast ones, stop at the town. (233)

In bribing voters with *constituent services*, Indian politicians are hardly unique. When compared to those from the advanced world, however, thanks to their enormous powers, Indian politicians can deliver much more. On anyone that helps them to win elections, these politicians lavish money, power, and influence that they have accumulated while in the office. Of course, if all this fails, they resort to direct action. In 1989, because of charges of ballot stuffing and intimidation of voters, the election commission ordered votes to be recast at ninety-seven polling stations in the Amethi area. (234)

In any event, winning a seat in the legislative body happens to be just a first step. To become the chief executive (of a state or the nation), one needs the constant support of one's colleagues in the legislature. Among other things, this involves dishing out a lot of money, jobs, lucrative contracts, and everything else one can get one's hands on. As N.T. Rama Rao—then the chief minister of (the state of) Andhra Pradesh—found out, it would also help to have a few plum posts to throw around. Recently (1989), Rao faced a revolt from within his party. Fortunately for him, he still controlled the candy jar. By appointing the dissenting members as the chairmen of the various state-owned corporations, this former movie star won them over. A reporter for *India Today* adds, "The wily Chief Minister's most winning move, however, was his promise of giving cheap government land to legislators for building houses." (235)

While Rao was putting out these fires, his nemesis, Rajiv Gandhi was hardly sitting on his hands. Rajiv was busy approving a multi-million rupee petrochemical plant in the opposition-ruled state of West Bengal. After delaying it for several years, Rajiv was simply trying to bribe voters in this state as a part of his efforts to contest in one of those general elections which, once in a few years, rocks India. These elections are noisy, gaudy, and, yet, spectacular affairs. Each one involves fighting over nearly a half billion votes. It decides who will inherit the giant machine and control its output. The whole thing boils down to a no-holds-barred contest. (236)

Each election gets more expensive than the previous one. There are 542 parliamentary constituencies in India. During the campaign, 50,000 vehicles each travel at least 100 km. a day for at least twenty days. The total fuel bill alone runs into tens of millions of rupees. Besides, to hire musclemen, shepherd voters, capture booths, rent megaphones, pay for posters and graffiti writers, and give directly to slum lords, politicians need a lot more money. In addition, during 1989 Congress(I) spent 400 million rupees to hire professional advertising staff—a hallmark of the eighties. (237)

The ruling politicians can easily raise that kind of money. Between the majestic Himalayas and the shining Indian Ocean, they own everything and everybody. Within six months prior to the 1989 elections, the Congress(I) government cleared twenty mega-projects (such as the petrochemical plant in West Bengal) that had been languishing for years. Total investment in all the projects: a cool 200,000 millions rupees. Alleged Rupa Chinai of the *India Tribune,* "Deals struck in the last few months, relating to sugar, edible oil, vanaspati (hydrogenated oil), and the diamond industry, the dereservation of plots in Bombay and the floating of mega issues, raise strong suspicions that Rajiv Gandhi government has been on a fund raising spree. The target, insiders say, was a whopping Rs.5,000 millions." (237,238)

The donors did quite well. Officials granted a few of them exclusive contracts for the importation of edible oils. When diamond merchants paid up, the authorities returned confiscated gems worth thirty millions and also stopped tax raids. Thanks to the dereservation of plots, the developers could earn 2,000 to 3,000 million rupees. In return for a billion rupees, officials allowed many companies to go public and float mega-issues. At a cost of tens of millions of rupees to the treasury, they exempted some of the new licensees from sales and purchase taxes. To accomplish all this in a short time, the ruling party moved with the zeal of an American real estate agent. It had every reason to. It hoped to walk away with three to five percent of all this money. (238)

Businessmen who help politicians around election time also earn a few intangibles. Without any fear of reprisals from the law enforcement apparatus, they can engage in all kinds of illegal activities. Says a reporter for *India Tribune*, "If their [private] vehicles are used for Mr. Rajiv Gandhi's rallies each time, which officer can ever ask them to follow rules? The trucks for the [usually staged] rallies don't come free. Some sort of a price has to be paid." (237,238)

More than any element, this marriage between politics and money-power totally compromised the law and order. From hawkers at the famous Taj Mahal and taxi drivers at airports to top industrialists, everyone pays *the usual* and carries on with whatever he is doing.

As to be expected, corruption has become such a natural order for India that any and all attempts to rid the country of it are resisted from almost all quarters. If, due to some sort of miracle, any of these attempts ever succeed, one can't imagine how many lives it will disrupt. Surely a major upheaval will follow.

"What was happening within these four crucial days was a replay of Indian Politics at its filthiest and grimiest. Money,

muscle, treachery, self-interest, blind ambition, and machina-
tions of two men…" Inderjit Badhwar and Prabhu Chawla, reporters from *India Today*, were simply talking about the national front of the anti-Congress parties which the frustrated
voters were using to replace the already-discredited Rajiv Gandhi
and his Congress(I) at the center. (239)

In early 1990, V.P. Singh, who succeeded Rajiv Gandhi as the
prime minister, decided to, once and for all, do away with corruption. (240)

His government introduced a bill in the parliament requiring appointment of a three judge committee—*Lok Pal* or,
People's Commission. Justices from the supreme court would
supervise its functions. This commission was expected to look
into allegation of corruption against prime minister or his council
of ministers. (240)

How a group of three people, however honest they are, can
cleanse a society so riddled with nepotism, corruption, and
criminal politicians is open to question. What if these supremos
decide to abuse their powers? Maybe another commission
consisting of God, Mother Theresa, and Superman's father will
supervise these supervisors. Maybe it will banish the bad guys
into outer space.

Out of desperation, and believing that the leaders who have
come up just happen to be corrupt and need someone to look
over their shoulders, many people go along with such quick
fixes. More importantly, what everyone is really acknowledging is that the normal electoral processes have failed.

They, however, have failed miserably for one simple reason
that has little to do with "lack of good leaders." Instead of allowing for the election of a few among their countrymen to
perform a few basic functions—which are so limited as to make
these leaders amenable to voter supervision—the founding
fathers of modern India have envisioned and created an all-
encompassing government and bestowed on its leaders

overwhelming powers. The earlier leaders have hoped that only saints will come up in the system, and that out of the goodness of their hearts these elected officials will place the interests of their countrymen ahead of their own. As to be expected, the whole system works just the opposite. It has created a situation in which, not only one has to be totally brain-dead to resist all temptation, but, also, even if one does so and stays honest, one will have been eliminated by those who use their powers and money to get elected. Such an honest person can not win elections in his back alley, much less his parliamentary district, state, or the nation.

Arun Nehru, then (after the 1989 elections) the minister of commerce, knew as much. Thanks to his new position, he controlled export licenses worth billions of rupees. He naturally had to distribute them to the satisfaction of everyone who had helped him along the way and, more importantly, everyone who would keep him there. (241)

The reporter of *India Today* says, "Nehru now has the task of deciding the new favorites, not an easy one by any means, since each constituent of the ruling alliance has a list of its own." (241)

---

[13]There was a long waiting list to buy cars in this shortage-plagued and protected economy.

# CHAPTER 8
## *A Country Breaking Apart at Its Seams*

DECIDING FAVORITES, OLD or new, came naturally to Indira Gandhi. Besides all the political experience she had gained from observing her father, Nehru, she possessed strong instincts. With a flair, she conducted the politics of redistribution. She was to the process what Zubin Mehta is to conducting an orchestra.

Indira Gandhi knew that in order to help her favorites—politicians, regions, or groups—she had to control the flow of capital. To this end, she nationalized many banks in the late sixties.

That suited Janardhan Poojary, a central finance minister in 1987, just fine. To improve the prospects of his Congress(I) party in the opposition-ruled (state of) Karnataka, he distributed 300 million rupees as loans through a number of these banks. The government routed 85,000 loan applications thorough *social workers*. Without collaterals or firm repayment schedules, it doled out the money. (242)

85,000 sounds like a lot of loans, but such programs help only a tiny fraction of the tens of millions who live in Karnataka.

Only those who are close to Congress(I) politicians (a.k.a. social workers) benefit from such handouts. The rest in the state
and the country wait for their turn, which seldom arrives. (242)

Naturally they get mad. Very, very mad. Time and time again,
their anger boils over. It rips the nation apart. So much so, an
editorial in the *Illustrated Weekly of India* describes the country
as, "a loosely knit nation unwinding itself and becoming a mean-
ingless tangle of states, groups, individuals…" (243)

It was not supposed to end like this.

After the British left, for the first time in its history India came
together under a single administration. Socialism would usher
in a new era of equality, uniformity, and social peace; these
common goals would unite Indians, who for a long time remained splintered along the lines of region, religion, caste,
sub-caste, and language. So hoped its leaders.

Unfortunately, however, their policies had the exact opposite effect on the national psyche. The restrictions that invariably came with their planning process made sure that very few
Indians would be able to take the initiative to earn a decent
standard of living. Being victims of this legal apartheid system,
the rest were left to pin their hopes on politicians and their
promises. To get elected, politicians dangled in front of the
voter everything from jobs, health care, cheap rents, and quality food to condoms. There was a slight problem with such
promises. They gave rise to expectations that were as genuine
and limitless as one's dreams. And few governments would
have the funds to satisfy everyone's needs, not certainly the
one in India with its stunted economy.

Unable to meet the unlimited demands of the voters, officials arbitrarily chose whom amongst the citizens would get
the handouts. On a few selected regions, they bestowed steel
factories and irrigation dams. Soon after his election as the
country's prime minister, for example, V.P. Singh picked (the
state of) Assam as a beneficiary, because its government

supported Singh. It would get a fourth oil refinery and increases in oil royalties by fifty percent. To establish a paper mill in Assam, Singh handed out a *gracious* grant of 660 million rupees. (244)

Besides confiscating the capital from all over and handing it out to their favorites, there's another way by which Central leaders such as Singh can decide the patterns of distribution of wealth and poverty. This has something to do with the excessive concentration of economic powers in the hands of Central government. It has to approve almost every economic decision in the states. Prinay Gupte, the author of *India: The Challenge of Change,* explains: "At present, more than 95 percent of all industrial output in India is directly controlled and monitored by the Central government—even small items like razor blades, gum, match sticks, soap, zip fasteners and domestic appliances cannot be produced without formal clearance from Delhi." (245)

In states governed by their political allies, the national leaders clear the licenses with a comparative ease and allow for economic growth and relative prosperity. Their countrymen, however, fail to understand such things as politics and ever-changing bedfellows. Most people get cynical. They suspect that, without *their own* people at the helm, their state or region will lose out in this game. Each time a new cabinet is announced, many an Indian reflexively looks for his own. He wants to know how many from his group are sleeping with the prime minister.

By having a political ally of the prime minister batting for it, a state might get more funds and licenses. How much good all this will do an individual, however, depends upon how close he or she is to this political ally and his friendly state leaders. These local officials have the same problem as the national leaders. The former seldom have enough stuff to give away to everyone. At everyone else's expense, they, too, satisfy only a few. The rest feel helpless. They blame their plight on discrimination. They feel that *the others*—usually those who speak a different language, or belong to a different region or caste—are benefiting at their expense.

Naturally, many in the country heed the calls for any and all agitations. They have little hope of getting a shot at decent life. They haven't got much to lose. They start to fight for a separate state. By having *their own* at the top in their brand new state, many hope to receive their "fair share" of jobs and everything else.

Within a few years after independence, these dynamics drove many to the streets and led to very turbulent times. The first successful mass agitation along these lines took place in the southeast. It was led by Potti Sreeramulu. For people speaking Telugu, he wanted a separate state carved out from the state of Madras. After he died fasting in 1953, Telugus were granted the first linguistic state: Andhra.

I was only a toddler then and was becoming a Telugu speaking person (according to my mother, very slowly). Ever since, I heard many explain why Telugus needed a separate state. They had to protect *their jobs* from "the dominant Tamils from Madras state."

Soon this trend became contagious. People from various regions in different states started to agitate for separate states. To avoid bloodshed, Nehru did what he had to do. He allowed for formation of quite a few states. What Nehru allowed for, however, was an increase in the number of states. His planning process was incompatible with transfer of real power—the economic kind—to the states. In other words, if the states enjoyed the powers to collect and spend large sums of money, where would he find the capital to build giant steel plants and hydroelectric projects or indulge in his favorite experiments such as the green revolution?

Unable to dole out such goodies to every state, region, district, and town, however, he and other leaders in Delhi had to play favorites. The more they did so, the more the states fought among themselves. They haggled over such things as irrigation dams and river waters. Even administrative units of the national railways had to be separated based on language and region.

Most people came out of these fights feeling like either losers or bigger losers. The universal disappointment soon spilled into elections. Politicians had a field day stroking these passions. They championed the cause of each diverse and unhappy group and built semi-permanent constituencies. As a result, during the sixties the opposition parties registered quite a few victories. They even gained the control of a few state governments.

Gorbachev knows by now that charisma can't put potatoes on dinner tables, but it brings hope to people and maybe votes to its owners. By virtue of the strength in his beliefs and his refined behavior, Nehru was certainly charismatic. At the same time, the anti-Congress parties lacked sorely in that department. More importantly, they failed to offer any viable alternative policy. Their linguistic or religious chauvinism was hardly a match for the ideological pull of Nehru. As a result, the Congress Party did retain its shaky control of the central government. Most every decision it made, however, pleased a few and angered many more. Soon it realized what every parent had known instinctively: It had the mandate to distribute, but not how to do it.

Agitations continued to rock state after state. Just about as surely as the seasons changed, unions, students, government workers and every other powerful group went on periodic strikes. At the expense of the silent majority, the more each group gained with its militancy, the more it helped the others to develop this agitation habit. To maintain order, Nehru had to use force. But his democratic ideals stood in the way. Also, he had to mediate between the fighting factions in his own party. Such meddling went against his grain. He hated to give up on his ideals such as federalism (in the political sense, of course). Owing to all these contradictions, Nehru wavered. His own countrymen perceived him to be weak and indecisive. Defeat in the 1962 war with China proved to be the last straw for this great man.

Indira Gandhi, who succeeded her father after a brief interlude, realized that her support in the ever-feuding Congress Party was very shaky. Repeatedly, its old guard challenged her authority. To gain control over the party, she had to fight. This she did with flare. She was also smart enough to learn from her father's predicament. She had few illusions about such things as federalism and democracy. As she saw it, she needed more powers to get the job done. Only by having her own puppets in the states could she push her economic program. With a heavy hand, she suppressed dissent within her own party and started to pick and choose the state and local leaders.

Rajiv Gandhi even bettered his mother. Between 1985 and 1988, in nine states ruled by his party, he changed fifteen chief ministers; one of the states went through three changes. Both these Gandhis wanted to make sure that no local leader would get entrenched in his position and pose a threat to their authority. To this end, they and their aides simply mastered the game of "political dissidence." (246)

The game plan was simple and repetitive. A member of Congress party would become chief minister of his state by doing two things. From a few of the aides closest to the prime minister, he would obtain blessings; the state leader would also bribe his co-legislators to support his bid. Even before or immediately following the swearing-in ceremony, his own party colleagues would launch a movement to dislodge the poor man or woman. They would make frequent trips to Delhi. They would try to win over the disgruntled legislators that had found out that the chief minister couldn't give every one of them a minister's post, or, at least, a board chairmanship. Most chief ministers—bless their hearts—tried to increase the numbers of both. But they failed to satisfy everyone. It was a physical impossibility.

Meanwhile, from the royal court of the Nehru-Gandhi dynasty, another aide—who had preferred an alternative candidate and lost—would be working to dislodge this chief minister. With a lot of help from the dissidents that had paraded to Delhi, he would convince the prime minister that it was time for a change. On a not-so-fine morning, the chief minister would find himself facing a delegation from the high command armed with a simple message: "Resign." In no time, he would become a future dissident.

Naturally, over the years, power gravitated to a handful of aides close to the prime minister. Chief ministers of states began to feel like puppets. Some of them publicly said as much. The people, who had agitated for and gotten their own state, found out how it felt to win empty victories. In the selection of their state's chief minister and his cabinet, their votes mattered very little. They were still ruled from Delhi. To protect their interests, they could ill-afford to trust the yo-yos that it had imposed on them.

Non-Congress parties exploited these feelings to the hilt. They maintained that only they could champion the local interests. They ran on the platform of injured pride and took away control of many more state houses. They, too, were hamstrung by the powers of the central government, but that suited them just fine. These anti-Congress leaders discovered a nice little scapegoat. They couldn't fulfill their promises because of "discrimination by the center."

They made alliances with each other and started to eye the ultimate prize of ruling the Central government. As to be expected, Congress fought back. To topple the opposition-led governments, its members pulled any and all tricks. How they did it and the way the opposition responded with a few dirty tricks of its own could form a legend by itself.

A lot of skill and street smarts go into playing this political football.

Congress(I) members possess plenty of both. To teach a lesson to N.T. Rama Rao, then an anti-Congress chief minister of Andhra Pradesh, and gain a vote or two in the process, in 1988, they picked a backward region in the state called *Rayalaseema*. A few Congress members from the region went on a hunger strike demanding more water for the region. They blamed Rao for "neglecting" this region. Rama Rao, despite his trademark saffron robes, was hardly a saint. He raised the ante. To embarrass Congress(I), then the ruling party at the Center, he dispatched a few members from his Telugu Desam party to Delhi. Protesting, "the central government's policy of stalling several crucial developmental projects for the state," they staged a demonstration. These lawmakers broke the security cordon and

invited reprisals from the police. In return for a few blows, however, they reaped a publicity bonanza for their chief minister.
(247)

This was hardly the first time N.T. Rama Rao locked horns
with Congress (I). Rao won on the issue of linguistic pride and
a promise of 25 kg. of rice to each of 9.6 million families with
monthly incomes of less than 500 rupees. He would sell them
the rice at a subsidized rate of two rupees per kg. To get his
bowl of rice, however, Rao had to go to the central government which first collected rice from the states and distributed
it among them. Rao claimed that, even though his state was
one of the top suppliers to the central pool, it was treated the
same as the others that did not contribute. He complained,
"The Congress (I) has mortgaged the interests of the people."
(248)

In reality, Rao never had enough rice to keep his promises.
He also had a problem curbing false income certificates and
thus keeping the list of potential beneficiaries short. Some of
these "poor families" owned television sets and refrigerators.
For all these reasons, he had to reduce the ration to fifteen kg.
per family. Congress(I) correctly criticized his impossible populist programs, but it, too, suffered from a credibility problem.
In the neighboring (state of) Tamil Nadu, it went along with an
expensive mid-day meal program by a friendly party. (248)

Naturally, all these claims and counterclaims confuse the hell
out of the voter who has few ways of verifying them. Recently,
for example, in (the state of) Mizoram, Congress(I) defeated a
regional party—Mizo National Front (MNF). The former claimed
that it had won based on a lottery scandal. Congressmen alleged that the ex-chief minister, Laldenga (of MNF), made a
lot of money by accepting bribes from agents who would conduct lotteries. To explain his defeat, however, Laldenga postu-
lated his own theory. He said that the Congress(I) won only
because it had rigged the election with the help of the
centrally-appointed governor. (249)

If, indeed, it had done so, this was hardly the first time that
it had misused its clout over the governor, the constitutional
head of the state. In theory, other than during times of crisis,

the governor should function just as a ceremonial figurehead. Many a time, however, Congress(I) used the governors to perform ceremonies of a different kind—funerals of the opposition-led governments. It deposed quite a few such governments that still enjoyed a majority in the legislature.

True to this tradition, Rajiv Gandhi deposed a state government in Naga Land. The high court, however, threw a stink bomb in his party. It ruled that the governor's report, recommending dissolution of assembly, was unacceptable. The opposition was hilarious. Said Vamuzo, president of the Naga Land People's Conference, "The judgment will help us, as the Nagas feel cheated." He went so far as to claim that Indian colonialism had placed the "Naga identity" in danger. (250)

Vamuzo knew what he was talking about. When the court decided that a popularly elected local government had been thrown out by such a cynical use of the constitution, voters in the state would feel further alienated. More than likely, the deposed leaders, such as himself, would become heroes. Despite their past sins, they would become the rallying points against the center. All this could fetch a lot of votes for the leader; much more than he could get by explaining to the *cheated* Nagas (or others) what he would do to improves their lives. *(250)*

Congress had a time-tested formula to combat such trends. To raise money and woo support in Naga Land, it hastily handed out government contracts to pro-Congress businessmen. (250)

In Naga Land, the judiciary stood in the way of Congress(I). In (the state of) Andhra Pradesh, even the judges lent a helping hand to the central government in its attempts to dismiss Rama Rao, the chief minister. A five-judge bench of the state's high court ruled that Rama Rao had abused his position on five counts and that the actions of his government on two other charges were arbitrary and illegal. (251)

The court's inordinate haste and timing made people smell rotten seafood. It handed down its verdict during the harvest festival, and that, too, on a Sunday. The judges moved this case ahead of 3,000 other public interest litigations. More importantly, even before receiving a few documents that they themselves had requested earlier, the judges made up their minds. (251)

When the stakes are so high, even acute human tragedies turn into political weaponry. After floods in Assam, Rajiv Gandhi toured the state and blamed the opposition run government for the magnitude of damage. The state government promptly reminded the press that, as the country's prime minister, Rajiv Gandhi controlled the purse and its strings. This logic played well with the locals. Rajiv faced protesters carrying placards against "discrimination by the Center against their state." (252)

Said a local politician, "The rural folk are now smart enough to see through the game. They are well acquainted with the politics of flood relief." (252)

In a couple of states, Punjab and Kashmir, this game of politicians trying to gain power by fanning the flames of mass discontent got totally out of hand.

Earlier leaders, such as Nehru, wanted to make Punjab a showcase of their Green Revolution, not a bloody revolution. The central government poured billions of rupees into this state. It built canals and dams and distributed fertilizers and good-quality seeds (developed by scientists such as Norman E. Borlaug of Rockefeller University). Owing to the high yields, farmers in Punjab prospered. (245)

Sikhs,[14] a majority in the state, on average did quite well. A few of them dominated industries such as road building. Many occupied important positions in the bureaucracy and military. To many Indians, the spectacle of a Pakistani general and his 90,000 troops surrendering to a Sikh army officer after the Indo-Pakistani war of 1971 still remains a fresh memory. (245)

Just as in other states, however, for each military officer, rich farmer, and road contractor, there were several who felt left out. Like most Indians, they, too, hoped to prosper in a separate state based on their own language—Punjabi. Akali Dal, a local party, picked up on these feelings. In 1960, it launched an agitation for a separate state. Many Hindus from Punjab suspected that in such a state Sikhs would dominate. To census takers, these Hindus claimed Hindi as their language.[15] This widened the rift between them and the Sikhs. In 1966, the central government finally formed Punjab with fifty-two percent of its population as Sikhs. In the neighboring Haryana, they composed five percent. Both of these states would share the capital city, Chandigarh. (245)

Many Sikhs felt disappointed. For them, this Punjab was much smaller than expected. They hated to share Chandigarh. They also feared a heavy migration of Hindu workers from the neighboring states. Such a movement could surely reduce Sikhs to a minority status in their own state. Meanwhile, due to such things as an increase in fertilizer prices, the Green Revolution started to fizzle out. Farmers no longer felt rich. Like their brethren elsewhere in the country, they charged that the government was paying too little for their crops. Many Punjabis also complained about the diversion of funds to other populous and vote-rich provinces in northern India. They had forgotten that, during the Green Revolution, Punjab had received a lot more money from the rest of the country. Who says that we block off only painful memories? (245)

They could have directed some of the anger toward *their own* in the state government. Like most in the country, however, these Sikhs knew who held all the economic strings. For example, Punjab *exported* seventy percent of its cotton and sixty percent of the molasses for processing to other states. The reason: The central government refused to clear licenses to construct the plants in this state. (245)

Such restrictions on investment stunted the economy. They choked the growth that was badly needed to absorb the increasing numbers of educated Sikhs. Many of the Sikhs felt hopeless. They naturally became much more receptive to the charges that the center, dominated by Hindus, discriminated against them. Their religious leaders, who were alarmed by the increasing "Westernization" of Sikhs, also joined in the chorus of discontent. (245)

To increase its appeal to the already unhappy Sikhs, Akali Dal inflated its demands. For Punjab, it asked for more of the river waters and to incorporate Punjabi speaking areas from the surrounding states. It would rather not share Chandigarh. In 1973, in a (*Anandpur Sahib*) resolution, Akali Dal outdid itself. With regards to Punjab, the Central government should limit itself to only a few areas such as defense, currency, communications, and foreign affairs. (245)

This strategy paid off well for Akali Dal. Following the *emergency*, in 1977 the anti-Indira wave swept this party to power. In three years, however, Indira Gandhi got back into the saddle redeemed and renewed. She started to focus on one mission, to route the opposition. She dismissed the Akali Dal government. As a part of her master plan, she encouraged a very inconspicuous militant—Sant Jarnail Singh Bhindranwale. He was supposed to make more militant demands on behalf of Sikhs and make Akali Dal look weak. (245)

Bhindranwale succeeded beyond her expectations. His militant demands gained more converts, mainly unemployed youth. He also received financial support from many Sikhs living abroad. Over the next few years, he used it to fan popular discontent among Sikhs. Just like the Hindu Goddess Durga, Indira hoped to ride this tiger. Bhindranwale, however, proved to be a tough customer. He reduced Indira Gandhi to a mere mortal. He washed his hands of her and embarked on a journey for a separate country for Sikhs, Khalistan. He started a campaign of terror on local Hindus and uncooperative Sikhs. Indira Gandhi soon realized that she had created a Frankenstein. To make up for her tragic miscalculation, she backed down. She accepted a few demands by Sikhs. Government-owned All India Radio would broadcast Sikh religious services. On domestic flights, male Sikhs would be allowed to follow their tradition and carry a knife (*kirpan*), but it should be smaller than six inches. (245)

Akali Dal, much more than before, locked in a competition with militants, brushed aside these concessions as token. The terrorists stepped up their attacks and killings. They disgusted most Indians, especially Hindus. Indira Gandhi saw a chance to gain the Hindu vote. She promised to handle the situation with "a firm hand." (245)

She invoked a few national security laws and destroyed the checks and balances that had worked only halfway even under normal circumstances. Police abused their powers. Their excesses alienated the locals some more. With each wave of repression, more and more Sikhs were converted to the militant cause. Moderate Sikh politicians were caught in the middle. Instead of looking like sellouts, many just quit politics. The civil disturbances continued and invited more repression. More arrests meant more heroes. More deaths meant more martyrs and more recruitments to the cause. (245)

This cycle landed militants in the holiest of Sikh shrines, the Golden Temple in Amritsir. They posed a further challenge to the authorities and created a law and order nightmare. To flush them out, the army attacked the Golden Temple. The operation was personally approved by Indira Gandhi. She picked Lieutenant General Ranjit Singh Dayal, a Sikh himself, to lead it. (245)

It was an instant military success. Indian troops killed one thousand militants. Just as she had done after the Bangladesh War, Indira Gandhi reached the peak of her popularity. Even the opposition leaders applauded her actions. Soon, however, the whole story became a Shakespearian tragedy when her own Sikh bodyguards assassinated Indira Gandhi. (245)

"By doing this (attacking the Golden Temple), they created as many extremists as there are Sikhs," boasted a Canadian Sikh. Anti-Sikh riots following the death of Indira Gandhi brought this assessment closer to the truth. In the name of avenging her assassination, mobs in Delhi—allegedly supported by Congress(I) politicians and definitely ignored by security forces—indiscriminately attacked Sikhs and created carnage. In four days of rioting, according to the government's estimate, 2,733 Sikhs died. The Citizens' Justice Committee claimed the number to be 3,870. (253)

As usual, the numbers would tell only half the story. Mobs attacked trains and houses looking for Sikhs. The rioters dragged, hacked, and burned men in front of their families.

They raped women. Said one, whose husband and two sons aged eighteen and twenty-one were killed, "My son died crying for a glass of water as flames enveloped his body." (253)

In July of 1985, Rajiv Gandhi, under pressure to solve the Punjab problem, reached an accord with Sant Harchand Singh Longowal, a member of the endangered species—the Sikh moderates. Rajiv went as far as any Indian leader could go. He agreed to change the boundary of the state, assure a Sikh majority, be lenient to Sikh political prisoners, and withdraw sweeping powers given to the army. Chandigarh would go to Punjab. He also promised a greater share of river waters and rapid industrialization of the state. The issue of autonomy would be handed over to a commission. (245,254)

The militants started to lose momentum. They got worried. In less than a month after the signing of the accord, they assassinated Longowal. But Akalis formed their government. After about eighteen months, citing increasing terrorism and violence, Rajiv dismissed it. He imposed the Central government's rule and appointed a hard-line governor. Akalis denied his charges vehemently. Escalating violence and terrorism after their departure from power made them look better: Within eighteen months of the Central government's rule, terrorists killed more people (2096 vs. 790 under Akalis) and were killed in increased numbers by the police (496 vs. 118). (245,255)

Naturally, the atmosphere in Punjab got more vitiated. Ordinary villagers found themselves at the mercy of police extortionists during the day and terrorists and killers by night. Scared stiff, some villagers gave rides and food to terrorists and faced charges of collaboration. Asked one, "Can you deny food or shelter to a band of heavily armed terrorists?" Forty local government leaders resigned to protest the "state terrorism." A few parents even paid bribes to get their sons arrested and formally charged. By doing so, they could at least protect their boys from the usually dangerous illegal detentions by police. (256,257)

✦    ✦    ✦

"Kashmir is at war with India," declares Inderjit Badhwar of *India Today* (Apr. 30, 1990), "In Kashmir nobody, either out of fear or out of total alienation that pervades the region, now talks for India or even a settlement with the center." (258)

Kashmir happens to be India's northernmost state. It is flanked by Pakistan and China, traditional enemies of India. That alone makes the secessionist movement in Kashmir the most serious challenge to the integrity of India. Like the others, this movement, too, is rooted in economics—roads, water, industries, power supply and....

"There are no jobs," a local shop keeper tells Badhwar, "Look around you. For forty years, despite promises, there has been no improvement. Everything is filthier and grimier." Quzi Nassar, whom Badhwar describes as "an ex-radical turned moderate," backs such sentiments, "But their real anger is about jobs—every third person here is unemployed. About not being represented beyond class 1V [the lowest level] in the central government. About rampant corruption and the failure of the government to usher in any development. About the violation of civil rights. Kids below 10 have been arrested under the anti-terrorism act." (259)

Xenophobic protectionism also hurt the state. Much the same way as India restricted foreign holdings in its industries, Kashmir (under article 370) restricted the property rights of those from out of state. The reason given for this madness: "to preserve the unique culture of Kashmir." Without the guarantee of property rights, private investors stayed out. And so did the jobs. Government's funds acquired even a bigger role as a source of capital and, thus, economic growth. (260)

Citing "the strategic importance of Kashmir," national leaders did spend a lot of money (close to 8,000 million rupees a year) in the state. What happened to all this money? The same thing that had happened to the massive amounts of government-to-government aid that was showered all over the third world. The funds ended up in the pockets of powerful elites in Kashmir, primarily a coalition of government contractors, politicians, engineers, and other officials. While bridges, roads, schools, hospitals, and relief works lay rotting, the state

officials spent a lot of money on a cable car project and a golf
course that they couldn't even finish. At a cost of 6,000,000
rupees, the government built a hospital which later on developed a crack in the middle. After spending two years and millions of rupees, a road—named after Indira Gandhi—remained
unfinished. (259)

The only legacy of these monies was a malignant corruption. For fraudulent manipulation of a roster for medical college admissions, judges passed several injunctions against the
state's ministers. One of the ministers was even accused of involvement in a gang rape. Said a Kashmiri youth, "India sends
us money, but it only leads to corruption and moral degradation. We would rather be poor in liberty than rich in bond-
age." (261,262)

Militants received training and arms, including automatic
weapons, from Pakistan. They intensified an anti-India agitation. But of course, it was not just a few militants and fanatics.
Even the shop-keepers and professionals talked of "liberating
Kashmir." The whole state became an Indian Lebanon. Only a
few officials, who would need constant protection, and the
army represented India. The militants unleashed waves of terrorism on local Hindus. About 140,000 of them would flee to a
neighboring state. (258,259,263)

By keeping other Indians out, Kashmiri Hindus hoped to
maintain their cultural purity. In the end, however, they lost
their homeland and became refugees in their own country.
Nevertheless, it seemed that they were the luckier victims.
Showing how such agitations had little to do with helping
Muslims or Buddhists, said Rakesh Khar (of the *India Tribune*),
"And the plight of innocent Kashmiri Muslims is no less miserable—sandwiched as they are in between gun-wielding militants and the security forces." (263)

Mulayam Singh Yadav, then the chief minister of Uttar Pradesh,
knew exactly what was behind India's problems. He said, "The

English language is the biggest curse on this country and the state. The language breeds corruption." (264)

To exorcise the state, he threatened to close down its English-medium public schools and missionary schools. He also decided that the bureaucrats should only use Hindi in conducting their business. In the absence of any proof to the contrary, we can safely assume that the officials still demand bribes, but probably, they have started to do so in Hindi. (264)

Among all the Indian intellectuals, language-oriented men and women are truly a breed apart. They come up with fantastic suggestions. Kushwant Singh, a famous author, says, "If Roman was made the official script, we could solve the problem of entire nation by writing all languages in Roman." Citing the example of Turkey, Singh concludes, "In short, most thinking nationalists support Roman: only a few cranky chauvinists oppose it." (265)

Roman?

Early on, Turkey did switch to Roman script. As a result, however, very few of its citizens can read the rich Arabic texts languishing in their libraries. Besides, without anyone imposing from above, India will always have one more language than it needs. Its people are the ones who pay for such social engineering. And the price involves much more than throwing money to convert all the "important" books and re-educating close to 800 million Indians. Any such major overhaul is sure to touch many emotional buttons. As recently as October of 1989, for example, the state government of Uttar Pradesh, designated Urdu—primarily spoken by Muslims—a second language. In the resulting riots, many died. (266)

The history of such meddling goes far back. Within a few years after India had settled down from the partition tremors, language became a major issue. While on one side most Indians were demanding separate states based on their language, in the name of promoting unity, their national leaders got busy with full-fledged attempts to impose Hindi, spoken by the majority.

Roughly speaking, Indian languages are as diverse as the European ones. To many, Hindi is very alien, as alien as German to an Italian. What transformed the age-old diversity into a shattering conflict, however, were again the bread and butter (or, shall we say rice and curry) issues. The minorities feared economic discrimination. They felt nervous about competing with the Hindi-speaking majority on its own turf and about being left out of government jobs. For example, the officials—especially the high-ranking ones—controlled how government would invest *developmental* funds. If proficiency in Hindi was used as a yardstick, more of these officials would come from the northern half of India. They would be able to decide such things as where to build roads and factories. What if they would channel the public sector jobs away from the minorities?

Recommendations, such as the one to hold all civil service examinations in Hindi, did little to curb these phobias. Also, the government linked pay raises and promotions to literacy in Hindi. Suddenly, middle-aged officials, who previously took these benefits for granted, became nervous students. I remember my father, a devout nationalist, dozing on his Hindi textbook at the age of forty. He dreaded the upcoming examination. The uneducated felt even worse. They were more scared of being left out of the mainstream.

The backlash started in the south. The more the authorities pushed Hindi, the more they alienated the *others*. Political parties that appealed to language chauvinism started to gather support in the public. Congress could ill afford to ignore these feelings for long. It had to slow down its Hindi drive and even allow for formation of states based on language.

Each of these states reserved jobs for *its own*. They passed the so-called son-of-the-soil laws. Thanks to these laws, an Indian who left his states had only a slim chance of getting a job or a college seat. Under the quota system, in some states, even by leaving one's region, district, or university one would become ineligible for most jobs and college seats. Many an Indian felt like an alien in his own country. He faced less discrimination in New York than in Bombay or Calcutta. Those who could sought opportunities in other countries.

Relatively very few, however, moved to other Indian states. The majority limited themselves to their mini-forts. They clung to *their own* . As fewer and fewer mingled freely with *the others*, physically and psychologically the age-old divisions got more entrenched. An attitude of "us versus them" pervaded the society. It became an integral part of the national psyche. Even after leaving India, many formed regional organizations and partied within them.

Instead of promoting common bonds through a free movement of people seeking opportunities, the government tried to homogenize the country by shoving Hindi down the throats of the minorities. Owing to the compulsions of the democratic processes, however, it had to defer to the popular sentiments. It had to sever the linkage between Hindi literacy and hiring and promotions. It, however, refused to totally give up and started to throw money at the problem. As recently as the summer of 1990, to infuse Hindi into the public sector, it formed special cells. About 25,000 Hindi officers worked on the project and tried to replace some common English words with new Hindi terms. Through painstaking research, they came up with such gems as *hast padnak snaini vastra khand*—a piece of cloth for wiping the hands, also known as a handkerchief. (267)

Their Hindi coaching classes—conducted twice a week during the office hours—disrupted what little work that was being done. Said one employee, "We get a holiday to appear for the exam. That's a major incentive." The plan also called for cash bonuses of 400 to 600 rupees to each employee who would pass a Hindi examination. (267)

Politicians came up with a brand-new excuse for their worldwide junkets, to investigate how the various embassies were using Hindi. In a country that was filled with shortages and joblessness, they employed language chauvinism as an easy and convenient diversion from their unfulfilled promises. When asked about his party's economic program, an official belonging to Telugu Desam—a regional party based on the linguistic pride of Telugus—answered, "Both capitalism and Marxism are unacceptable to us." (268)

It's futile to blame these leaders. They never have had a real economic plan or even pretended to have one. Besides their populist programs—such as the provision of midday meals for school children or selling one kilogram of rice for a rupee or two, they have come to power promising to protect their language and culture. They also have this irritating habit of calling those who speak their language "brothers and sisters."

Besides reserving jobs in their respective states for their *brothers and sisters* at the expense of the rest in the country, they passed laws promoting the native tongue. The governments mandated its usage for official business. Even the signs on buses and trains were to be written only in the local language. Such one-language policies lead to massive confusion. Because of my inability to read signs written in local languages, for example, I feel more overwhelmed in Indian cities such as Madras than in New York. I also have to give up on my favorite pastime—haggling with cab drivers and shopkeepers.

In (the state of) Tamil Nadu, the labor department ordered all non-Tamil names of shops be replaced by new names. The new ones must be in "pure Tamil." Contamination from other languages would be disallowed. One could fret about this encroachment of governmental authority over private lives. The shopkeepers, however, had a more immediate problem. Said the report, "They cannot remember the new names of their shops." (269)

After conducting extensive research, Makrand Mehta—president of the modern Indian section of the Indian History Congress—reached a conclusion that would forever change the fate of the universe.

He concluded that Swaminarayan, a sect leader from the early nineteenth century, conspired with his followers to project himself as a god. What else is new? And who cares? Obviously, one and a half million followers of this sect did. They considered Mehta's revelation a blasphemy. They wanted to sue both the journal which had published these findings and Mehta— who, anyway, should have been sent to his room for wasting the public funds on such a pointless endeavor. (271)

To sue, however, they needed government's permission.[16] But there was no problem. Most of the sect members were rich and naturally well connected. The government gave them the permission to sue and injected itself into a controversy that pitted the proponents of religious and academic freedoms on opposite sides. (271)

This story, however, has little to do with either of these freedoms. It's about the right to sue. It's about the number of laws that cover everything. It's about the extent to which government meddles in the affairs of private citizens. Without permission from its officials, one can't even ask a court of law to decide if one's rights are violated. What if a politically weak sect were involved? The case would have been shut before it was ever opened.

In such a statist society, one needs connections not only to earn a living and enjoy the fruits of one's labor, but also to practice one's religion, pursue education, speak one's language, and, obviously, to seek justice in the courtrooms. For only the elites and the strong are these basic freedoms inalienable.

The others feel vulnerable. They huddle into groups. Hoping to derive strength from numbers, they form voting blocks based on religion, caste, or even sub-caste. They vote for a leader that voices their concerns. Blindly and repeatedly, they back the party that champions *their cause*. The Muslim League tries to round up Muslims. RSS (Rashtriya Swayamsevak Sangh) and its political affiliate BJP (Bharatiya Janata Party) espouse the Hindu causes. As to be expected, RSS talks of "Hindu Raj." Recently, it has issued a stamp of Greater India, which includes Pakistan, Burma, Sri Lanka, and even parts of Thailand. (273)

All along, Hindu leaders have maintained that the Muslim loyalties are suspect and that someday, because of mass conversions and family planning, Hindus will become a minority. To back up their theories, they use the 1951 census in which Muslims had been under-counted. If they use the 1941 census as a reference, however, they will find out that the growth rates of both Hindu and Muslim populations have stayed roughly equal. By and large, economic factors, rather than the religious or cultural ones, influence the birth control practices of either community. (272)

In real life, few politicians waste time on such trivia. Most appeal to the gut. They inflame the passions of those who feel a constant flame in their gut, such as the unemployed youth. The results are often tragic. In the city of Aurangabad, for example, when a court case related to an election marred by religious controversies was adjourned, one group attacked Muslim localities. The Muslims attacked back. Quite a few people died in these clashes. (274)

For many seasoned politicians, inciting such riots is just politics as usual. It's their shortcut to power and the wealth that such power brings them. In private, some even boast of how many of their *own* they control and how many of *the others* they have killed. Diwakar Raote, chairman of the standing committee of Bombay Municipal Corporation, bragged how, in the cities of Bhiwandi and Ahmedabad his party organized the killings of nearly three hundred Muslims in communal riots. Raote belonged to another Hindu party, Shiva Sena. He recorded these boasts on a cassette and sent it to a few Gujarati traders. He just wanted to impress them with his prowess so that they would donate large sums to his party. (275)

Small wonder that the minorities have learned to distrust the officials. Often, when attacked by a mob from a dominant community, not only do the minorities receive little help from the authorities, but a few policemen, themselves, might join the attackers. The minorities feel vulnerable. Quite a few organize themselves. In many previously peaceful cities and towns, trivial issues, such as the route of a religious procession, escalate into devastating conflicts. They leave more wounds that rarely heal.

For a long time, Congress depended on votes from secular-minded Hindus. Also, without improving the lot of the majority of Muslims, it got their support by constantly appeasing a few Muslim leaders. Constituting more than twenty percent of the electorate in about ninety-eight crucial constituencies, Muslims have been the party's dream vote bank. (272)

A notable exception was in 1977. After lifting *the emergency*, Indira Gandhi lost. She felt betrayed. Despite "all that she and her father had done for Muslims," they voted for an anti-Congress Janata party. She printed her own Hindu card and played it in the next elections. Indira Gandhi talked about "rights of the majority." Her party men likened her to the Hindu goddess, Durga. In less than three years, she rode back to power. (276)

Rajiv Gandhi tried to rise above the politics. During one of his reformist seizures, he flirted with the idea of emancipation of Muslim women. He tried to liberalize the draconian divorce laws. The supreme court backed his progressive measures.

Power, not emancipation, interested Muslim leaders. They led mass demonstrations. Rajiv woke up to the stark realities of Indian politics. Without the "Muslim vote," he would surely lose. He panicked. At what many consider the turning point of his prime ministership, he took two steps backward. His party passed a law making divorce even harder on Muslim women. (277)

Hindu leaders saw a small opening to enlarge their base. They promptly drove a tank through the hole. If, under communal pressure, Rajiv could reverse himself and the supreme court ruling and pass a retrograde *Muslim Women's bill,* he could certainly help Hindus settle their age-old score with Muslims; so the Hindu leaders argued. (277)

This old score had something to do with Ayodhya, the birthplace of the Hindu God, Rama. At this site, Babar, the first Mogul emperor in India, allegedly demolished a temple and constructed a mosque. For centuries, Muslim invaders before and after Babar did such things all over India. Until very recently, very few demanded a redress. The all-promising and all-powerful politician then arrived on the scene. Always in search of a vote bank, he led many influential groups to believe that the power of state was at their disposal. All they had to do was to vote right and push a few correct buttons and these groups could get whatever they want. (272)

Leaders of Hindu organizations specifically wanted the government to overturn an order issued by the state's high court, to maintain the status quo in the mosque/birth place case, and hand them the site. They wanted to demolish the mosque and build a temple for Rama. The resulting clashes led to a lot of riots, loss of life and property, and even the fall of a government or two. (272)

To be sure, these fights had little to do with either Rama or Mohammed.

They had everything to do with an entity higher than Allah and Rama put together—money. Asks Syed Shahabuddin, a Muslim leader, "Why is it that in Hyderabad City, where 60 percent of the Muslim population stays in the old town, only 15 percent of municipal expenditure goes there? Why is it that when you build village roads, the villages with Muslim concentration do not get priority?" (276)

By promising such amenities and, more importantly, jobs and other economic benefits, these leaders attract even the semi-believers. They tell anyone who hopes to stay out of the politics that he could lose big in the distribution game. And this game certainly involves a lot of chips. During the mosque/birthplace controversy, a few Muslim organizations got together to form the National Political Convention of Muslim Indians. It made a few demands for Muslims: the right to employment, an unemployment dole of 150 to 250 rupees per fortnight and a minimum wage of 25 rupees per day for rural laborers, quotas for Muslims at all levels (including the parliament, police, and the intelligence machinery), a special anti-riot force that would derive at least fifty percent of its members from the minorities, and amendments to an act that sought to take away powers from the Muslim courts (and from these leaders). Reflecting their distrust towards the authorities, the leaders demanded liberalization of arms licensing in riot-prone areas. Included in their list were a few token religious demands. (276,278)

Before and immediately after independence, many forward-thinking leaders from various communities helped to forge a secular India. But for them, the country would have suffered a lot more deaths and destruction during the partition tremors. These days, editorial writers seem to miss such leaders. They ask, "Now that the country needs them the most, where are the secular leaders?"

It's hardly as if such moderates have disappeared. They have been simply pushed into the background. They have been edged out by the likes of Shahabuddin—the products of the culture of state-sponsored solutions for all problems. These new leaders practice politics of group rights, promise jobs and other economic benefits, and gather support easily. Shahabuddin wrote a piece about the tactics, "This strategy will work if and only if the Muslim voters vote unitedly and solidly at the constituency level. The political maturity of a minority lies not only in identifying whom to vote for but in organizing cent per cent voting for him." (276)

Translation: "Screw the moderates and the secular nerds."

"The appointment was possibly motivated by Rajiv's wanting a duo of Rajput and Brahmin to run the state [of Bihar] and the party. For once even Rajiv Gandhi has got his caste arithmetic straight," said Farzand Ahmed and Uttam Sen Gupta of *India Today*. (270)

Newspapers routinely include such calculations in their political commentary. They have to. To win elections, politicians exploit the influence of caste and religion to the hilt. With stakes being so high and because of their preeminent position in the society, their juggling becomes newsworthy.

By law, people belonging to Scheduled Castes and Scheduled Tribes—formerly untouchables—are entitled to a portion of all government jobs. After independence, a majority of Indians did support such quotas, but that has changed. In the past four decades, increasing levels of education combined with a not-so-rapidly-increasing job market left many Indians unemployed, poor, and angry. The principle behind the quotas would no longer appeal to them.

Besides, close to eighty-four percent of the Scheduled Caste members live in villages. They benefit very little from these quotas. Those who take away their jobs and college seats are none other than the children of their caste members who have previously benefited from the quota system. Maiku Ram, a former untouchable and now the top cop (Inspector General of Police) in (the State of) Bihar, explains why his children should enjoy these special privileges, "They [his children] studied in the best schools but still developed an inferiority complex." (279)

For poorer members of the Scheduled Castes, it's hardly a question of complexes but one of survival. They not only lose out to the more-privileged members of their caste and get little out of these quotas, but also suffer a backlash from members of the other castes. Poor people belonging to the other castes question why they should be left out. In devising the quota system, why not use the economic status of the individual? For a few rupees, however, practically anyone can cook up a false income certificate. If jobs are reserved for the poor, the unscrupulous rather than the untouchable will prosper.

Besides helping those that are well off to get even better off, these quotas offered many leaders from the affluent and powerful castes a convenient way to gather more support. These politicians promised to get their castes designated as the "Other Backward Castes (OBCs)." (280)

In any other country, to be called backward can be considered as an insult. In India, however, such a designation brings jobs for the caste members and votes for their leaders. After losing the support of a top leader from his coalition, V.P. Singh sought to boost his electoral base in this grand tradition of Indian socialism: He sought to create his very own vote bank. In August of 1990, Singh wiped dust off a flawed Mandal Commission report. (280)

On the basis of out-dated[17] and very limited information, the commission had issued its recommendations in 1980. The commission, itself, said, "This survey has no pretensions to being a piece of academic research." The survey covered only two villages and one urban block from each district of the country.

Its questionnaire, meant for the general public and placed in leading English and vernacular newspapers, received an abysmal 1,872 responses. (280)

Nevertheless, the Mandal Commission used the data to categorize 3,743 castes and sub-castes as the Other Backward Castes (other than the former untouchables). It recommended to include these OBCs in the quota system. Some feared that this plan could generate mass confusion. Said a 1990 report in *India Today,* "As it is, government departments use a complicated 40-point roster with a combination of weightages and percentages and multiplications in order to identify which sub-caste to assign handicaps over the others in hiring and promotions. And the states already have their own lists of backward castes and reservations. There are many castes which figure in one state's list and not in that of its immediate neighbor's." Also, according to 1988 figures, approximately 55,000 central government jobs came under the Mandal quotas. This meant that each caste would qualify for a mere fifteen jobs. What if 5,000 people belonging to a caste applied for these jobs? Government had two choices: Either benefit a tiny fraction of these unemployed youth, or ask each person to work one day a year. (280,281)

As the country's prime minister, Singh promised to back these vague ideas with the definite force of law. By doing so, in the words of one of his opponents, Singh divided India in a manner even the British could not do. Many young men and women from the non-backward castes revolted. They threw stones, blocked roads, and destroyed property. Some even committed self-immolation. As they saw it, there wasn't much left to lose. One Muslim student union from Aligarh University demanded that Muslims be included in this quota system. Many Christian organizations joined in the protest. Sharad Yadav, then a cabinet minister under Singh, urged his supporters to go on the streets and demonstrate their support for the enlarged quota system. All this raised the specter of a full-scale caste war. (280,281)

Singh couldn't care less. He always knew that very few of his rivals could oppose his move. All along these politicians *fought for the oppressed.* They had to either follow Singh or come out looking mean-spirited. Most responded to this crisis by essentially criticizing "the way it was done." (281)

Nevertheless, true to Singh's calculations, the politics of vote banks ripped every major political party apart. Many in Congress(I) did support the quotas. Its leaders such as Shankaranand and Shiv Shankar asked, "The Congress has always fought for the downtrodden. How can we oppose Mandal report now?" Vasant Sathe, another Congressman, wasn't so sure. Scared of losing votes from the forward castes, he said, "V.P. Singh is reviving the caste system.[18] The [Congress] party must fight it." BJP, a member of the Singh's coalition government, tried to divert the attention to the mosque/birthplace issue. (281).

Within the country, the arguments ran in every direction. "After several centuries of exploitation, giving up 55,000 jobs seems like a fairly small price to ask of the higher castes," said a letter to the editor of *India Today.* Said another one, "The 52 percent of our population which stands to gain if the Mandal report is implemented have been denied all this while because of self-centered politicians." (282,283)

If there was ever a gold medal for absurd-speak, K. Karunanidhi, chief minister of (the state of) Tamil Nadu, would have won it hands down. While inaugurating the "wildlife week", he said: "When we are prepared to accept reservation of places for animals, some of us do not accept reservation of seats for men." (284)

At best, this plan would have taken care of a very tiny fraction of the unemployed Indians. Singh knew as much. He couldn't think of a way to create hundreds of millions of jobs for the rest, but he did know of a faster, easier, and time-tested way to win their support—bait them with promises of a few thousand jobs. As if enough damage hadn't been done already, and as if there were not enough restrictions on the economic enterprise—which, if allowed to expand, would have employed many more than this quota system ever could—the Commissioner of Scheduled Castes wanted to enlarge this policy of "positive discrimination" to the private sector also. (285)

Naturally, the supreme court was clearly worried. It said, "This approach alone [caste based quotas] would legitimize and perpetuate the caste system. It does not go well with our proclaimed secular character as enshrined in the preamble to the Constitution." (280)

"What glue will hold [a country]?" asks Michael Barone of *US News and World Report*. (286)

He knows what won't, "But a common language does not a nation make: trilingual Switzerland is one of the world's most cohesive countries, but Ireland finally succeeded in winning its independence from Britain just after almost all of its peasants switched from Gaelic to English." (286)

A single culture isn't the answer either. East Germans wanted to join West Germany, but the Austrians didn't. Besides, it eludes a precise definition. (286)

A host of complex factors, such as wars, historic accidents, and the will of a few individuals, have led to the formation of nations whose existence we all take for granted. For their sustenance, however, most countries depend upon the strength of a few ideas. Barone talks of one such idea based on civility and civil liberties now flowering around the world. He asks, "If minorities are treated fairly and can leave when they want, why fight to let distinguished gentlemen sit around a table and indolently, irresponsibly draw new lines that may create as many problems as the old ones?" (286)

One thing is certain. Rarely, if ever, do the groups that compose any nation fight to show their supremacy or settle a theological dispute. Out of their efforts, they hope to win something tangible—usually something economic. As a matter of fact, even when they fight over land, river waters, or the loin cloth of a prophet, the cause behind these causes can often be spelled as "opportunities." Instead of allowing for its citizens to create their own opportunities, when a government seeks to distribute them, it generates enormous tensions. It matters little whether the country in question is Canada, Ireland, or India. When a government distributes based on groups' rights, members of each group have no alternative but to fight over such things as licenses, jobs, or college seats. The age-old divisions that separate the people acquire a sharper edge.

In contrast, individual rights are non-discriminatory. They are simple and predictable. Most of us can relate to them. Regardless of our differences, we tend to unite against any perceived encroachment. Group rights, on the other hand, lead to endless charters of demands. They pit the various groups against each other. Due to infighting over the spoils, even the victorious group gets splintered further.

The heat such fights generate can melt the very glue that holds together any nation.

"Like an invincible cancer, the violent protests have traveled from the cities and towns of North India into the rural heart land, pitting neighbor against neighbor, friend against friend," Farzand Ahmed (of *India Today*) was reporting on the aftermath of the Mandal quotas fiasco. (287)

This is no accident. From all the tussle over the distribution, the average Indian has learned something: If her group doesn't push, someone else's will push her out. When a person finds out that having *his own* at the top fails to automatically guarantee a job for him, however, suddenly the definition of *his own* group changes. From people belonging to his religion, it narrows to those from his caste or even sub-caste or from those who speak his language to those from his district. Small wonder that over the years, most in the country have learned to regard men, women, and even children from areas, castes, religions, language groups or sub-sub-castes other then their own as the "others." At a gut level, the people have learned to distrust. These feelings have become an inseparable part of the national psyche. They stay with many Indians for life, or maybe even beyond.

Ironically, this separatism without an endpoint first reared its head in Andhra, the first linguistic state in the union. People from nine districts of its Telangana region wanted their own state. A local leader, Chenna Reddy, took up their cause. He did so for a good reason: Because of allegations of voting irregularities, the courts barred him from contesting in elections; he regarded the separatist movement as his ace, his only hope for political revival.

Reddy's plan worked very well. The agitation paralyzed this state. Indira Gandhi had to buy back peace by easing Reddy back into the political process. He went on to become the state's chief minister. People from Telangana, some of whom saw their family members die in the agitation, mostly stayed poor and backward.

Time and again, this script has catapulted many unknowns into leadership positions. Mostly using poor, unemployed youth, they stir up an agitation and render life miserable for the public and the state or region ungovernable. Government buys them off with concessions; a few that benefit the leaders personally and a few token ones for the group. Showing off the latter and with the help of a newly-gained notoriety, these leaders go on to win elections, usually for seats reserved for the group. They gain power and money.

Ambitious leaders, such as Reddy, keep on inventing new constituencies. Each and every day, they champion new causes. As many groups can form as there are Chenna Reddys. This is an endless process. India, known for its diversity, fell into this trap when its leaders thought that they could devise a magic formula for distribution of wealth that would redress all the past inequities. Instead, they created new ones. They ended up pitting one Indian against the other on the basis of religion, caste, sub-caste, language, region, and length of one's nose. Their policies destroyed the remarkable unity that their countrymen had displayed during the independence movement.

In less then a half century, this socialist experiment imperiled the very concept of an Indian Union.

[14]Followers of Sikhism—an off-shoot of Hinduism—founded in Punjab in the late 15th century AD by Guru Nanak.

[15]Rather than Punjabi, the language spoken by the majority in the state.

[16]Act 295A of the Indian Penal Code, which deals with offense to religious sentiments.

[17]It used the census data gathered by the British in 1891 and 1931.

[18]Multiple factors—including occupational differentiation, family worship, racial and ritual differences, taboo, and prohibition of intermarriage—splintered Hindu society among various castes and sub-castes. The New Encyclopedia Britannica defines: "A caste is, in general, an endogamous hereditary group of families, bearing a common name; often claiming a common descent; as a rule professing to follow the same hereditary calling; clinging to the same customs, especially regarding purity, meals and marriages; and very often further divided into smaller endogamous circles."

# CHAPTER 9
## *Fast Track to Fiefdom*

JUST LIKE THE most of us, prime minister Rajiv Gandhi probably enjoyed simple pleasures, such as a stroll in fresh air. If that were the case, one should have felt sorry for him. By simply taking a walk outside his tightly guarded home, the prime minister would have run into crowds. (288)

These were friendly crowds. They belonged to his party, Congress(I). These politicians gathered outside his home to find out which of them would get the tickets to represent the party in the upcoming (1989) elections. At stake were more than 500 seats in the national parliament and thousands in the various state assemblies. (288)

In doling out these tickets, Rajiv got plenty of help, much more so than good-old Santa Clause. Collectively, his helpers called themselves "the party high command." To accomplish their task, these commanders depended upon an army of domestic intelligence agencies. These state organs put the aspirants under a microscope. These agencies took into consideration such factors as the ability of each contestant to relate to the dominant caste, religion, and political faction in the area, and made their recommendations to the high command. Trusted aides to the prime minister scanned through these reports and chose among the tens of thousands of candidates. (288)

The high command did pick quite a few rotten mangoes. Many corrupt politicians, who were kicked out in the past, had to be let back in because, in the words of a senior Congress(I) member, "They led powerful factions in many states." If rejected, they would "sabotage the party's candidate."

All this would have shocked the authors of the Indian constitution. Using domestic intelligence agencies for political espionage was farthest from their ideals. To precisely curb such an abuse of power by the ruling class, they adopted many checks and balances characteristic of the Western democracies.

The framework that would serve as the backbone of their constitution, primarily materialized in Britain (and in America) back in the late eighteenth and nineteenth centuries. It was based on a slow but eventual realization that the rulers—even the elected kind—would pose the biggest threat to individual rights that relate to life, liberty, and property. Consequently, the British constitution (and, more so, the American constitution) tried to keep these rights beyond the normal reach of the elected representatives. To prevent despotism, it created a government of checks and balances, for example, the separation of powers, independent judiciary, multi-party democracy, the various avenues for ousting an unpopular administration and, of course, a fiercely free press. Owing to these hurdles, running a government involved a lot of debate, discussion, consultation, and even confrontation. Except during times of national emergencies, such a government was slow to act. This, however, caused little harm. Because government largely limited its functions to those that are not covered by the private initiative (law and order, issuance of currency, and national defense), it could afford to be slow and deliberative.

Such a limited government bred a different kind of politician. He enjoyed very little control over the economy. He had few permits or licenses to sell. For anyone who just wanted to make money, commercial endeavors offered better and faster avenues to wealth than government service. To engage in business, he needed very few connections, if any. Most politicians made their living elsewhere. Perhaps, many were simply bored with their lives and entered politics looking for excitement. What else could one do for kicks in a Victorian village anyway?

Most entered the public arena with a passion to serve rather than to survive. Even after a minor scandal or an allegation of mismanagement, many resigned. They could afford to. Government service was often a drain on their time and money.

Shortly after independence, quite a few Indian politicians followed these healthy democratic traditions. They tried to honor the checks and balances. This phase, however, turned out to be short-lived owing to a mismatch: The liberal political framework (with its checks and balances) that the founding fathers had chosen for India proved to be too ill-equipped to handle their socialist economic policies. It proved to be too slow, controlled, and inefficient to undertake such tasks as building giant irrigation dams and power plants, distributing fertilizers, and deciding who were the best tribal dancers. Government had to use force to implement such measures as land reforms and nationalization of private properties. The leaders had to choose. That they did, of course after some hesitation. They sacrificed their ideals of a liberal democracy on the altar of their economic program. They compromised the democratic institutions, one by one.

Also, thanks to the socialist planning, many a politician found out that he could make money faster and easier selling permits than petrol. Anyway, to sell petrol he needed connections. Why would he get his hands dirty and smelly? Many became wealthy without creating any wealth. These dynamics gave birth to an era of the professional politician who depended upon his position to thrive. Asking him to quit was like asking a lawyer or a doctor to turn in his license. Not surprisingly, with passing time, fewer and fewer politicians resigned even when the courts had convicted them of felonies. Many politicians became so bold as to openly admit they were corrupt, albeit to a lesser degree than their opposition. They viewed the democratic niceties and the constitutional guarantees of freedom as inconvenient hurdles in their march to prosperity. They were more than happy to abandon these relics from the bygone era. In no time, the country was largely reduced to a medieval serfdom.

There was one exception. These lords and ladies of Indian politics had to still contend with once-in-a-few-years elections. To survive this nuisance, they jumped to use their hold on the state apparatus. In (the state of) Uttar Pradesh, for example, Congress(I) used buses belonging to the UPSRTC (the government bus system) for electioneering. As a result, the party owed 26.7 million rupees to the UPSRTC. When asked about the repayment, a Congress worker responded, "As it is, we are struggling to collect funds for the coming elections. Where is the question of paying anything to the UPSRTC at the moment?" (289)

Actually, the ruling politicians did much more than to just use government's material, media, and men to blow their horns. They used its awesome powers of coercion to intimidate any and all opposition. Anyone who failed to toe their line faced their wrath. In 1969, Indira Gandhi ordered raids against the Birla group (famous industrialists and, for many years, the richest family in India), which allegedly sided with her adversaries. Her younger son, Sanjay Gandhi, turned out to be her best campaigner. Famous for his strong-arm tactics, he used the various government agencies to further his mother's cause. In those days, a close aide to both these Gandhis routinely gave instructions to the director of the CBI (Central Bureau of Investigation). With the premier spy agency under their thumb, they could easily nullify the checks and balances of the system. (290)

To destroy intra-party democracy, for example, Indira Gandhi routinely used CBI to dislodge many a Congressmen who was too entrenched for her liking. To this end, she established the healthy tradition of spying on her own party colleagues. Mrs. Gandhi knew her Machiavelli both backwards and forwards. Under her microscope, she even placed quite a few Congress politicians with whose support, early on, she had survived a bitter power struggle within the party. She summoned to Delhi one such chief minister, Brahmananda Reddy of Andhra Pradesh, for *consultations.*

Back in his state's capital, rumors filled the air, "Reddy will be sacked." When he returned from Delhi, a majority of his legislators gathered at the airport to demonstrate their support for Reddy. He was visibly moved. He tearfully requested them to back another candidate chosen by the prime minister. He had to. Indira Gandhi allegedly confronted him with a dossier (of his illegal activities) prepared by the secret service.

A chief minister (of the state) of Sikkim, too, disliked what he saw in his unauthorized biography. At that time he belonged to an opposition party. He simply joined the Congress(I). Just like that, all the charges against him soon vanished. (291)

The intelligence machinery that makes such political skullduggery possible is truly awesome. Says an editorial in *India Today*:

> *Few countries have laws that arm investigation and prosecution agencies with the kind of summary powers that India does. Indeed, few countries have a plethora of such agencies as this country does: the Central Bureau of Investigation(CBI), the Enforcement Directorate, the Directorate of Revenue Intelligence, the Economic Intelligence Bureau, and so on. Many of the Government's prosecuting agencies have often been half-jokingly referred to in the past as persecution agencies. This is because of the selective and motivated use of tax raids, and the institution of dubious cases by the CBI that eventually do not yield very much.* (293)

In the first place, government erected this machine "to maintain law and order, protect the nation from foreign agencies and catch and punish *economic offenders.*[19]" As it turned out, however, these agencies were too busy to carry on these assignments. They occupied themselves with one business: deterring the political crime of disagreeing with those in power. Congress (I) was exceptionally good at using them to destroy its opponents. The following is a partial list of such infractions by one such agency, the Criminal Bureau of Investigation (CBI):(290)

- It grilled Chandraswamy, one of the informants of the *Indian Express,* in the Bofors arms purchase scandal, and persuaded him to switch sides.
- It prosecuted Nusli Wadia, an industrialist, who had apparently financed an investigation against Amitabh Bachchan, a close friend of Rajiv Gandhi.
- It prosecuted S. Gurumurthy, a columnist for the *Indian Express* (opposed to the Congress rule), for violating the *Official Secrets Act* when he quoted a few official documents in a report.
- It arrested Sanjay Singh, a prominent opposition leader, on a murder charge and proceeded with selective leaks to implicate him.
- It charged R.L. Jalappa—home minister of (the state of) Karnataka, then ruled by an anti-Congress party—with conspiring to murder a lawyer, Abdul Rasheed. After Jalappa had resigned, it stuck with two minor charges.
- It investigated a report by the *Indian Express* about illegal foreign accounts of a Congress MP (Kamalnath). Even though the documents quoted were found to be authentic, it soon shelved the probe.
- It initiated proceedings against Arun Nehru, whom Rajiv Gandhi considered his Judas. While serving as a cabinet minister under Gandhi, Nehru allegedly caused a loss of 1.9 million rupees to the government in a deal to buy Czech pistols. Only after he had joined the opposition, however, did the CBI file the charges.

Its favorite tactic was to file such charges despite the lack of evidence and leave the victim dangling in the air.

Before the 1989 elections, Congress(I), then the ruling party, aimed at the heart of the opposition parties. It picked their national leader, V.P. Singh, as its main target. It hoped to implicate him in a scandal and finish him for good. (294,296)

According to a story in a newspaper, *Telegraph*, Ajey Singh, son of V.P. Singh, had a foreign account worth $21 million in the Caribbean tax haven, St. Kitts. The report implied that V.P. Singh had made this money while serving as finance minister under Rajiv Gandhi and stashed it away in the Caribbean. (294,296)

M.L. Akbar, who would become a Congress(I) MP later on, edited the *Telegraph* at that time. In conducting this *investigative journalism,* he allegedly received help from several government officials and agencies: then foreign minister P.V. Narasimha Rao (who went on to become the country's prime minister), foreign secretary S.K Singh, Rajiv's aide, R.K. Dhawan, cabinet secretary T.N. Seshan, the enforcement directorate, and a host of other mid-level officials. Indian diplomats in the US and St. Kitts received direct orders from Delhi. The story also contained the ingredients of a third-rate spy novel. It implicated an American businessman (Larry Kolb), a former managing director of the, now defunct, First Trust Corporation (George McClean), a controversial god-man (Chandraswamy), and that scandal-prone Adnan Kashogi. (294,296)

This report, however, had more holes than a mosquito net. V.P. Singh promptly challenged it. Congress(I) feared a backlash. As fast as it had surfaced, the whole affair faded into the background. (294,296)

After the 1989 elections, Congress(I) sat in the opposition benches. In May of 1990, it accused the government, now headed by V.P. Singh, of harassment. The vigilance department apparently raided the houses of pro-Congress politicians and bureaucrats. Singh came up with the usual: "Nobody is above the law." Congress(I) members disagreed. They created noisy scenes in the parliament, protesting this "political vendetta." (295)

Early on, the judiciary did protect many innocent people from vendetta—political or otherwise—of the other branches of the government. It certainly stalled the situation from getting worse. The supreme court even convicted Indira Gandhi of using the government's machinery for political campaigns and voided the election results. Gandhi refused to give up. She showed how far a ruling politician would go in her quest for everlasting power. Despite the absence of any unusual threats to the country, she imposed a state of national emergency. After a few years, owing to a sheer miscalculation, she lifted her seize and conducted elections in which she lost. Charan Singh, one of her opponents, tried to copy Mrs. Gandhi. As the new home minister, he used the country's investigative agencies to harass her. (297)

A couple of years or so before she was convicted, Indira Gandhi displayed a prescience about all this. In April of 1973, she appointed A.N. Ray as the chief justice of the supreme court. In doing so, she bypassed three of his seniors. They promptly resigned. (297)

The appointment of Ray was too little and too late to prevent the conviction of Gandhi. Many commentators, however, regarded this as a watershed event in the decline of Indian judiciary. Owing to this unprecedented interference by the executive branch, the idea of separation powers started to lose its promise. Most judges learned a simple lesson: Few could remain isolated from the corrupt politics that infiltrated every nook and cranny of the country. (297)

Much more so than before, many of them started to trade favors with the politicians. What's alarming is that these judges have behind them the full power of the constitution. Only an impeachment by the parliament can remove any judge belonging to a high court or the supreme court. Unlike the politicians and the other bureaucrats, the judges could hit anyone who accuses them of wrong doing with a charge of contempt of court. Very few dare to speak up. (297)

What little deterrence the politicians had faced from the judiciary in the past, ceased being a factor in their calculations. With judges on their side, they felt emboldened, engaged in more corruption, and destroyed the political freedoms of anyone who would stand in their way.

In addition, the more government had reached into the private affairs, the more it would drown the courts in huge workloads. They had to rule on violations of a multitude of laws dealing with such matters as rent controls, price controls, land ceilings, building codes, false birth certificates, and injured religious sentiments. The courts were so bogged down that most of the time the justice was too delayed to protect those who were wronged by the state or the other individuals.

To make matters worse, the fees were astronomical. Here again government had its hands deep into the pockets of the citizens. Ramakrishna Hegde, chief minister of Karnataka in 1989, for example, found out how expensive it was to seek justice. All he wanted to do was to sue Subramanian Swamy, another politician, for defamation. Court fees in Karnataka were so high that this chief executive of the state filed his suit in the neighboring (state of) Maharashtra. (298)

To contact, then, the Egyptian president, Nasser, Jawaharlal Nehru, needed a special envoy. For this honor, Nehru chose his personal friend Karanzia, who also happened to be the editor of a national magazine, *The Blitz*. (299)

Karanzia returned such favors. He toed the official line to the point of supporting the emergency imposed by Nehru's daughter, Indira Gandhi. He lectured his colleagues about "social responsibility," a.k.a. working as government's mouthpieces. (299)

Besides Karanzia, many others in the media worshiped Nehru. After India's humiliating defeat in war with China, however, most journalists sobered up. For trusting the government's propaganda, they felt like suckers. Many developed a healthy case of skepticism. After the war, they grilled Krishna Menon, Nehru's defense minister. Nehru had to move Menon, his friend and a trusted aide, to another department. (300)

Over the years, many Indians, including journalists, started to question the official line for another reason. Day in and day out, rising corruption and official ineptitude, which contrasted sharply with the positive images promoted in the media, stared in their face and mugged these Indians into reality. Most in the country concluded that their leaders would do and say just about anything to stay in power. (300)

Of course, there were those who continued to question the need for a free press in a country "plagued by poverty and superstition." They came up with fascinating arguments. A questioning press would spread cynicism, weaken the administration, impede the developmental process, and render this diverse country ungovernable. Compared to freedom of speech, even leprosy had a better reputation. (300)

What these skeptics were really saying was that the policies and politics of distribution wouldn't survive an open debate. People who were left out of the handout process would raise their voices through the free media. Their dissent would weaken the leadership and splinter the country. Indira Gandhi preferred "a third way," something "that lay between the Western and the communist models." She called it *developmental journalism.* She praised *responsible* journalists who had supported her. She told a conference of station directors of (the state-owned) All India Radio that she never understood the concept of an unbiased radio. There was no doubt in her mind that it was a government organ. (300,301)

Despite such paternalistic (or is it maternalistic?) reasoning, Indira Gandhi committed the final act that boosted the cause of freedom of press. During the *national emergency,* her government took advantage of its newly acquired draconian powers; once and for all, it tried to destroy what little freedoms the press had enjoyed. Its attempts to cover up the official excesses during this period showed what Indira Gandhi really meant when she had called for "developmental journalism." (300,301)

Later on, an investigative panel (Shah Commission) brought to light many of the horror stories of this emergency period: Officials kept a close eye on many newspapers. They scrutinized everything from reports on the parliamentary proceedings and court judgments to birthday greetings to an opposition politician, Morarji Desai. One of the editors, A.D. Gorwala (of *Opinion*), couldn't find a press crazy enough to print his reports critical of the government. To publish his magazine, Gorwala had to use a laborious and primitive method called cyclostyling. The officials also cut off electricity to a newspaper office. They delayed a few editions of another one just long enough to kill the news value of the paper's stories. For once they figured it right. Nothing is as old as yesterday's paper. (300,301)

Of course, they employed such despotic measures only against a few newspapers. Out of fear, however, the rest capitulated. They failed to report on such "developmental activities" as thousands of forced sterilizations. While the officials were throwing the poor out of the urban slums in the name of beautification, most *responsible* journalists stayed mum. (300,301)

Most, but not all. *Indian Express*, despite the frequent harassment of its owners, defied the authorities and kept on reporting. After the emergency was lifted, even its competitors praised *Indian Express*. Suddenly the printed word acquired a new credibility, more so because the government continued to own the only radio and television networks in the country. From the excesses of the emergency period, many learned that, to get the real story, they had to look elsewhere.

They certainly looked with a vengeance. Within the next few years, there was literally an explosion of periodicals, dailies, and magazines. By 1984, the total circulation jumped to a record sixty-one million. Advertisement revenues went up to 6,000 million rupees in 1988, a 1,000 million increase in just one year. (302)

Politicians, however, continued to regard free speech as a fly in their ointment. They refused to let up in their attempts to silence their critics, including a few light-hearted ones. For making fun of Rajiv Gandhi's mannerisms and for lampooning the national anthem, Johnny Lever, a stand-up comedian, was arrested. Early on (in 1974), for speaking against police brutalities and oppression, a Marxist revolutionary poet had been charged with sedition. The authorities continued to detain him without any bail. They implicated him in twelve cases of which he was acquitted in three; one case was discharged and two were quashed. By 1989, the officials failed to even file the charge sheets on two of the six remaining cases. Meanwhile, his family was shadowed, systematically harassed, and isolated from any help. (303,304)

Stand-up comedians are hardly a craze in the country, and revolutionary poets support freedom of speech only until the arrival of *the dictatorship of the proletariat*. To get the mainstream press, however, the authorities had to use a more discrete and subtle approach. Especially after the emergency period, they labored under a few democratic formalities. As much consummate professionals as they were, they found a way. They simply employed the same regulatory powers that they had used to control the other businesses.

Their tactics made it impossible for Vinod Mehta to continue as editor-in-chief of *The Indian Post* (a Bombay daily). Finally (in 1989), he resigned. Mehta explained, "I was informed by the management that certain reports appearing in *The Indian Post* against prominent persons had caused Raymond's group [the post's owners] serious problems and embarrassment and jeopardized the group's [other] business interests." (305)

These owners had business investments worth 6,000 million rupees on line. Just like everyone else, to conduct their businesses, they needed the ruling party's blessings. The management repeatedly advised Mehta not to carry adverse reports on Rajiv Gandhi and his aides, but Mehta refused to listen. One of these aides even asked the owners to sell the paper to an industrialist close to the Congress(I) party. Before he finally left, Mehta commended his employers. After all, they had lived with eighteen months of his attacks on prominent members of the ruling party. (305)

*The Statesman,* another famous newspaper, had reported on a corruption scandal involving a close friend of Rajiv Gandhi and the Sumitomo Corporation of Japan. In retaliation, the government allegedly delayed the clearance for a multi-story office building that the newspaper owners were planning to erect in Delhi. The authorities scrutinized income tax and foreign travel documents of one of its editors. The officials also investigated a few stockholders of the company. The adverse publicity hurt the stock value and fed the rumors of a possible takeover. On its front page, *The Statesman* had to declare that it was not for sale. (306,307)

Newspapers and magazines also depended upon government for, among other things, newsprint. Close to 35% of their newsprint, they bought through the government's State Trading Corporation. The government raised both prices and import duties of newsprint. Due to such measures, over the two years prior to 1989, while the world prices for newsprint were going down, those in India increased by 60 to 100 percent. Because newsprint took up more than half the direct production costs, these price hikes hit many papers hard; especially, the small ones fared poorly. By 1989, close to seven thousand small newspapers faced an imminent shutdown. (308,309,310,311)

Manufacturers of newsprint lobbied heavily for price increases. Naturally, they were happy. So were the officials of the television network. Owing to the increased costs of magazines and newspapers, advertisement on TV was expected to picked up. Instead of demanding such measures as a reduction of duties, the newspaper owners called for rationing. That suited the officials fine. They loved to ration in favor of their friends. They also more than loved to shut down the rest of the press. (308,311)

On occasion, they did so literally. When a family dispute caused a minor scuffle at the offices of a newspaper (*Dainik Bhaskar*), the police took over the building "to prevent any possibility of breach of peace." On many occasions prior to this one, this newspaper had *breached the peace*: It had adversely reported on Arjun Singh, the state's chief minister. (312)

Recently (1989), editors of the *Indian Express* started to transmit their reports using couriers; they stopped using their teleprinter and telex lines. The Congress(I) government tapped these gadgets. This should surprise few. Of all the newspapers in the country, the one Congress(I) loved to hate was *Indian Express*. Congress(I) politicians accused Ramnath Goenka, chairman of the paper and a prominent industrialist, of being fervently anti-Congress. They branded the paper as a mouth piece of the "Goenka empire." They also made sure that, by the end of 1989, *Indian Express* had 300 court cases pending against it. (310,313)

During a raid on the paper's offices in the same year, the income tax officials went straight to a particular desk and asked for a specific ledger dealing with the purchase and sale of newsprint. Managers at *Indian Express* realized how, all of a sudden, the tax department developed such psychic powers. They got busy looking for the mole(s). (314)

By and large, such tactics happen to be just an exercise in overkill. Politicians catch many more flies with honey.

And they control plenty of the sweet stuff, for example, up to twenty-four percent of the total advertisement revenues in the country. Because government owns a lot of industries and employs a huge advertisement budget, politicians and bureaucrats get to decide who in the media get the business, and, of course, the big bucks. *Jansatta,* a newspaper from (the state of) Madhya Pradesh, reported how these funds promoted corruption, if not outright thought control. *Jansatta* claimed that editors of small weeklies regularly approached the chief minister's office looking for these handouts. (310,315)

*All India Small and Medium News Papers Federation* felt betrayed. Its members held demonstrations and called for a boycott of *Jansatta.* They also did something that should make every journalist, living or dead, tingle with pride: They demanded that the government should take action against this daily. (315)

Besides doling out all this advertisement money, the officials can also lavish regulatory relief on the owners. In a few towns in (the state of) Madhya Pradesh, for example, they waived the various rules that had governed the use of land in press complexes. By flouting these laws, newspaper owners had been making profits all along. After the waiver, they would selectively enjoy the official blessing for their actions. (316)

When they can, the officials also insert themselves into such things as labor disputes and enhance their control over the media. Just like the other workers in the country, journalists lobbied Rajiv Gandhi, then prime minister, to increase their wages. They wanted the government to tighten a few screws on the management. Ruling politicians love to oblige such requests. More likely than not, the journalists who plead for higher government-imposed wages will feel obligated to the politicians. (317)

If a journalist plays saint and shuns the awards and special titles that the officials can bestow upon him, it hardly means that he can maintain his independence. Brahmadeo Singh Sharma, an editor in (the state of) Bihar, discovered this the hard way. In his city of Dhanbad, Jagdish Raj, the police superintendent, disliked Sharma's report on police brutalities. On charges of failing to appear when summoned, Raj arrested Sharma. Sharma, however, claimed that he had never received the summons. Only after the intervention of the state's chief minister, was Sharma even taken for a bail hearing. (318)

To be fair, Congress(I) was hardly alone in doctoring the media. In (the state of) West Bengal, for example, the ministry of information and cultural affairs of the Marxist government produced and distributed pamphlets describing the violent ways of Congress(I). In (the state of) Andhra Pradesh, Rama Rao, then the chief minister, decided to use the taxpayer's funds to launch a fortnightly publication. Its sole purpose was to highlight Rao's achievements. (319,320)

Many who back *responsible* journalism and "society's" control over newspapers claim that, unlike the consumers from the West, the majority of Indians are too illiterate to police the media. But the consumers in this state proved such cynics wrong. The readers refused to spend their hard earned money on this piece of propaganda. Finally Rao's government sold the paper by weight. (320)

Notwithstanding the constant pressure from the ruling politicians, the print medium has to cater to the consumer. In any competitive market, to be able to sell, the message has to be believable. Few readers will plunk their hard earned rupees down to buy a paper that they consider a pack of lies. On many occasions, even the usually pro-Congress(I) papers have had to choose credibility over the party's interests.

But the broadcast networks have no such competitive pressures to deal with. True to its role as the master planner and provider of most services, government owns and operates the (until recently) only radio (AIR) and television networks (Doordarshan) in the country. Every ruling party used its control over the broadcast media to the hilt. It set the agenda, prescribed the limits, conducted the debate, and stifled any and all dissent. The main goal was to create its own reality. Even the slightest of deviations from the official position resulted in threatening phone calls from the minister's office. In a recent (1989) poll, close to sixty percent of the sample population considered Doordarshan biased. At that time, Congress(I) was in power. A surprising forty-two percent of its supporters acknowledged the slant towards their own party. Krishna Kumar, then (1988) an information and broadcasting minister, made no bones about it. He said, "The government's achievements have to be projected. This is the legitimate work of the Information and Broadcasting Ministry." (322,323)

Especially before elections, the likes of Kumar shift into a higher gear. Hoping to drown out any and all dissent, they create a lot of noise. For months before the 1989 elections, Doordarshan treated its viewers to hours of programming on sexy subjects such as the "new employment scheme" and "local administration" *bills*. The audience had to sit through hours of patriotic plugs. The national flag showed up on the TV screen a little more often than usual. The symbolism was hard to ignore. The country's flag closely resembled that of the Congress party. (324)

A few opposition politicians did manage to show up in the newscasts. A photograph showing these gentlemen in the company of a known heroin smuggler got a full forty seconds coverage on the national TV. One of them, Satya Prakash Malaviya, claimed that this picture was taken at an unscheduled tea party and that he did not know the smuggler. Soon, M. Yadav, another non-Congress leader, produced a photograph showing Rajiv Gandhi (then prime minister), two former Congress chief ministers and *the same smuggler.* Doordarshan ignored the new picture. It failed to air demands by the opposition leaders that both they and Rajiv should be simultaneously investigated for any ties with this smuggler. (325)

The network lost interest in this story. Soon, it moved on to other interesting topics. To protest the Congress(I) rule, then the united opposition staged a strike. Doordarshan spent eighteen minutes to cover it, but only to show what a flop it was. In four states ruled by its opponents, Congress(I) prevented the TV crews from covering media events sponsored by local governments. (325,326,327)

To be subjected to censorship by this network, one need not necessarily belong to an opposition party. Doordarshan interviewed Indira Jaisingh, a feminist leader, about a controversial Muslim women's bill—largely favored by Muslim leaders. She told the interviewer that the bill was unconstitutional and anti-women and it violated woman's right to equality before the law. This interview was prerecorded. Later on, when she saw it on television, Jaisingh probably choked on her popcorn. Before they aired the piece, the officials edited out all her criticisms of the bill. She sued Doordarshan. Bombay high court agreed with her. It cited the network. (328)

Officials feel that only they can decide what this idiot of a consumer can handle. As to whom to offend, only they get to pick and choose. They edited out Singh's critique of the bill because Muslim leaders, with their vote banks, had failed to make it to their (officials') list of those that needed to be vilified.

So did the police. The television officials rejected one movie because it showed policemen in bad light. *In the Dust of Development*—a movie by Meera Dewan, an internationally acclaimed movie maker—also bit the dust. The official reason: "It offers no solutions." "They make you feel so unpatriotic," says Dewan, "One puts more energy in dealing with the bureaucracy and in running around to government offices than in the film itself." (329)

To ward off such criticism, the officials employ another simple trick. They pay the producer. They assure her that the show will be aired "when a slot becomes available." And the bureaucrats simply use their *editorial prerogatives*: They make sure that for controversial shows—covering such topics as aviation disasters—the slot seldom opens. As to the wasting of money, who's counting? (330)

After defeating Congress (I) and coming to power, in December of 1989, Janata Dal did introduce a bill to reform the broadcast media. A corporation, headed by four full-time and seven part-time governors, was supposed to supervise the television and radio networks. Based on recommendations from the vice-president, chairman of the press council, and a nominee of the government, the president of India was supposed to appoint ten out of these eleven governors. (331)

The *media reformers* rejected any solution that would solely rest upon intelligence of the consumer and the power of his choice. They dismissed, out of hand, such ideas as multiple privately owned radio and TV channels. Said B.G. Verghese, a media expert, "Commercial channels dish out rubbish. It would be a perversion." (331)

Such officials also presume that the president and vice-president are above the day-to-day politics. In reality, however, both the president and his vice (no pun intended) are beholden to the legislators who had elected them in the first place. For example, prior to the 1989 elections, S.D. Sharma, then vice-president of India, refused to release a magazine as planned because of the nature of its contents: It contained a few anti-Congress(I) articles. (336)

Also, the ruling party would continue to have its fingers on the remote control of these *autonomous corporations*. With their revenues at 2,300 million rupees and expenditures at 8,600 million (1989 figures), parliament must vote funds for these broadcasting corporations. Amrit Rao Shinde understood what it meant to be controlled by the officials. He said, "Instead of *mantralaya* [ministry], you will say board of governors." He ought to know. Shinde was the director general of All India Radio. (331)

In other words, if implemented, this proposal would have made the bird cage a bit larger. It lulled many critics of government's media policy into a false sense of security. They reasoned that because Congress(I) was thrown out, everyone had learned his lesson, those anti-Congress leaders would be above using the media to their advantage and all that was needed was minor tinkering.

Soon, however, the new rulers revealed their true colors. In early 1990, Chutala, then chief minister of (state of) Haryana, apparently led hordes of gun-wielding hoodlums and captured booths in his assembly constituency—Meham. Quite a few died in the riots. A few independent producers captured the attacks on camera and offered the footage to Doordarshan. This government owned television network refused to use it. It gave the story a very limited coverage. (332,333)

Around this time, Thomson Press (printers of *India Today*) experienced a blackout. Also, in (the state of) Haryana, where Thomson press was located, one journalist was handcuffed and paraded through the streets and another was charged with arson. (334,335)

These journalists and Thomson Press had one thing in common. They reported on the poll-related violence in Meham and implicated Chautala in it. Chautala and his father, Devi Lal, then deputy prime minister of India, belonged to an anti-Congress National Front headed by V.P. Singh. All these reports made Singh look bad. After all, while in opposition, he and his colleagues protested such behavior by Congress(I). Apparently Singh hated to look bad. He pressured Chautala to resign. (334)

That upset Devi Lal, Chautala, and members of a union supporting him—LMS (*Lok Mazdoor Sangh*). For their blues, however, the LMS members found a miracle cure; beating up those who had caused it. LMS people picked, as their targets, workers at Thomson Press, who incidentally belonged to a rival union—HMS (*Hind Mazdoor Sangh*). Police in the state knew better than to cause grief to Chautala and his friends. Despite many complaints from the victims, the authorities refused to file charges against the members of LMS, but they did file

against a few members of HMS. In the absence of police protection, workers at Thomson Press feared attacks by LMS. They
failed to show up to work. (334)

By then, members of Congress(I)—who, while in power
could have authored a book titled *One Thousand and One Ways
to Muzzle the Press*—were sitting in the opposition benches
and hated every minute of it. They loved to embarrass the new
administration. They caused an uproar about the blackout in
Thomson Press, which the government blamed on "technical
problems." (334)

It was entirely possible that technical glitches did cut the
juice off at Thomson and the journalist did commit the arson.
Such coincidences, however, spooked the reporters. It was a
habit born out of experience. Whoever was in power always
considered them to be more of a nuisance than they really
were; the rulers did whatever they could to silence the press.
Once out of power, the same politicians found it to their benefit to recite the Bill of Rights. They created uproars about funny
looking blackouts.

Awatef Rehman, a professor at Cairo University, points out how
this kind of media manipulation has backfired on the third world
governments. It's like *if you don't talk to your child about the
facts of life, she will get her education from her high school buddies anyway.* Rehman says that, by suppressing the national
press, these governments have made their people easier targets for domination by the Western mass media. (321)

Rehman seems to be a very perceptive man. When the going gets tough, many Indians switch on their shortwave ra-
dios. During the Indo-Pakistani War (1971), I remember listening to the BBC just to find out what was really going on. The
officials at the All India Radio (AIR) care a lot about the political
implications of what they put on the airwaves. They have little
use for such ideas as the quest for truth and prompt reporting.
For a few hours after the Western media had reported on the

assassination of Indira Gandhi, AIR carried on as if nothing had happened. No announcements, no mourning, just farmer's shows, love songs… the usual programming. (351)

This is hardly new. Whomsoever was in power always followed the motto: "World according to Raj."

They used their ownership of the radio and television networks to decide which of the world events the public should know about and when it should know. Government also tailored the message to fit its needs. Out of habit, it wrapped its intentions in pretty package. P. Upendra, the information and broadcasting minister, said in 1990, "You have to think of friendly nations…. Ultimately freedom of information can't go against the national interest." (333)

He did so when asked about the role of Indian TV and radio in playing down the remarkable events of the communist world during 1989 and 1990. Upendra saw no reason to embarrass his friends in the communist party of India. With this *national interest* in mind, this anti-Congress politician choose propaganda over truth. (333)

For the same reason, Congress(I), too, glossed over the demise of these leftist dictatorships. More importantly, both Congress and its opposition professed socialism in one form or other. All along they had mouthed the official line from communist countries and denigrated capitalism. They claimed that communism worked well except that it was a bit undemocratic. Based on these arguments, they embraced the happy medium—democratic socialism. The collapse of communist economies together with the phenomenal success of capitalism in Southeast Asia, however, challenged this orthodoxy. Indian politicians hated *glasnost* in any shape or form.

Besides driving them to scramble for an ideological cover, Glasnost also removed the wind behind their policy of non-alignment, which, based on a strange logic, equated the imperfect Western democracies with the brutal Stalinist dictatorships. The Indian officials worried that the voter might found out how they rode with one leg on each horse and landed the country in its current limbo. In the face of a severe shortage of fig leaves, Doordarshan resorted to a valiant rear guard action.

In 1989, it decided that the rapid changes that were reshaping the world were going against the "national interest" and simply scrapped its program, Weekly Glimpse of the World. (337)

Officials used their control over the media, doctored the facts and projected their view of the world for a simple reason. That way they could do as they pleased. Without first convincing the voter that the country would benefit from their adventures, for example, they could gain a few foreign policy *successes*. These adventures were more than a luxury. They served the officials as their very own decoy. Any *success* abroad diverted the attention from the tough problems at home. It would be a definite crowd pleaser. Indira Gandhi, for example, became very popular after the 1971 war in which she successfully split Pakistan into two; off the three-pronged threat to India from its hostile neighbors, she, thus, crushed one prong. Without delivering on her grand slogan of, "Ban poverty," largely owing to this victory, Indira Gandhi won handily in the next elections.

Because the economy continued to be weak, however, the rulers always needed such decoys. In their quest for cheap popularity, they soon started to view India's other not-so-hostile neighbors as a fair game. Politicians, who were used to muzzle criticism from inside the country, started to deal forcefully with these small countries. In 1975, Indira Gandhi incorporated into India the sovereign state of Sikkim. (339)

Such behavior lead the *Illustrated Weekly of India* to run (in 1989) a cover story with a question: "Is super-India emerging as the big bully?" The magazine raised this question after India had blockaded Nepal, a mountain kingdom in the Himalayas. Nepal had traded with India for a long time. It had exported raw materials such as jute, rice, timber, and sugar and imported fuel, medicines, machinery, and manufactured goods. In 1988, alone, it ran up a trade deficit of more than $200 million. For a few years before 1989, however, India and Nepal hadn't seen eye to eye. India was unhappy with Nepal's intentions to buy arms from China. India vetoed a Chinese bid to build a highway in Nepal. Nepal's decision to float a proposal declaring itself "a zone of peace" also irritated Indian officials. They feared that such a proposal would preclude a possible stationing of India's military forces in Nepal. (338,339)

More importantly, Nepal became the victim of a few political calculations in New Delhi. Beset by scandals and after steadily losing in the public opinion polls, Rajiv Gandhi's government was looking for ways to redeem itself when it suddenly discovered Nepal. Indian government refused to sign an agreement initialed by both sides six months before. Its rhetoric jumped to a fever pitch. Suddenly it canceled the transit rights for its landlocked neighbor. (338,339)

It did so when trade talks between these two countries had failed, as they had routinely done between many other countries before. Europe and the US, for example, had disagreements over farm subsidies and India, itself, had its share of fights with the US. On occasion, such disputes might make it to the front pages of newspapers or even figure in idle conversations. They, however, rarely led to blockades. Also, like most other countries, India and Nepal had, all along, treated trade and transit as separate issues. International law guaranteed such rights of transit. Rajiv Gandhi's government ignored these norms. It shut down all but two of Nepal's twenty-one trade and fifteen transit points. Goods such as medicines, kerosene and baby food became scarce in Nepal. Due to the embargo on petroleum products, factories and vehicles came to a standstill. (338)

Despite the human misery, in a crazy way all this worked in favor of Nepal. It catalyzed an upheaval which would ultimately deliver to the people of this country a parliamentary democracy. Indian politicians neither predicted nor claimed such a change as their purpose.

Speaking of claims, when questioned by the media about the origination of terrorist activities by Tamils in Sri Lanka, Indira Gandhi claimed that no such training camps existed in India. While she was vehemently doing her denial, many ex-military officers—with the knowledge and support of the various government agencies-were training the Tamil guerrillas; so concluded reporters from *India Today*. Owing to a brilliant piece of investigative journalism, they uncovered a few training camps teeming with guerrillas who vowed their allegiance with such radicals as George Habash of the PLO (Palestine Liberation Organization). The reporter, Sekhar Gupta, described the political views of these Tamil guerrillas as "extreme leftist." (340,342)

Hoping to please voters from the southern state of Tamil Nadu, the national leaders soon deepened India's involvement in Sri Lankan affairs. Under the protection of its air force jets, India air-lifted twenty-five tons of relief supplies to Tamil rebels in areas blockaded by Sri Lankan forces. This display of might softened up Sri Lanka. It agreed to accommodate *Tamil aspirations of autonomy and equality.* But many Tamil leaders objected to the deal mediated by India. It foreclosed on their demands for a separate state. A few Tamil groups felt that they were not consulted enough. One Tamil leader claimed that he had signed the accord because he "had no choice and was pressured by Delhi." Soon, it became known why a few of his colleagues *had no choice.* Indian officials gave them a bribe of five million rupees. (340,341,343)

Many Tamil groups refused to disarm. They escalated the violence. A struggle that was instigated in the name of Tamils' rights deteriorated into brutal clashes. Extremists and moderates among the Tamils killed each other. In an ironic twist, these terrorists used the arms, money, and training that they had received in the jungles of south India to kill members of the 50,000 strong Indian peace—keeping force and mastermind the brutal assassination of Rajiv Gandhi.

Despite India's own economic problems, its leaders wasted precious resources in these misadventures. More importantly, in light of its own separatist agitations, the country found itself in a morally defenseless position. Says a report in the *Economist,* "Unfashionably, Asia appears to be giving birth to an embryo super power with expansionist ambitions at a time when the real super powers of the world are at least trying to look less menacing." (339)

The report explained the motive behind such aggression: "An adventurous foreign policy is the last hope of a worried government." (339)

Following the tradition of "worship the leader," S. Kesari, a treasurer of Congress(I), extolled the importance of Rajiv Gandhi to India. Kesari said, "We must eliminate all those who dare to malign the youngest prime minister." Hermann Goering [20] couldn't have said it better. (344)

Kesari had every reason to extol. Just like Goering, he benefited from all the powers which his leader had gathered. So did Bhuta Singh—another inner circle type and then (1989) home minister under Rajiv Gandhi. A reputed newspaper compared Singh to Beria, head of the dreaded secret service under Stalin. Singh headed an invisible but omnipresent security force. Allegedly, he had collected incriminating dossiers on most everybody. The likes of Kesari and Singh love to use the government and its organs to trample on whomever or whatever happens to be in their way. By equating the welfare of their leader with that of the nation, they justify their actions. Rajiv Gandhi himself declared, "Our enemies are not the enemies of the Congress alone. They are also the enemies of the nation." (345,346)

Within a few days after a similar speech by Rajiv, one of the student organizations affiliated with his party staged a violent demonstration at the residence of a prominent opposition figure, Ram Jeethmalani. Their conduct even worried a few Congress(I) members who felt that their party might have created its version of "political storm troopers." (347)

The *Illustrated Weekly of India* couldn't help but notice the slow evolution of political life toward dangerous authoritarianism. It opened its report on Gandhi's information minister with a question: "Has Rajiv found his new Goebbles [21] in Professor K.K. Tewari? He (Tewari) works hard, bars no hold when it gets down to a street fight, and swears undying loyalty to his Fuhrer." (348)

In the ensuing interview, Tewari did little to allay such fears. He dismissed all the talk of an Indian Glasnost as "nonsense." As far as he was concerned, freedom would lead to anarchy. When pressed about the role of the radio and the TV, he said,

"Their business is not to criticize the government. They have other things to do." (348)

Tewari alleged that, in order to destabilize the incumbent Congress(I) party, a foreign intelligence agency had bankrolled the *Indian Express* and all the opposition parties. Such leaders did much more than attempt to tarnish the reputation of those who disagreed with them. Reminiscent of attacks on unfriendly industrialists in Nazi Germany, members of Congress(I) party, while in power, harassed many corporations, including the owners of *Indian Express.* (348)

This kind of aggressiveness towards opposition—from in and out of the country—is the hallmark of most distributive systems. So concluded Friedrich Hayek in his (1944) book *Road to Serfdom.*

By reading this book, the earlier leaders of India could have foreseen the consequences of their policies. Hayek pointed out how the inherent distributive nature of socialism made the use of force rather inevitable. This is true not just in communist dictatorships. When well meaning socialists (such as Nehru and those of Weimar Republic in Germany) try to reconcile the irreconcilable ideals of democracy and of forced distribution, they face insurmountable odds. Unwilling to use the force needed to distribute, they hesitate. That makes them look weak and indecisive. In due course, they are replaced by those who are corrupt and/or authoritarian, and are ready and willing to use their enormous powers to stay in office indefinitely. Eventually, the voter is left to choose from among the least desirables. As such, he becomes too powerless to prevent an ultimate slide toward some form of totalitarianism. (349)

Of course, in the face of the electoral defeat of Congress(I) in 1989, such warnings might sound a bit hysterical. The subsequent events, however, proved otherwise. The new rulers, too, captured voting booths and harassed their opponents. The former also bickered among themselves. By his attempts to develop his own vote bank, each deepened the divisions in India. In less than a year, their government collapsed.

All this left news reporters in the country feeling disgusted. The *Statesman* predicted a bleak future for India. The *Indian*

*Express* blamed all the parties "for the squalid levels to which the country's politics had been reduced to in these two months." It added that the political system had almost been reduced to shambles by a combination of "unbridled play of personal ambitions and the crassest kind of populism that has stirred up dormant animosities." (350)

The reporter from the *Illustrated Weekly of India* who had interviewed Tewari predicted as much. Several months before the 1989 elections, the reporter said that the opposition (to Congress-I) would deliver an equally obnoxious government and "that's the tragedy which may well breed the kind of malevolent nationalism men like Tewari boast of." (348)

---

[19]Judged by the multitude of laws and regulations, most every citizen would fit this description.

[20]Goering, Hermann Wilhelm (1893–1946); German Nazi leader under Hitler, premier of Prussia, minister of aviation and president of Reichstag.

[21]Joseph Paul: Minister of propaganda for the German Third Reich under Adolph Hitler.

# CHAPTER 10
## *It Doesn't Matter; It Will Do;*
## *It's Okay; Yes master;*
## *and Poor Chap*

MURAD ALI BAIG, a public relations executive for Escorts, Ltd., lists the words that often come up in conversations among (Hindi speaking, in this case) Indians: *Parwa Nahin; Chalega; Thik Hai; Jihuzur; and Bichara*, or respectively, it doesn't matter; it will do; it's okay; yes master; and poor chap. (352)

These words reveal the attitudes of carefree tropical islanders who live off trees, not those of members of a nation that are willing to do whatever it takes to survive. Besides Baig, many other Indians complain how lazy their countrymen are. After recommending a massive grassroots campaign to clean up the environment, Prinay Gupte, author of *India: The Challenge of Change,* pulls back to say, "And I am not so sure that Indians are often inclined to galvanize themselves to work for causes whose rewards aren't easily forthcoming." (351)

Quite a few of these *it-doesn't-matter-it-will-do* folks, however, go abroad, prosper and confound their critics. Says Baig, "The ultimate irony is that outside our sacred land, Indians are recognized as being among the hardest working and most intelligent people in the world...They cut through foreign corporations like knives through butter." (352)

It's debatable whether these carpetbaggers are smarter or work harder than any other group of emigrants. One thing, however, is certain. Most of these Indians do make frequent trips back home. They hand Air India unsolicited business and go on to complain about the service. Many of them also bitch about the arrogance of customs officials, stupidity of bank bureaucrats, mosquitoes, heat, dust, and the road conditions because of which it takes half a day to visit one's beloved grandmother who only lives forty miles from one's home town.

What annoy our typical traveler the most, however, are the *attitudes* of many that live back home. He notices that, in managing their day-to-day lives, few engage in any kind of planning. Rather than doing whatever it takes to earn money, unemployed young men and women moan and groan about the quotas and lack of *influence*. Quite a few routinely blame other individuals—usually a few leaders that happen to be in charge at the time—for whatever goes wrong. Our traveler encounters many people who seem to alternate between feelings of apathy and helplessness and those of frustration and rage. He also notices that, to an unbelievable degree, they display a kind of numbness toward the ever-increasing violence that manifests itself as paralyzing strikes and destruction of property and toward degradation or even loss of human life.

After all, our emigrant-turned-vacationer grew up with the same attitudes, but he finds it hard to accept them now. In his heart he also realizes something else: Over the years, it's he, not people from *back home*, who has changed. He suffers from new perspectives. Explanations that have made sense before no longer do so. They sound like mere excuses.

This is not to say that everyone in a country thinks and acts the same way. In most countries, however, a sizable segment of the population tends to exhibit a degree of uniformity in its behavior. So much so that it reveals a few underlying common patterns of thinking. When a majority of people act out of their commonly held beliefs, they form the so-called consensus.

Consensus lead to such things as political promises, party platforms, government policies, and passage of laws.

In each country, what gives this whole process its own unique spin is the prevailing legal-economic system. Each system rewards certain actions and punishes others. It, thus, modifies the behavior of most individuals in its own way. When most people in a country behave in a certain way, they produce certain results and conditions in their society. Based on what happens to them in these conditions, the people adjust their future behaviors, attitudes, and beliefs, which in turn mold the future laws and dictate future conditions. The process feeds on itself.

To demonstrate the power of an economic system to modify the general behavior and attitudes, Sweden serves as a good example. Until recently, many countries (including those in eastern Europe) viewed Sweden as their model. They thought that it had successfully combined socialism and capitalism. Its social welfare state guaranteed employment, education, child care, health care, and retirement benefits. This sounds great. But what should Swedes work for? Their gambling money? And why should they work at all? With an unemployment rate of 1.8 percent, few worry about losing their jobs. (353)

Swedish planners have all along ignored such questions. Says Nils Lundgren, a local economist, "The whole point of a welfare state is to make sure that whatever happens to the state doesn't affect the welfare of the individual." Experience in his own country proves that, because a state is obviously a collection of individuals, such an insulation is impossible. In the absence of incentives, for example, Swedes behaved like the rest of us and started to work less and less and produce less and less. To get more out of the shrinking pie, workers resorted to strikes, demanding better wages and benefits. While organized labor got more, the rest had to be content with less. (353)

Even King Carl XVI Gustaf, who was expected to normally stay above the fray, told his countrymen that the one reason for their country's problems was that their work ethic was "not the best." A report by Knight-Rudder Newspapers quotes a bus driver: "I know lots of people, they wake up Monday morning and say 'Oh, boy, I don't feel like going to work to-day.' So they call in sick. They go hunting, they work in the garden, they paint the house." (353)

Still, they get paid. Government sends as much as ninety percent of the salary as sick pay directly to the employee. The employer has few incentives to check whether the employee is truly sick or just plain goofing off. The average Swedish worker takes twenty-seven sick days a year. He also enjoys five weeks of vacation. The report goes on to say: "On any given day, it is not uncommon for one-fourth of a factory's work force to be out; on a sunny Monday in summer, the figure might be closer to one half." (353)

✦    ✦    ✦

King Carl XVI Gustaf sounded like someone who would be least impressed by the work ethic of the Soviet citizens. In a Moscow news poll (in 1990), only thirty seven percent of the workers said that they would be willing to work harder for higher pay. (354)

These Soviet citizens suffered through severe shortages. Despite this, the majority were unwilling to work harder. The reason was simple. Their legal-economic system offered few guarantees—otherwise known as property rights—that such work would improve their lot. Through his reforms, Gorbachev tried provide the reassurance. Besides his self-serving insistence on wanting to reform "within the socialist framework," he faced a major problem in the attitudes of his countrymen. Owing to repeated and massive destruction of property rights, through such measures as forced collectivization, and owing to the promises of cradle-to-grave protection, a common pattern of thinking and, thus, behavior had evolved among most Soviet citizens. They became very apathetic, very dependent on *Big Brother*, and, yet, very suspicious of his promise of property rights. Most would rather sit around and wait for his handout than to take the initiative and make a living by producing goods and services. These attitudes doomed *Perestroika* before it had any chance.

To the extent they abridge economic rights, discourage enterprise, and restrict competition, the various governments in India also retard the development of a work culture. Even a simple venture such as street vending can be tough, futile, or even dangerous. For not having a license or breaking some silly law, the vendor lives with the constant threat of harassment (see chapter 2) by the authorities. By not trying at all, the poor man might remain hungry, but he is safe in his hut. Only the very stubborn venture out to make a living. For the most part, however, to prod an unemployed person in India to get moving and start even a low capital business such as vending is very tough. It's as tough as prodding a water buffalo out of a cool pond on a hot summer afternoon. Both instinctively know that they will step into hell.

By whatever means, a few Indians do overcome such obstacles and succeed in their ventures. These businessmen, however, get little credit for providing goods, services and jobs and alleviating the poverty. The popular consciousness, pervaded with leftist ideology, regards them as greedy and exploitive. Even his employees feel that they are toiling just to make the businessman rich. They simply ignore that their work creates wealth and caters to the needs of the consumer. Consequently, most workers view their own contributions as anything but positive, suffer from low self-esteem, and deliver poor performance. Besides, it's hardly as if they must work hard and beat the competition. The business owner is usually well connected; only then can he survive in this legal framework. With plenty of help from the state apparatus, he owns a guaranteed share in the market. He and his workers lead a kind of privileged life. They, too, catch the *taking it easy* syndrome.

Of course, if ever taking-it-easy is made into an Olympic sport, the government officials can bag more gold than the former East Germany and Soviet Union combined. Most of these bureaucrats come to office only to kill time. They discuss everything from politics to sports and take everlasting coffee and lunch breaks. As a matter fact, by working hard in a government office, one risks becoming a bit of an oddball. Naturally, the sky has to fall before many move to their feet.

Sometimes, even when the sky falls, they move slowly and awkwardly. After the fatal attack on Indira Gandhi by her body-guards, her aides shouted orders to each other. They couldn't use the specially-equipped ambulance outside the prime minister's residence, because a short while before the driver had left for tea and taken the ignition keys with him. A couple of the officials lifted her body into a car. After a four-kilometer, twenty-minute ride, they reached the All India Institute of Medical Sciences (AIMS). Amazingly, it had not occurred to anyone to call AIMS by telephone and prepare the hospital authorities for her arrival. The hospital guards didn't know who she was. They took another three minutes to realize her condition and open the gate to let the car in. After another five-minute delay, the attending physicians showed up and took her to the operating room. (351)

According to most news accounts, Indira Gandhi had died well before she was brought to the hospital; even the most efficient management would have made little difference. The officials that the prime minister had surrounded herself with, however, represented the *cream of the crop.* In their ineptitude, they were only matched by their colleagues who, following the assassination, wavered for two days before they imposed any curfew. Meanwhile, thousands of Sikhs were slaughtered in Delhi. Between them, these top officials revealed how far down the path of lethargic mental programming the bureaucracy had traveled. (351)

That should surprise few. The immensely privileged and all pow-erful bureaucrat—a hallmark of every socialist system—can rarely be accused of being efficient.

He derives all his perks and privileges without ever having to deliver. Naturally, he has become an object of envy and awe from the rest. Most talented students aspire to step into his shoes. Because the corporate type is thoroughly discredited, amounts to little, and mostly stays in the background, the government official pretty much serves as their role model. In due course, some of these once industrious students join the government service. They, too, get caught in the *Maharaja* culture. They, too, become inefficient and arrogant. They, too, go back and inspire another batch of young Indians to follow their footsteps.

These young bureaucrats learn fast. Their survival and progress have little to do with their performance. They absorb the atmosphere of *nothing matters.* They are least accountable to their consumers, so *anything goes.* An absolutely minimum level of quality is expected of them. They usually say *"chalega"* or *"it will do."* To those, who can't even do as much as show up regularly, the boss says, *"thik hai"* or *"it's okay."* Owing to the job guarantees of civil servants, the boss can seldom fire them any way. To protect his behind and that of his subordinate who fails to deliver, the boss says about the latter, *"bichara"* or *"poor guy."* The only standard the boss expects from his subordinates is a facade of obedience. To avoid being hassled by him, his minions behave as if they have taken up the survival mantra: *Yes, master.*

Such things as being subservient to those above and to the extent possible using one's position to trample over the rest become essential skills in this culture. Very few dare to question the authority. Those who do, risk sliding into the ranks of misfits. They get transferred to remote places and not so *lucrative* positions. Most people play it safe. They learn to keep quiet and follow orders. Clerks and peons rarely, if ever, sit in front of their officer. When his boss comes to inspect his work, the officer in turn displays his obedience by assuming the early *Homo sapien* posture with folded hands. Doing the personal chores of one's superior becomes an accepted norm.

Slowly, such subservience has spread to outside the government circles. When they visit government institutions, such as nationalized banks, private citizens grovel before the officials. Naturally, after being shouted at in the office by their superiors, or (in the case of private citizens) insulted by the usually arrogant bureaucrats, few dads and moms come home and teach their children to be questioning. The young and old alike have mastered the art of mindless obedience which has become the society's greatest virtue, its creed.

For those who want to study the intellectual oppressiveness and destruction of creativity that pervades the various public institutions, any of the hundreds of professional and post graduate colleges in the country can be a good place to start. These citadels of higher learning live and breathe blind obedience. In most medical schools, for example, it is considered indiscreet to even question the clinical findings of a chief physician. The boss takes out his stethoscope, listens to the patient's chest and announces the diagnosis. The fact that few objective ways (such as sophisticated lab tests) of verifying his findings are available has little bearing on what goes on next. Most students accept the findings as gospel. Those who dare to challenge, risk the wrath of the professor. First, they might suffer through a good dose of tongue-lashing. And it can get worse. During the final examination, they might face the same professor wearing the hat of an examiner.

After passing through such a grist mill, most students end up losing some of their self-respect and confidence, but they accumulate two valuable assets: an unquestioning obedience to authority and an unsurpassed ability to memorize. Rarely, if ever, are they creative. Such concepts as scientific inquiry mean little to them. A few educators do feel embarrassed by the deterioration of quality of scientific studies. Says Dr. Raja Ramanna, a Minister of Defense, "After being told to cultivate the spirit of scientific temper for 40 years, we have allowed ourselves to depend on various types of obstructionist practices which clearly show signs of a lack of confidence in ourselves." Ramanna catalogs the consequences of such self-imposed limits. He talks about how India has developed sophisticated missiles and reactors and says, "yet when it comes to the maintenance on distribution of water supply, roads, houses and traffic, our scientific sense seems to have evaporated." (355)

He exhorted the students to do everything to "increase the scientific quality of life and thinking." If any of them follows this advice and starts to question his professors, however, the student will end up without his doctorate or diploma or even a job. Most students are very smart. They mostly sleep through such sermons. (355)

Besides students and their moms and dads, many others who interact with the bureaucracy pick up on the various attributes of its culture. For example, anyone who tries to be punctual ends up waiting for the other guy that takes it easy. What's the point in hurrying up? Very few plan their days. And fewer plan long-term. Eventually those, who have learned to take it easy at work, bring their lethargy to the other activities. Each also spreads his apathy to a few others. Like a virus, mediocrity infects every arena.

This certainly includes professional sports. When the athletes return with very few medals and trophies, they add to the general disillusionment that blankets the country. After the Seoul Olympics, Murad Ali Baig (of Escorts, Ltd.) said, "Whether it is Olympics or industry, India has failed to respond to an increasingly competitive world. Little Guyanas and Surinams show up the ineptitude and indecisiveness of our policies, while tiny Taiwans and Hong Kongs far outstrip our exports, despite our vastly greater resources and potential." (352)

What brings the best out of these producers from Hong Kong, Taiwan, or any such country is none other than the so called *ruinous competition.* A Japanese automaker, for example, can't wait indefinitely for new designs. He needs them yesterday. Otherwise his competition will outsell him. If a construction project is delayed, the American developer ends up paying additional interest to the bank. In the face of stiff competition, he can pass on very few of these costs to the home buyers. He starts to make money only after he finishes the project. He has little use for tardy subcontractors who, in turn, stay away from lazy workers.

It's an old story that free competition and fear of failure push people to work harder and better. Such a commercial culture, however, produces much more than sleek cars, accurate watches, and that worst nightmare of every parent—a new and improved Nintendo game system each year. The culture also promotes such societal attributes as wide-spread efficiency, accountability, and individual responsibility. Under its influence, for example, the inhabitants of nineteenth-century Britain and that of present-day Japan have made hard work and punctuality an integral part of their consciousness. So much so, these traits have come to be identified with the character of the particular nation. Most of us have virtually made the wristwatch a part of our bodies, but we fail to realize that such an emphasis on value of time is a by-product of the competitive commercial culture of early Europe

Volunteerism, another attribute of the nineteenth century West (see chapter 13), caught up with Parameswara Rao, a nuclear physicist in the US. To start an organization which would primarily push the concept of self-help, Rao returned to India. (356)

The World Bank recognized his pioneering work. One of his projects involved developing marshlands to manufacture salt. Rao haggled with the skeptical bureaucracy and got it to lease the necessary land to his organization. This program worked well and employed many. When he tried a similar strategy to start a sugar mill, however, his luck ran out. The local sugar lobby used its influence over the authorities and killed this project. Like most of us, the sugar mill owners liked social work until it strayed too close to home. (356)

Besides Rao's group, a few other voluntary organizations in India serve the needy. Some clamor for more governmental involvement—quotas, special grants, and so on. Others believe in self-help. A group called Child Relief and You (CRY) also belonged to the second category. Seven people each contributed seven rupees to start CRY. They printed greeting cards and calendars and raised money for poor children. (357)

Owing to such hard work, in ten years prior to 1989, CRY grew: Its collections had increased from 900 rupees to five million. Various companies donated eighty percent of these funds. Five percent came from larger trusts set up by big corporations. Indians living abroad donated another five percent.

Only ten percent came from individuals living in the country. (357)

Indian religions have always emphasized the virtues of charity. In this agrarian society, to turn away hungry beggars was considered evil. Recently, however, this philanthropic flame has dimmed a bit. Notwithstanding efforts by the likes of Rao, woefully very few individuals engage in social service. For one thing, because so many of the public institutions are riddled with politics and corruption, donors tend to be a bit more skeptical. Says a representative of CRY, "There is so much of corruption around that one does not know who to trust." (357)

Besides, in an atmosphere of shortages it's tough to be generous. Excessive taxes and hyper-regulation stunt economic growth and hurt the poor in two ways. Fewer jobs mean that the poor have fewer opportunities to take care of themselves. Even those with jobs just get by. They refuse to fork out money to help the less fortunate. More importantly, in a socialist society, government is already engaged in *charitable* work. It taxes the rich and the middle class. Taking care of the poor and the needy, it proclaims as its mission. It distributes the funds to beneficiaries of its choice, and their ranks rarely include the very poor. The well-to-do hate to pay from both their pockets. Socialism fosters a mindset among the wealthy that taking care of the poor is not their responsibility but the government's.

Many of these rich folks, who rarely donate to charities, know how to influence God. They go beyond offering coconuts to dieties.[22] Nowadays, they also offer huge amounts of money, mostly black money, to temples. In this land of poverty, there is Tirupati—one of the richest pilgrimage places in the world. In income, it is rumored to be second only to the Vatican.

My cousin never believed in bribing God with coconuts or bananas. She told me, "I worked hard all my life. I earned my post graduate degree. All I want is a job. I am tired of depending upon my parents." She wondered, "Why can't the

government limit each family to one job? People like me need
the money much more than all those well-to-do women who
come to work only because they are bored at home. All they
do is to talk about saris and jewelry."

I had known her since she was a little baby. I always thought
her to be smart and sweet. Never before, had I seen her this
depressed, or this bitter. I asked her what she was doing to
climb out of her pit. As she saw it, she had two prospects:
landing a government job or seeking her opportunities outside the country. She hoped that her name would show up in
the soon-to-be-released list of appointees to government jobs
by the Public Service Commission. Soon, however, she learned
that she was not on the blasted list from the blasted Service
Commission. She promptly chose the third avenue which she
was smart enough to keep hidden from me and her parents.
She hanged herself.

She obviously counted on getting this job, but she was hardly
the kind of a person who would end her life after one such
reversal. Based upon our conversation, I concluded that a se-
ries of disappointments had left her feeling that she lacked any
opportunities and, thus, control over her future. Obviously, she
felt terminally hopeless.

Many young men and women like my cousin live in a kind
of limbo. Unlike their parents, they are too *Westernized* to leave
their future to fate, but very few of these kids enjoy the kind of
opportunities that those in the West have and take for granted.
The gap between what they can be and what they are creates
a lot of tension in those who lack the opportunities. It makes
them feel very despondent. On occasion, it pushes them over
the edge. Because they look up to their government as the
only source of hope, when the prospect of landing a government job recedes, they feel as if their life has to come to an end
then and there.

They know of no one else to turn to for hope, certainly not
to themselves. Over the years, the socialist legal framework
has hatched a kind of giant conspiracy against self-reliance. It
has done so by erecting all kinds of barriers along the path of
self-employment and by programing the people to look to *Big*

*Brother* for everything from jobs, cheap rice, and low rents to art shows. To this end, the government has built a huge public sector, legislated price controls and minimum wages, and established art academies. By deciding how much of a certain chemical for a certain detergent is to be produced, it tells the investor that he can avoid the trouble of finding out for himself what the consumers need or want. To anyone, who wants to take his chances and conduct his business his own way, *Big Brother* screams, "No!"

By leading many people to think that they are too weak and too dumb to take care of themselves, he tries to enter a protective relationship with them. Day in and day out, he convinces them to cede more control over their lives by giving up a few more of their economic rights. In the end, however, many—who have traded their basic freedoms for guaranteed opportunities—have neither.

Certainly, they enjoy very few freedoms. As for the opportunities, the officials hand them out to only a few selected beneficiaries. In this scheme of things, no matter how smart a person is, how hard he works, and no matter how many risks he takes, he has little control over what happens to him. In short, his fate becomes predetermined. Why try and try only to fail time and again? Lack of belief that one has any control over one's environment destroys self-confidence and discourages one from taking any initiative. It leads to premature detachment. It enhances one's belief not in one's initiative but in some superhuman force.

Naturally, the study of human affairs takes a backseat to that of cosmic events. In spite of the increasing literacy, astrology is a booming profession in India. Students want to know in advance about their careers and love lives. Fathers want to make sure that their daughters are protected. They marry the girls off to boys with good horoscopes and, of course, government jobs.

Even those who benefit from the arbitrary government policies credit their betterment in life to some superhuman force. Says a poor laborer of his son when the latter has been admitted to a residential school under the quota system, "I don't have land or money. God has done so much for him. He will do more." Such individuals, who feel that someone else is controlling their lives, refuse to take responsibility for anything that happens to them. They don't create their successes. Their choices and decisions have little to do with causing their happiness; someone else's do. They are like leaves drifting in a wind. (358)

If a person feels that he doesn't create his successes, he does not own up to his failures either. For every mishap, he learns to blame the external forces. The bad position of the stars has caused the car accident, not his silly attempts to pass a truck on the heavily traveled road. Because *his own* have failed to make it to the state's cabinet, he has missed his chance to be on that special list published by the Public Service Commission. Rather than the economic and political choices he and his countrymen have made, it's the overpopulation that has caused the shortages. Because too many people live too long, he can't get cement, rice, sugar, or a college admission.

Owing to the belief that external factors such as overpopulation are at the root of their troubles and to a desensitization to the misery that constantly surrounds them, many in the country have developed a kind of cavalier attitude toward life; their own, and more, importantly that of other people.

In (the state of) Karnataka, for example, in 1988 mobs killed six Sikh students. The trouble started when some of the students refused to donate money to celebrate a Hindu festival. For the killings, a local politician came up with a ready-made explanation. He blamed the victims for "failing to become part of the local community." Sikh leaders saw the murders in a different light. Plans by their community to build a medical college had aroused the jealousy of local people. The leaders claimed that a few people belonging to a rival college incited the trouble. (359)

Such a claim is far from outrageous. Most students, who view these seats as tickets out of poverty, are easily aroused by the cries of "someone else taking over our state." Politicians promised a judicial inquiry into the killings. Sikh leaders responded with a few demands of their own—compensation of

500,000 rupees to families of the deceased and new student hostels for Sikhs. (359)

In the view of the attackers, the cynical politicians who explain away such attacks on minorities, the leaders (of the minorities) that try to profit out of such misery, and the usually apathetic public, life itself has acquired a certain disposability. Simply, it has become devalued. Train accidents, floods, and other catastrophes fail to arouse most people. They are no longer bothered by little children who work dangerous jobs just to survive.

Also, parents who part with their children for a few rupees no longer shock the sensibilities of the general public. Recently (1989), an investigation initiated by Bombay police exposed an international gang involved in exporting Indian children to the Middle East. The children, mostly below five, were smuggled out of the country to places such as Dubai to participate in camel races. The children were tightly strapped to the backs of camels. The animals were whipped into a gallop. Alarmed by the cries of the children, the camels would run even faster. Kids who resisted participation were tortured. In the first place, the smugglers lured the families into yielding them custody of the children with promises of good jobs for the parents and free transportation and free "American education" for the children. And anyone who thinks that all the talk of economics is just an intellectual body massage should realize that poverty starves both body and spirit. (360)

"It's a girl!" The person yelling from the delivery room could be a grandparent or just a friend helping out. She could come from a poor family or the middle class. She might even possess a college degree. In any event, it's hard to miss the disappointment in the voice.

If a man's life is cheap in India, that of a woman is even cheaper. She is born into the midst of worries about her dowry.[23] Her parents feel that she takes a lot from them but returns little. They believe that it's more respectable to starve than to go and live in their daughter's home. A son, on the other hand, is expected to take care of his father, mother and everyone else in the family that needs any kind of assistance, for example, his unmarried or widowed sister. Far too frequently, their sons turn out to be the only financial security many parents have in their old age. Instead of asking, "Who will take care of me when I am old?" those without sons euphemistically ask, "When I die, who will set torch to the pyre?"

Many Indian intellectuals sneer at the materialism in the West, especially its lust for life. They, however, ignore how material concerns affect the human interactions in their own country. Unfortunately, in many cases parents' love for their daughters falls into this category. Quite a few parents wish to have just sons and escape the financial burden of providing for daughters. Some go beyond wishing. They abort female fetuses. According to a study in Bombay, in 8,000 abortions that followed amniocentesis, 7,999 of the fetuses were females. Such a bias is hardly limited to villagers. Dr. Gita Pandya (of the Foundation for Research in Reproduction and Reconstruction) estimates that, of her patients who engage in the sex selection, as many as sixty-six percent come from the business community, seventeen percent from industry, ten percent from the service sector, and seven percent from the ranks of professionals. (361,362)

For all this, one can certainly blame the procedure itself and point out how untamed science promotes unethical behavior. The female devaluation, however, precedes amniocentesis or any such technical advance. In villages, unknown numbers of babies die from negligence. Many girls who beat the odds and make it past the newborn period face serious neglect. For them, medical care is usually delayed until it's too late. Safdarjang Hospital in Delhi reports the ratio between boy and girl mortality rates to be eleven to seventeen. No wonder that between 1931 and 1981, the ratio of females to males dropped from 950/1,000 to 933/1,000. (361,362,363)

Compared to eighty percent of the boys, only fifty-four percent of the girls get enrolled in primary schools. Just fifteen percent of the girls finish high school. Each day when they go home from school, many of these girls engage in back-breaking work. You see. As "future housewives," they need all the training they possibly can get at their parents' home. A few relatives and friends take it upon themselves to remind these girls that, by pursuing higher education, they are wasting their time. These futurists say, "All you need to know is how to write a letter to your husband and maybe the grocery list." (363)

Quite a few girls, however, overcome such negative reinforcement, do well in school, join a professional college, and/or take up a career. These women face a lot of criticism. Instead of looking for ways to provide opportunities for both men and women who are willing to work, many blame the women for taking the jobs away from men, "whose job it is to support the families." (363)

In reality, it's the woman's work that supports many families. Bachi Karkaria (of the *India Tribune*) estimates that, in rural areas, little girls work 315 days a year. On average, they toil nine hours a day. They perform much more than household chores. Their sweat accounts for approximately twenty percent of the country's agricultural work. According to the 1981 census, girls compose 8.35 percent of the mainstream work force, while boys make up 4.17 percent. The former work in various industries such as embroidery, gem polishing, and carpet weaving. Nevertheless, these are the lucky ones, especially when compared to the girls who are sold and forced to engage in prostitution, some as young as fourteen. (363)

Women from the middle and upper class families, too, suffer from the devaluation, albeit of a different kind. Instead of giving them a share in the property, their parents pay a dowry to their bridegrooms. Like the most of us, these otherwise bright young men find it hard to shun all this easy money. Besides, few of these guys believe in themselves and their abilities to build a life through their efforts. Probably, the dowry taking prepares a few for real life. These soon-to-be government officials learn how it feels to make money for what they are, not for what they can produce. To many a young man and his parents, this money-grab supersedes all the other aspects of the marriage. Instead of becoming a joyous occasion, the wedding is marred by disputes about money and gifts. Such fights might even outlast the nuptials, and vitiate the family life. They can lead to suicides or bride burnings. And the trend is alarming. During 1985 and 1986, for example, the total figures for bride burnings in India went up by a third, from 990 to 1,319. And these were just reported cases. (364)

"Make disinheriting a daughter illegal and the problem will go away in no time," advise many social workers. India, however, already has such laws on its books. In 1956, for the first time women obtained property rights. Giving and taking a dowry became offenses punishable by imprisonment of up to two years. The laws also decree that any unnatural death of a woman in the first seven years of her marriage should be investigated both by the police and the magistrate. The constitution guarantees: "The state shall not discriminate against any citizen on grounds of race, caste, sex, place of birth." (364)

These laws and guarantees have yielded at best some marginal benefits. If anyone uses them and obtains a divorce or sends her husband to jail, she runs the risk of becoming a social outcast. She, along with her children, has to come back to her parents for support—financial and otherwise. Because their parents have spent money to marry them off in the first place, many of these women feel guilty. Rather than become "a burden on the family for the second time" and stigmatize it with their divorce, quite a few choose to suffer at their husbands' hands. All they can do is keep their husbands happy, at any cost.

In any thriving economy, such a victim has another option. She can move out as far as she likes, live by herself, and spare her family the financial burden, not to mention the stigma of a divorcee living at home. She can choose to do so only because she can find a job with a relative ease. This choice, by itself, affords most women—married or otherwise—a sense of independence and self-worth. It gives them back control over their bodies and their minds. In its absence, the divorce and property laws are as useful as rubles in empty supermarkets.

For an Indian woman—or, for that matter, an Indian man—even with the full support of the family, it's hard to get a decent job. If she won't use connections or pay bribes, she can just forget about it. Naturally, she is at the mercy of her family and its social compulsions. If, by chance, a lucky soul finds a job, moves away, and lives by herself, more than likely she has to fear for her safety from every robber and rapist. She can hardly depend upon the usually-corrupt law enforcement agencies. Mostly, such perpetrators own the system and get away with their criminal acts. A woman activist accused Z.R. Ansari, then a minister of environment, of attempting to molest her. It seems that, of all the places, Ansari picked his ministerial chambers in New Delhi as the site of his adventure. The ruling Congress(I) party not only failed to initiate an inquiry, later on, in the 1989 elections, it gave Ansari a ticket to contest as the party's candidate. (367)

Such cynicism has infected the society from top to bottom. This includes its venerable institutions. In March of 1989, a judgment was issued convicting a few policemen on the grounds of wrongful confinement, using force, causing hurt, and trespassing into Pararia—a small village in (the state of) Bihar. The judge, however, acquitted them of a mass rape. A.K. Chatterji, the officer in charge of the police station, absconded after allegedly supervising the Pararia operation. In just a year, he got his job back. (365)

It was unclear whether these women were raped or not. Newspapers, however, raised a few questions about this case, especially about the way the victims were treated. They accused the investigative agencies of sloppy performance. More than anything, what Judge O.P. Sinha wrote about these victims revealed quite a bit about the widely-held attitudes: "It can not be ruled out that these ladies might speak falsehood to get a sum of Rs.1,000 which was a huge sum for them." The defense council concurred with the judge. The former said that these women could not be equated with "such ladies who hail from decent and respectable society," because "they were engaged in menial work and were of questionable character." (365)

Such poor women might not get a break even in the country's highest court. During the seventies, in Mathura rape case, the supreme court let the alleged rapists off the hook by citing "immoral character of the victim." (366)

To each of its workers, a factory recently issued what one might call a mixed up pair of work shoes—one green and the other gray. My kids might yell, "funky!" But the management had little interest in making any fashion statements. Previously, it had lost several pairs of identical work shoes. To prevent the employees from grabbing some more, it resorted to this color mixing. (368)

Every Indian who owns anything of value can empathize with this management. Both labor under an ethical system in which grabbing as much as one can has become the norm. Such a code of conduct seems to be a natural offspring of an economic philosophy which, despite all the fancy names, great intentions and semi-scientific theories, works with this basic premise: Government owns all the wealth in a country. Only that portion which it lets one keep, one has the right to enjoy. The rest it's free to confiscate and distribute.

By constantly robbing one apostle to pay the another, politicians and bureaucrats give a simple and clear message to each and every individual. He is entitled to services and goods; he need not earn any of this stuff by voluntarily exchanging something of value. The government will be more than happy to get him what he needs. Very few can resist the lure of this message. Most endlessly covet the other's possessions and pocket whatever is in their reach. Tenants refuse to vacate the houses or raise the rents. Employees feel little guilt about taking the company's shoes or, if possible, the whole company.

Few of the landlords, owners of these companies, or, for that matter, holders of any other property, give up what is theirs without a fight. In order to overcome the resistance, the leftists use the force of the confiscatory laws. They employ such instruments as price freezes, rent controls, and worker owner-ship programs. Most Indians not only tolerate such a use of force but actually go along with it; especially those, who hope to receive the loot, love the whole idea. If on a rare occasion the rulers hesitate, the various groups exhort them to act. In 1989, the opposition leaders in India asked the government to raid sugar warehouses. To control sugar prices, they wanted the stocks sold at half the market rate. (369)

In the name of addressing the economic disparities, when government repeatedly used force, it effected a major change in the popular psyche. Over the years, most Indians came to regard the use of force as a solution for all the other societal problems. It became a way of life. To cure such ills as over-population and AIDS, for example, even the gentlest of the souls routinely prescribed the use of force. Avtar Singh Paintal, then (1988) director general of the Indian Council for Medical Research, proposed to make it illegal for locals to have sex with foreigners and NRIs (non resident Indians). He just wanted to prevent the spread of AIDS. Paintal claimed that individuals didn't have the right to have sex with anyone if it could destroy the country. He added, "Fear of the law is what Indians understand." (370)

O.S. Shrivastava, an economist, thought along the same lines. While advocating the use of force to control the population growth, he said, "Compulsions are necessary. Whosoever wants jobs in government or in organized sector, whosoever wants any permit for anything, whosoever wants a loan, a plot of land, a subsidiary, or admissions in college etc. must undergo family planning operation after three children...Whosoever speaks against them [these disincentives] should be considered violating the National Defense Act." (75)

Once the majority in the country have signed on to using such forceful means to achieve seemingly desirable ends and entrusted the government with all the necessary powers to carry out the programs, the people could do precious little when the elites use force indiscriminately, and even illegally, and get away with it. Police attack poor people who defy them; politicians use force to win elections; many hooligans help them by stabbing and shooting the opponents and capturing the booths.

Small wonder that many in the country have concluded that using force works. They believe in it. To address all their grievances—real and imaginary—most jump to use it. All this has filled every nook and cranny of the country with violence, some with a clear purpose and the rest totally mindless. During their strikes, students burn busses, force shop owners to close down, and attack cars whose passengers refuse to *donate* to the strike fund. Unemployed youth demanding job quotas shut down the whole state. Unions harm anyone who dares to cross their picket lines. Farmers attack officials who come to their villages asking for repayment of loans or electricity dues.

The victims of such attacks feel powerless and enraged. When, and if, their turn arrives, they, too, engage in violence and perpetuate the cycle. It has gotten to the point that, after any kind of provocation, many are ready to burst. In the spring of 1989, awaiting for the arrival of the chief minister of (the state of) Tripura, the Indian Airlines staff delayed a flight. Finally His Highness showed up. One of the passengers started to argue with the officials and blamed them for inconveniencing so many people. When the situation was getting out of hand, wife of the irate passenger tearfully intervened. She informed the bureaucrats that she and her husband were attending their son's funeral and every second mattered to them. This sad tale failed to mollify the officials. They refused to tolerate such a challenge to their authority. They continued to harangue the passenger until a few others on the plane got involved. Enraged by the insensitivity of the officials, these hitherto on-lookers—in the words of the reporter—"rose as one to fight them." (371)

Over the years, the Indian army has practiced strict discipline and remained a bulwark against a complete breakdown of law and order. Sometimes, however, even its members lose their cool. On July 4, 1989, a group of soldiers were scheduled to board a train at Lalgarh station in (the state of) Rajastan. A railway official, fittingly titled as "the movement control officer," wanted one of his buddies to be accommodated in a special compartment reserved for these soldiers, a routine request from such an officer. For some strange reason, the soldiers refused. Soon the arguments turned physical. A fight ensued, pitting the railway police on the side of the bureaucrat against the soldiers. (372)

Word got around. Soldiers from a nearby army base arrived with crowbars and hockey sticks. They attacked railway police and then went on a rampage. Fifty to one hundred people—a few railway employees and passengers, including women and children—were hurt. One victim lost his eye. (372)

V.S. Naipul, a famous author of Indian descent, said, "People are not ready to be individuals in India. It will take several generations for that to happen." (373)

Naipul grew up outside India. If he had spent a few years surviving the oppressive atmosphere in the country, however, he would have found out that, repeatedly and persistently, the all powerful state had subdued many Indians to the point that they had lost their sense of self-worth and individuality.

He would have understood that one could only take so much abuse, and that, beyond a point, one would lose all hope, become desperate, and behave in ways that would make little sense to any sensible visitor from outside the country. Certainly, the elders from the village of Morve (in Satara district from the state of Maharashtra) would have horrified such a guest. They decided that, instead of wasting money on useless elections, it was better to auction off the posts of heads of the village administration. On the election day, the highest bidders got the jobs. (374)

The legal structure that had paved the way for such a grotesque demoralization spared few other socialist countries. In the Moscow news poll mentioned earlier, fifty-five percent of the Soviets had no vision of the future. (354)

"The biggest of problem I see is a helplessness in society," says Olga Belukanova, chief of the letters department at the weekly newspaper *Argumenti i Facti*. She adds, "Very few people write that they are doing something. They are waiting. They are accustomed to getting everything from the state. For more than 70 years [of Communism] we got used to it this way." (375)

---

[22]A widely followed Hindu tradition.

[23]The money or property a wife brings her husband at marriage.

# CHAPTER 11
## *From France With Love*

WHEN MOTHER TERESA tried to open a home for the needy in
(the state of) Arunachal Pradesh, she found herself violating, of
all laws, the state's "Freedom of Religion Act (1978)." (376)

George Orwell (author of the book *1984*) would have loved
the name. Yes, this law was about religion, as discovered by
the minorities in Arunachal Pradesh, however, it had little to
do with the freedom to choose one's faith. As a matter of fact,
it specifically forbade them from converting to Christianity.
Alarmed by the high rates of conversion, and to preserve the
tribal religion from extinction, legislators of this state passed
this law and tried to prevent Christian preachers from entering
and conducting services. The ruling politicians, on the other
hand, extended their full support to Hindu missionaries such
as the Ramakrishna Mission and the Vivekananda Kendra to
set up schools and hospitals. (376)

Thankfully, however, like many other laws, this Freedom of
Religion Act too was flouted. The missionaries continued their
work, albeit by more ingenious ways. They set up churches,
schools, and hospitals along the border with Assam, a neighboring state. (376)

The reason why many people had converted to Christianity in the first place was a textbook example of the effects of materialism over the spirit. These poor tribals found their ancient religion to be very expensive. Owing to its emphasis on rituals of animal sacrifice, an average tribal family had to spend over 15,000 rupees a year—an astronomical figure even for the middle class. The tribals who joined Christianity, on the other hand, received food grains and cash from the missionaries. To a greater extent than their Hindu counterparts, the Christian missionaries also provided essential services such as education and medical care and enticed these tribals to convert. (376)

These converts soon discovered the only way to enjoy the right to practice their faith. As their numbers grew, they started to flex their political muscle. Tomo Riba, a former chief minister and a non-Christian, proposed a reversal of the law. He had to. Over forty percent of his electorate were Christians.

Hindu extremists, however, view such *sellouts* with contempt. Time and again, these fanatics have called for a ban on the proselytization. Finally when they prevail, they go on to prove that, in a statist society, the poor and the powerless might not even own their own souls. BJP (Bharatiya Janata Party), a Hindu-based party, did prevail in (the state of) Madhya Pradesh. After its victory in the 1989 elections, it gave priority to this burning problem. The state's assembly, dominated by BJP, passed a resolution calling for "immediate steps to check conversions done by foreign missionaries by use of force or allurement." (376,377)

Barely in office for a few months, these politicians were ready the use the enormous powers of the state to improve their standing with the Hindu vote bank. All such politicians care about is to somehow win in elections. They then go on to collect money and following. Naturally, they have few problems with stripping the individuals of their fundamental rights. They mostly go after the poor and those who refuse to develop or use connections or organize themselves as vote banks.

As much was discovered by Ronald Joffe, who sought the permission to film a Dominique Lapierre's book (*The City of Joy*), and by Lapierre himself, who hoped to make a documentary on Mother Teresa. Upendra, then a minister of information and broadcasting, denied the requests by Joffe and Lapierre, by declaring, "There is no need to show only the slums of Calcutta." (378)

One can be sure that somehow Joffe and Lapierre will survive this rejection. The same goes for their potential consumer who loses the right to judge for herself whether or not there is any need for movies that depict the slums of Calcutta or drug addicts in New York. Despite their pronouncements, however, the likes of Upendra are rarely content to just ban the works that arguably show the country in bad light. By and large, they decide what's good and what's not. They censure all "offensive" forms of expressions. While most nations with Christian majorities let their citizens decide the merit or lack thereof *The Last Temptation of Christ*, for example, Indian officials simply banned the movie.

It was as if only these officials were wise enough to judge. It was as if the consumer was too stupid. It was as if he needed to be protected from ever having to make a decision to see the movie or not. Such a father-child relationship between state and the individual is a hallmark of all statist systems, including democratic socialism. Under the guise of protecting the group rights of Christians, tribals, Hindus, or Muslims, the ruling politicians slowly render the individual rights of each and every citizen null and void. On occasion, the officials impose their will without even giving any explanation. Chidambaram, then a home minister, refused to divulge why he banned a book. He claimed that any explanation would threaten "the national security." (379)

In their zeal to ban books, Indian authorities even outpaced Khomeini. Well before the ayatollah issued his famous death threat against Salmon Rushdie, they banned *Satanic Verses*. For many Muslim leaders, the issue presented a great political opportunity. They tried to consolidate their following with statements such as, "While the West is defending one individual, the Imam [Khomeini] is defending the rights of one billion Moslems." (380)

Such demagoguery by Muslim leaders, who more than likely have not even read the book, inflamed passions. Despite the ban, more than twenty people died in India and Pakistan in the ensuing riots by mobs protesting against Rushdie and his supporters in the West. For three days, these riots paralyzed (the state of) Kashmir. All this violence vindicated many who, early on, fearing widespread unrest, supported the censorship. In their view, the possibility of loss of life was too high a price to pay for the principle of freedom of speech. The well-meaning censors ignored the simple fact that these fights had little to do with Rushdie or his book. They sprang from a hunger for power. Even if government banned all books, movies, and cartoons, demagogues—in search of a loyal following and, thus, power—would literally spin controversies out of air. In India, they did as much. The very next year after *Satanic Verses* was banned, they revived the dormant issue of birthplace of Rama and lead to killings of many more. (380)

As for the rights of billions of Moslems, Christians, or Polynesians, no one has held a gun to their heads demanding they read the book. By chance, if any of them reads a book that he finds blasphemous, he can use his freedom of choice and in the future boycott the source of the *filth*. He can use his freedom of speech (which many of his leaders want to see vanish into thin air) and urge other like-minded citizens to boycott the material. The group leaders, however, gain little from such an empowerment of the individual. What if their followers learn more and start to question the motives and methods of these leaders? These high priests of book-banning do rather well amidst ignorance. And they hate information.

After a great performance which the audience had loved, the eminent choreographer started to relax in my car. He had led a busy life and had a few stories to tell.

For example, a former president of India got upset with him when the artist refused to perform in His Honor's private function, free of charge, of course. My passenger accused Rama Rao, then the state's chief minister and the choreographer's colleague from the movie industry, of going back on a promise to sponsor the artist's tour to America.

Undaunted, the dance maestro auctioned his home. He withdrew his savings and undertook this tour. He was known for such rash actions. Despite his modest means, early on, he had built two art centers promoting classical dance. The American tour had an impact on him. For example, he used to worry about *the brain drain*; during the visit, however, he started to view Indians living abroad as potential art patrons.

Just like opera singers in America, in general, such artists enjoy a limited appeal. Many, such as myself, have never spent the time necessary to learn to appreciate Indian classical music and dance. Tons of acquired taste and a wealth of background knowledge are a must before one can be hypnotized by the magic of this art form. Hundreds of millions of poor and lower-middle-class Indians are also too busy to spend that kind of time. Acquiring the bare necessities of life tops their priorities. When they can, most prefer to relax in movies.

By and large, patrons of the classical arts are very learned. They also happen to be very well placed and, as such, enjoy a lot of influence over the government. They dislike paying for their fun and have found a better way. They generously let the taxpayer pick up the tab to support the traditional dance, drama, music, and literature. Naturally the public goes along. Just like everything else, preserving the culture is also government's business.

Being the products of a society which thrives on government planning, artists themselves often beg the authorities to get involved. Among other things, they ask for funds to support works which they wouldn't be able to sell to willing consumers. The former also love the free publicity that comes with government awards and medals. At their request, when politicians butt in, inject corruption and nepotism into the field, and deprive the artists of their freedoms, however, these artists complain.

"The academy has been constituted in such a way that the vice-president has no role to play. The minister is the sole master. Arts cannot flourish in a closed system," said Jashwant

Thakar, a stage artist, when (1988) he resigned from (the state of) Gujarat's Music, Drama and Dance Academy. Early on, Hasmukhbhai Patel, the education minister in question, had tightened his grip over the government-controlled art academies in the state. He had simply packed their administrative bodies with politicians. (381)

When all else fails, the artists run to the Big brother himself. Recently, a group of them begged the prime minister to get involved in the affairs of Lalit Kala Academy, India's most prestigious fine arts body. They just wanted him to rein in its bickering leadership. Shankho Chaudhari, its chairman, had been fighting with the members of the academy for more than four years. Chaudhari was a sculptor by profession. His detractors accused him of carving out a few benefits for his relatives. He allegedly handed over a photography contract worth 17,000 rupees to his nephew's advertising agency. Chaudhari responded by accusing his accusers. He claimed that the vice-president and the secretary bought paintings worth 273,000 rupees without proper approval. (382)

The strife at the academy had gotten so bad that it caused a lot of confusion and paralysis. The Academy delayed an Indian arts exhibit in the Soviet Union and canceled another exhibit to be held in Mauritius. Many artists received their invitations to its functions very late—after the event had taken place. (382)

As if all this interference was not enough, the government also issued quotas for "artists," reserving, for them, jobs in the public sector and seats in various professional colleges. The principal of my medical school got most of his children admitted to the school despite their lackluster academic performance. One was admitted under the sports quota, and another under the arts quota. Their respective skills in these areas turned out to be the best part of the joke.

Besides bringing the usual doses of nepotism, corruption, and inefficiency to arts and art academies, government also inflicted a different kind of damage. It removed from arts what one might call the subjectivity, the essence of art appreciation. A rickshaw-puller might spend his hard-earned five rupees on a movie, or he might choose to spend his time listening to a song or watch a roadside snake show. A middle-class man and his wife might enjoy reading a magazine story. A filthy rich Indian might enjoy a special live concert by Lionel Ritchie (such a concert was actually arranged for a marriage). In each case, the individual has determined what is art and how to enjoy it.

In other words, each of us subjectively decides what is it that lifts his spirits. If it happens to be a wild flower or a child's smile, we enjoy it without reaching into our pockets. On other occasions, we pay for our entertainment. We pay to watch a movie, buy a cassette, or commission an artist to do a portrait. And we pay on a voluntary basis. We support the artist for the quality of his work, not because he is someone's brother-in-law. The artist, for his part, can't fall back on his influential friends and relatives. He has to try his best. To create his own niche, he has to be different. Out of his efforts burst out experimentation, creativity, and, on occasion, even excellence.

On the other hand, as taxpayers, when we pay through government, we lose the power to decide what's art and how much it's worth. Someone else, usually an official or his crony, decides for us. Either has few reasons to take a chance, seek new material, and risk criticism. Just as they do in other areas, such bureaucrats either follow fixed and usually traditional formulas and keep promoting the same old material, or they choose based on political considerations.

The artists that have failed to make it to their list (of subsidized artists) get upset. They denounce *the chosen ones* as mediocre. Of course, instead of all this whining, the former could go to a voluntary organization and obtain patronage. In a statist society, however, such organizations are hard to come by. Very few people give donations to establish private agencies. Most regard art patronage, just like everything else, as primarily the government's responsibility. Also, after paying their taxes in the belief that some of the money will be spent in art promotion, people are much less inclined to pay for the second time.

In many other countries besides India, government involvement diminishes the arts. In the US, each year the National Endowment for the Arts (NEA) chooses fifty or so pieces for awards. When the judges—instead of the consumer—pick these out of the thousands of works presented, promote these pieces and patronize the artists in NEA exhibits, they push the rest of the artists into the background. All along, NEA officials had bestowed an unfair advantage on a chosen few. Only when an activist group got involved recently, the whole mess became public[24]. As to be expected, this group employed its political clout to influence the outcome. It just about coerced the judges into supporting the works that many people considered as pornographic and obscene.

Every artist who has created these so-called obscene works has the right to question such a characterization. He also has an inalienable right to make a living through the sale of his works to a willing buyer. When government gets involved and funds his work, however, he also acquires the right to reach into pockets of those who refuse to recognize his work as art and are actually offended by it.

Many people support government's sponsoring of arts, because they distrust the only viable alternative; an economic democracy, in which consumers—a lot more in number than the few officials and certainly not as arbitrarily chosen—support the work they consider as art with their money. The elites feel that such a commercial culture devalues the arts; in it only *trash* raises to the top; it's primarily unfair, because the poor will be left out in the cold; and because they have more money to spend, the rich will pretty much decide who the artists are and what kind of work should be patronized. In reality, however, in any commercial society, most of the popular arts and artists thrive only on widespread support. Most singers earn their big bucks from record sales and public concerts. Successful movie stars, television personalities, and even magicians need a big audience. On the other hand, when government gets mixed up with arts, the artists can pretty much afford to ignore the average consumer and his tastes. At best, they self-indulge, or, they simply cater to the elites, pressure groups, and politicians to whom they owe their positions. Little of the high brow material these artists deliver fits the tastes of the poor who are supposed to receive a *fair* shake in this noncommercial culture. How often does one see Joe Six-Pack enjoying symphony orchestra or a puppet show, of course funded by his taxes? His counterpart in India—our rickshaw puller—rarely sits before the television set to watch a free program of classical dance promoted by his government. He would rather fork out a few bucks and go to a movie, incidentally a product of the commercial culture. As to quality, isn't it very subjective?

Such an economic democracy has few of the dangers inherent to the alternative—marriage between arts and government. In a way, this alliance is like the one between religion and government. When mixed, each ends up poisoning the other. Arts patronage not only distracts government from its legitimate functions and increases official corruption, it also lessens the democratic process by giving politicians yet another chance to put their spin on thought control. The NEA exhibits, for example, were used to ridicule the so-called conservatives and "their tastes in women.[25]" Along the same lines, in 1989, the Marxist government of (the Indian state of) Kerala restructured the state's cultural bodies and packed them with its supporters. It also gave literary awards and prizes to movies and books with leftist leanings. The state's Film Development Corporation dropped from its 50-year celebration all movies that were critical of the communist rule. (384)

At the same time, government's involvement in arts retards the development of private, volunteer based art institutions. It corrupts arts and artists. It destroys creativity and taints the field with divisiveness. Recently (in 1992), after stepping down as the chairman of the NEA, John Frohnmayer hoped to return to private life and work "for quality art, for less hate and for a generosity of spirit that allows us to live with our differences in real community." (383)

In India too, government's patronage of arts promoted quibbling over creativity. It pushed the charlatan ahead of the genius. It reduced the importance of arts as a whole. Even newspapers left the arts promotion mostly to the government. S. Nihal Singh (of *India Today*) complained that most newspapers used their art criticisms just "to fill holes." (385)

There is another kind of damage that further devalues arts in India—the physical kind.

Just as it owns everything else, the government owns most of the art treasures. The Archeological Survey of India is the sole custodian of the country's priceless idols, sculptures, and paintings. They cannot be sold in any form. (387)

Also, in the egalitarian spirit of socialism, the government reneged on many of its earlier promises to various small and medium rajahs (kings) and permanently took away their palaces and other valuables. It took care of these art treasures just as it took care of other public properties. Under its protection, some of these treasures suffered irreversible damage, and quite a few were lost without any trace. Every year, more than 400 idols and paintings are stolen and smuggled out of the country. Even though such smuggling had always existed, thanks to the emergence of a culture of corruption, after independence the pace accelerated. Explained a CBI (Central Bureau of Investigation) spokesman, "Now the smugglers operate hand-in-glove with the customs authorities and temple priests or senior museum officials." (386,387,388)

In 1986, twenty-seven ancient masterpieces sent to the Festivals of India in the US and France returned damaged. So did thirty five of the 861 sent to the Soviet Union in 1989. And that's a shame. Some of these pieces date back to 100 B.C. (387)

Early on, the Archeological Survey of India had loaned the art pieces to the National Museum to organize these exhibitions. Government officials played down the damage. To hide it from the public, a few even attempted to glue and touch up the wounded treasures. For damages costing hundreds of thousands of rupees to art pieces that were insured for millions of rupees, insurance companies paid just five to ten thousand rupees. The various government agencies meekly accepted these low payments. (387)

Meek or not, the authorities have little personal interest in these art pieces. Judging by the widespread corruption, it's hard to blame anyone who speculates that the insurance companies have bought off the officials. At one time or another, most of us have haggled with insurance companies. We know that they try to pay the least amounts they can get away with. Because we own the items they have insured and because we have paid the premiums through our noses, we fight these companies for *a* just compensation. A private art owner in India, Thakur Saheb of Sohapur, proved that he was just like the rest of us. Unlike the government officials, he contested a 50,000 rupee award to cover the damage to one of the idol's bells. (387)

More importantly, such private collectors guard their art investments with utmost care. Otherwise, their losses would be unbearable. Whether it is a car, house, agricultural land, or an art piece, a property is best preserved when an individual believes that he owns it. On the other hand, when *the society* owns, it deteriorates very fast. A single generation, which lets its government takeover the country's art treasures, can pulverize the work that their ancestors have created over thousands of years. N.K. Singh of *India Today* says, "Due to the myopic policies of the government, some of the country's most ethereal pieces of sculpture now look like wounded icons from a forgotten past." (387)

A volunteer-based museum would have taken care of these pieces much better than the government, if for no other reason than those who get involved in the task are expected to believe in art and its preservation. Due to a dearth of volunteer spirit and abdication of all responsibility to the government, however, there is little support for a movement to build museums in the country.

Many of the art pieces returned damaged to India after they were sent out as a part of cultural exchange programs. On occasion, these arrangements take a few strange turns. Recently (in 1988), Indian officials cried foul because their French counterparts allegedly went back on their earlier promises: The French failed to send to India a lot of famous paintings, including the *Mona Lisa.* (389)

[24]NEA's promotion of explicitly homosexual photographs by Robert Mapplethorpe in its exhibits prompted demonstrations by his detractors and supporters. (383)

[25]Caption of a photograph of a naked obese woman implied that conservatives dream about such women.

# CHAPTER 12
## *Hares and Hounds*


BY THE MID-EIGHTIES, India's fortunes definitely turned north.

By then, the reform winds, set in motion by the Thatcher/ Reagan duo, were gaining momentum around the world. Rajiv became a convert. His government started to dismantle the *license Raj* by reducing restrictions on enterprise. Previously, to invest a mere $16 million, one needed clearance from the central cabinet. Every Indian knows what this means. From minister to peon, every official could hold these plans hostage. Rajiv raised this requirement to $40 million. In March of 1985, his government delicensed twenty five areas. It freed thirty-four groups of industries to make changes in their product mix without seeking fresh licenses. (390,392)

During the next few years, such reforms kept rolling out of the government. By 1988, to all but twenty-seven specified types of industries, government extended delicensing. The company could enjoy this freedom, as long as it would invest within certain limits. These limits varied from area to area. In centrally-declared backward areas, for example, only companies investing more than 500 million rupees needed an industrial license. Outside a certain distance of twenty-one cities, this figure was 150 million. Projects requiring foreign exchange (for importing raw materials and components) of less than 30 percent—up from a previous 15 percent—for the first year of commercial production, faced less regulation. (392)

For a very long time, the government had regarded many small to medium companies that produced more than twenty-five percent of goods in a particular sector as monopolies. Using the MRTP (Monopolies and Restrictive Trade Practices) Act, it allowed them to expand only into what the planners considered as core industries—fertilizers and petrochemicals, for example. If a company saw profit in an *uncore* industry and wanted to get in, it faced many hurdles. In 1988, Rajiv's government freed sixty-nine companies from this anti-growth MRTP act. They could now freely invest in new areas. (391)

Many of the small and medium-scale companies that exercised their newly acquired freedoms turned out to be pretty efficient. They gave the big boys a run for their money (see below). Despite its name, MRTP had entrenched the monopolies. A retreat from it increased the market competition. (391)

*The Wall street Journal* was very impressed by all these reforms. It called Mr. Gandhi "Rajiv Reagan." True to Reagan's legacy, Rajiv slashed the marginal income tax rates from 98.5 percent to 50 percent. These cuts, coupled with the regulatory relief, brought in a rash of new investments to start thousands of businesses. Previously, to protect and preserve their black money, the investors used to spend close eight to ten percent of it per year. After the cuts, many more used this money to invest in legal businesses. Also, many companies issued stocks and raised a lot more capital (80,000 million rupees in 1989 alone). After the reforms, the stock market experienced an explosive expansion. (393,394,395,396,397)

Naturally, the economy moved into a higher gear. Between 1985 and 1989, the real GDP went up by 5.1 percent a year. The industrial output climbed by eight percent and agricultural production by fifteen to twenty percent. In real-life terms, all this meant a better availability of jobs, goods, and services. Earlier, people used to wait to buy scooters, cars, or telephones. There was a huge black market for cement, tires, and fertilizers.

In the post reform years, the consumer could buy most of these items without the delays. (396)

Actually the country gained a whole lot more. For instance, it came through the drought of 1987, which, in terms of rainfall, many consider as the worst of the century, with flying colors. Prior to this one, India had suffered its share of droughts. Invariably the economy shrank. Millions suffered. By comparison, the 1987 drought proved to be very tame. The country maintained an astonishing growth rate of six to seven percent. Said one official, "Indian economy has clearly acquired a lot of underlying strength." Vikram Lal, chairman of a tractor company, knew why. He said, "I think we are seeing the effect of years of liberalization, of competition and better efficiency." (398,399)

By fostering economic growth, the reform program helped the country to successfully weather the worst drought of the century. It thus showed that capitalism is one of the most humane of all the human inventions.

To keep this fact hidden from the public, the leftist media called the program *liberalization*. What Rajiv did, however, was to, ever so slightly, enhance the economic freedoms of his countrymen and women. In other words, he embraced capitalism and promoted free enterprise. In this, he simply imitated the likes of Thatcher and Reagan.

Thanks to the policies of both Labour and *Conservative* governments in the past, Thatcher, too, inherited what many had called the "sick man of Europe." Britain had all the elements of a socialist state, including a huge public sector, high tax rates, militant unions, and a population that looked up to government for every thing. In the name of providing its subjects everything from health care to housing, the government squandered a lot of resources. The National Health Service, for example, took in more and spent huge sums on administrative costs, but generated fewer and fewer services leading to the now-famous, long waiting lists, not to mention the decimation of the consumer choice. In the field of education, politicians neglected school buildings which lacked many essentials, and in many areas, even leaked. Instead, they spent a lot of money to pay salaries to the powerful unionized teachers. These unions resisted any and all attempts to inject teacher accountability, such as vouchers for school choice. They refused to yield the power back to parents. (400,401)

The earlier governments had provided houses for the poor. In the absence of an interested ownership, these dwellings suffered physical deterioration and ended up as nothing more than concrete ghettos. Even if any of the poor folks wanted to fix their house, however, they couldn't afford the repair costs. The monopolistic unions, with the help of politicians, jacked up the costs to three to four times the market rate. Owing to an anemic growth of the economy, occupants of these public projects had fewer prospects of finding jobs and leaving their ghettos. The welfare state trapped them, both physically and psychologically. (401)

Thatcher tried to reverse these trends. Her reforms increased the proportion of owner occupiers from fifty-two percent to sixty-six percent. She also cut taxes and sold many companies such as British Gas and British Telecom to private investors, mostly stockholders. Since 1979, five million more British citizens owned stocks. During the decade of the reforms, the average living standards in the UK improved by twenty-three percent. Of course, the critics observed that the rich got richer. They implied that the poor got poorer, but the statistics showed otherwise. The gross earnings of the lowest-paid ten percent increased by eighty percent. Of the one million who bought their council houses since 1979, forty-four percent belonged to the skilled, manual working class. (401)

Thatcher, Reagan, and other reformers such as Rajiv Gandhi, however, faced two formidable hurdles. For one thing, the vested interests that had benefited from the status quo, such as the bureaucrats, organized labor, and protected industrialists, did everything in their power to stall the reforms.

The bigger problem for the reformers was the public mindset. Thanks to the non-economic effects of decades of socialism, most people had come to view the state as the major provider of their needs. They wanted it to fully take care of them regardless of their efforts. They tried to win higher unemployment doles, mandated union wages, and more funding for education, housing, agriculture, and health care. During the three decades of socialism, even the once capitalistic, independent, and adventurous Britons became too attached to their government. They had gotten too dependent to take a chance and better themselves in a free market economy. They wanted to do well, but only within the safety network of the social welfare system. And the media echoed such thinking. It blamed Thatcher for failing to make such an inherently inefficient system brim with efficiency.

Such attitudes proved to be very formidable for these reformers. The mindset dampened their results and made these leaders look bad. As a result, voters replaced them with politicians, both rightist and leftist, who only differed with each other regarding the pace of increasing the role of state in private affairs.

Notwithstanding, the reformers also scored their biggest victories in the realm of consciousness. By the time they arrived, the experts had thrown their hands in the air and declared that the worldwide stagflation of the late seventies was incurable. But for the economic revival of such countries as the US, Great Britain, and West Germany, many of these experts would have reached the next logical conclusion—the Western economic systems had failed for good. The pundits would have blamed the problems in the first, second and third worlds on the usual suspects: overpopulation and shortage of resources.

In reality, it was this leftist wisdom that had failed. The reformers showed what aspects of these economic systems would work and what would not. For example, the tax cuts did increase the revenues, but not enough to finance the galloping increases in government spending. The deregulation did cause healthy rates of growth and provide jobs for many. It worked better than any make-believe job program of the leftists and shook the foundations of the welfare state. Consequently, the leftists not only had stomachaches but also second thoughts. For example, every chance they got, Labourites attacked Thatcher; their party, however, had to slowly move to the center. It tried to shed its loony left image. Its members shied away from proposals of higher marginal tax rates of more than fifty percent, let alone the pre-Thatcher figure of eighty-three percent. Few of them talked of nationalizing the industry. Neil Kinnock reportedly said in 1989, "Capitalism is the system we live in, and we've got to make it work more efficiently, more fairly, and more successfully." (402)

Quite a few of the Democrats in the US have also undergone a similar change of heart. They tried to shed the label of "taxers and spenders." By embracing such Republican initiatives as NAFTA and welfare reforms, Bill Clinton billed himself a new Democrat. He successfully distanced himself from the socialist policies of the old Democrats and won the presidency. He took credit for the economic growth, which resumed after a brief recession[26] even before he took the oath of office.

Shimon Peres, head of the Labor party which firmly set Israel on its own road to socialism, was more honest. He said: "If we want to distribute money like socialists, we have to make money like capitalists." Peres added, "There are rules to the game, and you cannot turn your back on it." (402)

"Lord Curzon, [a British viceroy to India], acknowledging it [Indian Civil Service] as the most honorable and the proudest service in the world, also observed in it some of the meanest and most malignant types of disappointed humanity it had ever been his misfortune to meet; a view doubtless arrived at when his own transcending arrogance had collided with something similar in one of his officials," said Geoffrey Moorhouse, the author of *India Britannica*. (403)

Several decades later, Rajiv Gandhi probably wondered what made the honorable species become extinct. Much more so than Reagan and Thatcher, he had to contend with the opposition from the bureaucracy. The officials were smart. They refused to take on the popular prime minister right away, and they lay low for a while. Slowly, they used everything they had to delay, dilute and ultimately reverse, the reform process. Owing to the partial nature of the reforms, they still enjoyed the powers to sabotage the program. (390)

To be fair, one could say that their opposition had stemmed from much more than just malignant meanness. These officials built their whole lives around the status quo. They had commitments to meet. With kids in college and daughters to be married, few could survive on the salary alone. They needed *the usual* and had no wish to be reformed into the poorhouse. Many of them mistook their personal well being for that of their country. One official said, "Seventy-five percent of the time we are battling his [Rajiv's] mad ideas." (390)

With his reforms, Rajiv also victimized a few others. They too had little use for "his mad ideas." For example, previously, the influential businessman who had obtained an exclusive license enjoyed a virtual monopoly over his area. Owing to the deregulation, quite a few brand new investors started businesses with relative ease and exposed him to competition (see below).

Both workers and consumers benefited from the reform process. They, however, failed to connect their good fortune with the changes in the legal/economic structure. All along they had believed that most good came from the top and the only way to prosper was to get a government job, license, or ration. Most people were unwilling to embrace the new ideas which depended upon such things as taking risks, individual initiative, and a desire to succeed. They refused to give up their support for the Robin Hood approach. Previously, only those that missed out in this distribution complained. That was all they wanted to change. The various groups kept up the pressure for more handouts. Farmers demanded a waiver of their loans and power at subsidized rates. The unemployed sold their votes for promises of new employment schemes. When a new labor law that would favor workers over unions was proposed, the unionized labor screamed bloody murder. Despite turning the communist-ruled states into a working class hell, union leaders said, "In free India, Rajiv Gandhi thinks of banning strikes. Even the British didn't do this." (404)

Limited by this mindset, the reform program went as far as it did. Despite the impressive results, it was hardly the magic wand most were looking for. It left many wanting. The largely left-leaning media reinforced the unease: It dumped on Rajiv and labeled him as *pro-rich*. His Congress(I) party started to suffer defeats in mid-term polls. Its politicians started to panic. Many of them, who had previously supported the reforms only halfheartedly, spoke up. They urged the government to do the only logical thing; rededicate itself to socialism. In the fall of 1988, the Congress(I) party passed a resolution which promised for the poor, among other things, employment opportunities for at least one adult member of each rural family, adequate nutrition for children, provision of two saris to adult women (free to destitutes and at subsidized rates to others), and essential commodities such as food grains, pulses, edible oils, and kerosene oil at *reasonable* rates. Reminiscent of the heyday of Indira Gandhi, the party members attacked monopoly houses (big corporations). And they hailed the public sector. (405)

Actually, the ruling politicians did more than just hail this black hole. They kept pouring money into it. Always with an eye on the upcoming national elections, for example, they unveiled a rural employment program named after Jawaharlal Nehru. Under it, the government would provide for *housing and shelter upgradation.* In some 120 backward districts, it would employ one person from each poor family for 100 days a year. Of course, the politicians made sure to include quotas for women and the Scheduled Castes. How much might all this cost the taxpayer? The initial estimates hovered around 5,000 million rupees. (406,407)

Owing to such spending, the deficits soared. To bridge the gap, government did two things. It increased the money supply and pushed inflation into double digits; it also went back to the good old standby, tax increases. In ten years, its 1989 budget had the stiffest tax increases. Rajiv's government levied a three percent increase in *employment surcharge* on people making more than $3,000 per year. It doubled some of the hotel taxes. It raised excise duties on a lot of goods such as cars, electronic components, and television sets. (407)

Some of the taxes underscore the power of state to enforce its social values on the individual. Excise tax on motorcycles (often used by young men) went up by five percent. But scooters were left alone. A spokesman from the finance ministry explained: "They [scooters] are family vehicles." (407)

Harsh Goenka, a prominent industrialist, said' "I pay Nadkarni a courtesy call every month." (408)

It was not as if Suresh Nadkarni was sick or lost a loved one. The only reason for such courtesy calls was that every year he could give away 30,000 million rupees to his friends: Nadkarni headed IDBI (Industrial Development Bank of India), one of the country's four premier financial institutions. Along with the other three—Unit Trust of India (UTI), the Life Insurance Corporation of India (LIC), and the Industrial Credit and Investment Corporation of India (ICICI)—it parceled out loans that could easily bankroll a small country. Such a power can also produce mini-earthquakes. At eleven o' clock each morning, for example, officials at UTI decide the stocks they are going to trade. With a lot of funds to invest, on many days they probably decide which way the market is going to go. (408)

The ruling politicians repeatedly promised that these public institutions would be autonomous. In comparison, Bill Clinton did better with his marriage vows. Said one former chief executive, "The decisions are political. Orders come from the finance ministry and we implement them." The officials followed a loan policy that was anything but narrow, simple, and predictable. They decided on *a case by case basis*. They waived 210 million rupees in interest owed by the once-ailing Andhra

Pradesh Rayons, but sat tight on a similar request from Punalur Paper Mills. (408)

In their universe, such discretion yields power. Because all along the legal framework has retarded the development of large, privately owned financial institutions, the local industrialists have very few other places (besides these government institutions) to turn to for big loans. These businessmen have to cater to the ruling politicians who find such power too alluring. Rajiv and his band of reformers proved to be no exception. (408)

Even as the reform process was unfolding, these officials became more and more adept in pulling the strings every way they wanted to. To get the loans, the companies had to sign agreements that would allow for conversion of the debt into equity. Most officials find such clauses handy. After all, they are in the business for more than just making a profit on these loans. They hope to control the company. At the time of their choosing, the officials use the automatic ownership clauses to appoint directors to the company's board. Backed by the huge government machinery, these directors and their political bosses blackmail the businessman and help their friends takeover his outfit.

A few companies which slept with them woke up naked. Shaw Wallace, for example, was taken over by Manu Chhabria, then a well connected tycoon. The officials also backed Vijay Mallayya's bid for Best & Crompton. After Dhirubhai Ambani (of the Reliance Corporation) had acquired a twelve percent stake in Larsen & Toubro (L&T, India's largest private sector engineering firm worth 10,000 million rupees), the institutions used their controlling interest in L&T to help Ambani swallow it. Explained an institutional source: "Dhirubhai Ambani asked his friends in Delhi to speak to the institutions and the company fell into his lap." (408,409)

Besides sponsoring such takeover battles, the officials discovered a few other ways to directly benefit from the privatization drive. After a few investors close to Bhuta Singh— then an union cabinet minister and an adviser to Rajiv Gandhi— had purchased a *sick unit* from the government, Singh faced charges of favoritism. Early on, the government did try to auction the unit. It arrived at a sale price of nine million rupees. In such a mega-deal, however, the officials gave the letter of intent to a corporation which showed an initial capital of only 700 rupees, the cost of a dinner for four at a five star hotel. (410)

The auction was carried out improperly and without minimum bidders (contrary to the rules of the Investment Corporation). Allegedly, the deal cost the taxpayer close to twenty million rupees. The other charges included selling the unit without a proper evaluation of the assets, waiving dues of ten million rupees under the pretext of helping the sick unit, handing over the land after receiving only thirty percent of the price, and reducing the state-owned Investment Corporation's equity from agreed upon twenty-six percent to ten percent thus virtually giving total control to the new owners. (410)

In the long run, such private owners might end up reviving the sick units. Many of them, however, acquired the units using their connections. The whole arrangement smacked of crony capitalism. From all this, one might conclude that when a country had traveled far on the road of socialism, it would end up with so much corruption that its officials would even stink up the reform process.

Vaçlav Klaus, a Czech finance minister, repeatedly said that his country needed investment, not aid. Czechoslovakia along with Poland, China, Hungary, and even Russia, happily sent Lenin and his theory of how multinationals exploit poor countries packing. They rolled out their welcome mats to these companies and asked them to help rebuild their economies. (411)

These countries know that the multinationals can do much more than make computer games or housecleaning robots. These investors can bring in the necessary capital and technology and play a big role in the country's efforts to provide basics for its people. Owing to transportation and storage problems, for example, a good part of food that is produced in India gets spoiled. The country grows ten percent of the world's fruits and vegetables, yet over thirty percent of the produce rots every year. Gokul Patnaik, managing director of (the state of) Punjab's Agro Industries Corporation, laid his finger on the problem when he said: "At present the industry suffers from lack of state-of-the-art technology in processing, packaging, and marketing." (412)

Rajiv Gandhi knew who had the state of the art. To attract these companies to India, in the fall of 1988, his government promised to slash taxes on processed foods and packaging materials. To clear the transportation gridlock, it eased restrictions on foreign-owned airlines and let them pick up some cargo. (412)

The government also took a few other tentative steps to attract outside investors. Its bureaucrats still carried the begging bowl, but their political bosses instructed them to scoop up a few investors along the way. After lunching with these official delegations and listening to their speeches, a few foreign investors did start to eye the country with interest. In theory at least, it made more sense to do business in India where the property rights were much more secure than in countries such as China. Soon, however, these investors discovered the simple truth: The reform process was a mile wide but only an inch deep.

These investors faced a kind of Oedipus complex. A few politicians who lived in the front lines greeted them with delight. S.S. Ray, then the governor of the troubled state of Punjab, said, "Punjab [secessionist movement] is not a law and order problem alone. Most of those arrested for terrorism are unemployed. Pepsi will give jobs and a farmer with five acres will earn Rs.50,000 a year." (413)

The investor also had to deal with the other kind of politician who knew that protectionism was a gold mine of good slogans and great politics. What such officials said, or more importantly did, could still make or break the outside investor. As Pepsi found out (see chapter 5), there were hardly any preset criteria that he could fulfill and open his business in the country. Thanks to the halfhearted reforms, each investor had to work out a separate deal with the government; the officials still enjoyed the powers to decide *on* a case-by-case basis. They held the multinationals at their mercy. The companies that somehow received the approval had to still deal with the many archaic laws of the country. For example, government had previously reserved the manufacturing of bottling machinery for small-scale companies. Pepsi gave the order to a big company. That was a big no-no. So was the importing of machines that Pepsi was supposed to buy in the local market. (413,414)

Being the products of a administrative and legal setup, which had relied heavily on central planning and was biased against private property and investment, such laws easily survived the partial liberalization. Thanks to them, the officials retained their control over the foreign investor. As a result, Pepsi watched its fortunes waver in the political winds. The minister for textile and food processing, Sharad Yadav, who came to power after defeating Rajiv and his Congress(I), asked to review the Pepsi file. He said, "We will look at how the project benefits farmers." As a throwback to the seventies, Yadav promised not to allow the multinationals into food processing. Translation: "Let the fruits rot and potatoes spoil. I need my votes." (415)

Also, as if it were bad to promote economic growth throughout the country, the officials limited many incentives to the so-called export promoting zones. These halfway measures yielded, at best, halfway results. To improve backward regions, for example, government established these zones in areas with poor infrastructures. More importantly, all the remaining restrictions, coupled with the political posturing, demonstrated to the investor how shaky his property rights were. As he saw it, what little the government gave, it could take away too. Naturally, very few of the foreign investors came into these export processing zones (EPZ). By 1989, for example, of the 115 established in the Kandla zone, only eleven units had attracted foreign equity. A few domestic producers did come in. They were simply escaping the relatively more oppressive business atmosphere elsewhere in the country. These small and medium units did miserably. They lacked the necessary finances, marketing skills, and knowledge of the export markets. (416)

To attract capital, the country has to guarantee property rights not just to a chosen few selected on a case—by-case basis, but to all of the investors. The ruling politicians, however, repeatedly pulled away from even the partial reforms. They, thus, further scared off the outside investors. After a bid by Coke to come in was rejected by V.P. Singh's government, reported the *India Tribune,* "The word in the American business community is it that the Coke rejection may prove to be a trend-setter viz the policies of the Indian government in that it sent negative signals to prospective investors." (416,417,418)

Compared to the previous year, in 1989, the US and Japanese investment in India went down. Despite their pronounced objective of playing a bigger global role, Japanese invested 100 million rupees in India, a miniature figure compared to their investment of 34,000 million in Thailand. A group of Japanese businessmen explained that they were "concerned, uneasy, and anxious" about the [Indian] government's "socialistic and populist approach." Said another businessman: "All we end up doing is filling forms." (419)

While welcoming a group of West German industrialists to invest in India, a finance minister from India warned that they would face "a few problems of bureaucratic nature." (420)

In harassing the outside investor, however, few of the bureaucrats behave like racial bigots. Most plague the nonresident Indians (NRIs) as thoroughly as they do the other groups. Recently a few NRI investors talked of the various bureaucratic hurdles. Many had problems with repatriation of profits. Others disliked the high interest rates charged by the financial institutions. (351)

One of their biggest complaints, however, dealt with confidentiality—more precisely the lack of it. Per the regulations, many had submitted detailed proposals about their projects in India only to later find these plans in the hands of their competition. They lost control over both economic and technical information. They found out that when an official talked of transfer of technology to India he really meant, "give me your project designs and your trade secrets so that I can pass them along to whomever I want to." (351)

The influential domestic producer not only obtains *soft loans* from government, enjoys protected market share, and evades taxes, he also gets to eavesdrop on the competition. He can choose to copy it or even better it. Said H.P. Punwani, president of the Association of Basic Manufacturers of Pesticides, "There is virtually no patent protection for the pesticides industry in India." (421)

The outside investor, who enjoys very few safeguards for his material possessions, has even fewer protections for his intellectual property. Just like a friend of mine, who hates to wear his Rolex watch downtown, most investors hate to take their valuables to any country that has a track record of confiscation. Rather than give out the findings of their expensive research, most simply stay out. Mr. Hansen, director of the U.N. Center on Transnational Corporation (UNCTC), said that the Indian government's stand on trade-related intellectual property rights and investment matters might pose a deterrent to foreign investment. (422)

Transnationals account for ninety percent of the technological innovations and ninety percent of the world trade. For a good reason, they are happy to take their best technology to a country which has adequate safeguards in place. The more they can use their technology, the more these companies can effectively compete in the world markets. By simply guaranteeing intellectual property rights, the host country benefits immensely. It gains exports and foreign exchange. Its people get jobs, and they get to use the best technology. In the long run, this policy also benefits domestic manufacturers. They give up their hobby of stealing. Just to survive, most shape up and start innovating. Sounds like a fairy tale? Hardly. After Japan had tightened these rights, its companies switched from copying to innovating. The rest as they say is history. (421,422)

The Indian elites, on the other hand, clung to their outdated notions of managed markets and self-sufficiency and refused to guarantee intellectual property rights. The officials behaved as if growth was good as long as it was *planned*. These politicians put in place partial measures and halfhearted cures. They and the bureaucrats discovered the remaining regulations and laws to be a gold mine. The illusion of a liberalized atmosphere gave them control over more investors—domestic and foreign—and more pockets to pick.

In short, the officials managed to limit the scope of Indian *Perestroika*, dilute its results, taint it with their corruption, and give it a bad name.

Mr. Prodl, an Italian industrialist, said that, in his country, private companies operated more efficiently than the state-run enterprises. Gorbachev asked why that was so. Prodl replied with a question: "Why does the hare, small and weak, consistently outrun the hound?" (423)

The Soviet leader was puzzled. "It is because the hare works for himself while the hound works for masters," explained Prodl. (423)

Gorbachev laughed appreciatively. He said that he would tell this story to the politburo. If he went on to do so, probably the politburo members would have asked him, "What else is new?" Every day, the results of their failed experiment stared in their faces. They knew a thing or two about incentives; they had little use for rabbit stories or pig tales. (423)

So did leaders of many other countries that had tried socialism. If Gorbachev told them this anecdote, narrated by Karen Elliott House of the *Wall Street Journal*, they probably would laugh appreciatively too. Within the next few decades, the gap between what they know already about the hares and hounds of their countries and what these leaders can do to harness the power of individual efforts through free market policies could prove to be crucial. It could well decide the fate of each of their countries.

Using the cute label of "liberalization," many of these politicians did try small doses of capitalism. They, however, faced a tough transitional period. Unsure of their new course, and upon failing to see the light at the end of the tunnel, many of them hurried back right after the very first bump on the head. Very few of their countrymen and women questioned this retreat. Most people also shared these phobias and doubts. They, too, agonized over the question of whether it was proper to try free market policies without knowing for sure that these ideas would work in their country.

In a way, it's like asking whether penicillin should have been used in a third world country without first conducting thorough research in the country itself. Without any hesitation, doctors tried this miracle cure for the first time in every nook and corner of the Third World. Based on certain immutable natural laws which applied to all humanity, they simply guessed that it would work wonders. And it did.

According to many political economists, such laws also apply in the realm of economics. These worldly philosophers attribute both the failure of collectivism and the success of free markets to the so-called *invisible hand*, driven by natural laws governing human behavior. It seems that, regardless of the color of our eyes or the coloring agents we use in our food, we humans exhibit uniform responses to such things as the power of incentives, the propelling force of self-interest, and the discipline imposed by competition.

It's reasonable to question the analogy between these laws and those that pertain to the efficacy of penicillin. How immutable are the natural laws that govern economics? For example, one could ask whether Indians are as entrepreneurial as Japanese or Koreans, whether eastern Europeans are as hard working, or whether consumers in Africa are as literate and discriminative as those in the West to protect their interests in a *laissez-faire* economy.

How do we know that the free market policies actually improve the average standard of living in a third world country? What if the capitalist measures nurture monopolies, as predicted by Karl Marx? Won't that lead to more polarization of wealth, class conflicts, widespread social unrest, and an ultimate breakdown of law and order?

The recent reform program in India did help quite a few, but disappointed many more. Despite its shortcomings, however, it worked as a sort of mini-experiment. In its results, a close observer might find an answer or two to these important questions.

I was about twelve, when my father bought our very first radio and thrilled me and mother. My only disappointment was that it was not Phillips, then a household name in India.

Of late, however, many of its once-loyal customers switched to its competitors. Owing to the recent reforms, they had plenty of alternatives to turn to. Said an industrialist about Indian economy: "The oligopolistic structure is disappearing in one sector after another." (424, 425, 428)

Its detractors called the reform program pro-rich and pro-business. Very few of the existing businesses, however, found it to their liking. Mainly because some of the freedoms were pretty nonselective, the program helped tens of thousands of the least known and not so well connected investors to enter into legal ventures and compete successfully with the established companies. For example, after the government delicensed production of electric bulbs, some 200 or so new manufactures entered the field. They sold more bulbs[27] at lower prices and inflicted major losses on big companies such as Elmi, Bengal Lamps and Peico Electronics and Electricals—formerly known as Phillips. (425)

Said D.R. Putatunda, Peico's senior vice-president and director (of lighting division), "In 1984, our lamps division was a money spinner. In 1988, it was one of the reasons for the company's record loss [200 million rupees]." Assured of a hefty share in the previously protected market, the management had become very sclerotic. It was slow to adopt to the new realities. A slew of labor troubles also hurt Peico's ability to compete in the open market. Faced with heavy losses, the management did get serious about revival. It pruned the employee rolls from 9,035 to 8,095. It phased out several losing divisions such as home appliances, computer peripherals, and batteries. Soon these efforts paid off. In the twelve months prior to March of 1990, the company showed profits of 54 million rupees. (425,426,427)

Besides Peico, a lot of big companies saw their bottom lines swim in a sea of blood. Of the largest ten private sector companies in the country, nine reported a drop in profits in 1986–87. Actually the big boys sold more, but made less: The top 100 companies had nine percent higher sales but their profits dropped by twenty-four percent. Small wonder that these business owners liked the competition as much as a kid would like his booster shots. They started to complain. Ratan Tata, a noted industrialist, observed, "People who were crying from the roof tops for liberalization are now making just as many representations seeking protection." (428)

As long as the cries for protection fell on deaf ears, one by one the big businesses got out of their easy chairs. It was as if the reform process lit a fire under them. Very soon, the companies started to show profits. According to a study by the Center for Monitoring Indian Economy, in the first half of the financial year 1989-90, gross profits of 327 companies rose by thirty-nine percent. (430)

The reforms also energized Tatas—the Indian version of Howard Hughes, the Rockefellers, and a few more like them rolled into one family. Their industrial empire is akin to a conglomeration of US Steel, General Motors, Dow Chemicals, Union Carbide, and Proctor and Gamble. One could even say that, as Tatas go, so goes India. (429)

Once before, Tatas took advantage of their new economic freedoms and enlarged their operations. After independence, freed of British protectionist laws, they built steel mills, cargo trucks, power plants, oil refineries and a group of luxury hotels known for their outstanding service. Their factories made everything from soap to cement, chemicals, and fertilizers. Among their prized possessions was what used to be the forerunner of the now-famous Air India. (429)

Not any more. In 1953, as a preview of the events to unfold, Nehru nationalized the carrier. Just as it did with the other industries, by dousing the flames of entrepreneurial spirit with regulations and by guaranteeing monopoly rights, his socialist program put Tatas into a deep slumber. The reforms of the eighties, however, woke up the irrepressible Tatas. Said a merchant banker, "I don't remember a single public issue by the Tatas in the second half of the '70s, but now they display great confidence and continuously raise money from the market." (429)

Tatas used these funds to initiate quite a few modernization programs, such as the one in Tata Steel involving ten billion rupees. The list of new projects they looked into or started in three years prior to 1988 included a new line of light commercial vehicles, passenger cars, a possible Daimler Benz export unit, oil drilling, computers, telephone instruments, telecommunications, and fertilizers. For all this growth, Ratan Tata gave credit to the new legal structure. He said, "What you see at the moment is just the pent up ability to undertake these expansions and diversifications, coming into the open now that government policy allows it." (429)

Besides Tatas, many others put to good use their *pent up abilities*. They expanded or entered into new areas. Previously, six companies had made two-wheelers. The number went up to fifteen. The number of producers in telephone instruments went up from one to several dozen; those making polyester yarn rose from six to two dozen. Car models jumped from two to seven. Working within the legal structure suited the investors well. They became efficient and produced more for the consumer. In a matter of five to seven years, the number of two wheelers doubled, refrigerators tripled, and cars quadrupled (45,000 to 160,000). (431,432)

Many of these producers were small companies. Previously, government tried to nurture small companies by handing out subsidies and protecting them from competition from the big ones. This strategy propped up a few businesses with well connected owners. It particularly worked well to deprive the consumer of quality products, for instance, decent eye glasses for more than forty-five million Indians who had serious eye problems. Government reserved this business exclusively for small companies.[28] (433)

These companies lacked the necessary capital and technology to keep up with the latest advances. As a result, besides Egypt, India was the only major country which used the less-accurate windowpane glasses to make more than half of the twenty-five million pairs of lenses produced each year. In keeping with its culture of force, during the seventies the union cabinet tried to ban such usage. Owing to a lack of alternatives, however, this ordinance got nowhere. Even the ministers saw that the windowpane glasses were better than no glasses. (433)

Rajiv's government reversed the blind policy. It let the large companies produce contact and hard resin plastic lenses. It also allowed the local companies to collaborate with foreigners such as Bausch and Lomb. Together they set out to leave windowpane glasses where they belonged—in windows. Their customers probably failed to see the connection between the legal changes and their new glasses. But they could see everything else better. (433)

Obviously, the reforms worked wonders where the force of law had failed. By letting the market plan itself, they proved that it was unnecessary, or even impossible, to reserve a particular field for small, medium, ultra medium, or super-ultra-medium scale industries. While the large ones did well in certain areas, the small companies excelled in others. In some areas, both thrived. Various factors—size being just one of them—influenced the outcome. When allowed to choose, the consumer bestowed on the efficient company sales, profit, and longevity, regardless of its size. In other words, he *reserved* not just each area but each task to the appropriate producer.

To attract and keep him, the producers had to improve the quality. For the first time in several decades, for example, auto manufacturers upgraded their models. Their products began to look less and less like those from used car lots. Besides the cosmetic changes, the manufacturers also improved fuel economy. They planned to reduce emissions and noise levels, showing how efficiency born out of free competition could help to clean up the environment. (435,436)

Indian industry also started to export more. In one year before the spring of 1987, textile exports went up from 6,341 million to 9,213 million rupees; exports of gems and jewelry increased from 5,351 million to 7,761 million rupees and that of petroleum and marine products grew by sixty percent. These trends continued for the next few years. Exports of manufactured garments jumped from 18,570 million in 1987 to 31,180 million rupees in 1989, and that of engineering goods from 9,540 million in 1985–86, to 35,000 million rupees in 1989–90. Besides the falling rupee, what helped to create a sustained boost in exports year after year were the improvements in quality brought on by competition. Reflected a drug company executive on his newly found wisdom: "Importers insist on quality." (437,438,439,440)

He knew from experience. His firm exported base drugs such as ampicillin and ibuprofen. Within the four years before 1989, pharmaceutical exports from India shot up by a whopping 700 percent. A few commentators attributed the success to a weakening of the patent laws by the government. Improvements in quality, however, were hard to miss. These products were so good as to even satisfy the notoriously tough FDA (The US Food and Drug Administration). One executive said, "It's a great success story. A decade ago we were still finding our feet in the international bulk drugs market. Today we are walking tall." Soon, the US manufacturers started to complain about the exports from India and ask for protection. (440)

Such exporters proved that, once freed of government shackles, the Indian businessman could compete successfully in the open market. They also tossed a few other previously-held concepts on their heads. In 1977, for example, Bijon Nag, a first generation entrepreneur, founded IFB Industries, Ltd., an engineering firm. Between 1984 and 1987, IFB increased its turnover from 25 million to 250 million rupees. Nag applied for the government's permission to set up a eighty-million-rupee plant in England. He wanted to produce safety-critical, engineering components for passenger cars. For its British concern, IFB planned to supply most of the capital equipment from its units in India. (441)

Inquired a reporter: "Somewhat like reversing the history of colonialism?" (441)

One nationalized bank came up with a brilliant idea: meditation rooms for employees so that they could come up with some more brilliant ideas to improve the bank's performance. (442)

Commercial banks in India have no time for such fun and games. They are too busy enjoying their new highs, their high profits. Also, they have little need for meditation rooms or massage parlors. All along they knew how to perform. To provide the necessary capital for economic growth, all they needed was the freedom to follow their own instincts. (443)

As a part of the reform program, the Reserve Bank of India (the country's central bank) did relax its restrictions on them. For example, it allowed these banks to issue certificates of deposits and fix their money market interest rates. Interest rate ceilings on inter-bank lending (previously at 10 percent) and commercial loans (previously at 16.5 percent) were also lifted. Freed of burdensome regulations, many Indian banks watched their bottom lines improve. (443)

So did two dozen or so foreign banks that took advantage of the new openness and established close to 150 branches in the country. These foreign banks also brought in new ideas, improved efficiency, and energized the whole business. For example, they introduced such concepts as electronic banking (through across-the-board computerization), automatic teller machines, and zero coupon bonds. Through car and scooter loans, these banks reached out to the middle class. (445)

To compete effectively, local banks had to follow suit and become aggressive. This included even the government owned State Bank of India (SBI), which launched its famous drive for NRI (Non-Resident Indians) deposits. D.N. Ghosh, the bank's chairman, conceded as much when he said that the competition from foreign banks made him less complacent. Owing to the increased competition, much more so than before, private banks valued credibility. Many voluntarily sought evaluation by credit rating agencies and showed how self-interest can lead to self-regulation. (445)

Along with the exploding stock market, the deregulated banks helped to provide the capital to fuel the phenomenal growth of the late eighties and beyond. In this, they were greatly helped by the increased household savings during the eighties. Owing to the reforms, the average Indian made more money. That left him more to save. According to a recent (1989) report by the Planning Commission, household savings as a percentage of total savings in the economy went up from 68% in the sixties to 75% in the eighties. (444)

The banks also took advantage of their newly-acquired channels to capital from outside the country. Previously, only nationalized banks and the big financial institutions had access to foreign money. Of late, banks such as Grindlays, Citibank, and Canara Bank and industrialists such as Modis, Birlas, and Mahindras have tried to raise their own funds. They primarily work with financial firms in the US and Europe that control large pension funds. (446)

Besides bringing in capital and technology, such foreign investors also help India in its relationships with the outside world. They become its good-will ambassadors. Christopher Sinclair, president of Pepsi-Cola International, tried to become one. In the spring of 1990, he asked the Bush administration not to retaliate against India under the US Super 301 trade action.[29] (447)

In the face all the competition, foreign and domestic, businesses scrambled to reach the consumer. This included many previously little known companies. Some gained ground by word of mouth.

Others advertised heavily, luring the consumer away from the safety of the established companies. For example, Nirma, a detergent maker, went on an advertisement blitz and captured sixty percent of the market by 1989. It beat Hindustan Lever, a past leader in the field. Lever responded with a huge marketing program. Many other companies—new and old—which made everything from coffee, soft drinks, and cooking oil, to electric fans followed this strategy and gained ground. So did several newspapers, showing how economic freedoms nurture the process of democracy itself. (448)

Previously, very few besides a few industrial giants advertised. The upstarts were at a definite disadvantage. Many were doomed from the outset. During the late eighties, however, several small companies spent heavily on product promotion in TV, radio, and newspapers and put down their roots in no time. In other words, the advertisement program helped the reforms to work and cause the economic boom. Heavy marketing by all these companies, in turn, boosted the revenues of the advertisement industry. These revenues received world-wide attention. For the first time, *Advertising Age*, an American journal, reported the 1989 billings (1,010 million rupees) of the largest advertising agency in India, Hindustan Thompson Associates. (448,449)

The advertisement wars made a few people nervous. A reporter for the *Illustrated Weekly of India*, for example, was as thrilled about them as I was about my teenage son's driving. The reporter said, "Wherever you look, you see them. Blood and gore on newsprint. Vicious attacks on the tube. All in the name of comparative advertising, which is a euphemism for marketing mayhem." He concluded, "Gone is the belief that success came along with a good product." Never mind that the consumer had decreed the products to be *good*. (448)

Many of us have such apprehensions about the advertisement industry. We consider the advertisers to be mostly a slick bunch. What if they trick all the people all the time? Even in countries with high literacy rates, most consumer advocates work on such a premise. A lot of them do a splendid job of disseminating information about defective products. Others simply lobby their governments to ban such items as dirt bikes and lawn darts. These activists have a simple mission in life—to protect the dim-witted consumer from his habit of buying dangerous and poorly made objects.

The typical consumer might not be that stupid after all. Conceivably, he might be tricked by a cleverly-made advertisement.

Owing to a sales pitch from his favorite rock group, he might try the brand new cola for the first time. Only when he considers the product to be superior to its competition, however, does he keep coming back. Few companies can realize long-term profits on first-time buyers alone. During the seventies, American car companies learned this the hard way. Despite a massive advertisement campaign, they lost heavily to imports. Only after they improved the quality did some of them stage a comeback.

Besides, a company could spend bundles of money and work for years in building consumer loyalty. By failing to maintain its standards, however, it risks losing it all. Ask Perrier, once a best seller of bottled water. Its employee mistakenly used a product containing benzene to clean grease from a bottling line. Soon, traces of this potentially toxic chemical showed up in a few of the bottles. Perrier recalled its bottles from worldwide distribution. It had a rough time making a comeback. (450)

The whole idea of market discipline works only if the consumer exercises her judgment wisely. Regardless of her education, economic status, or cultural background, she has to assess the competing claims of the producers and choose a winner among them. Only then she can force them to deliver value. The consumer has to accomplish this on her own, without any help from *Big Brother*. For a country like India, this might sound too radical. How can a poor, illiterate villager survive all the smoke and mirrors of this advertisement carnival? But then, how can someone, who is unable to decide which particular detergent gets her clothes the whitest, judge which of the politicians profess sound policies and have a solid track record? How can she know whom to vote for? Relying upon the collective wisdom of the governed to choose their leaders saved all of us from a lot of despotism. This strategy works for the market too.

By offering wider choices to its people, post-reform India proved to be a good testing ground for such theories. Its consumers came from different backgrounds. Most barely knew how to read or write. In the past they rarely switched brands. This was, however, hardly an ingrained trait. Because in large part they had to choose one piece of crap over the other, most bet on the bull they knew. When, owing to the increased competition, she was allowed to choose freely, the Indian consumer gave up her past loyalties. She went for value. Despite the high rates of illiteracy, even villagers proved to be very choosy. Said Vinod Dhawan of Cadbury's company, "The rural consumer is ready to pay for quality products." (455)

Companies that bet more on consumer wisdom rather than just a big advertisement campaign worked to enhance the value of their products. They improved quality and sold at competitive prices. To find out what the consumer wanted and to serve her better, more and more went for market research. Market surveys, however, happen to be just a tiny part of the communication network that exists between the consumer and the producer in any market economy. Every minute of every day the consumer speaks. She does so with her money rather than her mouth. Each time she chooses one brand of shoes, detergent, or television set over the other, she tells the producers what she wants, in what quantities and at what price. Only those companies that listen survive the competition. Such a consumer democracy is hardly a winner-take-all proposition. In it, every vote counts. It counts regardless of one's sex, race, color, or size of the midline. (451)

Of late, more and more of the consumers have been exercising their voting rights. Even a casual observer can spot the signs of rising consumerism in India. In crowded sari shops, restaurants, and movies houses, it comes through loud and clear. The people have more money to spend than before. Even the modest economic growth of the late eighties did improve the average income and push many of the poor into the ranks of the middle class. Various estimates place the numbers (belonging to the middle class) anywhere between 125 and 190 million and claim that these figures are increasing at a rate of twenty million a year. (452)

One also hears a few Indians complain how even children of household servants wear good cloths, study in schools and go to movies. The underclass too seems to be making more and spending more. From its national sample survey data on expenditures by people from the bottom 40 percent of the Indian population, a Planning Commission report (1989) claims that their incomes have gone up. Using these monies, the poor are participating more and more in the market. Buying food still takes up a lot of their income; but its once preeminent position in the hierarchy of priorities is being eroded by non-food consumer goods such as clothing and durables. (453)

Indian villages have become hotbeds of this consumer revolution. Between 1984 and 1988, the rural market for consumer items has more than doubled from 7,330 million to 15,000 million rupees. These villagers—usually extolled by the-return-to-nature-Gandhian types—buy sixty percent of the toilet soaps, forty-eight percent of the monocassette players, and forty-eight percent of the mopeds (motorized bicycles). At an increasing rate, they also gobble up scooters, refrigerators, electric fans, air coolers, washing machines, and color television sets. (454,455)

The villagers do surprise many a smart businessman. When Pratap Roy of the Godrej Company traveled to a few remote villages in (the state of) Maharashtra, he found out that a hair dye made by his company was in great demand. That rural India was fighting its graying every inch of the way was a vicious rumor. Actually, the farmers were using the dye to color their cattle. All they wanted to do was to make their livestock look "younger and healthier." (455)

As if their only mission in life is to please the rural consumer, quite a few companies innovate. For example, LML, Ltd. has introduced a scooter with a more powerful engine—aimed at the farmer who wants to transport goods. And Cadbury's hopes to develop a chocolate that won't melt easily in heat. There is hardly any need to worry about the decaying of rural teeth from eating too much chocolate. Colgate Palmolive has supply vans which show video films on oral hygiene and offer free samples. (455)

✦      ✦      ✦

"Making a choice is a satisfying experience," declares Vispi Doctor of *Young Minds*, the children research wing of Ormax Consultants, a market research group. (451)

After getting hooked on the freedom to choose in the much-expanded market of the eighties, the consumer tried to wiggle his way out of the chains of the ultimate monopoly—the public sector. Few can blame him for trying. It's hardly a secret that the government institutions treated the consumers—especially the poor and the disadvantaged—with disdain. Said the owner of a private hospital, "Even an auto-rickshaw driver knows that he will not be looked after in the government set-up unless he bribes doctors and nurses. So he comes to us, because we have only one bill and superior service and equipment." (456)

To improve the performance of a few of the 214 or so state-owned units, Rajiv' government attempted to expose them to market competition. As to be expected, officials in these industries hated getting off their behinds. Using a few outdated notions about the cultural characteristics of Indians, the bureaucracy attacked the private companies and their products. Said M.R. Naidu, chairman of HMT, a public sector watchmaker, "Indians prefer sturdy, reliable watches that are hand wound. Quartz watches sell only in throwaway societies." (457)

For decades, Indians swallowed such throwaway arguments. They bought their drab *reliable* watches from the state-owned monopolies such as HMT. The only other option the consumer had was to go to the underground markets. Smugglers sold plenty of timepieces—first Swiss, then Japanese brands, Seiko and Citizen. By cashing in on the demand, they captured one third of the market. (457)

Everything was going well for these smugglers and the public sector officials. Now, looking back, they probably wish that the eighties had never come. Largely owing to the reforms, newly-formed companies, such as Titan[30], jumped in to cater to the consumer. By 1989—within three years of its existence—Titan introduced 400 models, including many stylish and designer watches. Consumers liked what they saw. They rewarded

Titan with sixty percent of the country's quartz watch market. (457)

Despite their name recognition, for the first time, the state-owned units such as HMT and Hyderabad Allwyn started to lose the market share. They had to drop their silly ideas about Indians disliking the more accurate quartz watches and increase their quartz watch production. These companies had little choice. Their forte, the hand-wound watch market, was declining at a rate of eight percent per year. The consumer preferred buying from Titan than from the smugglers. In 1989, customs authorities recovered watches worth only 427.5 million rupees—down from 1,350 million rupees of the previous year. By matching the quality of production of Japanese goods, the likes of Titan laid waste to the notion that somehow, Indians only made bad pins, bad textbooks, and bad everything else. (457)

The new entrepreneurs also brought their versatility to delivering the various services to the consumer. Said Simran Bhargava and Salil Tripathi (of *India Today*), "Take a look at what they're offering customers today: an industrial license, a temporary secretary [or an office], designer letterheads, freelance drivers, someone who will buy your groceries, pay your phone bills and even walk your dog." (458)

The manufacturing boom of the eighties fueled growth in services such as accounting and telemarketing. In order to survive, however, these service sector pioneers had to force a change in the way the consumer thought. They had to break down a lot of resistance on his part to pay for intangibles. It used to be that most people hated to pay for a physician's consultation without receiving an injection or at least a prescription. Noted Sanjiv Sachar, a telemarketing executive, "When we first tried a phone survey, we were told to shut up." Fortunately he didn't. Within two years, his company realized a turnover of 600,000 rupees. Also, service providers such as management consultants attempted to forge a new kind of work culture. They offered stress counseling, sensitivity training, and team-building sessions for executives. Says K.N. Randeria, a management consultant, "When you lose a person you are writing off an asset." (458)

The burgeoning service sector created a lot of jobs. In 1970–71, it accounted for 25.5 percent of the economy. By 1987–88, the figure went up to 33.2 percent, well past the-often touted manufacturing sector (26%) and close to that of the primary sector (agriculture and mining etc. at 34.6%). Within the next two decades, the various service-based businesses could generate more jobs than the other two areas of the economy combined. Reminding one of Carl Sagan, said a member of the All India Management Association: "It is a tremendous market out there for services of these types. Billions and billions of rupees. By 2000 A.D. services will form a 50 percent chunk of the economy." (458,459)

How this job growth has already advanced the meekest of them all—domestic servants—reports Mahdu Jain (of *India Today*): "Just 10 years ago, a word to a friend and by the next morning two or three people would materialize [to provide domestic help] at the doorstep." (460)

Not any more. Nowadays employers are the ones who do the materializing. They show up at the finding agencies to enter their names in the long waiting lists of people seeking domestic help. The reason behind this sea of change is simple: demand for such help has simply outstripped the supply. Owing to economic growth, a lot of couples have found jobs. They desperately need help at home and push up the demand. What happened to all those who used to serve? Guess what? They too found jobs. At least in cities and towns that have enjoyed a brisk economic growth, these erstwhile servants bid good-bye to a few of the medieval notions that still haunt the rest of India. Says Jain, "With job opportunities opening up, that sense of destiny—call it fatalism—that the son of a servant could only be a servant has all but disappeared." (460)

These household workers no longer feel like bonded slaves. Without the help of any government decree or minimum wage law, the employers pay them 500 rupees a month and provide food, shelter, and clothing. Even though it's still meager, the salary is several times more than what it used to be just a few years ago. (460)

The employers pay because they have to. For the same reason, they treat their help with decency and respect. Jain says, "Today people beg, borrow and steal—even from their best friend—and employers will go to any length to keep a servant: teach them driving, get them jobs in private companies or in government offices." Naturally, the workers feel needed; they feel better about themselves. "With the growing aspirations of servants, employers often treat them as part of the family, even having them at the dining-table," adds Jain. (460)

He says, "Today, a raised eyebrow or a harsh voice and he's gone." (460)

The government of (the state of) Madhya Pradesh wanted to attract investors, domestic or foreign, to come its way. (461)

Its officials peddled a few backward regions for investments. They promised the necessary licenses and clearances and abundant power. Owing to these and other inducements, between 1985 and 1989, Malanpur, a town in one of the backward regions, attracted forty large and small factories. The investors poured in 13,000 million rupees. Within the next two years, they planned to invest another 40,000 millions. (461)

The villagers couldn't be happier. Their land prices soared. Many built houses to rent out to workers at a rate of 300 rupees per room—a tenfold increase in just two years. These rents went up because of demand. Owing to the boom, a lot of people found work in this village and needed places to stay. (461)

This story might not be a shining example of the success of capitalism since growth was channeled into one village. This *planning*, however, required little force. In other words, to fuel the boom, the officials didn't have to push banks to lend on their *priorities* or the businessmen to invest in only certain *essential* areas. It was all voluntary. All these officials had to do was to let go. Investors who trekked into this village did so on their own. They simply followed the smell of profit. They obeyed the dictates of the market and met consumer demands. In the process, they created wealth and employed many. (461)

This, in essence, is the story of the whole reform program. To the extent allowed, it worked in India and demonstrated the power of human initiative. Once freed of regulatory chains, and when allowed to keep a larger portion of their money, many investors, small and big, efficiently produced goods and services and created plenty of jobs. The program worked to raise the average standard of living better than all the subsidies, protectionist measures, and all the five-year-plans put together. In the open market, the producers competed with each other fiercely. The resulting consumer sovereignty worked better to control prices and improve quality than any bureaucratic price control or quality requirement. Regardless of her education or economic background, the Indian consumer has demonstrated that she is capable of enforcing such market discipline on her own. In this, she has needed little help from the *Big Brother*.

Most importantly, these producers and consumers have dispelled any doubts one might have about the suitability of capitalism to a backward country such as India. The success of these reforms—however limited—has shown how futile it is to complain about lack of leadership, overpopulation, or even shortage of resources.

It has also shown that the economic freedoms represent the only hope for the millions of Indians who, day in and day out, suffer from degrading poverty and utter desperation. And such a plan is their only avenue to regain their dignity and self-respect. This is best illustrated by an anecdote narrated by Prinay Gupte, author of *India: The Challenge of Change*. This story starts with Sudha Pennathur, who left her $150,000 a year job at the Levi Strauss Co. to venture into the *liberalized* India. She went on to combine her experience in mass merchandising with the skills of artisans from India and the other Third World countries. By exporting specially-made jewelry, accessories, and home furnishings to the West, this middle-woman linked these artisans with their faraway consumers. (351)

"A Marxist would look at Pennathur and denounce her as a clever merchant capitalist ripping off Indian peasants—which is why development economists in droves are throwing out *Das Capital* and returning to *The Wealth of Nations*," says Gupte, "The money she pays these underemployed artisans does more to raise their standard of living and enhance their self-respect than all the programs ever devised by Delhi bureaucrats and politicians." (351)

---

[26]Brought on by the Gulf War and Bush tax increases; the vibrant and deregulated Reagan economy shook these demons off and surged again only after a few quarters of recession.

[27]In four years prior to 1989, the production capacities increased by fifty percent from 300 million to over 450 million.

[28]Companies wirth less than 3.5 million rupees during the eighties. During the fifties, this figure used to be 0.5 million. (434)

[29]Super 301, first authorized in a 1988 trade act. Allows the U.S. government to list the foreign nations with "the most unfair or most burdensome overall trade barriers" and to impose 100% tariffs on exports from these nations unless they satisfy the U.S. demands.

[30]A joint venture by Tatas and the Tamil Nadu Government.

# CHAPTER 13
## *The Good Samaritan*

"ENTERPRISE, A FEW natural advantages, the readiness to build upon them and a booming export market have transformed Ludhiana from a once-sleepy town into one of India's premier industrial centers," says Surajeet Das Gupta of *India Today*. (462)

More than likely, visitors from the other sleepy towns in India are also equally impressed by this brand-new Ludhiana. If any of them visits Tokyo, Singapore, or New York, however, he will be more than impressed. He will lose his breath to the unfolding of these massive skylines. He will probably just stare and wonder. After several hours of in-flight food and entertainment, these travelers are too numb to think.

Such visitors do take a few days to snap out of their awe. To explain away the affluence that surrounds them, most of them fall back on their creed: It might be that these countries have had more resources, or their leaders have planned better. Is it anyway possible that somehow they have stolen all this wealth from the poor countries?

Recently, a senior Burmese officer, who had returned to Singapore after an absence of several years, caught himself wondering along these lines. He was hit hard by the contrast between his backward Burma and the host town with signs of prosperity written all over it. (463)

None of the above excuses could explain this disparity. By any stretch of imagination, Burma had more resources, and Singapore was never a colonial power. It was true that the planners of Singapore did a great job, but their *planning* included few grain boards or five-year plans. All it did was to let the natural desires of their citizens thrive and create these miracles. During his fateful trip, the Burmese officer discovered that this kind of planning worked better than any leftist planning. After all, he witnessed closely how decades of socialism planned Burma into utter poverty. (463)

Our Burmese friend started to cry. His return to his native country was reputed to be the beginning of widespread unhappiness with the Burmese strongman Ne Win and his socialist-military government. (463)

While few go that far, a lot of Indian emigrants to the US can relate to this officer. They, too, know a thing or two about stagnation. Especially during the seventies and the early eighties, when they visited India they saw little betterment. The few changes that they noticed in their cities had to do with the population growth and new stars in movies. A photograph of Madras taken in the late seventies would only be slightly different from a similar one from the fifties.

Of late, however, Madras has been changing. Various investors had plans to build commercial space worth 2,000 million rupees. Already, this city sports quite a few shopping complexes. The first such mall I visited had many stores that sold everything from books, shoes, utensils, and electronic goods to ready-made garments. Previously, to impress his wife, a brand-new husband had to buy strings of jasmines from street vendors. Nowadays, such a lovelorn man could go to a florist in one of these malls and choose from a variety of fresh blossoms. (464)

It was not as if Madras or Ludhiana just lucked out. By fueling economic growth, the reform program gave many other Indian cities each its own version of a facelift. The economic freedoms accomplished this by primarily altering the thinking and behavior, just as they had done in the developed countries. In other words, whether in Hong Kong, Bangkok, or Tokyo, the skyline might be impressive, but it's more like a nice book cover. Beneath it lies the fascinating tale of the phenomenal changes that have taken place deep inside the minds of the people, particularly those of the investors and consumers who have simply broken out of their traditional mold.

Based on such changes that are already taking place in the minds of its people, one could predict a brighter future for Madras. For example, it seems that nowadays more and more of Madrasis are eating out. They are also spending more on clothes, movies, and television sets. They are giving the businessmen a new courage to invest in the economy. Ask Vijay Gulechha, a partner in a construction firm which is sinking 100 million rupees into building a shopping plaza. He claims that the city's residents "are no longer the tight-fisted simpletons of yesterday." (465)

Ultimately, the likes of Gulechha realize decent returns on their investments only if these simpletons-turned-fun-lovers keep buying from these various shops. Only then, the investors can reinvest their profits, fuel some more growth, and fill the cities with glitter and glamour. The people they employ in the process spend some more and encourage building of more businesses. The new attitudes developed by consumers and producers, thus, mutually reinforce each other.

In the past, such habits as eating out or risking money in huge developments have been vaguely attributed to Western civilization. These traits, however, have shown up in a big way in as faraway and unlikely places as Tokyo, Bombay, Seoul, and Los Angeles. Where the sun rises or sets has little to do with their origin. They only signal a dawning of a commercial civilization.

As much as I want to glorify eating out, these changes go deeper than simple gluttony; they involve much more than being able to buy a brand-new washing machine; and they are a lot more rewarding than bringing home fresh flowers. Such a growth in consumption reveals a rising optimism. These Indians from boom towns feel confident that will do better financially. They believe in their future. At a subconscious level, they realize that more and more they, not some bureaucrat, can decide what happens to them. They feel less like nuts and bolts in a giant cogwheel. The opportunities give them a new sense of self-worth and individuality. In short, they feel in charge.

In a way, those from the post-reform India behave not unlike their countrymen who have emigrated to the US To the extent he is freed from the statist past and warped into a market economy, the emigrant knows that he is more or less responsible for what happens to him. With a lot more ease than before, he can start his own business or find a job in the thriving economy of his host country. Unlike before, he can ill afford to fool himself in the belief that somehow the government will step in and rescue him from his mistakes. In his dealings with others, he has to be alert. Otherwise, those that are trying to get ahead—his employer, employee, consumer, or grocer—will benefit at his expense. They simply exploit his mental laziness. Left to fend for himself, unhindered in seeking opportunities, and allowed to keep a larger portion of his wealth, he employs all his faculties to improve his lot. With each success he senses more optimism. He starts to believe in himself. Sandwiched between the rewards from his successful efforts and punishments from any blind dependence on someone else, he starts to look inside himself for guidance. For him, self-reliance becomes a survival necessity, an ingrained part of his day-to-day behavior, almost a religion.

Over the past few years, in the far corners of India quite a few rays of such self-reliance have been shining from behind the clouds of statism. Slowly, more and more young Indians seem to be getting tired of waiting for government jobs. They are starting to explore the other avenues. Some are finding jobs in the much expanded economy. Others are starting their own businesses. They are inspired by and adding to the growing ranks of entrepreneurs who have taken advantage of the recent unshackling of the businesses and prospered.

"You don't require an invitation where there is a profit," says Dhirubhai Ambani, an entrepreneur's entrepreneur. (466)

Of late, Ambani has been hitting the headlines frequently. Before him, for a very long time, a few families—such as Tatas and Birlas—dominated the Indian industrial scene. And they took time to get there. Ambani was short on patience. By doing whatever it took to succeed, in a few years he rose to the top and challenged the old-timers. (467,468)

Behind his rise there lies a tale, not so pretty, but as authentic as any ink-stained fingers to riches story.

Ambani, barely a high school graduate, started as a clerk in a French firm in Aden at a comfortable salary of 300 rupees a month. He left the firm in eight years. By then he had nearly quadrupled his salary. During the early sixties, he opened his company with 15,000 rupees (about $2000). In 1967, he started Reliance Textiles as a private, limited company with a capital of 150,000 rupees. In 1977, Reliance offered its shares to the general public. Many pundits in and outside the media ridiculed the venture. They predicted that the bubble would burst any time. (468)

Ambani was the one who busted their bubble. By proving his critics wrong by the widest margin possible, he crushed their crystal ball. By 1985, his empire was worth 100,000 million rupees. Ambani owned 1.5 percent of this loot—a cool 1,500 million. In terms of sales and total assets, Reliance ranked third among the country's corporate giants. (468)

Besides his zeal and daredevil attitude, what helped Ambani to get ahead were his friends in high places, especially those from the ruling Congress(I). Ambani used their powers to the hilt for everything from obtaining licenses, and relief from import duties and competition to takeover battles. This made many people jealous. His enemies attacked him; even a few of his friends turned on him. They questioned his methods. He reportedly called one of his colleagues and asked, "You accuse me of black marketing, but which one of you has not slept with me?" (468)

Ambani had a point. Most people who accused him of illegal activities also tried to profit by bending the rules. He just proved to be more adept. Besides, it was unfair to blame the likes of him. To survive this game, they had to play by its implied rules. Otherwise, the mercantilist laws and taxes would have doomed every one of him. The legal framework left anyone who wanted to engage in a productive, profitable venture with little choice but to break the rules. In economies with more freedom, such investors spend their energies more in building their businesses than connections. They live honorably only because the legal system lets them do so.

Entrepreneurs who do whatever it takes to make a profit regardless of the system might look ruthless and greedy. They might fit poorly in our idealistic vision of the world. As long as they refrain from infringing on another individual's basic rights, however, there is little justification in raising hurdles along their path to create wealth. The more the legal system tries to restrain their creative impulses, the more they end up breaking the law. This is true in every society. Also, without these capitalists, capitalism goes nowhere. Especially in a shortage-plagued country such as India, they make life bearable, even though in the process of creating wealth and jobs they break many unnecessary rules. If, on the other hand, every investor, except those who followed every rule and regulation and paid all the taxes, left the country, there would hardly be any enterprise in the country. India would have been swimming in more shortages, and Ethiopia would have been more habitable.

For example, but for Ambani's companies, which make more cloth everyday than any other textile company in the country, the Indian consumer would have felt naked more often; but for the jobs they had generated, many more would have been unemployed and hungry. (468)

Even though Ambani used his connections to obtain special privileges in the form of regulatory relief, he built his companies with little money from the treasury. Time and time again, he showed that he could raise his own capital. One of his ways was to offer stocks. By 1985, his corporation had more shareholders than any other Indian company—1.2 million. Their meetings were so well attended—12,000 in all—that the company had to rent a football stadium. And that was one happy crowd. By 1985, Reliance paid more share dividends than any-one else in the history of the country. In eight years, the stock price rose by fifty times. Actually, with his stellar performance, Ambani (along with a few others like him) was instrumental in making the idea of stock ownership take hold in the country. After reporting that by the end of the eighties a record ten million investors owned stocks, said Mukarram Bhagat of *India Tribune,* "Perhaps, no other single person has contributed as much to the spread of the equity cult as Dhirubhai Ambani of Reliance who perfected this funding strategy [of raising funds directly from the public] into a fine art." (468,469)

The likes of Ambani are just droplets in the sea of humanity that fills India, but they have helped to fan the flames of entrepreneurialism in the country. Actually, few modern soci-eties came into being already filled with a lot of entrepreneur-ial spirit. The whole process starts out small. Just as the nine-teenth century *robber barons* (such as the Morgans, Rockefellers, and Vanderbilts) have done in America, a few that hit it big incite others to aim high, take risks, and succeed. Each of the latter gets a few more to follow suit. Most everyone learns to act out of *greed;* soon the whole idea spreads like wildfire. Un-less doused by government regulations, such a chain reaction gives birth to a "nation of shopkeepers." It eventually makes entrepreneurship an ingrained part of the culture.

In it, without even thinking twice, high school dropouts start businesses. Even career civil servants can hardly resist the temp-tation. "The thought of what my position would be at the age of 55 [used to be the retirement age for most bureaucrats] sent shudders down my spine," said Mahendra Swarup, who used to work as a sub-divisional magistrate in Uttar Pradesh. Later on, he bought a running sawmill in Calcutta. Apparently he never looked back. By 1990, Swarup's Paharpur cooling towers enjoyed a fifty percent share in the 800-million-rupee cooling towers market. He also got into other areas such as synthetic bag manufacturing and flexible packaging. (470)

What helped the likes of Swarup, who were not as well con-nected as Ambani, to virtually start from scratch, run businesses with a lot more ease, and succeed was, again, the reform program. They took advantage of the economic freedoms and made it big in steel, plastic, shipping, fertilizer, electronics, and petrochemical industries and offshore construction. (470)

These high-fliers confounded the experts who had doubted whether a tradition-bound society such as the one in India could support risk-taking. Not unlike the earlier pioneers of the various developed countries, these Indian businessmen displayed a frontier spirit. When allowed to flourish in a liberalized atmosphere, they, too, pushed a few more boundaries.

This included many women. Proclaimed Inderjit Badhwar (and et al. of *India Today*), "Slowly but surely, and in what is widely described as a lower and middle class urban phenomenon no more than a decade old, Indian women have began to chip away at one of the last and most enduring bastions of male dominance—the no woman's land of business entrepreneurship, of risk taking, of financial adventure." (471)

They owe their successes primarily to that ever-increasing malady for which many social scientists are bent on finding a cure: consumerism. By simply catering to the needs of the customer, these businesswomen established themselves in such areas as food, leather, garments, handicrafts, and interior decoration. According to a study done on businesswomen in Delhi and its outlying areas, a highly-significant forty percent refused to conform to this stereotypical image of a woman entrepreneur. They ventured into such areas (previously monopolized by males) as electronics, engineering, consultancy, chemicals, circuit breakers, amplifiers, transformers, and microphones. (471)

These women have little use for a quota system or an equal rights amendment. They have learned to perceive themselves as individuals rather than belonging to a group. Says Kiran Majumdar, managing director of a biotech company: "Some women expect preferential treatment, just because they are women. That is wrong. You have to relate on a one to one basis." According to Purnima Mathur, a professor in the Department of Humanities and Social Sciences, IIT (Indian Institute of Technology) in Delhi, such women "have become more independent, achievement-oriented and career-minded." (471)

That they have succeeded in a society in which many college students still consider teasing their female colleagues as an innocent fun and their elders treat women as weak and fragile is all the more remarkable. But for the opportunities afforded by the relatively freer market, however, very few of these women could have dared to take such risks as starting a new business venture. Even now, to the extent they have to depend on the government, they are snubbed by the bureaucracy, which displays little interest in their success and is hardly immune from the prevailing attitudes of male orientation, if not domination. Malabika Shaw of the *All India Management Association* points out, "The deck is stacked against her from the very start. If you are a woman applying for a license or a loan, and you pick up a form on which the first question you have to answer is, 'son of....', what do you do?" (471)

Owing to the recent delicensing, such entrepreneurs have to deal with the bureaucracy and its sexist forms to a lesser degree. These women are finding out that the higher the level of deregulation, the freer they are; fewer of them are at the mercy of another person, his prejudices, and arbitrary decisions. Freedom lends self-respect, a hard commodity to come by in a country where female degradation is intolerably widespread (see chapter 10). Remarkably, all this spreading of wings has very little to do with any new bill or law giving special preferences to women. (471)

These businesswomen realize that they have succeeded for what they are, not what someone else thinks they ought to be. In a recent news account, a government official keeps introducing Madhura Chatraparthy, "meet Madhura, a woman entrepreneur." After a few times, she admonishes him, "Please introduce me as an entrepreneur. They can see I am a woman." (471)

✦    ✦    ✦

In the late thirties, author Norman Cousins prescribed a simple remedy for the high unemployment that was plaguing America. The employers should fire all female workers—all ten million of them—and hire unemployed males who numbered, strangely enough, ten million. (472)

At one time or other, female devaluation has reared its ugly head in every country. Good old Norm was just proclaiming what most everyone thought. In a poll conducted around that time, eighty percent of Americans disapproved of a woman working if she had a husband capable of supporting her. Much had changed in the ensuing years, especially after the Second World War. For one thing, women workers were desperately needed to fill in. That forced many people to soften their attitudes towards female workers. If war was the only reason why women became liberated, however, quite a few bras would have been burned soon after Aryan tribes invaded India, or at least after the Hundred Years' War. (472)

Michael Harrington, a devout socialist, explained what has happened ever since: "Prior to capitalism, one or another kind of authoritarianism was pervasive. Then capitalism created, not the full reality of freedom—and certainly not of justice—but a space in which men and women could fight for and win democratic rights and even make advances towards justice." This was as far as any self-respecting socialist could go in defense of capitalism. By freeing serfs from their landlords, the laws establishing and protecting widespread ownership of property provided for many individuals to make a living on their own. This led to a heightened sense of individuality, which in turn paved way for the widespread acknowledgement of the inherent worth of each human being. Naturally, support for his basic rights gained ground. (473)

Support for *her* basic rights, however, took a few more centuries to gain ground. As a matter of fact, it mostly happened after women started to enjoy the possibility of making their living independently. For one thing, owing to the high levels of economic activity brought on by advent of capitalism, the working woman was no longer an artifact or expression of new thinking, but a dire necessity. The employers would have to scale down or even close their operations without the availability of a large numbers of workers, both men and women. Whether as patients in hospitals or parents of school students, the consumers had to deal with and appreciate the woman worker. Through their jobs, women gained much more than their paychecks and respect. They learned to be self-reliant. What each of them could accomplish made many other women believe in themselves. Slowly women learnt to affirm their rights. The society had little choice but to soften its attitudes toward all women, whether working inside or outside the home.

Most feminists, however, ignore the contribution of capitalism towards women's liberation. As far as they are concerned, a few of the pioneers of their movement just happened to be born in the past one hundred years. These revolutionaries just happened to inspire or even push the rest to think like themselves. It was as if women's liberation were some kind of historic accident. During an argument, asserted a female acquaintance of mine, "It [capitalism] only helps white males"

Soviet women might disagree. Says an AP report from 1991, "The Soviet Union observed the [International Women's] day with marching bands, flowers and folk dancers, but some women watching the festivities in Moscow said unequal pay, poor living standards and the scarcity of consumer goods made women second-class citizens." "We are on the lowest level of society," said Valentina Zavyaskina. "It's bad when you have nothing to wear, when there are no cosmetics, when you don't know if you will have a job tomorrow or not." Having access to mascara from Lancôme [Paris], blush from Esteé Lauder or Jordache jeans might matter little. Having a productive job, however, certainly goes a long way. In its absence, Soviet women stood in long lines in the shops. Most put in a hard day's work doing nothing more than just fighting for consumer goods. To each of them—or an Indian woman who can only get a job with the help of her family—the talk of woman's lib. or woman's day has little meaning. (474)

Many, who agree that having access to a productive job is the first step toward equality, nevertheless question why women should be paid less in comparison. The activists demand that the government should step in and correct the imbalance. They, however, ignore the price we all pay when in pursuit of forced equality, we expand the power of state. The resulting regulations invariably shackle the enterprise some more, hamper economic growth, and limit our opportunities. In such a sclerotic bureaucratic economy, the truly disadvantaged fare particularly worse. On the other hand, the women and the minorities, who are willing to work hard to improve their lot, do much better in a competitive productive economy with plenty of jobs. In a tight labor market, they enjoy considerable bargaining power. To perform better than the competition, the businesses desperately need these productive workers. Naturally, those employers that value efficiency strive to retain their best and the brightest, both men and women.

The employers that fail to do so pay the price. They lose their productive talent to the competition. A 1990 study done on professionals from Fortune 500 companies by Wick & Co.— a Wilmington (Delaware) consulting firm—revealed that seventy-three percent of the American women who had quit their jobs went to work for other companies. At the time of the survey, seven percent were looking for new jobs. Another seven percent had left their jobs to stay home. Fully thirteen percent had started their own businesses. (475)

Owing to a ready availability of productive jobs—such as the twelve million new ones that American women have gained during the eighties—the workers are able to leave their jobs with much more ease during times of economic growth than other times. They enjoy more control over their future. The freer is the economy, the better are the chances for a woman or a minority worker to start her own business and create her opportunities and say to her boss: "take this job and…" (476)

Such independence brings about a curious change in social values and mores. Because, for her survival, she is less dependent on someone else's mercy, this newly liberated individual follows her mind. She is free to reexamine a few of the long-standing collective values that have been imposed upon her by either a few powerful elites or the despotic majority, mostly of men and quite a few women who think like these men. Few but the liberated woman set her value system. She could live with this status quo, dare to be different, or wander in between. She could even risk a conflict, if there is a need for one.

In this regard, what is happening in an increasingly enterprising India might hold the interest of those in the West who like to travel in time, go back and watch their own women's liberation unfold. As more and more are taking up jobs and starting businesses, these Indian women are increasingly ascertaining their rights. To a greater degree than before, each of them seems to follow her own individual values. Mostly, this involves choosing what she considers as the best ideas, whether they come from the East, the West, or outer space.

On occasion, this might result in a wholesale revolt against tradition. The divorce rate in India, for example, is rising at an annual rate of five percent. After exercising her inherent right to escape what she considers as a hopelessly miserable, tension-filled, or even abusive relationship, however, the woman needs a paycheck to carry on. Otherwise, such a choice amounts to a cruel joke. It seems that, much more so than before, Indian women are able to support themselves. According to a Pathfinder poll, in 1983, women from seven percent of the households in Indian cities held jobs. By 1989, this number nearly doubled to thirteen percent. To ascertain her independence, this new woman need not rush to a divorce court each time she has an argument with her spouse. But the ability to break free and survive by herself gives her more leverage. It gives her self-respect. She has fewer reasons why she has to take a back seat. Each of the newly independent women also transforms a few around her. Quietly and without much fanfare, she changes the prevailing attitudes. (477,478)

There are those who are genuinely worried about these "Western" values. They point to the high rates of divorce, illegitimate births, sexually transmitted diseases, and drug abuse in the West and predict the same future for India. Such deterioration, however, occurred not because the individual was free to choose his values, but every attempt was made to insulate him from the consequences of his choices. For example, by using mood altering drugs an addict harms no other person but himself; owing to the habit, however, when he loses his job, governmental programs take care of his basic needs such as food, shelter, and health care. He has few incentives to sober up and engage in productive work. In many instances, the programs actively encourage destructive behavior. By becoming pregnant, a single teenager from an inner city gains a home, food stamps, welfare checks, and a host of other benefits. Otherwise, she has to live with her folks, a prospect many an adolescent finds unappealing. In the name of compassion, one might justify some of these programs; one, however, must recognize the price a society pays for unconditionally protecting the individual from the consequences of her actions. To blame the results of such policies on a person's freedom to choose her values is highly misleading.

In a truly free society, not only should the individual be free to make her choices, commit her mistakes and live by her value system without coercion from others, she should be allowed to live with the consequences of her actions without *Big Brother* jumping in to help her whenever she screws up. The only other requirement in choosing one's value system and actions is that the one stays clear of the others' fundamental rights to life, liberty, and property. In such a society, just because they are free, most people are not going to abuse their freedoms. They adhere to the value system that they have developed, or voluntarily subscribed to, much better than the one imposed by the despotic majority or oppressive traditions.

Those who like to see equality take root in India through a change of heart rather than by force can take heart in a finding from a recent survey done by the *Illustrated Weekly of India*. In increasing numbers (sixty-nine percent of the female students, seventy-five percent of the male students and fifty-seven percent of the married men), the people expressed belief in sexual equality. (477)

In 1984, farmers in New Zealand were one angry bunch. So much so that they stormed the parliament in the capital city and slit the throats of their sheep. (479)

They did so to protest. What made these farmers see red was that their newly-elected government abolished the agricultural subsidies. It made 40,000 of them go cold—turkey. The prime minister estimated that about twenty percent of them would lose their farms. He, however, had little choice in the matter. He had inherited a mess which was forty years in making. By the time his Labor Party took over from the National Party in 1984, the accelerating spiral of subsidies—which amounted to one third of agricultural revenues—precipitated a run on the New Zealand dollar. The Laborites saw few alternatives to abolishing subsidies. To cure inflation, they also engineered high interest rates and squeezed farmers some more. (479)

As to what happened next, recounted Thomas Moore (of *US News And World Report*): "The results were right out of an economic textbook. The price of fat lamb dropped $20 a head to $8 in one year." Moore continued, "but the dire forecasts never came to pass." Notwithstanding the earlier predictions that 8,000 people would lose their farms, by 1990, fewer than 100 actually did. The rest cut costs, paid down their debts (piled up during the subsidy heyday), and searched for better land uses. Some of them tried to make money the old—fashioned way, by selling more. In response to the market demand, they increased the supply of livestock. Owing to all this belt tightening, average farm profits started to pick up. (479)

What picked up more was the farmers' morale. These once hooked-on-dole, sheep-slashing, and parliament-bashing protesters learned to rely upon themselves for sustenance. They loved being in control. Many swore off the subsidies. These born-again free marketers also pushed their government to deregulate the rest of the economy. Just as cigarette smoke offends many ex-smokers, handouts at home and abroad turn these farmers off. Says Owen Jennings, president of New Zealand Federated Farmers: "Farmers in the state of Iowa receive more aid in the form of subsidies than the World Bank spends on the whole of Africa." (479)

Besides the farmers in New Zealand, many groups in other countries (such as senior citizens and welfare recipients in the US, members of the scheduled castes in India and, of course, farmers in most countries) have also come to depend upon *Big Brother*, especially his promises of cradle-to-grave security. They have gotten hooked on the dole. Their physical and mental well-being revolves around its size and scope. Instead of looking at themselves for betterment in life, they look at him. If they screw up, he will bail them out. Won't he? At some point in time, however, when all the promises by the politicians empty the treasury and he is unable to meet his "obligations," the hitherto beneficiaries get upset, as upset as a drug addict on withdrawal.

To keep getting their hit, and if possible, to make it even bigger, they try to influence those in power by every possible means. These wards of state demonstrate. They strike. They get heavily politicized. The more statist is the country, the more these groups will try to put on pressure. Unless stopped by brutal oppression, they might resort to violent demonstrations, secession demands, or even terrorist acts.

Small wonder that countries such as the former Soviet Union and India have become highly fragmented and very turbulent. Practically every facet of life is riddled with politics. In this regard, both these socialist giants have plenty of company; Germany and Italy before the Second World War and most countries in present day Africa, South America, and central Europe.

Students of history might wonder why there is widespread violence and excessive interest in politics in these countries. They might even blame these traits on genes, food, climate, or that hard to define *culture*. All these countries, however, have one common denominator: An individual's survival, progress, and prosperity have little to do with his efforts. They solely rest upon his ability to influence those in power. They rest upon politics. Lech Walesa says, "We [Polish] want to rejoin the ranks of normal societies. It isn't an issue of ideology, it simply means we want a system where politics isn't everything and people can live normal lives." (480)

On the other hand, farmers in New Zealand have shown what happens if these countries embrace the so-called radical, free market programs. The beneficiaries are cut loose to fend for themselves. Mostly, a tiny minority which refuses to even attempt to better its lot fares poorly. After surviving the usually tough transitional period by whatever means, the rest rediscover their strengths. They snap out of the myth that all they have to do is to be politically active and a bunch of usually-uninterested bureaucrats will provide for them.

These ex-welfare recipients rather spend their energies to create their own opportunities by catering to the consumer who mostly rewards them based on the quality of their work. After trying their very best, they learn to live in peace with the results. And they are no longer afraid of being left out of the distribution game. They feel much less inclined to clamor for special privileges based on such traits as religion or color of skin, or their geographical location. They feel less volatile, arousable, and political.

After all, in every country, regardless of culture or geography, most people have the same priorities; earning a livelihood, providing for and taking care of their families, acquiring material comforts, and chasing after the so-called happiness. In a largely commercial society, because the government's role is comparatively limited, one could afford to ignore the politics and pursue these goals. Unlike in a statist third world country such as India, without even knowing the name of his congressman or senator, an American can get a job, start a business, buy a pound of sugar, or fish in a mountain stream (for the time being). Consequently, very few Americans get overly excited about such matters as who wins the elections. The only exception is the drama of presidential elections, hyped up every four years by the media constantly seeking higher ratings through sensationalism. Once these elections are over, however, people rarely harp on the results. Most are actually relieved to get back to their routines. Invariably, politics take a backseat to the other concerns.

This is not as bad as it sounds. It's true that a degree of citizen participation is crucial for the success of a democracy.

The problem is that in any country where most people believe that politics is everything and politicians control their lives, the public tends to be over-politicized. Election results dominate the life in the country. Most struggle to get "their candidates" into power. Supporters of the losing candidates are scared of being cheated out of jobs and other benefits. They get very emotional. Protesting the results, they burn busses and trash property. By demanding a separate voting district, or even a separate state for their group, they further balkanize their country. Such popular emotions can ultimately threaten the very survival of a nation.

On the other hand, the freer and more vibrant the economy is, the less people are affected by politics and politicians. The people have little need or desire to engage in violence and tear their country apart for political reasons. A glance around the world can demonstrate that such productive and apolitical people (such as the ones in Switzerland and American suburbia) constitute peaceful and prosperous societies.

In such a society, the individual is too busy tending to his immediate concerns. Reading papers or watching news becomes more of a hobby. Considering the quality of either, it's hardly surprising that he would rather go fishing.

"It is possible, but I think that we received here such impulse to work that we can overcome this. I hope." Ms. Zarharchenko, a Soviet attorney visiting the US, was responding to a question by Morley Safer (of CBS's *60 minutes*) of whether it would be more frustrating to deal with the Soviet bureaucracy when she returned to her country with all the "wonderful new ideas." (481)

One wonderful new idea that had come to possess Ms. Z and her colleagues was that they had to take responsibility for their welfare. Said Valentin Bluger, another Soviet attorney interviewed by Safer, "We're counting cholesterol. I never did it before, but I am counting it now." (481)

But then, never before he has lived in a liberal commercial society. In it, as a rule most people instinctively behave as if their actions and choices shape their futures. They do much more than watching cholesterol counts. Compared to those from other countries, for example, larger numbers of US residents refuse to smoke and they partake in regular physical exercise.

They also feel more secure about their future and that of their children's. Comparatively speaking, they have a lesser interest in the accumulating of or handing down huge amounts of wealth to generations to come. Instead, they try to enhance the quality of the life—theirs as well as other's. Many turn their attention to those that are less fortunate than they are. After spending some time on Duke campus, Hodding Carter said as much about the students:

> What I've witnessed is more task-oriented than ideological: students tutoring functional illiterates, helping establish shelters for the homeless, working at halfway houses and establishing nationwide networks of concern. There is virtually no passion directed at or toward the government. Instead, there seems to be a perception that government isn't going to provide solutions and so the solutions must be created on the ground, close at hand. (482)

From where does all this altruism come? Doesn't the popular media routinely call such young men and women *the self-centered American youth*? It also uses such labels as yuppies and Robber Barons (of the nineteenth century, for example) to describe some of us as money grabbing, selfish people chasing instant gratification. It categorizes the rest among the various other groups: victims, non-caring escapists, socially-conscious liberals, and altruistic philanthropists. In reality, all these entities just describe the various facets of the individual psyche. At one time or other, we all have experienced these emotions. Few of us can honestly say that we have never felt selfish, money grabbing, altruistic, or philanthropic. On occasion, we do believe that we are the victims of unfair actions of others. Chasing instant gratification is much more common than we care to admit. The level of an activity in a society depends more on how often its people feel like engaging in it than to what category each individual belongs.

For example, the amount of philanthropy depends upon how often the people feel like giving. When they are hurting or feeling powerless, very few are inclined to care about others. In such a society, volunteerism and philanthropy tend to be very limited. In countries where people succeed by their efforts, on the other hand, most feel in charge. They are confident that they can influence their environment. They know that they can lend a helping hand to the needy. Such confident and caring people are more inclined to donate their time and money. They also tend to be more tolerant and forgiving. Instead of demanding reparations, after both the World Wars, Americans helped the vanquished nations. The US has been the biggest donor nation during most of this century. But for its caring and giving, most relief organizations in the world would have gone out of business.

Even within the same country, such volunteerism and philanthropy fluctuate with economic conditions. During recessions and depressions, one hears of tales of sharing because of their novelty. During economic good times such as the eighties, levels of donations of time and money tend to go up. By the time the *me decade* had passed into the sea of history, for example, seventy-five percent of Americans were donating to various charities. Between 1987 and 1989 alone, the number of volunteers in the US rose by twenty-three percent. Many charities were worried about the effects of Reagan's tax cuts on such giving. Despite this, the sky is yet to fall on them. According to a recent (spring of 1993) report in *The Wall Street Journal,* for any country, in terms of absolute numbers and as a percentage of the national income, the donations in the US reached an all-time high. (483)

This was hardly the first time that Americans had engaged in voluntary, non-governmental efforts on a large scale. During the remarkably prosperous years of the late nineteenth century, with very little help from the government, private citizens established the library system, the school system, the Society to Prevent Cruelty to Animals, and the other "points of light," which many people now take for granted. Andrew Mellon bypassed his children to donate more than $31 million worth of art pieces and made way for the establishment of the National Gallery of Art in Washington, DC, one of the world's finest museums. (484)

While commenting on the subject of giving, Margaret Thatcher gave her own interpretation of the Good Samaritan story. She said that no one would have remembered him if all he had were just good intentions; he had material as well to give. Her critics countered by saying that it was for his good intentions that he was remembered. They branded Thatcher as hard-nosed and tin-hearted. Proclaimed one, "Thatcherism seemed to make a virtue out of base human nature rather than to desire its improvement." (485)

To find out what is it that causes such an improvement, let us sidestep the important question of who gets to define "improved human nature." Let us just use our Good Samaritan as a proverbial gold standard. Unlike most taxpayers, who are forced into being *generous*, he has given voluntarily. Just as the millions of donors from the various developed countries do each year, he has helped out of goodness of his heart. Just like them he had something to give. Unlike the farmers from New Zealand (prior to 1984), he believed in his ability to shape the future. This confidence led him to believe that he could help the person who was less fortunate than he was.

Just as he has done, most donors give to those who, in their opinion, are the most deserving. Just as the Good Samaritan has helped a Jew—a supposed enemy—these donors simply ignore politics. In the summer of 1990, for example, Americare, a totally privately-funded organization, sent a lot of relief supplies to Iran after a major earthquake.

To the best of his ability, the private donor stays away from freeloaders. He mainly helps those that are down through no fault of their own and are willing to pull themselves up. More than likely, he infects the beneficiaries with his ideas of individual initiative and self-help. For their part, they realize that, unlike the government funds which they feel are infinite, these monies can stop coming their way any time. Few want or can

afford to depend upon private donors for a very long time—
certainly not for several generations. Most recipients try to do
whatever it takes to build their lives. Soon, they and their benefactors move on to help other needy people.

Eventually, this virus of philanthropy and volunteerism becomes so widespread that it infects those who move to the
country from another culture. For example, the bug over-
powers the immigrants to the US in no time. Practically every immigrant group has an organization which thrives on
the voluntary efforts of its members. Today there are an estimated 300 periodicals serving the immigrant readers. Most
barely break even, but the work is done in the spirit of service. (486)

Quite a few Indians, who before coming to America had
taken little interest in other people's affairs, now keep themselves busy with various community activities. These volunteers put in long hours. They earn little personal gain. They
even take a remarkable amount of licking from their, sometimes, unappreciative customers and keep on ticking.

Of course, for some this is a kind of payback for their *fly now,
pay later plan* (see chapter 1). Their volunteer work with the
Indian associations has something to do with the sense of solidarity that one feels with *one's own* in a faraway land.

Even so, compared to the emigrants to Africa, Europe, or
the Middle East, the transplants to America seem to engage a
bit more in voluntary service. In the process, they also help
their country of birth. A few *adopt* villages in India. Others send
money to feed the hungry, build hospitals, or help victims of
various disasters. As long as they convince the donors of their
sincerity, few charitable organizations from India go back
empty-handed.

Recently (1987), a few doctors, lawyers, and psychotherapists
from Bombay offered a helping hand to abused women. To

this end, these volunteers started an organization called HELP—a night telephone service for women in distress. (487)

Litas, an advertisement agency, liked the idea. It wanted everyone to know about HELP and placed a half page advertisement in Bombay dailies, free of charge. Soon, many more women started to call. Each of them would talk to an anonymous listener, a volunteer just offering a helping hand. These volunteers seemed to have a healthy respect for the woman's ability to judge what was good for her. Rather than forcing a certain value system on her, they would inform the victim of her rights. Said Anjali Saxena, a clinical psychologist and co-founder of HELP, "It isn't easy for a woman to leave her husband. She knows it better than the feminists. That's her marriage, her world. My challenge is to make her realize that a husband who beats her thrice a day isn't worth living with." (487)

Even though the majority in the country still feel that it's the government's job to take care of the less fortunate, of late, the spirit of volunteerism seems to be catching up with quite a few Indians. Increasingly, more and more are realizing that they can and shall make a difference. Whether this is a result of better economic times or of globalization of ideas (for example, hitting the wife is no longer "an internal family affair" and the outsiders could and should help the victim) one can debate endlessly, but the beneficiaries couldn't care less about the inner mechanics. The ripples of voluntary efforts keep them afloat.

All this sounds wonderful, but such programs work only if a lot of people volunteer. How can one prod them to come forward? Not by keeping them poor and unemployed. Few who are scraping to meet their basic needs can afford to work for nothing. For example, during the fight for independence, the spirit of volunteerism did rush through the veins of Indians. Quite a few heeded the preaching of the Mahatma. They tried to help the poor and the downtrodden. They did so largely out of feelings of nationalism and selflessness; so selfless that, by and large, these volunteers were unwilling or unable to take care of their families. In no time, they, themselves, started to do poorly. Their enthusiasm for voluntary service ebbed; an overwhelming feeling of desperation took its place.

The recent seedlings of volunteerism seem to have a different origin. Far from being romantic idealists, most of the volunteers are very successful individuals in their personal lives. They have jobs and enjoy a decent standard of living. Because these men and women are practical to the point of being hard-nosed, it's entirely possible that their programs will endure.

# CHAPTER 14
## End of History?
## Or, is it the Beginning?

ABOUT THE POLITICIANS that the redistributive system has coughed up in India, said Arun Shouri, a prominent editor:

> But more than ideology, there is cold calculation—the premise that it is by advocating concessions which will benefit a particular section that one can get them to follow one…It isn't just that the demands they champion are sectional. It is that they champion them in a most divisive manner—it is always this caste as against that caste, Hindi as against English, farmers as against others. The hangover of what has failed everywhere—Marxism—is at the back of this of course. (488)

Shouri is quite unlike those commentators who claim that something is basically wrong with Indians so as to make them fight among themselves (see chapter 3). He points to the real culprit. It's collectivism. No country, state, or village, but perhaps a monastery, can survive the politics of distribution. Small wonder that the resulting tensions have imperiled the very concept of an Indian union.

Meanwhile, the culture of corruption engulfed the political process. It became hard to distinguish between criminals and politicians. These criminal-politicians rendered the checks and balances of the constitution irrelevant. The officials thus turned law and order into a joke, albeit a cruel one. The poorest and the weakest paid the highest price. They suffered terrible abuses of their basic rights.

This turn of events has confounded many champions of these rights. They wonder what has gone wrong. After all, the earlier leaders strived to guarantee legal protection of these rights. In this they were following the example set by the West. "And basic to this struggle [to establish the rule of law in America and Britain] was the inalienable right to life, liberty, and freedom of expression," comments an editor of *India Today*, "Indian democracy too is supposed to be based on the rule of law along the lines of the British and the Americans. But there the similarity ends." (489)

As to why, the answer lies in one missing phrase—*the inalienable right to property.*

Its absence is at the root of the problems of the typical hawker and the fruit seller who are constantly harassed by the authorities (see chapter 2). A lack of respect for the economic rights provides the ideological basis for the many laws that have made possible, among other things, nationalization, high taxes, rent controls, land reforms, urban property ceilings, and hyper-regulation. From this culture have emerged not only malignant corruption, deterioration of law and order, and breakdown of the fabric of the society, but also major changes in the individual psyche. Instead of optimism, self-reliance, feelings of self worth, individual responsibility, and philanthropy, such traits as pessimism, dependence on *Big Brother*, cynicism and a pervasive belief in force to cure all the societal problems have taken hold. In short, *right to property* holds the key to socialism and its affects—economic and non-economic. This is the missing grape that has soured the post-independent India.

The officials have always considered the right to own property as dispensable. Very correctly they view it not as God given, but as a human invention and an arbitrary setup.

But, so are the other rights, including the very basic one—the right to life. How can the Creator be so partial as to favor the tiger, but not its lunch, the deer, or the grass the latter eats? It's hard to imagine an omnipotent being that has bestowed upon a man the right to life but not upon the bugs he steps on everyday, or the bacteria that invade his body each time he brushes his teeth.

Rights are what we agree to give to each other. We hate getting killed or beaten up. Collectively and very arbitrarily, we have agreed to make murders and assaults illegal. The main purpose of our organizing into a society is to enforce such rights as the one to life. To this end, we punish, and sometimes even kill, the violators.

Our other arrangements which stood the test of time—such as marriage or letting our kids stay in our basements, even after they would finish their PhDs—were pretty arbitrary too. Nevertheless, all these arrangements and rights served as basic building blocks for human civilization. And so did the right to own property. The hunter/gatherer hunted or gathered only because he instinctively considered whatever he gained as his own. Also, neither the person that built the first tree house, nor the builder of the first skyscraper would have invested her energies if she knew in advance that her property would be confiscated. She would be left with few incentives to turn the natural resources into real wealth. Right to property, on the other hand, makes the individual work, produce, and consume what she wants to and exchange the rest. Simply put, no property rights means no economic material, which in turn means no bartering, no market, no society, and no civilization.

Most communist reformers ignored this basic tenant. Without adequately guaranteeing property rights, they tried *market reforms*. They forgot that one could only exchange something one owned. Invariably they failed. And so did their predecessors, who tried to build societies by abolishing individual property rights. Even Marx needed his pen, his papers, and handouts from Engles to excoriate these rights in his writings.

Only what you own, can you give. Without property ownership, there's no philanthropy. Also, if you feel robbed on a regular basis, you are in no mood to aid or comfort others. Recently (1990), readers of a Soviet newspaper were asked to list all that was bad and ugly in their country. Robin Knight (of *US News and World Report*) reported on the answers: "Along with empty shelves and rising crime, many mentioned 'bezdushi,' or heartlessness—the absence of decent human feelings." (490)

Leftist politicians in social democracies did distance themselves from the methods of Soviet government. They, however, had few problems with the idea of forced equality. In its name, they abridged the right to own property; the wealth they, thus, confiscated, they dangled in front of the voter, won his support, and stayed in power.

Margaret Thatcher finds this approach offensive. Says Paul Johnson, a British journalist and a historian, "To her, Labor was a party of moral fraudulence: It bribed its way into office by expensive schemes of public provision which, once installed, it abandoned since it could not pay for them." Thatcher believes in an honest day's work for an honest day's pay. She says, "It is not the creation of wealth that is wrong, but the love of money for its own sake. The spiritual dimension comes in when deciding what one does with the wealth." (491)

The free market ideology appeals to someone like her for two reasons. It yields results. More importantly, it operates on a higher moral ground. Compared to the alternative, which allows the officials to confiscate the fruits of the individual labor and use the money for personal and political gains, the economic liberalism rewards the individual's efforts to produce and lets him decide how to spend his gains. It makes him, not the state, responsible for his own good and that of the others. It makes him feel free and secure enough to care about his fellow men. Thatcher says, "Intervention by the state must never become so great that it effectively removes personal responsibility." Various politicians and theorists, who back socialism in one form or other, cover up the simple fact that their approach not only lets the individual off this moral hook of personal responsibility, it also benefits the privileged few at the expense of the many. (491)

To stay in power, however, these leftists need support from the many. They know it's all very tricky. How can you hurt someone and at the same time get him to vote for you? By doing a number on him without his knowing about it; by simply appealing to his good intentions; by packaging your designs in great sounding rhetoric; and by giving a great sounding label to your package. No matter where they come from, the socialist politicians own a dictionary full of these jewels.

In the US, they slogan about *America first*, and pass protectionist laws which curtail the consumer choice and depress his standard of living, while at the same time limiting competition to well connected producers-both owners and unionized workers. The American politicians also constantly try to enlarge the social welfare network by proclaiming such services as health care as *basic rights*; in the name of *full employment*, they always fund new bureaucratized employment and training schemes, even though, time and again, many similar programs have already failed.

Their role models, the various European politicians, are far ahead in this game of promising never-ending rights. In the name of *workers' rights*, most Europeans governments mandate benefits to those with jobs and raise barriers to starting new businesses. They, thus, keep a lot more unemployed and poor. In India, among other things, the politicians practice protectionism in the name of *self-sufficiency*. Their laws to "restrict monopolies" have actually kept the small players out and minimized competition to big houses. Their laws covering "Muslim women's rights" are the legal ways of stripping these women of their rights.

All these leftist politicians know that their glorious titles appeal to our emotions. No matter where we come from, we want our country to be nothing but first. We want it to be self-sufficient. We hate monopolies. And who can oppose the right to health care, full employment, or affordable housing or for that matter, workers' rights or Muslim women's rights? Only those that have grasped the details of a particular bill. The officials calculate that if they overwhelm the public with thousands upon thousands of such laws and regulations each year, fewer and fewer of these dictates will get the closer inspection they deserve; the rest will just slip by.

Using their word gymnastics, the socialists can mislead even the most discerning among us; they can also place their critics on the defensive. Anyone who questions the means of the leftists and points out that we all pay a heavy price when they enlarge the powers of state and that these laws produce the exactly opposite results, the officials paint as a cynic. They castigate him for opposing their worthy goals. They point out the imperfections of any alternative that he might propose, but never actually compare it with their prescription. In country after country, they dominate the political debate, pass their laws and even survive the abysmal results.

The statists can get away with their already failed and even despotic means because most of us in the public fear the only alternative to their intervention, free market. We fear that it only makes the rich richer by making the poor poorer. Says Nikolay Shmelyov, an economist at the Institute of U.S. and Canada in Moscow, "The groundlessness of this fear [of capitalism] is evident to anyone who realizes that classes exist in any society… Perhaps we will lose our ideological virginity [by embracing a free market program], but it now exists only in the fairy-tale editorials of newspapers". (492)

This romantic vision of a classless-problemless-utopian society is hardly limited to the fairy-tale editorials of the Soviet newspapers. To a varying degree, most of us harbor it. We have a certain image of the ideal world and how we should conduct ourselves in it. It's filled with selflessness, giving, and sharing. It's marked by a total absence of greed. Any form of confrontation—including the "cutthroat" competition, an essential element of a market economy—has no place in it. In short, this view of the ideal world happens to be very collectivist.

It also happens to be very naive. If anyone lives according to these ideals and totally and completely subordinates his well-being to that of others, he will end up in martyrdom faster he can say martyrdom. We instinctively know that selfishness and self-preservation are the two sides of the same coin. This realization keeps us rational. It helps us to protect our interests and survive. We compete with others who want the same thing that we do. To gain on them, we acquire and sharpen our skills, work hard, produce, and protect what is ours.

The gap between what we want to be and who we are, however, leads to friction. It creates tension. To deal with it, we hang on to our collectivist ideals, while at the same time do what we must do to survive. When delivered in a right package, the socialist programs naturally appeal to our unfulfilled ideals and present what looks like a shortcut to realize our cherished goals. They strike a chord in us. We hold these policies in high esteem. When they fail, we blame the particular leaders who happen to be in charge at that time.

What set us upon this trajectory are the common goals that we all agree on. Whether from New York, New Delhi or New Zealand, as an individual, each of us want to do well. We all want to be free. We want our government to protect our rights. We demand that it should ensure opportunities and decent living standards for those who are willing to work for them. And we hate exploitation.

We all know where to go, but the real debate is how to get there. We can live with the hope that a bunch of uninterested officials, whose only goal is to enhance their personal power, will achieve these ends for us. Or we can work with normal human behavior and let it respond to incentives and disincentives, enlarge wealth, and create opportunities for everyone. Using market mechanisms, we can build a system in which freely, voluntarily, and out of necessity, consumers, workers, and business owners treat each other fairly. In this scheme of things, capitalism means a little more than simply siding with those with capital; it means allowing those who want to create some and rewarding those who want to employ their human capital. In this lexicon, "pro-business" has little to do with just standing behind existing businesses, but supporting all productive ventures. And certainly, "pro-labor" is far removed from the unionism of organized, and largely privileged, workers. It really involves speaking out for all those who are unemployed or underemployed and whose only hope lies in creation of plenty of productive jobs in the legal sector.

Regardless of culture or geography, such a legal-economic framework can work wonders in any country. Indians—labeled by their own commentators as lazy, introspective, and quarrelsome—responded well even to a tentative and half-hearted reform program. (see chapter 12). To the extent they were left alone, they, too, utilized the opportunities to produce. The small insurgent new players in the business field successfully competed with the established producers who had all along led sheltered lives and hated competition in whatever shape or form it came.

Out of *greed* and to survive, these producers—both new and old—worked with efficiency. They made more cars, tires, soaps, TVs, eyeglasses, and everything in between. All this production, coupled with the new jobs, raised the standard of living for hundreds of millions. Consequently, many of them have ascended to the ranks of the middle class, which more and more resembles the one from an advanced country in that such things as a washing machine are fast becoming essential fixtures of the households. According to a recent (1990) estimate, demand for these machines has been growing by thirty percent a year. For many—especially working couples—such machines free their time and make life a little easier. (493)

More importantly, such rising consumption can create jobs for many more of the hundreds of millions of unemployed, disenchanted, bus-burning, secession-mongering, or self-immolating youth. Said a proud father (and a relative of mine), "The companies recruit from the campus itself. Nowadays, they desperately need post-graduates in chemistry."

The employer needs these young men and women as much as they need the jobs. To him, it matters little whether or not they belong to a particular religion, caste, or sub-caste. As long as they deliver, he is not even the least bit worried if any of them is from out of state. For their part, in search of better opportunities, the prospective employees do what they have to do and go where they have to go. Quite a few move out of their mini-forts (towns, districts, or states), and get to know the *others* (who speak a different language or belong to a different state than theirs) a little better.

The more complete is the economic liberalization, the greater is the chance for the individual to obtain his job or start his business without paying any bribes. In such a free society, how well he does depends upon what he can do rather than whom he knows. He learns to rely upon himself. He learns to believe in himself. He can safely disregard the promises of handouts and cast his vote based on performance. He can vote for the national politicians who, in his estimation, will effectively defend his country against aggression but refrain from unnecessary foreign adventures. On the domestic front, he can throw out the rascals that have inflated the currency and hit him with high prices. At the state level, he can vote for those who will best maintain the law and order. He can participate in local governments better and make sure that his kids get the best out of their schools. In short, he can better supervise a government whose functions are fewer and scope is narrower.

Despite all the betterment, however, he will be anything but content and static. He has learned to influence his environment. This ability makes him creative; it sets him free, but not entirely. Like a secular hound from heaven, it relentlessly pursues, challenges, and drives him into helping those that deserve to be helped. If the behavior of those that live in the relatively freer and more prosperous countries is any indication, he will join the other like-minded people and try to fill the cracks left by the market. He will donate time and money to feed the hungry, send supplies to the various disaster victims, or establish private libraries and museums, for example.

Such men and women can create a society in which politicians recede in importance and—in the words of Mario Vargas Llosa, a famous writer—politics become a purely formal, minor game. Llosa asks, "Do you know who the President of Switzerland is? I don't either. Not even a Swiss knows. That's civilization." (494)

Francis Fukuyama considers such a liberal democracy as the final form of human government. (463)

Fukuyama, deputy director of the US State Department's policy staff and a former analyst at the RAND Corporation, sees no viable alternative to the idea of economic and political liberalism. To him, this realization marks "the end of history as such: that is, the end point of mankind's ideological evolution and the universalization of Western liberal democracy as the final form of human government." (463)

He believes that the democratic freedoms foster general affluence. And it works the other way too. Fukuyama says, "In particular, the spectacular abundance of advanced liberal economies and the infinitely diverse consumer culture made possible by them seem to both foster and preserve liberalism in the political sphere." (463)

Notwithstanding his position at the US State Department, Fukuyama is hardly an apologist for capitalist interests. He actually views the end of history as "a very sad time." He laments the passing of ideological concerns. He refuses to get excited about a world filled with "economic calculations, the endless solving of technical problems, environmental concerns, and the satisfaction of sophisticated consumer demands." (463)

Fukuyama might be as thrilled about this vision of the future as someone who is going to have his root canal done. But he sees it as inevitable: The world is inching toward liberal democracy and away from socialism. He explains, "But those who believe that the future must inevitably be socialist tend to be very old, or very marginal to the real political discourse of their societies." (463)

At the same time, he concedes that the victory of liberalism has occurred primarily in the realm of ideas and is still incomplete in the real (material) world. He, however, is high on ideas. He believes that all human behavior in the material world, and hence all human history, is rooted in the *prior state of consciousness* (PSC)—the ideas and ideals that are deeply embedded in each society[31]. In other words, the material world is simply a product of the preexisting ideas and has a very limited impact on shaping these ideas. Fukuyama says, "Consciousness is cause and not effect, and can develop autonomously from the material world." (463)

He abhors the *matter over mind* philosophy of the both rightists and leftists. He excoriates Karl Marx for relegating the entire realm of consciousness—religion, art, culture, and philosophy—to a "superstructure" that is determined entirely by the prevailing mode of production of material. (463)

Fukuyama refuses to go easy on the free marketers either. He lumps them under the long-winded title of "Wall Street Journal [WSJ] School of deterministic materialism." He criticizes them for discounting the importance of culture and religion and seeing man only as rational, profit maximizing individual. Fukuyama feels that liberal economics work well only in the presence of a certain PSC. For the stunning success of economic freedoms in the Far Eastern societies, for example, he gives credit to a cultural heritage which emphasizes work ethic, saving, and family, "a religious heritage that does not, like Islam[32], place restrictions on certain forms of economic behavior," and "other deeply ingrained moral qualities." (463)

We all can fight over this issue. Which is first, mind or matter? Fukuyama may be right when he says that consciousness develops autonomously from the material world. Or, it's entirely possible that the legal-economic system—through its effects on the material conditions of the people—exerts a major influence on the individual behavior and consciousness: the ideas, ideals, attitudes, and morals. At each stage in the history of a society, the legal system can leave its thumb print on the PSC by helping the latter to evolve and incorporate a new set of ideas and ideals, which, in turn, can determine the behavior of the people and, thus, shape and content of the material world. In short, mind and matter constantly and continuously influence each other.

There are several ways to examine this proverbial egg-and-chicken question of mind and matter. One can start with a study by professor Sam Huntington (of *Harvard University*). It reports on thirty countries that, since the mid-seventies,

have made a transition from authoritarianism to fledgling democracies. The most significant factor behind the emergence
of political freedoms is that they have first lifted themselves up
economically. (495)

One can also look at the former East Germany and see how
forty years of communism has destroyed the PSC of its once
hard working and self-reliant Germans and turned them into
wards of the state. Most of these men and women still look up
to their government and expect it to take care of them. They
throw tomatoes at anyone who tells them that, in a free market economy, each person is on his own.

Or, one can study the behavior of emigrants from the various states of prior consciousness to America. Whether from
largely tribal and, thus, collectivist Africa, Confucian China,
Buddhist Sri Lanka, karmic India, or the 'restrictive' Islamic world,
these immigrants (just like the ones before) prefer to work than
to starve. Small wonder that, despite the odds, many prosper.
As to how his largely pacifist Jain religion (a.k.a. PSC) has influenced him, explains Parvin Mehta, one of those Indian merchants who have come from nowhere and in less than two
decades dominated the small diamond market in America, "We
[Jains] may be non-violent, but we are fighters." (496)

Out of an old habit (acquired in a statist society), such immigrants discuss politics, but most feel little need to get close to
the politicians. Relatively speaking, the carpetbaggers take better care of their bodies and minds and throw their fatalism (a
supposed characteristic of the old world) to the wind. When
they can, quite a few help the others to take care of themselves. As a matter of fact, most of these immigrants behave so
uniformly that they seem to have little respect for their individual PSCs. The only explanation has to be that their material
life in America—largely determined by the legal-economic system—did help to evolve their PSC.

When Indians among them go *back home,* they hear a lot
about the "brain drain." They learn about the many new ava-
tars of this old plague such as, *internal hemorrhage.* A.P. Mitra,
director general of the Council for Scientific and Industrial Research, explains how India is internally hemorrhaging: Science

students drift into civil services, managerial jobs, and banking. Mitra has a cure for this disease. He proposes forcing each of the 11,000 firms in the country with a R&D department to hire ten scientists, whether it needs them or not! (497)

Most expatriates realize that such ideas used to make sense, but not any more. They no longer care for such use of force. In more than one way, they find out how much they have changed. Many don't know why and that makes them feel uncomfortable. As a result, when they visit *back home* they complain about little things. With passing time, however, each of them gets more comfortable with his new self. They conclude that home is where you are happy.

Each gets busy with his life and with finding answers to important questions, such as, why despite all the dirt under the nails and a constant runny nose from working in the garden, it costs more to grow vegetables than to buy them in the super market.

At a subconscious level, these Indian immigrants realize that neither home-grown squash nor PSC is what it is cracked up to be.

---

[31]Fukuyama borrows this theory from Georg Wilhelm Friedrich Hegel, a nineteenth century German philosopher.

[32]Islam forbids such things as charging usury fees and interest. (463)

# Works Cited

1. Henry Grunwald; *Time,* Vol. 126 No. I, July 8, 1985, p. 101

2. *60 Minutes*—CBS, Vol. XXII No. 23, February 25, 1990.

3. James P. Sterba; *Wall Street Journal,* CCIX No. 18, Jan. 27, 1987, p. A31.

4. Bettina Bien Greaves; *Free Market Economics: A Basic Reader* (Irvington-on-Hudson, New York: The Foundation For Economic Education, Inc., 1975), p. 6.

5. Commentary; *The Illustrated Weekly of India,* Vol. CX 22, May 28, 1989, p. 6.

6. "Voices"; *India Today,* Vol. XIV No. 24, Dec. 31, 1989, p. 11.

7. Editorial; *Wall Street Journal,* Sept. 26, 1985.

8. News Item; *India Tribune,* Vol. 13/No. 27, July 8, 1989, p. 1.

9. Dilip Bobb, A. K. Menon; *India Today,* Vol. XIV No. 11, June 15, 1989, p. 10.

10. P. R. Brahmananda; *India Tribune,* Vol. 13/No. 48, Dec. 2,1989, p. 2.

11. Shabana Azmi; *The Illustrated Weekly of India,* Vol. CX 22, May 28,1989, p. 26.

12. M. Rahman; *India Today,* Vol. XIII No. 19, Oct. 15, 1988, p. 63.

13. Malcolm S. Adiseshiah; *India Today,* Vol. XIV No. 4, Feb. 28, 1989, p. 91.

14. News Item; *The Illustrated Weekly Of India,* June 11, 1989, p. 71.

15. S. Bana, S. Rajhans; *India Tribune,* Nov. 24, 1990, p. 16 & 18.

16. Dayanand Wagh; *India Tribune,* Dec. 1, 1990, p. 9.

17. June Kronholz; *Wall Street Journal,* Vol. CXCIX No. 89. p. A1.

18. Pankaj Pachauri et al.; *India Today,* Vol. XV No. 4, February 28, 1990, p. 75.

19. Javeed Anand; *India Tribune,* Vol. 14/No. 2, Jan. 13, 1990, p. 21.

20. Madhu Jain; *India Today,* Vol. XIII No. 22, Nov. 30, 1988, p. 80.

21. K. Srinivasan; *India Tribune,* Vol. 13/No. 37, Sept. 16, 1989, p. 9.

22. Raminder Singh; *India Today,* Vol. XIV No. 1, Jan. 15, 1989, p. 33.

23. News Item; *The Illustrated Weekly of India,* Vol. CX 19, May 7, 1989, p. 70.

24. Nikolay Shmelyou; *Wall Street Journal,* Aug. 26, 1987, Editorial page.

25. News Item; *India Today,* Vol. XIII No. 18, Sept. 30, 1988, p. 48.

26. News Item; *India Today,* Oct.31, 1988, p. 89.

27. N. K. Singh; *India Today,* Vol. XIII No. 10, May 31, 1988, p. 26.

28. Anuradha Dutt; *The Illustrated Weekly of India,* Vol. CX 21, May 21, 1989, p. 48.

29. Sudip Mazumdar; *India Tribune,* Vol. 13/No. 42 Oct. 21, 1989, p. 2.

30. News Item; *India Today,* Vol. XIII No. 5, March 15, 1988, p. 5.

31. Harinder Baweja; *India Today,* Vol. XIV No. 24, Dec. 31, 1989, p. 53.

32. Kamaljeet Rattan; *India Today*, Vol. XIV No. 12, June 30, 1989, p. 46.

33. News Item; *India Tribune*, Vol. 13/No. 46, Nov. 18, 1989, p. 5.

34. Farzand Ahmed; *India Today*, Vol. XIV No. 1, Jan. 15, 1989, p. 36.

35. Dilip Awasthi; *India Today*, Vol. XIII No. 10, May 31, 1988, p. 110–111.

36. Ramindar Singh; *India Today*, Vol. XIII No. 5, Mar. 15, 1988, p. 44–46.

37. Pankaj Pachauri; *India Today*, Vol. XIII No. 4, Feb. 29, 1988, p. 36–37.

38. Raman Nanda; *India Tribune*, Vol. 13/No. 38, Sept. 23, 1989, p. 8.

39. Editorial; *The Illustrated Weekly of India*, Vol. CX 22, May 28, 1989, p. 6.

40. Kushwant Singh; *We Indians* (New Delhi: Orient Paperbacks, 1982).

41. Hernando De Soto; *The Other Path* (New York: Harper & Row, Publishers, 1989).

42. News Item; *India Tribune*, Vol. 14/No. 2, Jan. 13, 1990, p. 18.

43. Shabana Azmi; *The Illustrated Weekly of India*, Vol. CX 22, May 28, 1989, p. 26.

44. Enno von Lowenstern; *Wall Street Journal*, Nov. 21, 1989. Editorial Page

45. News Roundup; *Wall Street Journal*, Nov. 13, 1989, p. A1 & A4.

46. Roger Thurow; *Wall Street Journal*, Vol. CCXIV No. 97, Nov. 16, 1989, p. A1.

47. Frederick Kempe; *Wall Street Journal*, Vol. CCXV No. 33, Feb. 15, 1990, p. A1 & A10.

48. The Associated Press; *Atlanta Journal And Constitution*, Dec. 6, 1989, p. A–3.

49. L. Brent Bozell III; *Wall Street Journal*, Jan. 2, 1990, p. A10.

50. George Melloan; *Wall Street Journal*, Sept. 9, 1991, p. A11.

51. Amity Shales; *Wall Street Journal*, July 24, 1989, p. A15.

52. Mathew C. Vita; *Atlanta Journal And Constitution*, Feb. 11, 1990, p. B–2.

53. Lech Walesa; *USA Today*, July 6, 1989, p. 9A.

54. Peter Gumbell; *Wall Street Journal*, Oct. 7, 1988.

55. Peter Gumbell; *Wall Street Journal*, Dec. 2,1988, p. A1 & A12.

56. The Associated Press; *Atlanta Journal And Constitution*, Jan. 29, 1989, p. A18.

57. Argumenti Fakty, Undated

58. Hedrick Smith; *The Russians* (New York: Ballantine Books, 1984).

59. Madeleine Kalb, Marvin Kalb; *The Atlanta Journal And Constitution*, Nov. 26, 1989, P. G–3.

60. Edwin O. Reischauer; *Japan: The Story of A Nation* (New York: Alfred A. Knopf, Inc., 970).

61. Milton Friedman; *Free to Choose* (New York: Harcourt Brace Jovanovich, Inc., 1980), p. 60

62. Frederick Kempe; *Wall Street Journal*, Dec. 3, 1987, p. A26.

63. Michael Harrington; *Socialism: Past and Future* (New York: Arcade Publishing, Inc., 1989), p. 197.

64. Knight-Ridder Newspapers; *The Atlanta Journal And Constitution*, Nov. 22, 1990, p. C–8

65. The Associated Press; *Atlanta Journal And Constitution*, Feb. 15, 1990, p. A–11.

66. Editorial; *Wall Street Journal*, Oct. 30, 1990, p. A20

67. Editorial; *Wall Street Journal*, Feb. 27, 1990.

68. David Lawday, Alexander Stille; *U.S. News And World Report*, Nov. 12, 1990, p. 50.

69. Milton Friedman; *Free to Choose* (New York: Harcourt Brace Jovanovich, Inc., 1980), p. 92.

70. Editorial; *Wall Street Journal*, Jan. 10, 1989, p. A18.

71. Jeffrey H. Birnbaum; *Wall Street Journal*, Sept. 17, 1990, p. A–16.

72. Milton Friedman; *Free to Choose* (New York: Harcourt Brace Jovanovich, Inc., 1980), p. 112.

73. *The World Almanac And Book of Facts*, (Pharos Books, A Scripps Howard Company, 1993, New York), p. 955.

74. John Hood; *Reader's Digest*, April 1989.

75. O. S. Shrivastava; *Economic Development and Planning in India*(New Delhi: Allied Publishers Private Limited, 1988), p. 33, 85

76. James Bovard; *Wall Street Journal*, May 22, 1990, p. A20.

77. Bruce Ingersoll; *Wall Street Journal*, May 1, 1990, p. A1 & A12.

78. Peter Truell; *Wall Street Journal*, May 16, 1990, p. A22.

79. Collin McCord, Harold P. Freeman; *The New England Journal of Medicine*, Jan. 18, 1990. p. 176–177.

80. L. Gordon Croviz; *Wall Street Journal*, June 13, 1990, P. A15.

81. David Whitman; *U.S. News And World Report*, Oct. 16, 1989, p. 28–32.

82. John Leo; *U.S. News & World Report*, Sept. 24, 1990, p. 37.

83. David Whitman; *U.S. News And World Report*, Oct. 16, 1989, p. 28–32.

84. A. N. Agrawal; *Indian Economy: Problems of Development And Planning* (New Delhi: Vani Educational Books, 1985), p. 105

85. Raj Chengappa; *India Today*, Vol. XIII No. 20, Oct. 31, 1988, p. 38–47.

86. A. N. Agrawal; *Indian Economy: Problems of Development And Planning* (New Delhi: Vani Educational Books, 1985), p. 101.

87. A. N. Agrawal; *Indian Economy: Problems of Development And Planning* (New Delhi: Vani Educational Books, 1985), p. 83–97.

88. Paul A. Samuelson; *Economics* (New York: McGraw–Hill Book Company, Eleventh Edition, 1980), p. 29.

89. Edwin O. Reischauer; *Japan: The Story of A Nation* (New York: Alfred A. Knopf, Inc., 1970).

90. A. N. Agrawal; *Indian Economy: Problems Of Development And Planning* (New Delhi: Vani Educational Books, 1985), p. 105.

91. News Item; *India Today*, Vol. XIII No. 18, September 30, 1988, p. 48.

92. Ben J. Wattenberg; *U.S. News & World Report*, Dec. 18, 1989.

93. Letter from Sunil Lahari; *India Today*, Vol. XIII No. 21, Nov. 15, 1988, p. 2.

94. A. N. Agrawal; *Indian Economy: Problems of Development and Planning* (New Delhi: Vani Educational Books, 1985), p. 84.

95. A. N. Agrawal; *Indian Economy: Problems of Development and Planning* (New Delhi: Vani Educational Books, 1985), p. 98.

96. Nikolay Shmelyou; *Wall Street Journal*, Aug. 26, 1987. Editorial Page

97. Michael Harrington; *Socialism: Past and Future* (New York: Arcade Publishing, Inc., 1989), p. 108.

98. Pranay Gupte; *India: The Challenge of Change* (London: Methuen. Mandarin, 1989), p. 119.

99. P. G. Mathai; *India Today*, Vol. XIII No. 18, Sept. 30, 1988, p. 54–57.

100. Amit Prakash; *India Tribune* Vol. 14/No. 5, Feb. 3, 1990, p. 12 & 22.

101. News Item; *India Tribune*, Jan. 13, 1990, p. 12.

102. Surajeet Das Gupta; *India Today*, Vol. I No. 2, Apr. 30, 1990, p. 58–60.

103. O. S. Shrivastava; *Economic Development and Planning in India* (New Delhi: Allied Publishers Private Limited, 1988), p. 30.

104. Hernando De Soto; *The Other Path* (New York: Harper & Row, Publishers, 1989), p. 206.

105. O. S. Shrivastava; *Economic Development and Planning in India* (New Delhi: Allied Publishers Private Limited, 1988), p. 28.

106. Michael Harrington; *Socialism: Past and Future* (New York: Arcade Publishing, Inc., 1989), p. 153.

107. O. S. Shrivastava; *Economic Development and Planning in India* (New Delhi: Allied Publishers Private Limited, 1988), pp. 35, 37, 38, 41 & 55.

108. Tim Carrington, Barbara Toman; *Wall Street Journal*, Feb. 6, 1990, p. A–1.

109. News Item; *India Tribune*, Vol. 14/No. 5, Feb. 3, 1990, p. 23.

110. Nikolay Shmelyou; *Wall Street Journal,* Aug. 26, 1987 Editorial page.

111. O. S. Shrivastava; *Economic Development and Planning in India* (New Delhi: Allied Publishers Private Limited, 1988), pp. 33, 45, 187 & 255.

112. Pradeep Puri; *India Tribune,* Vol. 13/No. 51, Dec. 23, 1989, p. 10.

113. Sudhirendar Sharma; *India Today,* Vol. XIV No. 15, Aug. 15, 1989, p. 77.

114. P. G. Thakurta; *India Today,* Vol. XIV No. 19, Oct. 15, 1989, p. 17.

115. Murad Ali Baig; *India Today,* Vol. I No. 5, June 15, 1990, p. 43.

116. Svati Chakravarty; *India Tribune,* Vol. 13/No. 39, Sept. 30, 1989, p. 9.

117. Kamaljeet Rattan; *India Today,* Vol. XIV No. 15, Aug. 15, 1989, p. 35.

118. Shekhar Gupta et al.; *India Today,* Vol. XIV No. 19,Oct. 15, 1989, pp. 14–21.

119. P. G. Thakurta; *India Today,* Vol. 1 No. 4, May 31, 1990, pp. 70–71.

120. S. K. Ray; *Indian Economy* (New Delhi: Prentice–Hall of India Private Limited, 1987), p. 141.

121. Dilip Awasthi; *India Today,* May 31, 1988, pp. 96–97.

122. David Devadas; *India Today,* July 31, 1988, pp. 76–77.

123. Bhaskar Roy; *India Today,* July 31, 1989, p. 32.

124. Anil Pratap, P. G. Mathai; *India Today,* Feb. 29, 1988, p. 60.

125. Paranjoy Guha Thakurta; *India Today,* Vol. XIV No. 4, Feb. 28, 1989 pp. 88–89.

126. S. D. Gupta, P. G. Thakurta; *India Today,* Jan. 31, 1989, pp. 68–69.

127. Surajeet Das Gupta; *India Today,* Aug. 15, 1989, p. 60.

128. Dinesh Singh; *India Today,* Apr. 30, 1989, p. 65.

129. Simran Bhargava; *India Today,* May 15, 1989, pp. 62–67.

130. N. K. Singh; *India Today,* June 30, 1988, p. 28.

131. Comment; *India Today,* Feb. 15, 1989, p. 7.

132. News Dispatches; *India Tribune,* Nov. 4, 1989, p. 9.

133. Prabhu Chawla; *India Today,* Jan. 31, 1989, p. 15.

134. R. Sasankan; *India Tribune,* July 1, 1989, p. 9.

135. Voices; *India Today,* Jan. 15, 1989, p. 71.

136. News Item; *The Atlanta Journal and Constitution,* P. A–4.

137. Jay Dubashi; *India Today,* Vol. X1V No. 6, Mar. 31, 1989, p. 100.

138. News Item; *India Today,* Vol. X111 No. 9 May 15, 1988, p. 64.

139. P. G. Thakurta; *India Today,* Mar. 31, 1989, p. 82.

140. P. G. Mathai et al.; *India Today,* Apr. 15, 1988, p. 60.

141. Inderjit Badhwar; *India Today,* Jan. 15, 1989, p. 43.

142. Voices; *India Today,* Jan. 31, 1990, p. 6.

143. News Item; *India Today,* Vol. XIV No. 16, Aug. 31, 1989, p. 8.

144. S. S. Gill; *The Illustrated Weekly of India,* Apr. 9, 1989, p. 6.

145. D. Singh; *News India,* Dec. 23, 1988. p. 12.

146. T. N. Ninan; *India Today,* March 15, 1988, p. 58.

147. Anthony Spaeth; *Wall Street Journal,* April 10, 1990, p, A–20.

148. News Item; *News India,* June 9, 1989, p. 12.

149. Inderjit Badhwar; *India Today,* Feb. 29, 1988, p. 56.

150. Sreedhar Pillai; *India Today,* June 15, 1988, pp. 66–67.

151. Payal Singh; *The Illustrated Weekly of India,* June 11, 1989. pp. 34–35.

152. Kamaljeet Rattan; *India Today,* Aug. 31, 1988, p. 60.

153. K. S. Ramachandran; *India Tribune,* Feb. 3, 1990, pp. 2 & 22.

154. Uday Mahurkar; *India Today*, May 15, 1990. pp. 78–79.

155. N. K. Singh; *India Today*, May 15, 1989, pp. 45–49.

156. News Item; *India Tribune*, July 29, 1989, p. 10.

157. M. Rahman; *India Today*, Mar. 15, 1989, pp. 78–81.

158. Press Trust of India; *India Tribune*, Jan. 20, 1990, pp. 10–11.

159. Pranay Gupte; *India: The Challenge of Change* (London: Methuen. Mandarin, 1989), p. 283.

160. Raj Chengappa; *India Today*, Jan. 31, 1989, pp. 62–64.

161. Bunker Roy; *India Today*, May 31, 1990, p. 87.

162. News Item; *India Today*, Oct. 15, 1988, p. 8.

163. News Item; *India Today*, Sept. 15, 1988, p. 6.

164. Pankaj Pachuri, Farzand Ahmed; *India Today*, Oct. 15, 1988, pp. 76–77.

165. News Item; *India Today*, May 15, 1989, p. 6.

166. Salil Tripathi; *India Today*, Nov. 15, 1988, p. 71.

167. Raj Chengappa; *India Today*, Oct. 15, 1989, pp. 64–66.

168. Prabhu Chawla, Raj Chengappa; ; *India Today*, Mar. 15, 1990, pp. 10–17.

169. Vipul Mudgal; *India Today*, May 31, 1988, p. 30

170. Guha Prasad; *India Today*, June 30, 1989, p. 86–87.

171. Bhaskar Roy; *India Today*, May 15, 1990, p. 30–31.

172. Raj Chengappa et al.; *India Today*, Jan. 31, 1988, p. 60–67.

173. Sharmila Chandra; *India Today*, Aug. 31, 1989, p. 105.

174. Raj Chengappa, Chidanand Rajghatta; *India Today*, June 15, 1989, p. 34–41.

175. Uday Mahurkar; *India Today*, Apr. 30, 1989. p. 34–35.

176. Salil Tripathi and N.K. Singh; *India Today*, Oct. 31, 1988, p. 74–77.

177. N. K. Singh; *India Today*, Oct. 31, 1989, p. 82–84.

178. Sudhirendar Sharma; *India Today*, Oct. 31, 1989, p. 84.

179. Surajeet Das Gupta; *India Today*, Nov. 30, 1988, p. 60–61.

180. News Item; *India Tribune*, Feb. 3, 1990, p. 8.

181. News Item; *India Today*, Aug. 15, 1989, p. 12.

182. Press Trust India; *India Tribune*, Mar. 3, 1990, p. 5.

183. Raj Chengappa; *India Today*, May 15, 1990, p. 38–41.

184. Partha Patnaik; *India Tribune*, June 2, 1990, p. 16.

185. Business; *U.S. News & World Report*, Aug. 27/Sep. 3, 1990, p. 37.

186. Mark M. Nelson; *Wall Street Journal*, Mar. 1, 1990, p. A1.

187. News Report; *Atlanta Journal And Constitution*, Mar. 11, 1990.

188. *60 Minutes*—CBS, Vol. XXII No. 23, February 25, 1990, p. 4

189. Editorial; *India Today*, Aug. 31, 1988, p. 5.

190. Khushwant Singh; *We Indians*, (New Delhi: Orient Paperbacks, 1982), p. 86–88.

191. News Item; *India Today*, Dec. 31, 1989, p. 10.

192. Voices; *India Today*, Oct. 15, 1989, p. 11.

193. Manoj Kumar; *The Illustrated Weekly of India*, June 11, 1989, p. 37.

194. S. H. Venkatramani; *India Today*, May 15, 1988, p. 18.

195. Dilip Bobb; *India Today*, Nov. 15, 1989, p. 35.

196. Prabhu Chawla, Bhaskar Roy; *India Today*, Nov. 15, 1989, p. 12.

197. A. G. Noorani; *India Tribune*, Aug. 19, 1989. p. 2 & 18.

198. News Item; *India Tribune*, Nov. 18, 1989, p. 12.

199. Dilip Awasthi; *India Today*, Jan. 31, 1990, p. 39.

200. Ramesh Menon; *India Today*, May 15, 1990, p. 32.

201. Bombay Bureau; *India Tribune*, Sept. 16, 1989, p. 12 & 22.

202. Uday Mahurkar; *India Today*, Mar. 31, 1990. p. 58–60.

203. Anand P. Raman; *India Today*, Aug. 31, 1988, p. 54–55.

204. P. G. Thakurta; *India Today*, Feb. 15, 1990, p. 89.

205. Raj Chengappa; *India Today*, Jan. 15, 1989, p. 47.

206. Anthony Spaeth; *Wall Street Journal*, April 10, 1990, p, A–20.

207. News Report; *India Tribune*, Nov. 18, 1989, p. 12 & 22.

208. Chidanand Rajghatta; *India Today*, Aug. 31, 1989, p. 74–75.

209. Prabhu Chawla, Lalita Dileep; *India Today*, Mar. 31, 1989, p. 68–72.

210. Salil Tripathi et al.; *India Today*, July 31, 1989, p. 22–27.

211. India Notes; *India Today*, May 15, 1988, p. 7.

212. N. K. Singh; *India Today*, Aug. 31, 1988, p. 50–52.

213. Rishi Singh; *India Today*, Sept. 30, 1989, p. 6.

214. *60 Minutes*—CBS, Vol. XXII No. 23, February 25, 1990.

215. Editorial; *Wall Street Journal*, Oct. 27, 1989, p. A–16.

216. Editorial; *Wall Street Journal*, Oct. 16, 1989.

217. David Gergen; *U.S. News & World Report*, Oct. 8, 1990, p. 84.

218. Gloria Borger et al.; *U.S. News & World Report*, Dec. 18, 1989, p. 22.

219. Claudia Rosett; *Wall Street Journal*, Apr. 10, 1989.

220. Kenichi Ohmae; *Wall Street Journal*, Oct. 25, 1989, p. A19.

221. Hernando De Soto; *The Other Path* (New York: Harper & Row, Publishers, 1989).

222. Khushwant Singh; *We Indians*, (New Delhi: Orient Paperbacks, 1982), p. 95.

223. M. Rahman; *India Today*, Apr. 30, 1990, p. 68–70.

224. Shekhar Gupta; *India Today*, July 31, 1985, p. 74–77.

225. Raj Chengappa, M. Rahman; *India Today*, July 15, 1990, p. 18–23.

226. News Item; *The Illustrated Weekly of India*, Apr. 16, 1989, p. 56–57.

227. Bombay Bureau; *India Tribune*, Sept. 16, 1989, p. 12 & 22.

228. Farzand Ahmed; *India Today*, Nov. 30, 1988, p. 64–65.

229. Navin Upadhyay; *The Illustrated Weekly of India*, Apr. 30, 1989, p. 30–33.

230. N. K. Singh; *India Today*, Sept. 15, 1989, p. 62–64.

231. Dilip Awasthi; *India Today*, Mar. 31, 1989, p. 32–33.

232. Bombay Bureau; *India Tribune*, Sept. 9, 1989, p. 12 & 22.

233. Dilip Awasthi; *India Today*, Sept. 30, 1989, p. 30–32.

234. Bob Deans; *Atlanta Journal and Constitution*, Nov. 26, 1989, p. A–3.

235. State Notes; *India Today*, Apr. 30, 1989, p. 53.

236. News Report; *India Tribune*, Dec. 30, 1989, p. 11.

237. News Report; *India Tribune*, Nov. 18, 1989, p. 12.

238. Rupa Chinai; *India Tribune*, Nov. 25, 1989, p. 12.

239. Inderjit Badhwar, Prabhu Chawla; *India Today*, Dec. 15, 1989, p. 10–16.

240. Press Trust India; *India Tribune*, Jan. 6, 1990, p. 1.

241. News Item; *India Today*, Jan. 31, 1990, p. 7.

242. Comment; *India Today*, Jan. 15, 1988, p. 4.

243. Editorial; *The Illustrated Weekly of India* May 28, 1989, p. 6.

244. News Report; *India Tribune*, Jan. 13, 1990, p. 6.

245. Pranay Gupte; *India: The Challenge of Change* (London: Methuen. Mandarin, 1989).

246. Dilip Bob et al.; *India Today*, Feb. 15, 1989, p. 24–26.

247. Amarnath K. Menon; *India Today*, Sept. 30, 1988, p. 44–47.

248. Amarnath K. Menon; *India Today*, Oct. 15, 1988, p. 29.

249. Onkar Singh, Vinod Behl; *The Illustrated Weekly of India*, Apr. 16, 1989, p. 30–31.

250. Ramesh Menon; *India Today*, Jan. 15, 1989, p. 28.

251. Amarnath K. Menon; *India Today*, Jan. 31, 1988, p. 22–25.

252. Ramesh Menon; *India Today*, Oct. 15, 1988, p. 26–27.

253. Harinder Baweja; *India Today*, Jan. 31, 1990, p. 27–29.

254. Editorial; *Wall Street Journal*, July 29, 1985.

255. Vipul Mudgal; *India Today*, Oct. 15, 1988, p. 25.

256. Comment; *India Today*, Mar. 31, 1989, p. 5.

257. Vipul Mudgal; *India Today*, Mar. 15, 1989, p. 32.

258. Inderjit Badhwar; *India Today*, Apr. 30, 1990, p. 10–16.

259. Inderjit Badhwar; *India Today*, May 31, 1989, p. 34–40.

260. Letter by Asit Kochru; *India Tribune*, Oct. 7, 1989, p. 4.

261. Inderjit Badhwar; *India Today*, Oct. 15, 1988, p. 18–21.

262. George Melloan; *Wall Street Journal*, Feb. 26, 1990, p. A–9.

263. Rakesh Khar; *India Tribune*, Dec. 22, 1990, p. 12.

264. Dilip Awasthi; *India Today*, Apr. 30, 1990, p. 24.

265. Khushwant Singh; *We Indians*, (New Delhi: Orient Paperbacks, 1982), p. 122.

266. Press Trust of India; *India Tribune*, Oct. 7, 1989, p. 7.

267. S. N. Vasuki; *India Today*, July 31, 1990, p. 54–55.

268. Amarnath K. Menon; *India Today*, July 31, 1985 p. 45.

269. News Item; *India Today*, Dec. 31, 1989, p. 55.

270. Farzand Ahmed, Uttam Sen Gupta; *India Today*, Mar. 31, 1989, p. 18–20.

271. Uday Mahurkar; *India Today*, May 31, 1988, p. 105.

272. Inderjit Badhwar et al.; *India Today*, Oct. 31, 1989, p. 14–22.

273. News Item; *The Illustrated Weekly Of India*, May 14, 1989, p. 71.

274. M. Rahman; *India Today*, June 15, 1988, p. 25–26.

275. M. Rahman; *India Today*, Sept. 30, 1988, p. 28.

276. S. Balakrishnan, Syed Shahbuddin; *The Illustrated Weekly Of India*, June 4, 1989, p. 22–25.

277. David Devadas; *India Today*, Feb. 29, 1988, p. 68–71.

278. Special Report; *News India*, July 21, 1989, p. 23.

279. Pankaj Pachauri; *India Today*, Feb. 28, 1990. P. 72–75.

280. Pankaj Pachauri et al.; *India Today*, Sept. 15, 1990, p. 36–39.

281. Pabhu Chawla; *India Today*, Sept. 30, 1990, p. 26–27.

282. Letter by Vivek Singh; *India Today*, Nov. 30, 1990, p. 6.

283. Letter by V. D. Sampath; *India Today*, Nov. 15, 1990, p. 3.

284. Voices; *India Today*, Nov. 15, 1990, p. 7.

285. Javed Anand; *India Tribune*, Jan. 13, 1990, p. 21–22.

286. Michael Barone; *U.S. News & World Report*, June 18, 1990, p. 35.

287. Farzand Ahmed; *India Today*, Nov. 15, 1990, p. 61–62

288. Moses Manoharan; *India West*, Oct. 27, 1989, p. 2.

289. State Notes; *India Today*, Aug. 31, 1989, p. 71.

290. Pankaj Pachauri; *India Today*, Sept. 15, 1989, p. 20–22.

291. Comment; *India Today*, Sept. 15, 1989, p. 5.

292. N. K. Singh; *India Today*, May 31, 1988, p. 26.

293. Comment; *India Today*, May 15, 1988, p. 4.

294. Prabhu Chawla; *India Today*, May 31, 1990, p. 26–27.

295. Press Trust of India; *India Tribune*, May 26, 1990, p. 6.

296. Prabhu Chawla; *India Today*, Feb. 28, 1990, p. 26–29.

297. Raj Chengappa, M. Rahman; *India Today*, July 15, 1990, p. 18–23.

298. Letter; *The Illustrated Weekly Of India*, Apr. 16, 1989, p. 4.

299. S. Nihal Singh; *India Today*, Apr. 15, 1988, p. 72.

300. Aroon Purie; *The Illustrated Weekly of India*, Apr. 16, 1989, p. 6–7.

301. Anil Divan; *India Tribune*, Jan. 20, 1990, p. 2 & 22.

302. M. V. Kamath; *India Tribune*, Dec. 23, 1989, p. 2.

303. S. Balakrishnan; *The Illustrated Weekly Of India*, Apr. 9, 1989, p. 26–27.

304. K. Narender; *The Illustrated Weekly Of India*, Apr. 9, 1989, p. 32–33.

305. M. Rahman; *India Today*, June 30, 1989, p. 93.

306. P. G. Thakurta; *India Today*, May 31, 1989, p. 75.

307. T. N. Ninan, David Devadas; *India Today*, Feb. 29, 1988, p. 67.

308. Surajeet Das Gupta; *India Today*, Apr. 30, 1989. p. 62.

309. News Dipatch; *News India*, July 21, 1989, p. 24.

310. M. V. Kamath; *India Tribune*, Dec. 23, 1989, p. 2.

311. News Dispatch; *India Abroad*, June 23, 1989, p. 10.

312. N. K. Singh; *India Today*, June 15, 1988, p. 16.

313. News Item; *India Today*, Apr.30, 1989, p. 7.

314. News Item; *The Illustrated Weekly Of India*, Mar. 26, 1989, p. 35.

315. State Notes; *India Today*, Sept. 15, 1989, p. 41.

316. N. K. Singh; *India Today*, June 30, 1989, p. 29–30.

317. S. Nihal Singh; *India Today*, Aug. 15, 1989, p. 78.

318. S. Nihal Singh; *India Today*, Aug. 31, 1989, p. 78.

319. State Notes; *India Today*, Aug. 31, 1989, p. 71.

320. Amarnath K. Menon; *India Today*, May 15, 1989 p. 29.

321. Press Trust of India; *India Tribune*, Sept. 13, 1986, p. 5.

322. Opinion Poll; *India Today*, Aug. 31, 1989, p. 28.

323. Madhu Jain; *India Today*, Oct. 31, 1988. p. 27.

324. Madhu Jain; *India Today*, Sept. 30, 1989, p. 84.

325. Dilip Awasthi; *India Today*, May 31, 1989, p. 30–31.

326. News Item; *India Today*, Sept. 30, 1989. p. 9.

327. R. V. Nayer; *India West*, Oct. 13, 1989, p. 4.

328. M. Rahman; *India Today*, July 31, 1988, p. 69.

329. Simran Bhargava; *India Today*, July 31, 1988, p. 78–81.

330. News Item; *The Illustrated Weekly Of India*, April 16, 1989, p. 71.

331. David Devadas; *India Today*, Jan. 31, 1990, p. 18–20.

332. Harinder Baweja; *India Today*, Mar. 31, 1990, p. 20–21.

333. Madhu Jain; *India Today*, Apr. 15, 1990, p. 73.

334. Harinder Baweja; *India Today*, Jan. 31, 1991, p. 32.

335. Harinder Baweja; *India Today*, Feb. 15, 1991, p. 53–54.

336. News Dispatch; *News India*, June 16, 1989, p. 11.

337. S. Nihal Singh; *India Today*, July 31, 1989, p. 73.
338. Harmeet K. D. Singh; *Wall Street Journal*, Oct. 4, 1989, p. A31.
339. Bharat Wariavwalla; *The Illustrated Weekly Of India*, June 11, 1989, p. 10–19.
340. Neelan Tiruchelvam; *Wall Street Journal*, Aug. 10, 1987, p. 27.
341. Editorial; *Wall Street Journal*, June 9, 1987. p. 34.
342. Editorial; *Wall Street Journal*, June 22, 1984,
343. Dilip Bobb, S. H. Venkatramani; *India Today*, Apr. 30,1988, p. 83–84.
344. S. H. Venkatramani; *India Today*, May 15, 1988, p. 22.
345. Prabhu Chawla; *India Today*, Feb. 28, 1989, p. 24.
346. Prabhu Chawla; *India Today*, Nov. 30, 1988, p. 14.
347. Pankaj Pachauri; *India Today* Apr. 30, 1989, p. 54.
348. Pritish Nandy; *The Illustrated Weekly Of India*, May 28, 1989, p. 10–19.
349. Friedrich A. Hayek; *The Road To Serfdom* (Chicago: The University Of Chicago Press, 1944).
350. News Report; *India Tribune*, Nov. 17, 1990, p. 8.
351. Pranay Gupte;, *India: The Challenge of Change* (London: Methuen. Mandarin, 1989). p. 38,286,32–35,293–295, & 262–266
352. Murad Ali Baig; *India Today*, Oct. 31, 1988, p. 50.
353. Knight-Ridder Newspapers; *Atlanta Journal And Constitution*, Nov. 22, 1990, p. C–8.
354. News Report; *U.S News & World Report*, Mar. 26, 1990, p. 13.
355. Staff Reporter; *The Hindu*, July, 14, 1990, p. 3.
356. News report; *India Tribune*, Dec. 16, 1989, p. 24.
357. P. G. Bharati; *India Tribune*, Jan. 20, 1990, p. 15.
358. Pankaj Pachauri et al.; *India Today*, Vol. XV No. 4 (February 28, 1990), p. 75.
359. Amarnath K. Menon; *India Today*, Oct. 15, 1988, p. 36.
360. News Dispatch; *India Tribune*, Sept. 23, 1989, p. 6.
361. Press Trust of India; *India Tribune*, Jan. 6, 1990, p. 23.
362. Rekha Basu, Salil Tripathi; *India Today*, Aug. 15, 1989, p. 46–48.
363. Bachi J. Karkaria; *India Tribune* Mar. 10, 1990, p. 15–16.
364. David Devadas; *India Today*, June 30, 1988, p. 58–60.
365. Uttam Sengupta; *India Today*, May 31, 1989, p. 44–48.
366. News Item; *India Tribune*, Jan. 20, 1990, p. 8.
367. Pushp Saraf; *India Tribune*, Nov. 11, 1989, p. 23.
368. News item; *The Illustrated Weekly Of India*, Apr. 16, 1989, p. 70.
369. Shekhar Gupta; *India Today*, Oct. 15, 1989, p. 14.
370. A. S. Paintal, Simran Bhargava; *India Today*, July, 31, 1988, p. 67.
371. News Item; *The Illustrated Weekly Of India*, May 28, 1989, p. 71.
372. Vijay Kranti; *India Today*, July 31, 1989, p. 35.
373. V. S. Naipaul; *India Today*, July 31, 1989, p. 48.
374. India Notes; *India Today*, Aug.31, 1989, p. 12.
375. *U. S. News & World Report*, Dec. 23, 1991 p. 45.
376. Ramesh Menon; *India Today*, July 31, 1988, p. 92–94.
377. N. K. Singh; *India Today*, Aug. 15, 1990, p. 30.
378. Eye-Catchers; *India Today*, Jan.31, 1990, p. 88.
379. Salil Tripathi; *India Today*, Mar. 15, 1989, p. 23.
380. Madhu Jain et al.; *India Today*, Mar. 15, 1989, p. 14–24.

381. Uday Mahurkar; *India Today*, Feb. 15, 1988, p. 31.

382. David Devadas; *India Today*, July 31, 1989, p. 34–35.

383. People; *U.S. News And World Report*, Mar. 2, 1992, p. 24.

384. Ramesh Menon; *India Today*, May 15, 1989, p. 40–41

385. S. Nihal Singh; *India Today*, April 30, 1989, p. 87.

386. N. K. Singh; *India Today*, April 15, 1988, p. 83–84.

387. N. K. Singh; *India Today*, Mar.31, 1989, p. 94–96.

388. Shantanu Ray; *India Abroad*, June 23, 1989, p. 39.

389. News Item; *India Today*, Oct. 31, 1988, p. 7.

390. June Kronholz; *Wall Street Journal*, Vol. CCVIII No. 92. p. A1 & A19.

391. Anand P. Raman; *India Today*, July 31, 1988, p. 62.

392. Anand P. Raman; *India Today*, June 30, 1988, p. 54–55.

393. Editorial, *Wall Street Journal*, Mar. 21, 1985.

394. S. Kumar; *The Illustrated Weekly Of India*, April 16, 1989, p. 11.

395. Mukarram Bhagat; *India Tribune*, Jan. 6, 1990, p. 13 & 16.

396. T. N. Ninan; *India Today*, May 15, 1988, p. 54–58.

397. P. R. Bramhananda; *India Tribune*, Dec. 2, 1989, p. 2.

398. T. N. Ninan; *India Today*, Jan. 15, 1988, p. 50–53.

399. P. G. Mathai, S. D. Gupta; *India Today*, Jan. 15, 1989, p. 74–75.

400. Tim Carrington, Barbara Toman; *Wall Street Journal*, Feb. 6, 1990, p. A–1.

401. Peter Jenkins; *The Illustrated Weekly Of India*, June 11, 1989, p. 42–45.

402. Editorial; *Wall Street Journal*, May 11, 1989.

403. Geoffrey Moorhouse; *India Britannica* (London: Harvill Press, 1983), p. 144.

404. P. G. Mathai; *India Today*, June 30, 1990, p. 48–51.

405. Prabhu Chawla; *India Today*, Nov. 30, 1988, p. 14–17.

406. L. C. Jain; *India Today*, Mar. 31, 1989, P. 77.

407. P. G. Mathai et al.; *India Today*, Mar. 31, 1989, p. 74–78.

408. S. N. Vasuki; *India Today*, Sept. 30, 1989, p. 66–69.

409. S. N. Vasuki; *India Today*, Apr. 30, 1990, p. 53–57.

410. Pankaj Pachauri; *India Today*, May 31, 1989, p. 14–16.

411. David Frum; *Wall Street Journal*, May 1, 1990, p. A18.

412. P. G. Mathai, S.D. Gupta; *India Today*, Oct. 15, 1988, p. 70–71.

413. T. N. Ninan; *India Today*, Mar. 15, 1988, p. 58.

414. Bombay Bureau; *India Tribune*, Dec. 2, 1989, p. 11.

415. Prabhu Chawla; *India Today*, Dec. 31, 1989, p. 21.

416. Press Trust of India; *India Tribune*, Oct. 28, 1989, p. 10.

417. News Report; *India Tribune*, Apr. 7, 1990, p. 1 & 22.

418. P. G. Thakurta; *India Today*, Feb. 15, 1990, p. 86–87.

419. S. N. Vasuki; *India Today*, May 31, 1990, p. 74.

420. Press Trust of India; *India Tribune*, Sept. 2, 1989, p. 11.

421. P. G. Mathai; *India Today*, Sept. 15, 1988, p. 70–71.

422. Tapan Das Gupta; *India Tribune*, Apr. 7, 1990. p. 8.

423. Karen Elliott House; *Wall Street Journal*, Feb. 6, 1989, p. A4.

424. T. N. Ninan; *India Today*, May 15, 1988, p. 54–58.

425. Raj Chengappa; *India Today*, Aug. 31, 1989, p. 84.

426. S. N. Vasuki; *India Today*, Jan. 31, 1989, p. 67.

427. S. N. Vasuki; *India Today* July 15, 1990, p. 74.

428. T. N. Ninan; *India Today*, May 15, 1988, p. 54–58.

429. M. Rahman, Ratan Tata; *India Today*, Oct. 15, 1988, p. 64.

430. Surajeet Das Gupta; *India Today*, June 15, 1990, p. 40.

431. T. N. Ninan; *India Today*, May 15, 1988, p. 54–58.

432. Feature; *India Tribune*, Jan. 6, 1990, p. 15.

433. M. Rahman; *India Today*, Mar. 31, 1989, p. 85–86.

434. O. S. Shrivastava; *Economic Development And Planning in India* (New Delhi: Allied Publishers Private Limited, 1988), p. 439.

435. Shiv Taneja; *India Today*, Nov. 15, 1989, p. 58–59.

436. S. N. Vasuki, S. D. Gupta; *India Today*, Aug. 31, 1989, p. 86–88.

437. P. G. Mathai et al.; *India Today*, Jan. 31, 1988, p. 54–55.

438. Trade Winds; *India Today*, May 15, 1990, p. 49.

439. Trade Winds; *India Today*, April 30, 1990, p. 49.

440 S. N. Vasuki; *India Today*, Apr. 30, 1989, p. 64–65.

441. Trade Winds; *India Today*, Mar. 31, 1990, p. 49.

442. India Notes; *India Today*, Feb. 15, 1989, p. 12.

443. S. N. Vasuki, Surajeet Das Gupta; *India Today*, May 15, 1989, p. 70–71.

444. Trade Winds; *India Today*, Sept. 30, 1989, p. 70.

445. T. N. Ninan; *India Today*, July 31, 1988, p. 54–56.

446. Shiv Taneja; *India Today*, Mar. 31, 1990, p. 55.

447. News Report; *India Tribune*, June 2, 1990, p. 8.

448. News Report; *The Illustrated Weekly Of India*, June 4, 1989, p. 10–19.

449. Trade Winds; *India Today*, June 15, 1990, p. 36.

450. The Associated Press; *Atlanta Journal And Constitution*, Feb. 20, 1990, p. D–10.

451. Shiv Taneja; *India Today*, Aug. 31,1990, p. 57–59.

452. Mukurram Bhagat; *India Tribune*, Jan. 6, 1990, p. 15–16.

453. Trade Winds; *India Today*, Sept. 30, 1989, p. 70.

454. Trade Winds; *India Today*, Mar. 15, 1990, p. 49.

455. Surajeet Das Gupta; *India Today*, July 15, 1990, p. 66–70.

456. Sreedhar Pillai; *India Today*, Jan. 31, 1988, p. 82–83.

457. Salil Tripathi, Amaranath K. Menon; *India Today*, Apr. 30, 1990, p. 50–52.

458. Simran Bhargava, Salil Tripathi; *India Today*, Sept. 15, 1988, p. 66–68.

459. Salil Tripathi, Shiv Taneja; *India Today*, May 15, 1990, p. 45–48.

460. Madhu Jain; *India Today*, Feb. 15, 1991, p. 82.

461. Surajeet Das Gupta; *India Today*, May 31, 1990, p. 66–68.

462. Surajeet Das Gupta; *India Today*, Oct. 31, 1989, p. 62.

463. Francis Fukuyama; "The End Of History," *The National Interest*, Summer 1989, p. 11, & 3–18.

464. S. H. Venkatramani; *India Today*, June 30, 1988, p. 53.

465. S. H. Venkatramani; *India Today*, Jan.31, 1988, p. 42–45.

466. Sutanu Guru; *India Tribune*, Jan. 13, 1990, p. 15.

467. P. G. Mathai; *India Today*, Aug. 31, 1989, p. 82.

468. T. N. Nanan, Jagannath Dubashi; *India Today*, June 30, 1985, p. 72–80.

469. Mukurram Bhagat; *India Tribune*, Jan. 6, 1990, p. 13 & 16.

470. P. G. Mathai, A. P. Raman; *India Today*, Aug. 31, 1988, p. 56–59.

471. Inderjit Badhwar et al.; *India Today*, July 31, 1988, p. 36–44.

472. *U.S. News & World Report*, Aug. 27/Sept. 3, 1990, p. 57.

473. Michael Harrington; *Socialism: Past & Future* (Arcade Publishing, Inc., New York, 1989) p. 3.

474. The Associated Press; *Atlanta Journal And Constitution*, March 9, 1991.

475. Cathy Trost; *Wall Street Journal*, May 2, 1990, p. B1.

476. Michael Barone, David R. Gergen; *U.S. News And World Report*, Apr. 9, 1990, p. 30.

477. The Weekly Cover Story; *The Illustrated Weekly Of India*, Apr. 30, 1989, p. 10–19.

478. Feature; *India Tribune*, Jan. 6, 1990, p. 15.

479. Thomas Moore; *U.S. News & World Report*, Sept. 24, 1990, p. 64–65.

480. John H. Fund; *Wall Street Journal*, April 2, 1990. p. A12.

481. *60 Minutes*– CBS, Vol. XXII No. 23 (February 25, 1990).

482. Hodding Carter III; *Wall Street Journal*, March 8, 1990, p. A15.

483. Susan Stewart; *Atlanta Journal And Constitution*, Oct. 23, 1990, p. D–1.

484. Calvin Tomkins; *New Yorker*, Sept. 3, 1990, p. 60.

485. Peter Jenkins; *The Illustrated Weekly Of India*, June 11, 1989, p. 44.

486. James Kelley; *Time*, Vol. 126 No. 1 (July 8, 1985), p. 95.

487. Salil Tripathi; *India Today*, May 31, 1989, p. 93.

488. Arun Shourie; *India Today*, Nov. 30, 1990, p. 53.

489. Comment; *India Today*, Apr. 15, 1988, p. 5.

490. Robin Knight; *U.S. News And World Report*, July 23, 1990, p. 10.

491. Paul Johnson; *Wall Street Journal*, June 9, 1988.

492. Nikolay Shmelyov; *Wall Street Journal*, Aug. 26, 1987, Editorial Page.

493. M. Rahman; *India Today*, Nov. 15, 1990, p. 55.

494. Miriam Horn; *U.S. News And World Report*, Nov. 5, 1990, p. 15.

495. David Gergen; *U.S. News & World Report*, May 27, 1991, p. 80

496. Pranay Gupte; *India: The Challenge of Change* (London: Methuen. Mandarin, 1989), p. 302.

497. Science Notes; *India Today*, Feb. 15, 1991, p. 81.

498. News Report; *India Tribune*, Mar. 11, 2000, p. 9.